ONE WEEK LOAN

About the author

Jo Beall lectures in the Department of Social Policy and Administration at the London School of Economics and Political Sciences (LSE). She does research on urban policy and gender and is a consultant to the United Nations Centre for Human Settlements (Habitat) and the European Commission, advising in particular on issues of gender and participation.

A CITY FOR ALL

Valuing Difference and Working with Diversity

edited by
JO BEALL

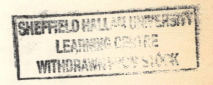

Zed Books Ltd
LONDON & NEW JERSEY

A City for All: Valuing Difference and Working with Diversity
was first published by Zed Books Ltd, 7 Cynthia Street,
London N1 9JF, UK, and 165 First Avenue, Atlantic Highlands,
New Jersey 07716, USA, in 1997.

This book was supported by the Overseas Development Administration (ODA) of the United Kingdom and the Women and Human Settlements Development Programme of the United Nations Centre for Human Settlements (UNCHS [Habitat]). However, neither the ODA nor the UNCHS (Habitat) can accept responsibility for any information provided or views expressed.

Cover designed by Andrew Corbett
Set in Monotype Garamond by Ewan Smith
Printed and bound in the United Kingdom
by Biddles Ltd, Guildford and King's Lynn

A catalogue record for this book is available from the British Library

Library of Congress Cataloging-in-Publication Data

A city for all: valuing difference and working with diversity /
edited by Jo Beall
        p.   cm.
    Includes bibliographic references and index.
    ISBN 1-85649-477-2. — ISBN 1-85649-478-0 (pbk)
    1. Cities and towns. 2. Cities and towns–Developing countries.
3. City planning. 4. Community development, Urban. 5. Housing.
6. Pluralism (Social Sciences). I. Beall, Jo, 1952– .
HT151.C5829 1997
307.76–dc21   97–3813
                                                                   CIP

ISBN 1 85649 477 2 hb
ISBN 1 85649 478 0 pb

Contents

List of Boxes

Contributors

Catherine Arnold completed her first degree in environmental sciences at Southampton University. She has worked in Bangladesh on rural income generation schemes and is currently working for the Overseas Development Administration in London.

Gautam Banarji has 11 years of experience as a programme officer with UNICEF. His last four and a half years prior to his present course of study at the LSE were spent with UNICEF Iraq, initially as project officer for primary health care and subsequently as the focal point for the Iraq Emergency Unit at the UNICEF Country Office, Baghdad.

Jeffrey Barron graduated from Columbia University in 1992 with a BA in history. Since then his focus has been primarily on Latin America. This has led him to work for a local newspaper and to teach in Santiago, Chile and complete an M.Phil. in Latin American studies at Cambridge.

Jo Beall lectures at the London School of Economics and Political Science in the Department of Social Policy and Administration, where she teaches a masters programme on social policy and planning in developing countries. Her specialities include gender and diversity issues in social and urban development as well as participation, urban poverty and social development in cities. She is currently researching a number of these issues in the context of solid waste management in South Asia. Jo also writes on South Africa and has worked as a consultant with a number of international development organisations, including Oxfam, ODA (UK), SIDA, OECD, UNDP and UNCHS.

Chittra Bunchandranon is originally from Thailand but now lives in the Philippines. She completed her undergraduate degree in economics at the University of Puget Sound, Tacoma, Washington, USA. She returned to the USA in the autumn of 1996 to study for a masters degree in political science at Stanford University.

Margaret Curtin is a paediatric nurse. She worked in general and paediatric hospitals in Ireland prior to joining the Irish NGO GOAL, for whom she worked on a refugee programme in Sudan, a street children's programme in Addis Ababa, Ethiopia, and relief and medical programmes in Angola.

Joanna Depledge completed her first degree in geography at Jesus College

Cambridge. Her main fields of interest are sustainable development and environmental issues in cities of the South. Her interest in these areas took her to the United Nations Conference on Environmental Development (the 'Earth Summit') in Rio de Janeiro in 1992 as an NGO representative. Jo has taught in Brazil and is currently an intern with the UN Secretariat in Geneva, working on the Framework Convention on Climate Change.

Allison Freeman received her BA from Mount Holyoke College in 1989. Since that time she has worked as a battered women's advocate in Cambridge, Massachusetts.

Tazeen Hossain has worked for the past three and a half years as a curriculum developer in the materials development unit of BRAC (Bangladesh Rural Advancement Committee). She also specialises in working with adolescents and young girls in both rural areas and urban-based schools of Bangladesh. She has recently worked at the University of Miskolc in Hungary as a research assistant on regional economics in the Department of Economics.

Gerard Howe is a research fellow at the London School of Hygiene and Tropical Medicine. He has worked in the Caribbean and in India and his research interests include the role of NGOs in the urban context, the urban environment and urban livelihoods. Fieldwork has included a study on solid waste management in South India.

Julie Jarman comes from the UK, where she has worked for five years as a community worker with homeless people and women and children fleeing violence. More recently she has lived in Tanzania for six years. She worked for three years with women's groups in Arusha Region, and for three years on a government water project in Dodoma Region funded by WaterAid. After completing her M.Sc. she joined WaterAid as their advocacy manager.

Elinor Jenkins graduated from University College Cork in 1986 with a degree in social policy and sociology. Initially she spent two years working with adolescents in London, after which she studied social work at the University of Edinburgh. She remained in Edinburgh for three years, working directly with homeless, ethnic minority women and children. Following this she moved to Bangladesh, where she spent two years working with homeless women and children in Dhaka.

David Jones is from Wales and gained a B.Sc. (Hons) in geography at Middlesex Polytechnic in 1987 and a PGCE at the Institute of Education, London University in 1988. He worked as a teacher and local authority representative for special educational provision for disabled children with the London Borough of Brent. He has worked in close collaboration with the Gambia Federation of the Disabled in an attempt to develop a more inclusive national policy initiative within the fields of education and rehabilitation. Since returning from West Africa, he has tutored on disability training courses for VSO.

Antonia Kirkland plans to work on women's rights, human rights and international law and to be the first post-modern feminist in the US Supreme Court or the International Court of Justice. She received a BA in international relations from Brown University, which included a year of study at L'Institut d'Etudes Politiques and the Sorbonne in Paris. She has obtained an M.Sc. in gender studies at the LSE and is pursuing her legal studies in the USA.

Andrea Lampis works and studies in London at the London School of Economics and Political Science, where he is reading for a Ph.D. in social policy. His thesis title is 'Access to health by low-income groups in Bogota, Colombia'. He obtained his B.Sc. in sociology in Rome, and his M.Sc. in sociology at the LSE. His main area of interest is urban poverty and health.

Loren B. Landau graduated in 1994 in political science from the University of Washington. He has worked in Washington DC with Human Rights Watch/Africa and Refugees International, where he was co-editor of *Refugee and Relief Alert*. In Seattle he was actively involved in efforts to provide the refugee and immigrant community with housing, health and education services. He is currently researching conditions for women-headed refugee households upon repatriation and resettlement.

Joyce Malombe is a lecturer and senior researcher at the Housing and Building Research Institute (HABRI), University of Nairobi, Kenya. She has been involved with the disabled people's movements for the last 15 years and regularly acts as a consultant to UNCHS (Habitat). She was a platform speaker at the special event for a DiverCity at Habitat II.

Inke Mathauer studied political and administrative science at the University of Konstanz (Germany). Her research interests are local government in developing countries and gender. She worked on gender integration and the institution of a network among organisations dealing with women's issues at the Regional Bureau of Women's Issues of the German Service of Development in Benin. She is now beginning a Ph.D. on the decentral-isation and promotion of subsidiarity in Uganda.

Rakesh Mehta joined the Indian Administrative Service in 1975 after graduating in history from Jawaharlal Nehru University, New Delhi. Since then he has been involved in development administration in India, in both rural and urban settings. He has worked in promoting community participation in a predominantly tribal area in the state of Arunachal

Pradesh in India, and has been involved in managing relief camps and the rehabilitation of flood-affected victims. He is currently dealing with rural development matters in the state of Goa.

Lourdes Mondragon Padilla studied physical anthropology at the National School of Anthropology and History in Mexico City. She has worked for the Mexican government for the last seven years, involved in social and regional development (the National Programme of Solidarity: Pronasol), rural education (CONAFE) and social assistance programmes.

Sandra Ng received her BA in political science from the University of British Columbia in Vancouver and her M.Sc. in social policy and planning in developing countries from the LSE. Her research interests include urban social movements, urban management and decentralisation from a social development perspective, with an Asian geographic focus. Sandra has worked with HOPE International Development Agency, a Canadian-based development organisation, at its head office and in its overseas operations. She has worked on a variety of projects in the Dominican Republic, Sri Lanka, India and Bangladesh.

Rajeev Patel worked in the UNCTAD Least Developed Countries Division and for an NGO in New Delhi delivering health care to slum dwellers. His first degree was in politics, philosophy and economics, and his interests are in the social and physical environments and their interconnections. He has done research for the Yale Institute of Environmental Policy and Law and for ACTIONAID, and is currently working again at UNCTAD.

Anita Payne is from England and gained her first degree through the Open University (UK), studying environmental and health sciences and international development. Her professional experience includes work in educational administration and in local government community disability programmes. For the last eight years she has been working in international development with VSO, specialising in disability issues and health programmes.

Anita S. Payumo did her undergraduate studies in management economics in the Ateneo de Manila University in the Philippines. She aims to move into social policy and planning after her degree.

Sophie Peace studied for her undergraduate degree in human sciences at Oxford University, after which she spent four months working for Ealing Family Housing Association and eight months in South Africa, where she worked as a volunteer for a Christian organisation in Cape Town. She would like to become involved in educating citizens of richer countries about the role they play in engendering Third World poverty and the ways in which they can respond to this situation in order to make a difference.

Francine Pickup graduated from New Hall College, Cambridge in 1989. She has worked alongside Zimbabwean women and in micro-enterprise in Venezuela and Guatemala. More recently, she has focused on the changing position of women in post-communist Russia.

Lamia Rashid completed her first degree in Third World development at Hampshire College in the USA in 1991. She has since worked in the development field in Bangladesh for four years, most recently at the Institute for Policy Analysis and Advocacy of Proshika: A Centre for Human Development, a national NGO.

Olga Segovia is an architect and a postgraduate student at the Royal Danish Academy of Fine Arts, Copenhagen. She is also a researcher for Sur Profesionales, Santiago, Chile. She has wide experience in the implementation of development projects and has published numerous articles on the living conditions of people in poverty in Latin America. She was a platform speaker at the special event for a DiverCity at Habitat II.

Sydney Smith joined the LSE from a career in international development and education. For the last five years she has worked on USAID-funded social sector reform programmes throughout Central and Eastern Europe, focusing on employment, training and social security programmes, including local initiatives for women and ethnic minorities. Her recent interest is the local control of social policy and programmes in transitional and developing economies.

Lucy Tacher completed her first degree in political science at Instituto Tecnologico Autonomo de Mexico. She has recently been working for the Mexican government as chief of the Department of Projects for the Capital Market in the National Securities Commission and as an adviser to the general director of Projects for the Securities Market.

Meenu Vadera is a postgraduate in rural management from IRMA (Institute of Rural Management, India). She is currently on one year's leave from ACTIONAID India, with whom she has been working for the past six years. She has also worked with a local NGO, the Urmul Rural Health Trust, in the Bikaner district of Rajasthan State, India. Her main area of focus has been working with grassroots women's groups. She has also been involved in training and capacity building at the programme and organisational levels in order to encourage a greater understanding of women's issues at policy and programme levels.

Alice Verghese-Choudhury was the education counsellor at the British Council. She has also worked for IUCN and has been a consultant to the Pakistan Women's Law Association and the Centre of Excellence for Women's Studies at the University of Karachi. Born Indian-Malaysian, she currently lives in Pakistan.

Amor Vieira is a Spanish student on the M.Sc. course in gender and development at the LSE. Her academic background is in sociology and anthropology. Her main interest is to study the contribution that the concept of diversity, specifically in its dimensions of gender and race, can make to social planning in development.

Gareth Ward completed a BA in social anthropology at Trinity College, Cambridge, and worked with street children in Guatemala City as part of his final dissertation. He has worked on behalf of Wrekin Council, UK on practical aspects of democratisation in local government in Gatchina in the St Petersburg region of Russia. He has recently taken up a new post with the Foreign and Commonwealth Office in the UK.

Preface

This book and the project from which it stems was prompted by the Second United Nations Conference on Human Settlements, Habitat II, held in Istanbul, Turkey in June 1996. I was involved in the preparatory process for this conference as a consultant to the United Nations Centre for Human Settlements – UNCHS (Habitat) – working at various times with the Urban Management Programme on urban poverty, the Women in Human Settlements Development Programme (WHSDP) on policy and planning with a gender perspective in human settlements development, and with the Best Practices and Local Leadership Initiatives Programme as a member of the Steering Committee and as chair of the Gender Steering Committee. In the period leading up to Habitat II, I prepared two papers (Beall and Levy, 1994; Beall, 1996) for UNCHS (Habitat) and participated in the Dubai Conference on Best Practices in Improving the Living Environment in November 1995. I was also involved in and wrote up the OECD Conference on Women in the City: Housing, Services and the Urban Environment (OECD, 1995) and gave a keynote address to the International Symposium on Citizens' Contribution to Sustainable Development in Osaka in March 1996. Obviously the thinking that went into these events and processes, as well as the experience that came out of them, fed into my teaching and research at the London School of Economics and Political Science (LSE).

On the M.Sc. programme in Social Policy and Planning in Developing Countries which is offered in the Department of Social Policy and Administration, I currently offer options both on urbanisation and social planning, and on gender, development and social planning. During the 1995/96 academic year, much interest was shown in the preparatory process for Habitat II by course participants taking these options. They were interested in the way in which issues of difference and social diversity, as well as the concerns of social development specialists more generally, related to processes of urban development. At the same time, I was discussing some of the ideas that were emerging from my teaching and research with people in UNCHS (Habitat), notably Catalina Hinchey Trujillo from the Women and Human Settlements Development Programme. This led to two connected activities. The students on the course asked if there was any way in which they could contribute to or participate in Habitat II and Catalina asked if I would think about taking my thinking on 'A City for All' to Habitat II in the form of a 'special event' for the parallel programme in the NGO Forum. I asked her if I could bring these two requests together, and the Women in Human Settlements Development Programme invited and sponsored us to present a Special Event on 6 June on 'Diversity in the City'.

In order to participate in the NGO forum, the students who volunteered to take part in this project registered their existing student organisations under one umbrella organisation, which they called LSE for DiverCity. As the majority of students on the course are foreign to Britain and come from countries across the globe, they were registered as an international organisation and were allowed five official representatives at the Habitat II conference. In preparation for this event, a much larger group participated in a series of workshops from November 1995 to May 1996 in which together we brainstormed the social development issues that related to the two main goals of the Global Plan of Action, or Habitat Agenda, namely *shelter for all* and *sustainable human development in an urbanising world*. Against a background of the papers I had prepared on gender and participation in the city (one of which appears as Chapter 2 in this book) and various drafts of the introduction to this collection, course participants produced theoretical essays or looked for case study examples of good practice in different areas of urban development. It is these that ultimately came to form the case study chapters of this book.

Thus apart from Chapter 1, in which I provide an introduction to and overview of the issues, and Chapter 2, which is reprinted with the kind permission of Oxfam's journal *Gender and Development*, all the chapters are written by those taking the 'urbanisation' and 'gender' options of the M.Sc. programme in Social Policy and Planning in Developing Countries during the 1995/96 academic year with the exception of Chapter 7, which was presented at Habitat II, as were the five boxed contributions. The difference and diversity discussed in the book are reflected in the composition of the authors. All course participants have some experience in or with countries of the South and many are themselves from cities of the Third World. Some are mid-career professionals with a depth of experience in government. Contributors to the book have, for example, worked in government in India and Mexico. Others have experience in international agencies and NGOs and authors represented here have worked for UNICEF, ACTIONAID, Save the Children, VSO, GOAL and CONCERN. Other contributors have had less direct experience in development organisations but have worked in countries of the South in various capacities, both as citizens and as visitors. Yet others brought to the table less experience but strong interest and analytical skills. This is reflected in the different weighting of the contributions. Some chapters take the form of case studies and reflect the actual experience of course participants or their organisations in the field. Other contributions are case studies drawn from the literature, or are more reflective pieces illustrated with selected examples.

Not all members of the group had equal familiarity with or understanding of the urban context, or shared the same understanding of gender and diversity issues. This led to long and sometimes difficult debates in which we developed and agreed a common language and conceptual framework. Some of this is discussed in Chapter 1, in which I attempt to give a flavour of the process as well as the product of these endeavours. Our commitment to process and to working through conflict reflected the kind of development practice we advocated, with everyone showing tremendous willingness to think through the issues, to review ideas and text and to participate in the numerous workshop and editing sessions in which papers were presented, critiqued, rewritten and revised again. The process has been exciting and rewarding and it fits with my commitment to teaching practice that makes room for student involvement and participation in ways that are both stretching and creative. It also sits well with the aims of the M.Sc. programme itself, which is concerned with the theory, methodology and applied practice of social policy, planning and participation in developing countries. Finally, it is the product of that generation of social development practitioners who will be involved in actually implementing the Habitat II Agenda. If they can own and articulate the issues involved, then it is more likely that they will willingly value difference and work with diversity in building future cities for all.

There are many other people to thank for making this project realisable. First a big thanks to Catalina Hinchey Trujillo, coordinator of the Women in Human Settlements Development Programme of UNCHS (Habitat) for encouraging our participation in Habitat II in the first place, for sponsoring the special event on DiverCity at Istanbul and for ensuring UNCHS (Habitat) contribution towards the publication of this book. Second, we are extremely grateful to Michael Parkes and Gayl Dickson of the Overseas Development Adminstration, UK for generous funding support, towards both the production and distribution of this book and the costs of attendance at the Habitat II conference for a student from the South. Thanks are also due to Professor Julian Le Grand of the Department of Social Policy and Administration for his moral and financial support towards LSE for DiverCity. Our gratitude is also extended to LSE Graduate Recruitment and LSE Research and Consultancy for their contributions to funding student attendance at the conference.

This collection could not have been produced without the commitment of all the students involved, and I feel very privileged to have enjoyed such a warm and enthusiastic learning process with them. In the process of conceptualising and writing the book, I have had as much to thank the participating students for as vice versa. An indispensable contribution to the process was the editorial assistance of Gerard Howe, who studied for

the M.Sc. in Social Policy and Planning in Developing Countries in 1994/
95 and who has been working on a research project in the department
during 1995/96. Enormous thanks are due to him, not only for his initial
edit, but for his creative and patient liaising between my various edits and
authors' responses. He played an additional and important role in ensuring
that the specific urban focus did not get entirely lost in the debates on
social development and difference and in good Freirian fashion provided
advice, moral support and encouragement when the process became
demanding. In addition to his skilful editorial eye, his role as a team player
was deeply valued by all of us. The time spent by Lucy Tacher and
Lourdes Mondragon Padilla on Spanish translation was invaluable and
much appreciated. The students who represented the group at Istanbul
worked particularly hard, both in preparation for and during the
conference, but their participation would not have been possible without
the generous goodwill and hard work of the whole group, who supported
the attendance of their representatives at the conference through
participating in fund-raising events and in many other ways, as well as
contributing to the book.

For my own part I am very grateful to David Satterthwaite, director of
the Human Settlements Programme at the International Institute for
Environment and Development (IIED) for agreeing to be a reader for
this book and for his helpful comments and global overview. Thanks too
to Naila Kabeer of the Institute of Development Studies (IDS) at Sussex
University and to Sylvia Chant and Gail Wilson at the LSE, who all cast
a critical eye over various chapters. I am indebted to colleagues at the
Development Planning Unit, University College London for refining my
skills as an urban specialist during the years in which I worked there. To
my colleagues teaching on the Social Policy and Planning in Developing
Countries masters programme in the Department of Social Policy and
Administration at the LSE, Anthony Hall and Hilary Byrne, heartfelt thanks
for their enthusiasm for and encouragement of the project and for helpful
comments on parts of the text. Nevertheless, the usual disclaimers apply
and responsibility for errors and omissions rests with me.

Finally, my concern with difference and diversity cannot be divorced
from my years in South Africa, my untimely departure from that country
and the struggles against apartheid in which I was involved – the struggles
against Apartheid with a capital A, the micro-level apartheid of everyday
life and inevitably the apartheid within. Thus this book also owes much
to people several steps removed from it and unaware of its production.
I reflect with nostalgia on those who were part of my personal encounter
with difference and diversity in Durban during the 1980s. I remember
with gratitude the support of the editorial collective of *Agenda* and of
colleagues at the University of Natal at the time, especially David Brown,
Bill Freund, Jeremy Grest, Heather Hughes, Ari Sitas, Alison Todes and

Astrid von Kotze. Special thanks to the reading group – Michelle Friedmann, Gerhard Mare, Blade Nzimande, Graham Hayes and Christopher Ballentine – for the intellectual challenges, the camaraderie and the certainty that valuing difference could not be divorced from the struggle for freedom from basic wants and fears. I will always be grateful to Shula Marks for her welcome and support when I returned to Britain. To Malcolm Alexander I offer thanks for his forbearance and community. Finally I want to thank my son Bud for his enduring love and support through many struggles.

Jo Beall, London
September 1996

Bibliography

Beall, J. (1996), *Urban Governance: Why Gender Matters*, United Nations Development Programme (UNDP), Gender in Development Monograph Series No. 1, March.

Beall, J. and C. Levy (1994), 'Moving towards the gendered city', paper prepared for the United Nations Centre for Human Settlements (Habitat) for the first preparatory conference for Habitat II, Geneva, April.

OECD (1995), *Women in the City, Housing, Services and the Urban Enviroment*, Paris: Organisation for Economic Cooperation and Development.

Abbreviations and Acronyms

AARP	American Association for Retired Persons
ACSP	Ashram Community Services Project (Birmingham, UK)
ADEMI	Asociacion Dominicana Para el Desarollo de la Microempresa (Dominican Republic)
ADOPEM	Asociacion Dominicana Pro-Desarollo de la Mujer (Dominican Republic)
BGPMUS	Bhopal Gas Peedit Mahila Udyog Sangathana (Organisation of Bhopal Women Worker Victims)
BJP	Bharatiya Janata Party (India)
BLRI	Blackbird Leys Redevelopment Initiative (Oxford, UK)
BPLP	Best Practices Local Leadership Programme
BRAC	Bangladesh Rural Advancement Committee
CASP-PLAN	Community Action in Slum Projects–PLAN
CBO	community-based organisation
CDS	Sandinista Defence Committee
CHC	community health coordinator
CIL	Centre of Independent Living
DIPAM	Disabled People's Association of Malawi
DPO	Disabled People's Organisation
DPU	Development Planning Unit
EFHA	Ealing Family Housing Association (UK)
EPZ	export-processing zone
FCSE	Forum for Street Children Ethiopia
FDPA	Fiji Disabled People's Association
FoH	Friends of the Handicapped (Lebanon)
FS	field supervisor
FSLN	Sandinista National Liberation Front
ICDDR, B	International Centre for Diarrhoeal Diseases Research, Bangladesh
IDDP	integrated district development plan
IHA/UDP	Integrated Holistic Approach/Urban Development Project Addis Ababa
IIED	International Institute for Environment and Development
ILO	International Labour Organisation
IMR	infant mortality rate

INSTRAW	International Research and Training Institute for the Advancement of Women
IPADEL	Institute of Local Government (Peru)
IUCN	International Union for the Conservation of Nature and Natural Resources
IUIDP	Integrated Urban Infrastructure Development Programme (Indonesia)
LSE	London School of Economics
MCH-FP	maternal and child health and family planning
MCN	Nicaraguan Communal Movement
MIC	methyl isocyanate
NCDPZ	National Council for Disabled People of Zimbabwe
NFSS	Nairobi Family Support Services
NGO	non-governmental organisation
NIC	newly industrialised country
NUK	Nari Uddug Kendra (Centre for Women's Initiatives, Bangladesh)
OCDA	Oxfordshire Cooperative Development Agency (UK)
ODA	Overseas Development Administration (UK)
OECD	Organisation for Economic Cooperation and Development
ORS	oral rehydration solution
PCTA	Pegasus Court Tenants Association (Oxford, UK)
PHC	primary health care
PJM	Program Jangka Menengah (multi-year investment programme) (Indonesia)
PRI	Institutional Revolutionary Party (Mexico)
Pronasol	National Programme of Solidarity (Mexico)
RADAR	Royal Association for Disability and Rehabilitation (UK)
SEWA	Self-Employed Women's Association (India)
SIDA	Swedish International Development Authority
SPARC	Society for Promotion of Area Resource Centres (Bombay)
SRB	Single Regeneration Budget
UCEP	Underprivileged Children's Education Programme
UHEP	Urban Health Extension Project (Bangladesh)
UNCHS	United Nations Centre for Human Settlements
UNCTAD	United Nations Conference on Trade and Development
UNDP	United Nations Development Programme
UNESCO	United Nations Educational, Scientific and Cultural Organisation
UNICEF	United Nations Children's Fund
UNO	United National Opposition Party (Nicaragua)
UPG	urban planning group
UTP	urban transport planning
VSO	Voluntary Service Overseas (UK)

WHO	World Health Organisation
WHSDP	Women in Human Settlements Development Programme
YBT	Young Builders Trust (UK)

PART ONE

Introduction

CHAPTER I

Valuing Difference and Working with Diversity

Jo Beall

To think of a democratic city is to think of a mode of inhabiting, participating in, building, creating, living, and imagining the city, the urban stage, new forms of space. To think of a democratic city, at least as possibility, means to do so along different dimensions which express the new relations that will exist among its inhabitants, the citizens (Alfredo Rodriguez, 1983, quoted in Friedmann, 1992).

You talk about difference and diversity in the city but for us, diversity is about cooking something different for our families every night out of the same old potatoes (Epry Suarez, Colombian participant in the special event, 'A City for All', Habitat II conference, Istanbul, 6 June 1996).

There are many ways of looking at the city. In the view of urban sociologists of the 1970s cities were sites of production, and later, of reproduction and collective consumption as well. More recently post-Fordist studies have traced the location and function of cities within the restructuring of the international economy and the twin processes of globalisation and decentralisation – centres of production, of services, and of financial and commodity markets (Castells, 1977; Harris, 1990; Harris and Fabricius, 1996; Harvey, 1973, 1989; Pickvance, 1977; Saunders, 1979). The role of cities in national development also constitutes a debate, in relation to their disproportionate contribution to national economic growth, as well as the economies of scale that potentially can be achieved in social development and welfare provision. While cities are among our greatest achievements, they are also host to some of our most pressing problems. By the turn of the century the majority of the world's absolute poor will live in cities of the Third World. On the other hand, cities are nodes of vast consumption, creating what William Rees (1992: 121) calls 'ecological footprints', which extend over immense areas beyond their boundaries. These parasitic dependencies on the hinterlands that functionally support cities may not be ecologically or geopolitically secure. At the same time, cities are not simply environmental negatives. The higher concentrations of people within cities reduce demand for land and conserve resources. Practices such as recycling and re-use hold the potential for further improvements in these directions (Hardoy, Mitlin and Satterthwaite, 1992).

A social development perspective on the city necessarily takes into account and cross-cuts all these elements: economic, political and environmental. It also has to take into account the different organisations and institutions that act upon the city and the social relations that underpin them, from the micro level upwards. However, cities are also physical spaces and the chapters in this book begin from the sense of cities as urban spaces. They are invariably linked to other spaces and are not the only, or even prioritised, spaces. Urban development includes not only megacities but small towns and cities of every size, while human settlements development applies to villages and rural settlements as well. But as urban spaces, cities have particular forms of physical, economic, social and institutional organisation. They have their own peculiar economic bases and human settlements, where sustainable livelihoods and habitats are pursued. In these urban spaces social identities collide, collude and accommodate each other. Social relations are built and challenged and social divisions occur while political coalitions and organisational linkages emerge and fade. Struggles for survival and power are played out in physical spaces and built environments that are spatial and organisational expressions of social relations and contesting realities.

Creating inclusive urban spaces that welcome diversity and meet the contrasting needs of different social groups is central to the goal of building 'A City for All'. The built environment of the city consists of a network of public and private spaces. These include buildings, streets, houses, institutions such as schools and hospitals, infrastructure and parks. Together they make up the building blocks of a complex urban mosaic. However, the physical structure of the city is the product of conscious decision-making and social relations and therefore can never be neutral. What gets built, where, how and for whom reflects relations of power and the often stereotypical assumptions of planners, architects and other urban decision-makers. Cities are literally concrete manifestations of ideas on how society was, is and should be.

The physical environment of the city is, in turn, the arena in which human activity takes place. The structure of urban space presents both constraints and opportunities which impact in different ways on the lives of the different inhabitants of a city. Women and men, the elderly, children, teenagers, disabled people, racial, ethnic or religious minorities, refugees and newcomers, migrant workers, the wealthy, people in poverty – all have contrasting needs and contributions to make and they experience and engage with the physical environment in different ways. The ways in which they participate in the social, economic and political life of the city will be diverse, and structures and patterns of urban governance need to accommodate this.

The arrangement of urban space has commonly been used by planners to 'put people in their place', defining appropriate spaces for particular groups and activities. The most extreme case of the translation of ideology into urban space is that of South Africa. Here the regime's apartheid policies included the forced removal of urban black communities into townships on the outskirts of urban areas, transforming South African cities into spaces of segregation and exclusion. However, even in the industrialised West, some housing estates or urban areas, whether by default or by design, have become associated with particular groups of people, be they an ethnic group or 'problem families'. And in cities throughout the Third World, poor communities are located on the periphery of cities, often in hazardous and isolated spaces, which marginalises them spatially and socially while cities of the North and South are characterised by inner-city slums.

The issue of urban space is one not only of where people are, but of how they get there and what it is like once they are there. The issue of mobility cross-cuts a number of chapters in this book and is specifically focused on in Chapter 14. The physical and social conditions in low-income settlements, including housing, infrastructure and basic services such as water and sanitation, health care, education and environmental conditions, are addressed. Access in the city – not only physical access but economic, political and social access – is also put under scrutiny in the chapters that follow. Against this background, the book explores two interrelated themes: a) the experience and organisation of difference as it relates to urban space and social relations in the city, and b) the practice in urban areas of social development that values difference and works with diversity.

The background and process

In June 1996 the Second United Nations Conference for Human Settlements, Habitat II, was held in Istanbul. Habitat II concluded a series of UN conferences that took place during the 1990s, with the aim of setting the development agenda for the new millennium. The City Summit, as it was also known, underscored the importance of understanding social, political, economic and institutional dynamics and linkages in an urbanising world.[1] It went further than the first Habitat Conference, held in Vancouver in 1976, in addressing social development issues. At Habitat II, strong emphasis was placed on the two themes of *shelter for all* and *sustainable human development in an urbanising world*. The goal of 'shelter for all' broadly reflects ongoing concerns in human settlements development since Vancouver, although perhaps today the theme might imply greater recognition of difference and diversity, alongside inequity. The focus on *sustainability* reflects the influence of the Earth Summit, the UN Conference on

Environment and Development (UNCED) held in Rio de Janeiro in 1992. It also reflects the incorporation of social concerns reflected in the idea that: 'The first step for rethinking ... urban development is to create a clear vision of the socially just, ecologically sustainable ... city' (UNDP, 1991). The use of the notion of *human development* embodies the combined concerns of the UN Conference on Social Development held in Copenhagen in 1994 (the 'Social Summit'), the International Conference on Population and Development held in Cairo in 1994 and the Fourth UN Conference for Women held in Beijing in 1995. While gender issues were on the agenda in Vancouver, at Habitat II they were well articulated and caucused, with greater efforts at mainstreaming them within human settlements development more generally.

In addition to the influence of United Nations conferences, however, concern with urban social development derives from the inevitable facts that, by the year 2015, over half of the people in developing countries will live in cities and poverty will have become a predominantly urban phenomenon. Perhaps the most significant aspect of Habitat II, then, is that the conference confirmed the transition to an 'urbanising world'. In the 20 years since Habitat I, the challenge of the inexorable process of urbanisation predicted in Vancouver has proved enormous. The dramatic growth of urban areas in the Third World presents an immense challenge to urban policy-makers and planners concerned with social and economic development in cities and with the provision of adequate infrastructure, services and facilities. While Habitat I assumed that national governments were able and willing to implement its recommendations – some of which were radical and implied a real transfer of power and resources to low-income people – the recommendations of Habitat II were perhaps more realistic in recognising the structural limitations on governments being able or willing to act 'in the public good'.

Nevertheless, the ever-increasing trend towards market-based solutions in development theory and practice was well reflected in the inputs and outputs of Habitat II. Thus, although there was a commitment to shelter as a human right, the conference confirmed the shift away from any idea that the public sector could provide housing, infrastructure and services and confirmed an 'enabling' or coordinating role for government. An important aim of current strategies is that of harnessing the full complement of human energy to the urban development project. This led to the conference acknowledging the necessity of a strong civil society in negotiating a better deal for low-income groups. However, as Nicholas You of UNCHS (Habitat) acknowledges, 'This requires a very different mind-set. It requires effective partnerships between public and private sector, between the communities' (You, 1996: 83). It requires a particularly different mind-set if urban partnerships are also going to be socially just and equitable engagements between diverse partners who are accorded equal value.

Otherwise partnerships can simply become mechanisms to increase the 'participation' of hard-pressed men and women in low-income communities so that they can provide for themselves in self-funded or self-help projects, where governments are no longer able or willing to provide.

With this in mind, a welcome preoccupation throughout the Habitat II preparatory process and conference was the focus on the institutional complexities associated with urban governance, urban management and participation. Recognising both the pressure of human need and the value of human creativity, initiatives such as Habitat II's Best Practices and Local Leadership Programme sought to disseminate lessons reflecting how cities, communities and different groups of actors within them have addressed some of the most pressing social, economic and environmental problems associated with urbanisation.[2] Award-winning projects included the Self-Employed Women's Association (SEWA) Bank in India, which has not only engaged in projects and programmes that directly improve the lives of women, such as a credit programme and the provision of clean drinking water, but has had remarkable success at the level of advocacy and organisational empowerment. Another example is the 'Don't Move, Improve' community development project from South Bronx, New York. This community-owned and -governed urban revitalisation project demonstrates that integrated urban development is possible, linking as it does health, education and day care with housing, transport, environment and capital development.

It was interest among my students in the Habitat II conference and preparatory process that gave rise to this book. For the past five years I have been a consultant to UNCHS (Habitat) on issues of gender, poverty and participation. I was involved in a number of ways in the preparatory process for the Habitat II conference[3] as a result of the work I have done for Habitat, in particular with the Women in Human Settlements Development Programme (WHSDP) on gender policy and planning and with the WHSDP and the Best Practices Local Leadership Programme (BPLP) on issues of gender and social exclusion in urban development and urban governance. As would be expected, I bring both my research and my practical experience in urban development into the classroom. In this instance I shared reflections and insights on Habitat II with students on the M.Sc. programme in social policy and planning in developing countries at the London School of Economics. A number of the course participants working with me on the urbanisation and social planning option or on the gender, development and social planning option were keen to know whether they might be involved in some way or participate in Habitat II. As explained in the Preface, we did indeed participate in the Habitat II conference, and prepared for and ran a parallel event which gave rise to and shared a title with this book.

Above all, 'A City for All' was a process. The book represents the culmination of a year of preparation, squeezed into early bleary-eyed sessions before Tuesday-morning lectures and immensely energetic weekend workshops throughout the 1995/96 academic year. It is the product of a self-conscious and reflective learning process in which there was a genuine sharing and in which my own ideas were able to crystallise as much as those of the student contributors. It was not always easy or harmonious, and our commitment to a development process that embraces difference and works with conflict was certainly put to the test. Resolve was challenged when deadlines loomed for essays and examinations. At these pressured times students questioned the wisdom of being involved in the process at all. Yet everyone remained committed throughout, often enhancing or adding sophistication to their academic endeavours through their work on the project. The process of preparation and production was both a stretching and a bonding experience for us all.

The conceptual framework for approaching difference and diversity in social development

Our first challenge in setting the framework for this book and for assembling case study material was to decide what we meant by 'difference', 'diversity', 'social development' and 'A City for All'. Some people in the group thought about urbanisation with ease and about difference with difficulty. Others felt comfortable with a diversity perspective but were unsure about issues of space, planning and urban development. Yet others felt deeply committed to gender issues but were ambivalent about dealing with difference more broadly, fearful that it might dilute the gender-specific concerns and struggles of women. Not everyone shared the same perspectives on social development or development, for that matter. Indeed, the agonies of consensus-building observed and critiqued within the UN conference system itself were played out in miniature in a classroom at the LSE.

Public action and identity politics It is the case that our understanding of *difference* derives much from debates among feminists over differences between women and men and among women themselves, as well as from the arguments underpinning the political challenge of women from the South (Barrett and Phillips, 1992; Marchmand and Parpart, 1995; Parpart, 1993). Debates on difference have underscored how gender as a social relation intersects with other social relations deriving from class, race, ethnicity, age and so on. Such debates, along with those on race, ethnicity and culture, have fed off and fed into post-structuralist, post-colonial and post-modernist scholarship and, for better or worse, have given rise to both a discourse and a politics based on identity (Carby, 1982; hooks, 1984, 1991; Marchmand and Parpart, 1995; Mohanty, 1988, 1992; Moore, 1994; Nicholson, 1990; Parpart, 1993).

However, these debates have largely remained in the realm of theory and as such have informed policy analysis more acutely than social planning and social development practice. While recognising difference seems to come comparatively easily to policy-makers, working with diversity presents enormous problems for social planners, professionals and activists. Public policy is defined here as deliberate public action by public institutions or organisations seeking to promote development and to address conditions or problems they indentify as important (Wuyts, Mackintosh and Hewitt, 1992). Social development needs to be seen as part of public policy, comprising an essentially political continuum from policy-making to implementation. It involves many actors working at different levels within governments, international agencies and organisations of civil society. This is an inclusive rather than an exclusive definition of policy, which recognises that organised consituencies of people have and act on different and competing interests. The question of who should make policy and for whom is contested almost as much as the issue of what sort of development policy is needed. Thus the conceptualisation of policy and planning as 'public action' is important because it embraces not only those who hold power but also those seeking to share or challenge power.

Anne Phillips (1993: 17) argues that while groups organising around interests may eventually reach accommodation with opposing interest groups, 'The intensity of identity politics is less amenable to a politics of accommodation or compromise, and is far more likely to encourage fragmentation or mutual hostility.' The task is further complicated for social policy-makers and social development professionals and activists by the fact that social identity based on gender, race or some other articulation of difference is not only about how individuals or groups might identify and present themselves, but about the way in which they are perceived and categorised by others and how these difference perceptions and presentations interface. Identity politics and social organisation on the basis of difference feed into public action and social policy and planning with considerable difficulty at times.

Defining difference and diversity Bearing in mind the complexities of identity politics, which according to some writers can lead to inaction rather than social change (Bourne, 1987), as well as the imperatives of social development at a time when macro-economic forces are squeezing welfare and social sector spending, I deliberately make a distinction between the concepts of 'difference' and 'diversity'. I believe this to be a helpful distinction when moving from social policy analysis to the practice of social development. As nouns the words mean much the same thing. They both refer to being different, dissimilar, distinguishable and unalike. But when these nouns become verbs, there is a subtle but important change in the actions implied. To *diversify* means 'to make diverse', 'to vary, modify, variegate', 'to guard against loss' whereas to *differentiate* means to 'make or become different in the process of growth or development', 'to constitute difference between' or 'to discriminate between'.[4]

In the context of social development, the act of differentiating can become a top-down process of social planning. At best, 'to differentiate' implies categorisation, prioritisation and potential hierarchies; at worst, it can imply discrimination or even social engineering. At a more basic level, 'to differentiate' implies 'labelling', 'naming' and 'othering'. Social development policies that target specific groups can be important and necessary in redistributing resources to the most needy. However, there is a danger that the process of identifying groups of people, or responding to the identities they assert at a particular time, can create and solidify these identities. For example, people with disabilities or female household heads can come to be seen only as disabled people or lone parents, without entitlement to other identities, interests, affiliations or causes. Thus a fundamental dilemma facing the social development practitioner when considering difference is that of 'naming', 'othering', 'categorising' or 'differentiating' which holds the danger of inducing the status or responses implied by the label itself. People choose to locate themselves among multiple and hyphenated identities that are fluid and contingent. Yet when social planners identify and respond to one or more of these identities with policies, programmes or projects, there is the potential for them to become codified and carved in stone as if they are immutable.

By contrast, the verb 'to diversify', in the context of social policy and planning, implies different *processes* rather than *identities*. The act of diversifying implies variation, modification and protection against loss. In the 1970s John Turner (1976) revolutionised the way we thought about housing, not as a noun but as a verb – something people struggled for and provided for themselves. Although not claiming the same sort of conceptual breakthrough as Turner, or even necessarily the same theoretical position, the verb 'to diversify' does imply action 'among' and 'by' people, rather than 'on' or 'for' them. It allows innovative interventions and interactions to flourish. What are argued for here, therefore, are policy approaches that recognise difference and do not deny it. But in the shift from analysis to action, I would argue that it is equally important that planning, management, partnerships and activism interact creatively with *diversity*, which is a more dynamic and flexible concept than the static one of *difference*. It is for this reason that the book is sub-titled *valuing* difference and *working* with diversity.

I attempt to illustrate this distinction between the actions of *differentiating* and *diversifying* through the example of ethnic identity. I have chosen this example partly because it is an area of difference that is not extensively covered in the case studies presented in this collection and therefore represents an omission in the illustrative material. However, the example of ethnicity also allows me to draw on the valuable work of a number of South African writers who have worked extensively on the subject (Boonzaier and Sharp, 1988; Dubow, 1994; Mare, 1993; Marks, 1986; Marks and Trapido, 1987; Wilmsen and Dubow and Sharp, 1994) and whose reflections can usefully inform our understanding of social development practice. In his study of ethnicity and Zulu nationalism in South Africa, Gerhard Mare distinguishes between categories and groups of people:

> A *category* … refers to the labelling of a number of people or things according to similar characteristics. A category of people is created by an outside observer and the 'members' of the category may have no idea of similarity or even be aware that they have been allocated to a category …
>
> A *group* of people, on the other hand, is aware of and accepts belonging together and being categorised as similar. Members of a group accept their inter-relationship, even though they may not all know other members of the group (Mare, 1993: 6–7; original emphasis).

What this points to is that just as identity politics might be a vehicle for marginalised, excluded and oppressed *groups* to assert their interests, identity can be a *category* used instrumentally by those with power, to suppress the interests of others. Thus before we 'celebrate diversity' too naively it is important to remind ourselves that working with diversity can be as destructive and divisive as it can be helpful. Documenting and detailing difference and fostering diversity was the life blood of the architects of empire. 'Divide and rule' tactics were a tried and tested strategy by which colonial administrators differentiated the colonised, pigeonholed bureau-cracies and retained power for themselves. This was not a one-way process. In the scramble for Africa and throughout the colonial era on that continent, tribal identities were destroyed, created and reinvented as some groups were conquered by, others colluded with and yet others resisted the colonisers (Ranger, 1983). The twin processes of denial and neglect of difference on the one hand, and assertion of difference on the other, have had some devastating and destructive historical and contemporary effects. The problems that can arise when difference is politically mobilised are testified to by the experience of present-day Bosnia or Rwanda or, in the case of cities, Sarajevo, Jerusalem, Los Angeles and Karachi.

The most obvious example of the political mobilisation of ethnicity and the social engineering around it is apartheid South Africa. The alloca-tion of national resources, the design and use of urban space and political and constitutional solutions were founded on the basis of race and are still being contested on the basis of ethnicity. Examining the prospects for a post-apartheid political dispensation in KwaZulu/Natal which has been characterised by Zulu ethnic mobilisation and violence, Gerhard Mare (1993) acknowledges the validity and importance of ethnicity in the con-struction and renegotiation of South African social identities. However, he argues that this should be 'separated from political mobilisation, manipulation and fanning of ethnic sentiments' and that ethnic groups 'should not be constitutionally rewarded for their group identity'. He goes on to argue that: 'In much the same way, no other *social* identity should be so rewarded. The ethnic identities held by individuals should be protected in a bill of rights based on individual rights and freedoms' (Mare, 1993: 107; original emphasis).

These sentiments echo Anne Phillips' compelling hope for 'democracy *through* difference; a politics that neither denies nor capitulates to the particularity of group identity' (1993: 5; original emphasis). Although perhaps a rather optimistic and dewy-eyed vision of society, it is one worth holding on to. Helpful in beating a path to this vision is the distinction made by Saul Dubow (1994) between two fundamentally different senses in which ethnicity has been treated in South Africa. He refers to 'the act of "claiming" on the one hand, and "naming" on the other' alluded to above, and goes on to say:

> By claiming, I refer to the strand of thought that conceives of ethnicity in a situational, contextual, and subjective sense. According to this usage, ethnicity is understood as a form of social identity that acquires content and meaning through a process of conscious assertion and imagining. By contrast, naming refers to the tendency to conceive of identity in primordial, static or essentialist terms. Crucially, it is often employed by one relatively powerful group as a means of defining other less powerful communities. The fact that those communities might take on aspects of this identity as a pragmatic means of defence or else for opportunistic reasons, should not obscure the power relations which overdetermine this process of ascription (1994: 368).

What this discussion of 'naming' and 'claiming' suggests for social development is that policy-makers, planners and practitioners can label and target people as 'the poor', 'vulnerable groups', 'children in difficult circumstances', 'lone parents', 'women', 'youth', 'elderly', 'disabled', 'minorities', 'refugees' or whatever. Ultimately, however, these groups will respond to the top-down ascription of identities only if it provides viable solutions for them out of the limited choices and options available, or if the labels themselves have resonance for them at a particular time in their life-cycle. For example, while identifying the particular needs of lone parents has been an important direction in social policy in Europe, the 'naming' of this group of mainly young and vulnerable single mothers has also led to them being 'blamed' for multiple social problems relating to children and youth, many of which are structural.

So the argument does not imply that policies and projects targeted at particular groups are all bad, but suggests that *identities* have to be recognised by all partners in the process of social development, which in turn implies consultative and participatory processes. It is the process of 'claiming' accompanying the 'naming' that ensures that social development practice does not work uncritically, unilaterally or without reflection. Thus it is important to get right the processes for working with diversity so that difference can be valued, without it resulting in suffocating and non-negotiable identities to which people are eternally bound. To return to Anne Phillips (1993: 21) again, 'Difference need not, but can, be a tremend-ous barrier between people, and there are few ways of breaching it other than through democracy itself.'

Defining social development   The very endeavour of social development is a contentious one when the entire development project is currently being fundamentally questioned and challenged (Chambers, 1983; Crush, 1996; Escobar, 1995; Latouche, 1993; Max-Neef, 1992; Parpart, 1993; Sachs, 1992) and when our own concerns see social development as contested terrain. However, while we reject 'top-down', predetermined and rigid definitions of social planning, the goal and practice of social development cannot be totally abandoned:

> Because social welfare, equity and opportunities for the realisation of human potential do not magically appear from nowhere, but are the results of the organised efforts of human beings, the attainment of these ideals ... requires a discussion of organisational arrangements and professional responsibilities ... both of which need to be clarified if these abstract ideals are to be translated into practical agendas for action (Midgley, 1984: 2).

We defined social development as a necessary process of organised and participative social change, designed to promote the well-being of present populations, while catering for for the future and for future generations. As such, social development embraces not only social sector policy but implies a social perspective integrated into all aspects of development, including economic, environmental and human settlements development. According to this definition, economic development does not have to imply accelerated growth. It does imply, however, that eco-nomic development would be pointless unless for the purpose of and accompanied by improvements in social well-being for whole populations. Social development as we understand it, therefore, critically examines and is centrally located at the intersection of social, economic and political processes. It is not just about 'meeting needs' but is informed by the concepts of process, agency and active social change and is linked to 'claiming rights' through a broader process of 'policy as public action' (Macintosh in Wuyts, Mackintosh and Hewitt, 1992).

Social development undertaken with difference and diversity in mind would necessarily be inclusive and participative, recognising people's vulner-abilities and capabilities and supporting them in maximising their life chances. Social development sensitive to difference would mean tackling social exclusion without necessarily insisting on integration. A diversity perspective would recognise that some groups might be unable to or unwilling to participate themselves and to work through representative structures, while others may choose to be different or to spurn mainstream development trajectories altogether. It would also recognise that some might benefit and gain strength from being separate, different or even excluded. For example, people working in the informal sector have largely benefited from being unregulated and overlooked, while people in India from scheduled castes suffer discrimination but have also gained sole access to particular jobs associated with their caste position. On a recent visit to Colombia I was told of a community which was located in a valley, not connected to the main road on the plateau above. In the context of decentralised decision-making processes around social funds, the community were asked if they wanted to spend their allocation on a road up the mountainside. They thought and consulted and came back with the answer that they would prefer donkeys. In that way, they reasoned, they could transport their produce up the mountain to markets, without having to have development come down the mountain to them![5]

The methodology of social development The methodology of social development engages with a process of change which includes three broad phases. The first is the *situation analysis* of existing social conditions and relationships. Second is the *process of change* itself. Using illustrations from the human settlements field, it can be spontaneous, such as the emergence of squatter settlements; it can involve planned intervention such as a programme of settlement upgrading or slum improvement; it can entail advocacy initiatives and resistance such as the rent boycotts in South Africa, which were protests for decent and affordable housing and urban services; or it can take the form of urban partnerships and linkages in public action. The third process of change is *evaluation* and impact *assessment*. In considering *best* practice in all these phases of social development it is important to stress that what we are really talking about is *better* practice, better rather than bad or worse because *good* practice is always iterative and reflective. It should be process- rather than goal-oriented and should not constitute blueprints, because practice that values difference and works with diversity cannot be formulaic. Thus it is never entirely replicable or transferable, but merely adaptable to specific contexts.

Nothing is more silencing and disempowering than invisibility. Good practice in situation analysis, therefore, would disaggregate aggregate categories such as 'the household', 'the family', 'the community' or 'people-centred development', be alert to both the vulnerabilities and the capabilities reflected in difference, and identify excluded or marginalised groups. Indeed, a number of the chapters in this book focus on who is included and who is excluded in the city. They also, through a relational analysis, identify who is doing the excluding. Good practice analysis has to be rid of assumptions and stereotypes that lead to 'othering' and 'labelling' and which induce relationships predicated on those categories. It also needs to stand above the public/private dichotomy and trace the linkages between the micro, meso and macro levels when examining policy impact.

Working with diversity primarily concerns the second methodological stage of social development, the process of change itself. Here best practice is policy, planning and participation that begin with the actual lived experience of women and men and that recognise and work with difference rather than disguising or ignoring it. A diversity approach also involves adopting a relational perspective which recognises the issue of power between individuals and groups. This in turn assumes conflict, and good practice would work with conflict as a creative, constructive and inclusive process. A creative approach to evaluation and impact assessment would include reflective and participatory methods of identifying winners and losers as well as inclusionary and exclusionary processes.

This is easy to say but difficult to practise. Dealing with difference is something that has tended to occupy policy analysts rather than social planners active in policy formulation and implementation, with some notable exceptions (Kabeer, 1994; Moser, 1993). The theoretical contributions of policy analysis are invaluable because how we conceptualise and theorise difference and diversity informs our practice. Nevertheless, *doing* social development is a more difficult and courageous affair than theorising difference and analysing social change, precisely because it is based on action. Getting it wrong can lead to more than an identity crisis: it can wreck people's lives in both direct and indirect ways. Mary Anderson (1996) has taken the concepts of difference and diversity into development planning and practice in a considered way, and discusses the costs of development assistance that fails to take account of difference. She argues that appreciating diversity means that local people assume responsibility for and ownership of development programmes; formulaic development approaches that ignore 'local contextual realities' are thus undermined (1996: 10).

However, she goes on to identify possible negative consequences of development programmes built on difference and diversity: 'If every place and every culture is different, then (some believe) we must empty our minds of past experiences as we approach each new area. The result is that there is no attention to accumulating and codifying lessons' (1996: 11). Moreover, attention to difference might mean only recognising vulnerability, or targeting only the most marginalised people, while missing differences within these groups (1996: 11). She also warns of the dangers of an ill-considered, programmatic emphasis on difference, reflecting that: 'In taking on the just cause of the poor, development programming has often promoted confrontation between those it is intended to help and those seen as perpetuating unjust systems' (1996: 13). These are sobering thoughts, but the difficulties involved should not paralyse us altogether because difference cannot be dismissed. As Anne Phillips (1993: 20) so aptly puts it in relation to politics in Britain: 'We can no longer construct a version of the political community that is premised on us having the same experience – all men together, all English together, all white together, and so on.'

There are now quite sophisticated and sensitive methodologies used in social development which are participatory and designed to involve different groups and include the less visible and vocal (Chambers, 1983; Gibson, 1994; Scoones and Thompson, 1994). Although they have been developed mainly in the context of rural development, their adaptation in urban contexts is under review (Mitlin and Thompson, 1995; IIED, 1994). In both rural and urban applications, however, participatory appraisal and evaluation can generate conflict and expose vulnerabilities in communities or settlements which, along with existing power relations, are then left behind to be sorted out for better or worse when the research initiators disappear. Although these issues are recognised and critiqued in the literature and in practice, the problem remains that organisations as remote as multilateral agencies, bilateral donors and international NGOs may not always be using participatory tools in participatory ways. They often act without reflection on their relative power, influence and limitations in this area.

Thus another important consideration in the practice of social development with a diversity perspective is organisational attachment or the location of the social development practitioner. This is significant whether he or she is using participatory methods out in the field, or formulating policy at head office. The differences in power, resources and access among international agencies, national and local governments, private sector organisations, NGOs and community-based organisations are considerable. Many well-meaning social development professionals, sensitive to difference and committed to working with diversity, end up advocating the right kind of development from a rather awkward platform. Doing social development is never a neutral exercise, and the organisational locations from which it is professed and in which it is conducted cannot be presumed away. Participatory approaches in social development can be considered good practice when they do not assume equality or parity among the different groups or organisations involved and when all development practitioners are sensitive to their own relative power.

Recognising and valuing difference in the city

On the question of difference in the city, for a long time urban sociologists and geographers have paid attention to who gets what in the city and why

(Castells, 1977; Harvey, 1973, 1989). Writers such as Doreen Massey (1984), Linda McDowell (1983) and Elizabeth Wilson (1991) have analysed the specific imprint of gender relations on the built environment and vice versa, while urban planners such as Clara Greed (1994), Patsy Healey (1995), Caren Levy (1996), Jo Little (1994) and Carol Rakodi (1991) have examined the relationship between gender and planning, broadly arguing that 'attempts to understand the implications of planning *per se* on women's inequality must acknowledge the way planning reinforces and is shaped by broader gender relations' (Little, 1994: 2). In our discussions on difference in the city, we agreed that from a planning point of view, we wanted to contest 'Le Corbusier's standardised "modular man", whose dimensions were to be at the core of all design, from furniture to city' (Healey, 1995: 51). From our perspective on social development, that meant challenging the mainstream to change and to accommodate different needs and diverse practices in the city, rather than difference being seen as deviance or inconvenience, and people deemed as 'other' having to adapt, fit in or have their needs met and catered for as victims or vulnerable groups.

An issue that vigorously exercised the collective mind of the group was 'Are some differences more basic than others?' (di Stefano, 1990: 78). For many participants in the project, their interest in social development derived primarily from a concern with poverty and so, explicitly or implicitly, issues of power or inequality were informed by a *class* or status perspective. They worried that seeing the city as a social and cultural mosaic held the danger of cultural relativism in which 'anything goes'. From the point of view of a social development perspective, they believed that this encouraged an *ad hoc*-ism that denied universal human rights or the need for collective belonging and action. For others, inequality and power could not be divorced from *gender* relations and they were reluctant to lose the political impetus generated by women's struggles, or to dilute the safe spaces, strongholds and extensive networks that gender and development staff, lobbyists and activists had created in international, national and local arenas. What was agreed was that class relations, like gender relations, intersect and combine with other social relations to constitute the identities and experiences of individuals and groups. The project of establishing a hierarchy of oppressions was considered unhelpful and we agreed that: 'Rather than the abstract ranking of relations of power inherent in class, race, gender and sexual orientation, the focus [has] shifted to the ways in which each of these relations intertwine, reinforce and contract each other in historically specific contexts' (McDowell and Pringle, 1992: 92).

These were important debates for practitioners working in post-modern times and it was good that we could agree that reductionist discourses based exclusively on class or gender have failed to explain the lived reality of many people in cities throughout the world, for whom, for example, their age, ability, ethnicity, race, occupation or national status have pre-occupied them more greatly at particular times in their lives. In a book on women and planning which looks at social relations in the context of urban space, Clara Greed (1994: 176) points out that: 'You can never plan entirely separately for women (or for men), and it is a sign of dichotomised thinking (and pillorisation) to imagine so. We all live in the same urban space.' This is echoed in the work of Patsy Healey, who has argued in respect of the city that:

> A major characteristic of our present period is the recognition of the diversity of lifestyles and conditions in our societies. We recognise variations in age, physical capacity, gender, colour, race, culture, interests, place and experience. This recognition is central to what is often called our 'post-modern condition' … This recognition has been greatly advanced by the growth of women's politics and feminist intellectual endeavour. This has pushed open a window not just on our social lives, but on our working arrangements and the organisation of public policy. Through this window, we have come to see that our societies massively discriminated against women. We have also come to see more clearly the many other discriminations which our ways of thinking and organising brought about because they emphasised homogeneity and universality, not heterogeneity and difference. The policy challenge is now to bring this perception to fruition in our thinking about the city and in all areas of public policy (1995: 50).

It is important to challenge social planning and development practices that perpetuate the myth of universal truths, based on the experience of dominant categories of people, while other categories are marginalised or regarded as 'other' (Mohanty, 1988). However, working as I do with some of the most deprived communities of the poorest cities of the world, while valuing difference I have also come to recognise and value what people have in common. They often share great deprivation, vulnerability and insecurity, together with remarkable resilience and capabilities. I believe, therefore, that as social development specialists we need, while working with diversity, also to hold on to the goal of achieving, at the very least, universal basic freedoms from want and from fear. When those basic freedoms are absent, it may be the result of class exploitation, gender oppression, ageism, child abuse, religious persecution, racial or ethnic discrimination or a combination of some of these. In all cases, however, it is caused by an undue exercise of power.

Accounting for power: working with diversity and conflict

However we deconstruct or slice *difference* and no matter how fluid and malleable it may be as a concept, signifier, label or way of delineating identity, the construction of difference, from above or below, cannot be divorced from the structures of power in which the process occurs. A recognition of the way in which power informs social relations and impinges on the way we *diversify* is what enabled me to answer, with an emphatic 'no', the question of a South African friend on hearing that I was working on this book: 'Is this going to be another celebration of the "rainbow nation"?' In looking towards 'A City for All' we are not simply celebrating social and cultural diversity, although this is welcome when it exists and can flourish and form in an open and equitable environment. Rather we are anticipating a city and an approach to urban social development which values difference and works with diversity, in the certain knowledge that power relations are superimposed upon both.

There is an obvious intersection between power and space. As cities grow, competition for space becomes increasingly intense. As ever, it is the poor and disempowered who tend to suffer as market forces combine with political indifference to displace or degrade their private and public spaces. The bulldozing of informal settlements to make way for the homes, shops and leisure facilities of more powerful groups is an all too common scandal. This is not just an issue for the South. In the cities of the North such as London and New York, the process of gentrification has also led to the destruction of communities. The renovation of run-down inner city areas for occupation by high-income groups means that the original inhabitants, often elderly people or ethnic minorities who have lived in these areas all their lives, are gradually pushed out by rising rents.

Although it is difficult to define, we are certainly aware when power is being exercised. It manifests itself as the ability to coerce, to ignore, to override, to force or control. It is the ability to dictate an agenda, or more positively, it is the ability to influence things. However, power is not monolithic, something used by those who hold it over those who do not. Nor is it something simply associated with jackboots and guns, or even laws governing rights, movement or access. It can be subtle, covert, multifaceted and fragmented (Foucault, 1976). It can be as readily found and exercised in the language and practice of social development as in the international arms trade or the excesses of a kleptocratic state.[6] Thus power is not simply the 'power to do' something nor 'power over' someone else (Lukes, 1974). Neither is it, on its own, what Kabeer (1994) describes as 'the power within'. The counter to the subtle and multifarious exercise of power is the process of empowerment, a concept 'clearly rooted in the notion of power and in its reverse, powerlessness' (Kabeer, 1994: 224). Naila Kabeer describes the explanatory strength of the concept empowerment over powerlessness thus:

> powerlessness suggests a total absence of power whereas in reality even those who appear to have very little power are still able to resist, to subvert and sometimes to transform the conditions of their lives. The focus has therefore

shifted to the more processual aspects of power – empowerment and dis-empowerment (ibid).

Mirroring Lukes (1974), Friedmann (1992: 33) sees an alternative development as predicated on households and their individual members being empowered in terms of social power, political power and psycho-logical power. Social power he associates with 'a household's access to the bases of its productive wealth', including information, knowledge and skills; political power he interprets as a household's access to 'the process by which decisions, particularly those that affect their own future, are made. Political power is thus not only the power to vote; it is as well the power of voice and of collective action.' Finally, psychological power, he posits, is best described as 'an individual sense of potency. When present, it is demonstrated in self-confident behaviour.' Feminist debates on the household have correctly pointed out that 'households' as such do not produce or have access to wealth, and do not vote or make decisions. Rather it is members within households that do this and the relations between them are not necessarily harmonious or equitable (Folbre, 1986; Kabeer, 1991; Sen, 1990; Wilson, 1991). Thus, in accounting for power, implicit in the analyses in this volume is an understanding that it operates on a variety of levels, within households, communities, cities, regions, countries and the international arena.

Coming to terms with culture Of all the complex issues involved in recognising difference, one that invariably emerges and indeed preoccupied some of our discussion was that of culture. The concept of culture often accompanies the notion of 'celebrating diversity' and is often understood uncritically or certainly outside of any concept of power. However, it is precisely the culturalist critique of development that has fundamentally questioned the very meaning or usefulness of the concept of development (Sachs, 1992), characterised simply as the imposition of European culture and a process of 'deculturation' of the non-European world (Latouche, 1993). Together the culturalist and environmental critiques have questioned the validity of development based on modernisation, industrialisation and economic growth. Adrian Atkinson and Paul Chamniern (1994: 149) argue that if the values of this approach were to prevail, we would 'return to a planet rich in multifarious cultures, leaving behind us the nightmare of a world steam-rollered into a monotonous uniformity of McDonalds and mirror-glass office towers'. Clearly a development that values difference and works with diversity needs to recognise culture(s).

Culture is a difficult issue for people engaged in social development who are often concerned with areas such as health or family planning, which impinge on the most intimate and private parts of people's lives. In acknowledging and working with difference, particularly gender but also ethnic difference, social development activists and professionals are told not to interfere in the culture of other people. This becomes particularly sensitive when they are from, or work for agencies from, the North. While sensitivity is obviously urged and culture to be respected, there are two caveats. First, macro-level development such as economic reform and restructuring has had a devastating impact on people's private and intimate lives. For example, there is considerable evidence now to suggest that the urban poor have suffered disproportionately under the impact of structural adjustment policies and that low-income urban women have borne the brunt of increased labour demands, reduced consumption and unstable and sometimes violent domestic relationships, disrupted and undermined by declining real wages, increased insecurity and a changing gender division of labour in relation to paid work (Chant, 1996a; Elson, 1989; Kanji, 1995; Latapi and Gonzalez de la Rocha, 1995; Moser, 1996). This can be more damaging to domestic lives and intimate relationships than any community development worker asking women about contraception!

Second, culture is not immune to conceptual complexity and, as Atkinson and Chamniern (1994: 149) themselves acknowledge, it is neither static, nor is it 'beatific or benign'. Culture reflects the social and political structures of time and place, it is dynamic and can be changed, but some aspects are especially resistant to change. We also have to be alert to the fact that culture is often invoked to justify oppressive practices, not least of all the maintenance of oppressive gender relations that seclude, oppress or otherwise disadvantage women. However, culture can also be protective and inventive and provide security, particularly for migrants or minorities. While recognising and acknowledging the importance of culture, therefore, we do not want to fall into an uncritical celebration of social or cultural diversity that denies or obscures the social structures and political dynamics within which it constantly evolves and reshapes itself. This is particularly pertinent in the urban context where, for a host of reasons ranging from a nostalgia for roots to competition for resources, some groups retain and even exaggerate their cultural identity and exclusiveness in the city. Others meld or inflect rural custom, ethnic identity or other aspects of 'traditional' consciousness with an urban or working-class culture (Freund, 1994; Sitas, 1996). Yet others assert distinctive contemporary *urban* cultures manifest, for example, in homeboy dress and talk and rap music in the United States.

Process, participation and partnership The examples of urban social development practice that are described as 'best' or 'better' practice in this volume seek to make people's experience of the city more equitable and accessible, through participatory processes and partnerships that facilitate full participation in social, economic and political life and the governance of the city. In this context it is important to bear in mind that participation does not imply an endless and relentless process of self-help and do-it-yourself projects, often synonymous with social and community development, especially for low-income communities. Participation may mean public action and organisation to get others to do things for you, especially if they can do things more effectively, efficiently and with fewer opportunity costs. The comparative disadvantage of single women household heads in upgrading and self-build housing projects provides a stark example of how all citizens are not equally prepared for all tasks (Moser, 1987). In order to ensure that women-headed householders have the same access to housing as men or women in other household structures, it is sometimes appropriate and useful to train women household heads to be bricklayers, carpenters and joiners so they can have a house and perhaps a job or a business in due course. This has been tried successfully in the Caribbean (UNCHS, 1990) where women are active and visible in the labour market but would not necessarily work in other contexts. An alternative approach was adopted by the Bombay-based NGO Sparc in India, which worked to empower women pavement-dwellers, through legal literacy and other means, to demand and lobby for housing themselves.

Under any circumstances and towards all forms of social development, full participation necessitates the empowerment of disadvantaged and disenfranchised people, on both personal and organisational levels, so that their engagement in urban development is around their own priorities and on their own terms, rather than according to an agenda the terms of which have already been set elsewhere (Shetty, 1991). If participation 'involves organised efforts to increase control over resources and regulative institutions in given social situations' (Pearse and Stiefel, 1979)[7] on the part of organised groups and movements, it may mean self-help and the contribution of people's time, energy and money towards the development of their communities. However, it may also mean the ability to prevail upon politicians, bureaucrats or others to participate as well. Thus participatory development and partnerships include active and participatory democracy from the local level upwards, resting on the concerns of communities or interest-based groups within them, or the legitimate exercise of authority by accountable elected representatives on behalf of their constituents. Effective and equitable partnerships and development processes are best accompanied by a robust and vibrant civil society and accountable and consultative government. A social development perspective that takes into account difference and diversity has to be sensitive, however, to the way in which agendas might be set in the interests of one group over another or challenged on the basis of one identity group in opposition to some 'other'. In short, a social development perspective has to address and not avoid the issues of priorities, power and conflict.

We began our working process challenged by the question of whether the urban issues we were dealing with gave rise to 'best practice' solutions. We concluded that there could not be best practice – there could be only good practice and better practice. Better practice is reflexive and adaptable and involves a broad spectrum of individuals and organisations. It is not just a bottom-up or a top-down process; it is both. Government-led initiatives are not intrinsically better or worse than community-led in-itiatives. Thus good practice includes both 'our practice' and 'their practice'. We have to accept that there may never be true equity in partnerships between groups with different levels of and access to power and resources. Thus we need to find creative responses to see how bottom-up and top-down initiatives can meet in the middle on more equal terms. This may mean creating horizontal coalitions in civil society to facilitate accountable vertical linkages with the public and private sectors. Accountability needs to work in different directions so that structures that are representative and transparent can hold to account those that are not. In some cases this may be organisations of civil society holding government to account. In other cases it might be the other way around.[8] Thus good practice that values difference and works with diversity in urban social development includes an *awareness* of power imbalances, a *willingness* to identify and hear all voices, an *acceptance* of conflict without out and out confrontation and deadlock, a *desire* to learn from our own experience and that of others and the *courage* to confront our own power in 'A City for All'.

Organisation of the chapters

Urban spaces often overlook the particular needs of different groups of women and men that arise from both their physical differences and their socially ascribed roles as workers, mothers, carers and decision-makers. Some of the problems that would need to be overcome in achieving a gender-aware city are explored in Chapter 2. Of course neither women nor men are homogenous groups of people and their gender identity is cross-cut by, for example, age, race and class. While women experience particular gender-related difficulties, they are not the only group whose activities in public space are constrained. Nevertheless, an introductory chapter providing an overview of gender issues in the city was considered important for two reasons. First, a diversity perspective should not obscure the fact that the 'gendered city' (Beall and Levy, 1994) is still an aspiration and not yet a reality. Although gender relations are only one set of power relations, they have not been fully or finally addressed and still need challenging. Women's priorities in the city are still not recognised by planners and few women are in government, even at local level. Neither are they there in any number in the strategic heights of the private sector, and they are often confined to the most insecure and poorly paid echelons of the labour market. Second, precisely because women are not the only people who suffer in the city, there is the opportunity for building alliances and making linkages.

Thus understanding the constraints and opportunities for women's participation in urban governance (Beall, 1996) is important in order to build coalitions that together challenge the shared experience of exclusion. With this in mind, in Chapter 2 I reflect on gender and participation in the city. Participation is understood in two ways, first as *entitlement* in the city, for example entitlement to a decent livelihood, secure shelter and a liveable habitat. Second, participation is also understood as *empowerment*, including participation in public office and in civil society and a synergy between the two. The chapter makes a case as to why, in both senses, gender matters.

In the course of the argument the importance of women as an organised constituency is linked to and contrasted with the importance of a gender perspective in urban development. The chapter points to the fact that a focus on broader issues of difference and diversity should not in any way diminish the priorities and activities of women as an organised constituency, or the goal of gender-sensitive urban planning and development practice. After all, the struggles of women have contributed towards opening the space and creating the opportunities for broader issues of difference and diversity to be put on the agenda. It is no coincidence, for example, that in the preparatory process towards Habitat II, it was the women's caucus that welcomed alliances with other groups concerned with difference and social justice in the city. In the context of mainstream development, it remains difficult for men in grey suits to see themselves as 'other'. It is perhaps no coincidence, either, that the special event we were invited to present at the Habitat II conference on 'A City for All' was sponsored by the Women and Human Settlements Development Programme of UNCHS (Habitat).

Part Two From a gender perspective the spatial organisation of the city has long been instrumental in defining appropriate spaces for women. Traditionally and on an almost worldwide basis, women have been associated with the private space of the home and men with the public space of the urban streets, women with domestic and community work and men with paid employment. The chapters in Part Two fundamentally challenge these stereotypes. Instead of this artificial dichotomy between home and work, people's income-earning activities and unpaid tasks are viewed holistically within a 'livelihoods framework' (Grown and Sebstad, 1989) so that neither women nor men are simply seen as housewives, unemployed or as workers and earners, as if no other responsibilities informed their identities, choices or opportunity costs.

In the same way, housing is seen as a social asset without which it is impossible to participate fully in society, and as a commodity that has a market value. It can also be seen as a productive resource. A house is shelter and it is a place that can accommodate income-earning activities both directly, for example in home-working, and indirectly, for example when it is used as collateral for credit. The importance of access to a safe private space is a key urban issue for all citizens. For many shanty town-dwellers, constant fear of eviction means that the home is anything but a secure place. Homeless people face discrimination because without a legal address they find it almost impossible to secure employment, obtain social benefits or even register to vote.

In Chapter 3, Allison Freeman, Francine Pickup and Lamia Rashid look at women's income-generating activities in the urban informal sector. They emphasise how women's work is often undervalued, not only in the labour force but in the home, where daughters, sisters and mothers release other women for paid work by taking on domestic responsibilities and childcare. Moreover, income generation often takes place within the home and can transform already overcrowded living quarters into cramped and poorly ventilated sweatshops that harbour serious occupational health hazards. The chapter concludes by looking at positive examples of practice and policy. The authors are keen to point out that often the very livelihoods and survival strategies of people working in the informal sector are contingent upon minimal interference or benign neglect on the part of authorities. They suggest, therefore, that in a world that is not ideal, policy interventions need to enable and protect, rather than regulate, particularly when informality helps women combine their multiple responsibilities at home and at work.

Chapter 4 reflects on women's 'domestic' and 'productive' labour. Loren Landau argues that the way the relationship between the two is conceptualised and understood can influence the design and provision of housing. Taking as his starting point Engels' (1972) *The Origin of the Family, Private Property and the State*, he asks why Engels' arguments still inform much of the work on gender and housing. Regarding the argument that the time dedicated to domestic labour acts as an obstacle to women's full social participation, he argues that the positing of domestic and productive labour as binary opposites is a position that has not stood the test of time. Globally, changes in production processes and the international division of labour have led to increased contracting out and home-working is already a feature of women's activities in the urban informal economy. Thus he suggests that the 'house' has ceased to be just private shelter (if ever it was) and has expanded its role as a link into economic activity. Because women are increasingly reliant on the house as a base for 'productive' economic activities they should have a *de jure* and *de facto* right to housing that is accessible and affordable and accommodates multiple usage.

Children are another group with particular spatial needs that are often overlooked. And yet, as Chapter 5 points out, children and youth are also vital contributing members to low-income urban households and are the urban citizens of the future. The authors make the case for a multi-dimensional approach to working with children, arguing that if they are narrowly defined by one particular aspect of their lives, such as work (child labour) or shelter (street children) or education, then development interventions will be blind to other influences on their lives. The challenge put forward to social development practitioners is to address children on their own terms, recognising that they have multifaceted lives and valuable insights on their own situation and the management of cities themselves. Case studies from Ethiopia and Bangladesh offer experiences of alternative ways to address the problems and priorities of urban street and working children, both for the present and with an eye towards their future.

In Chapter 6, Elinor Jenkins examines the relationship between work and housing for young women working in the garment industry in Bangladesh. While Landau presents housing as an economic asset, Jenkins emphasises the social value of housing. She makes the point that rental housing is important for people at particular stages of their life-cycle and for people in poverty. She applies this analysis to a project concerned with housing young women workers in Dhaka city who are not in immediate contact with family and kin. In an Islamic country where single working women living alone are an anathema, they are stigmatised and treated with suspicion. For them, therefore, safe and secure housing is a premium for which they are prepared to pay a remarkably high proportion of their limited incomes in the interests of social honour. She also makes the interesting point that young women who are not under the direct control of either fathers or husbands are a relatively new phenomenon in urban Bangladesh. This has created a space between 'girlhood' and 'mother-hood' which is giving resonance to a concept akin to 'adolescence', one that would have previously been unrecognised in this social context.

The final chapter in Part Two is not by a student on the MA programme but by Olga Segovia, who was one of the participants in the special event on DiverCity at Habitat II. She is an architect practising in Santiago, Chile and presented a paper on the relationship between women and space in low-income settlements in Chile: the way women use space, what it means to them, how it is negotiated among them and with others on the basis of gender roles and gender relations. She concludes by looking at the role of planners and how they might strive towards creating both public and private space that accommodates people and allows them to define and use their own space in constructive, supportive and collaborative ways. This chapter is followed by comments made by participants at the special event on the issue of gendered urban space (Box 2.1). These set the scene for Part Three which more directly takes up the issue of negotiated space, and how in the face of violence and urban conflict people seek to build secure homes and neighbourhoods.

Part Three   Liveable environments include not only homes but residential neighbourhoods and communities. Two sets of factors go to undermine people's efforts to build secure homes and liveable communities. One concerns the problems of inadequate housing and urban infrastructure and services, issues that are considered in Part Five of this collection. The second set of factors is dealt with in Part Three and concerns social divisions and conflicts that contribute towards disintegrating neighbourhoods, dangerous settlements and violent homes. It is the issue of violence that binds the different chapters that go to make up this part of the book. In an overview chapter on the causes and effects of urban violence, Rajeev Patel presents a sobering picture of the insecurity that characterises lives in homes and neighbourhoods in cities throughout the world. Urban violence is not just defined as physical violence but includes psycho-social violence, which would embrace the assault of exclusion and the denial of basic rights and freedoms crucial to building a liveable city. Patel shows how the poor are vulnerable but how wealthy cities are not immune. He describes and illustrates how particular groups – women, children, racial and ethnic minorities – are more at risk than others from different forms of violent attack and abuse from different sources, from the police to husbands.

In Chapter 9, Meenu Vadera explores the issue of violence against women, questioning the specifically urban dimensions of violent homes in violent cities. Drawing on experience from India, she discusses the situations of violence faced by urban women and the individual and organisational responses of women survivors and campaigners against violence. She describes in particular the experience of Shaktishalini, an organisation formed by the mothers of the victims of so-called 'dowry deaths' to support in various ways women subject to domestic violence. In looking at the socio-spatial dimensions of violence against women, she argues for safe streets and public spaces, and homes that are secure both physically and financially. Property ownership for women, as well as social support and physical shelter for women survivors of violence, are urged. The cases of urban and domestic violence provide examples of the intersection between private isolation and individual fear on the one hand and political and social invisibility on the other.

The issue of safe spaces for battered women is taken up in Chapter 10 by Antonia Kirkland, who examines good practice in providing domestic violence shelters. Drawing on material from cities in the North and the South she examines the factors that give rise to and exacerbate domestic violence in cities, such as poverty and high-density living. She looks at recent evidence that suggests a relationship between the social impact of economic restructuring and increased domestic discord at the household level and she shows that everywhere, without choices women often choose to remain in abusive relationships rather than face insecurity or social improbity. She illustrates the value of providing alternatives that allow women to have asylum from violence and the chance to renegotiate their relationships and their lives from a stronger position.

Chapter 11 in this section is by Amor Vieira, who describes and critiques a resettlement programme affecting a group of 300 Roma-Gypsies in Madrid. Ostensibly the programme was sensitive to diversity, providing different sorts of housing to meet the social and economic needs of different groups and lifestyles. However, in reality it denied diversity and, through the processes of assessment, allocation and implementation, constructed a hierarchy of livelihoods and cultures that resulted in virtual exile from the city for this group of Roma-Gypsies. The programme buckled under resistance from settled communities and the Roma-Gypsies ended up on an unserviced site adjoining the city's rubbish dump, where 'the only sign of the promised housing were units marked with white squares painted on the earth'. Vieira's case study reveals a classic case of 'othering' whereby the programme placed at the centre the norms and values of white Spaniards, living in nuclear families and employed in formal sector jobs. Against this 'normality', other lifestyles were judged. While difference was recognised it was seen as deviance and not valued. The assault of exclusion that resulted from social planners *differentiating* this community is resounding.

Part Three concludes with the testimony of the mayor of Apartado in Colombia, presented at the Special Event on 'A City for All' at the Habitat II conference. She is a remarkable woman who, as a community activist with strong legitimacy and no tainting affiliations, was prevailed upon to take office as mayor in a city rent by corruption and devastating violence. She represented the hope of many citizens longing for peace and seeking inclusive and constructive partnerships rather than a lifetime of futile destruction and rebuilding. Since her moving address at Istanbul and return home, the region in which she lives and works has been taken over by the military and she is currently mayor in name alone.

Part Four Cities create their own divisions and processes of exclusion. They are particular spatial and organisational expressions of social relations. Urban services, infrastructure, housing and public buildings are simply not designed with a view to the needs of anyone but the most robust, healthy and potentially productive. The young, old, disabled or frail are physically challenged by a system created by planners and policy-makers who are callous at worst, careless or uncritical at best. The chapters in this part of the book deal with the issues of access and mobility and how some people are denied these freedoms in the city. Social exclusion results from physical design that denies older and disabled people, or women caring for children or sick or elderly relatives, access to buildings, events and jobs. It also stems from social relations and attitudes that create artificial and invisible boundaries as well as real and tangible ones. The chapters in this collection point to the way in which spatial exclusion through confinement to private space leads to social invisibility and in turn to policy neglect. However, the physical environment of cities is not fixed or unchanging and nor are social relations in cities. Relatively disempowered groups are challenging the assumptions and power relations built into urban space and as the following chapters illustrate, where difference is valued and diversity worked with, positive changes result, providing the potential for creating more inclusive cities.

Chapter 12 on disability and diversity in the city starts off with the assertion that, historically, urban and state planning has tended to reflect the interests of politically powerful interest groups and has generally failed to allocate resources on the basis of fairness and equality. David Jones and Anita Payne argue that nowhere is this more applicable than in the case of the neglect of disabled people by mainstream planning. They go on to describe how the city constitutes an obstacle course for disabled people. They contest the 'othering' of disabled people and argue that urban management has a lot to learn from disabled people and their experience and perspective. Jones and Payne also stress the important lessons the disability movement offers from having taken identity politics into the arena of public action and social development. It has fought 'naming' and prejudice and has 'claimed' its place in mainstream society. At the same time it has taken on the considerable challenge of embracing difference within its own ranks. The personal impact of planning neglect and negative social attitudes towards disabled people and the value of their difference are confirmed in the moving testimony by Joyce Malombe, presented at the special event on 'A City for All', which concludes Part Four.

Older people are also valuable members of society. In households they are a resource and a support, contributing to domestic work and childcare and releasing other members for paid work. Many older people engage in paid work themselves or bring in pensions which are important contributions to limited household incomes. And yet, as is pointed out in Chapter 13, cities have failed to come to terms with both the value and cost of ageing populations, undervaluing the past and present contributions of older people. Thus in cities that cater only to the productive and woo the spending power of the young and energetic, ageing is often perceived in negative terms, and the contribution of older citizens who often have time, energy, experience and interest to invest in their communities is ignored. Despite this, the chapter also points to positive examples of policy and projects that have addressed the needs and worked with the potential of elders.

In Chapter 14 Gareth Ward, Sydney Smith and Jeffrey Barron present a 'best practice' example of city transport planning from Curitiba, Brazil.

Without suggesting that this specific solution can be directly transferred to other cities, through this illustration they point to the value of integrating a social development perspective into an area of urban development that has traditionally fallen into the planning domain of economists, engineers and technicians. They show how equitable and effective transport plays a crucial role in providing the mobility and access needed for diverse social groups to participate fully in urban life. For example, they show how the introduction of a 'social fare' prevented discrimination against people from low-income settlements, forced to travel long distances from the periphery of the city; and how difference was valued and responded to by allowing the socially stigmatised rag-pickers who scavenge for recyclable materials in the city dumps to trade waste items for bus tickets.

In Chapter 15, Jo Depledge also points to a success story, in this case an inner-city food-growing project in Birmingham, England called Ashram Acres. She shows how a project with explicit environmental goals – in this case a form of urban agriculture – can also be used as a vehicle to promote wider social objectives. The project provides a liveable recreational green space for people and has been described as a 'green oasis', especially for women, children and the elderly who were fearful of using the existing parks. At the same time it cultivates, at affordable prices, foodstuffs relevant to Asian and Afro-Caribbean diets, such as coriander, callaloo and fenugreek. A strength of the project is that it remains in local hands. It provides an informal advice and information role to a community wary of official structures and interventions. It is flexible in its organisation and its responses and as such holds the potential of adapting to changing circumstances, including the pressure to scale up.

Part Five Within the framework outlined by Mitlin and Satterthwaite (1996), this part of the book looks at how cities can be both ecologically and socially sustainable – where sustainable development is viewed as a 'commitment to sustaining environmental capital [which] has to be combined with a commitment to ensuring that people's needs are met' (Mitlin and Satterthwaite, 1996: 24). International interest in the environment has been primarily focused on the 'green agenda' (for example, global warming, biodiversity, resource depletion and deforestation), while many of the environmental issues in the South concern what has been dubbed the 'brown agenda'. The 'brown agenda' includes the most immediate and critical environmental problems facing cities in the Third World, such as lack of safe water supply, sanitation and drainage; inadequate solid and hazardous waste management, and air pollution including uncontrolled emissions from motor vehicles, factories and low-grade domestic fuels; all of which are closely linked to the poverty–environment nexus.

A focus on the 'brown agenda' reflects the priorities of a broad range of people concerned with social development and poverty eradication in cities and informs Chapter 16, by Julie Jarman. Her focus is urban water supply and sanitation which, she argues, has an important role to play in poverty reduction in Third World cities. Areas of poverty are usually areas of highest population density and fewest public resources. Jarman shows, for example, how the poor often pay a significantly higher price than the rich for their water because they are not connected to a subsidised water supply system but have to pay prices set by (monopolistic) water vendors. While water is a decreasing resource, in both quantity and quality, urban demand for water is increasing. She is critical of highly engineered systems based on expensive imported technology which is difficult to maintain and argues for participatory solutions, which are often accepted but seldom implemented. She says the water and sanitation sector can benefit from new understandings of urban poverty that emphasise not only vulnerabilities but capabilities among the urban poor, as well as the heterogeneous nature of urban poverty. She uses a case study from Addis Ababa in Ethiopia to show what these concepts may look like when translated into practice, and makes suggestions for further research.

After Jarman's review, which charts the complexities of installing appropriate and affordable urban services under conditions of resource scarcity, it is sickening to read of the destruction of urban infrastructure in Iraq as a result of the Gulf war, described by Guatam Banarji in Chapter 17. He shows how the destruction of infrastructure such as electrical power installations, telecommunication facilities, roads and bridges has had a devastating effect on urban social sectors. For example, water sewage systems have been incapacitated because they are dependent on electric supply. This, combined with the disruption of transport and communication systems, has lead to a spiralling chain of health hazards that has particularly impacted on the urban poor and on women and children. The destruction of war described by Banarji shows how cities cannot conduct their affairs in isolation from global forces. Increasingly cities are paying the price of human conflicts, not only those generated within their boundaries but those occurring outside them.

This theme is taken up in the next chapter by Rajeev Patel, who looks at the question of urban disaster management after the explosion at the Union Carbide factory in Bhopal in 1984. Although it was a localised disaster the events in Bhopal were the result of various interventions by *national* and *international* institutions, starting with the lack of attention paid to safety by a multinational corporation, and ending with efforts to mitigate the disaster being taken out of the hands of local people. Government and NGOs showed more concern with the international legal impacts of the disaster than with the immediate plight of the victims. The case of Bhopal is chosen not as an example of good practice, but rather as an object lesson in how *not* to proceed. Patel shows how gender, ethnic and income differences became fault lines for divided responses and the systematic exclusion of various disempowered social groups, not only within Bhopal, but in a wider political arena. This exclusion has continued long after international interest in the accident has waned. His chapter concludes with guidelines for better practice in urban disaster management through an inclusive process of intersectoral urban partnership.

Chapter 19, by Andrea Lampis, examines the relationship between the health of an individual and the social and economic environment. The chapter addresses the long-standing issue of how the disease patterns of the urban poor reflect their location at the interface between 'under-development and industrialisation', and identifies factors that have prevented improvements in the level and quality of access to health in urban areas. These ideas are explored through case studies representing the most commonly implemented approaches to extending health for all, a holistic approach and a selective approach. The holistic approach is explored with reference to the provision of specialist medical services to women and sexual minorities in Glasgow under the aegis of the Healthy Cities Project there, and the selective approach through exploration of a targeted project for HIV-positive people in Brazil.

The final chapter of Part Five is by Catherine Arnold and is also concerned with health. The emphasis is on the organisation and delivery of health care and family planning in urban areas. The author looks at the important role played by volunteer women in health and family planning initiatives promoted by an urban health extension project in Dhaka, Bangladesh. She makes the point that volunteer drop-out rates have been low, in stark contrast to the experience with rural volunteers. She usefully addresses the question as to why economically disadvantaged slum women should continue to work as community volunteers and what support they will need for their commitment to be sustained. She concludes that although primary urban health services cannot be based only on volunteers, volunteerism can provide a valuable reservoir of talent.

Part Six The chapters here all present practical case study examples where attempts have been made to put social development objectives into practice in ways that address difference or work with diversity. The experiences they discuss reveal that this is not always easy and that successful projects are not always replicable, transferable or even capable of being scaled up. However, together, they constitute a strong case for continuing to work creatively and reflexively in building and sustaining inclusive urban partnerships.

Chapter 21 examines urban management in two contexts, Indonesia and Peru. In both cases attempts were made to broaden the scope of urban management and to increase the range of actors involved, not with equal success. Neither the top-down approach adopted in Indonesia nor the bottom-up approach pursued in Peru imply the best route to diverse and equitable urban partnership. The Indonesia experience shows that while decentralisation of power to local government was important, non-involvement by the private and community sectors constituted barriers. In Peru, although the private and community sectors were involved, this did not automatically imply that differences within them were recognised and the interests of dominant groups still prevailed. The chapter concludes by arguing that urban partnership can facilitate a diversity perspective only when there are constructive mechanisms for recognising difference and resolving conflict, and this is contingent upon the presence of political will.

Chapter 22, by Sophie Peace, offers a short case study of a project proposal for funds from the Single Regeneration Budget in Britain. Addressing the problems of a deprived housing estate in Oxford where youth unemployment is high and social conflict an issue, the proposed project includes an integrated strategy to improve housing and the residential environment in ways that recognise and respect the needs of different groups of residence and provide short-term employment and longer-term opportunities for income earning.

The following chapter by Rakesh Mehta examines the role of an NGO in empowering a slum community in Tughlaqabad Delhi. He examines the relationship between the land-owning agency, the Delhi Development Authority, and the urban municipality, the Municipal Corporation of Delhi, and how their conflicts affected the slum community and the NGO advocating on its behalf. He looks at how informal land markets work when formal markets are monopolised by a single agency and the repercussions for communities when responsible agencies avoid providing basic civic amenities. The chapter concludes on an optimistic note, showing how NGOs can play a vital role in enabling slum-dwellers to command resources on their own account.

Chapter 24 by Lucy Tacher and Lourdes Mondragon Padilla looks at how a central government, in this case that of Mexico, has tried to promote new institutional arrangements and responsibilities in its social programme, the National Solidarity Programme (commonly known as PRONASOL). The programme was designed to invest in both physical and social infra-structure, but with the government no longer being seen as the only source of social welfare provision. The concept behind PRONASOL sets a new relationship between the government and citizens whereby mutual responsibility is established in the fight against poverty. The chapter discusses some of the potentials and constraints of this approach to social development, particularly with regard to the participation of women.

The book concludes with a study of participation and empowerment in Nicaragua by Leah Schmalzbauer. She looks at the Nicaraguan communal movement, in terms of its practical work in the areas of health, education and land distribution, as well as its engagement in mobilisation, reconciliation and coalition building. She traces its development from an organisation linked to the Sandinistas to an empowered and autonomous community-based movement, which owes its success both to the participation it has built in neighbourhoods and to the projection of its political voice, which is heard and respected by government whatever the dominant political party. Schmalzbauer concludes that if grassroots initiatives work in partnership with city and state, they can 'produce communities that are not only liveable, but prosperous, diverse, dynamic and kind'.

Notes

1. The Report is UNCHS (Habitat), *An Urbanising World: Global Report on Human Settlements* (1996), Oxford University Press. The main author was David Satterthwaite, director of the Human Settlements Programme at the International Institute for Environment and Development.

2. The Best Practices and Local Leadership Programme was set up and is coordinated by UNCHS (Habitat). From early 1995 over six hundred 'best practices' were submitted to and judged by a Technical Advisory Committee. Twelve awards were presented at the Habitat II Conference and a database of best practices was produced on CD Rom and disk. There is an ongoing process to evaluate and refine the criteria for good practice and to solicit further submissions and keep the database updated. There is also a continuing debate as to what constitutes 'best practice' and on the usefulness of the concept and the exercise.

3. I prepared two background papers for Habitat II. The first was written with Caren Levy for the First Prepcom held in Geneva in April 1994 and entitled 'Moving towards the gendered city'. The second paper is entitled 'Urban governance: why gender matters' and has been published by UNDP in their Gender in Development Monograph Series, No. 1, March 1996.

4. Definitions are from the *Concise Oxford Dictionary*, 7th edn, 1982.

5. I am grateful to Ana Lucia Munoz of *La Seguridad Social en Colombia* for sharing this story and her insight with me during my visit to Colombia in April, 1996.

6. Using the concept of 'the state' itself is problematic as it is a set of forces, interest groups or people and needs deconstructing as much as any other power category or set of institutional relationships.

7. This is the definition of participation used by the United Nations Research Institute for Social Development (UNRISD) and implies action 'on the part of groups and movements of those hitherto excluded from such control' (quoted in Burkey, 1993: 59).

8. I am grateful to Sarabajaya Kumar for bringing to my attention the fact that accountability is a 'two-way street'.

References

Anderson, M. B. (1996), *Development and Social Diversity: A Development in Practice Reader*, Oxford: Oxfam.

Atkinson, A. and P. V. Chamniern (1994), 'Urban environmental management in a changing development context: the case of Thailand', *Third World Planning Review*, 16(2), May: 147–70.

Barrett, M. and A. Phillips (eds) (1992), *Destabilizing Theory: Contemporary Feminist Debates*, Cambridge: Polity Press.

Beall, J. (1996), *Urban Governance: Why Gender Matters*, United Nations Development Programme (UNDP) Gender in Development Monograph Series No. 1, March.

Beall, J. and C. Levy (1994), 'Moving towards the gendered city', paper prepared for the United Nations Centre for Human Settlements (Habitat) for the first preparatory conference for Habitat II, Geneva, April.

Boonzaier, E. and J. Sharp (eds) (1988), *South African Keywords: The Uses and Abuses of Political Concepts*, Cape Town: David Philip.

Bourne, J. (1987), 'Jewish feminism and identity politics', *Race and Class*, XXIX: 1–24.

Burkey, S. (1993), *People First: A Guide to Self-Reliant, Participatory Rural Development*, London: Zed Books.

Carby, H. (1982), 'White women listen! Black feminism and the boundaries of sisterhood' in Centre for Contemporary Cultural Studies (ed.), *The Empire Strikes Back: Race and Racism in 70s Britain*, London: Hutchinson, pp. 212–35.

Castells, M. (1977), *The Urban Question*, London: Edward Arnold.

Chambers, R. (1983), *Rural Development: Putting the Last First*, London: Longman.

Chant, S. (1996), *Recession and Adjustment: Gendered Outcomes and Implications in Mexico and Philippines*, Research Papers in Environment and Spatial Analysis No. 31, Department of Geography, London School of Economics.

Cohen, A. (1969), *Custom and Politics in Urban Africa. A Study of Hausa Migrants in Yoruba Towns*, London: Routledge and Kegan Paul.

Crush, J. (ed.) (1996), *Power of Development*, London: Routledge.

Dubow, S. (1994), 'Ethnic euphemisms and racial echoes', *Journal of Southern African Studies Special Issue: Ethnicity and Identity in Southern Africa*, 20(3): 355–70.

Elson, D. (1989), 'The impact of structural adjustment on women: concepts and issues' in B. Onimode (ed.), *The IMF, the World Bank and the African Debt. Vol. 2: The Social and Political Impact*, London: Zed Books, pp. 55–74.

Escobar, A. (1995), *Encountering Development: The Making and Unmaking of the Third World*, Princeton, NJ: Princeton University Press.

Folbre, N. (1986), 'Hearts and spades: paradigms of household economics', *World Development*, 14(2): 245–55.

Foucault, M. (1976), *Power/Knowledge*, New York: Pantheon.

Freund, W. (1994), *Insiders and Outsiders: The Indian Working Class of Durban in the Twentieth Century*, Pietermaritzburg: University of Natal Press.

Friedmann, J. (1992), *Empowerment: The Politics of Alternative Development*, Oxford: Blackwell.

Gibson, T. (1994), 'Showing what you mean (not just talking about it)', *RRA Notes, Special Issue on Participatory Tools and Methods in Urban Areas*, 21, London: International Institute for Environment and Development.

Gonzalez de la Rocha, M. (1994), *The Resources of Poverty: Women and Survival in a Mexican City*, Oxford: Blackwell.

Greed, C. (1994), *Women and Planning: Creating Gendered Realities*, London: Routledge.

Grown, C. and C. Sebstad (1989), 'Beyond survival: expanding income-earning opportunities for women in developing countries', *World Development*, 17(7): 937–52.

Hardoy, J., D. Mitlin and D. Satterthwaite (1992), *Environmental Problems in Third World Cities*, London: Earthscan.

Harris, N. (1990), *Cities in the 1990s*, London: UCL Press.

Harris, N. and I. Fabricius (eds) (1996), *Cities and Structural Adjustment*, London: UCL Press.

Harvey, D. (1973), *Social Justice and the City*, London: Edward Arnold.

Harvey, D. (1989), *The Condition of Postmodernity*, Oxford: Blackwell.

Healey, P. (1995), 'Integrating the concept of social diversity into public policy', in OECD, *Women in the City: Housing, Services and the Urban Environment*, Paris: Organisation for Economic Cooperation and Development.

hooks, b. (1984), *Feminist Theory from Margin to Centre*, Boston, MA: South End Press.

hooks, b. (1991), *Yearning: Race, Gender and Cultural Politics*, London: Turnaround Press.

IIED (1994), *RRA Notes, Special Issue on Participatory Tools and Methods in Urban Areas*, 21, London: International Institute for Environment and Development.

Kabeer, N. (1991), 'Gender, production and well-being: rethinking the household economy', Institute of Development Studies Discussion Paper 288, May, Falmer, Sussex: University of Sussex.

Kabeer, N. (1994), *Reversed Realities: Gender Hierarchies in Development Thought*, London: Verso.

Kanji, N. (1995), 'Gender, poverty and economic adjustment in Harare, Zimbabwe', *Environment and Urbanization*, 7(1), April: 37–56.

Latapi, A. E. and M. Gonzalez de la Rocha (1995), 'Crisis, restructuring and urban poverty in Mexico', *Environment and Urbanization*, 7(1) April: 51–75.

Latouche, S. (1993), *In the Wake of the Affluent Society: An Exploration of Post-Development*, London: Zed Books.

Levy, C. (1996), 'The process of institutionalising gender in policy and planning: the "web" of institutionalisation', Development Planning Unit Working Paper Series 74, March.

Little, J. (1994), *Gender, Planning and the Policy Process*, Oxford: Pergamon Press.

Lukes, S. (1974), *Power. A Radical View*. London: Macmillan.

McDowell, L. (1983), 'Towards an understanding of the gender division of urban space', *Environment and Planning for Society and Space*, 1(1): 57–70.

McDowell, L. and D. Massey (1984), 'A woman's place?', in D. Massey and J. Allen (eds), *Geography Matters*, Cambridge: Cambridge University Press.

McDowell, L. and R. Pringle (1992), *Defining Women: Social Institutions and Gender Divisions*, Cambridge: Polity Press in association with Open University Press.

Mackintosh, M. (1992), 'Introduction', in Wuyts, Mackintosh and Hewitt (eds), *Development Policy and Public Action*.

Marchmand, M. and J. Parpart (1995), *Feminism, Postmodernism, Development*, London: Routledge.

Mare, G. (1993), *Ethnicity and Politics in South Africa*, London: Zed Books.

Marks, S. (1986), *The Ambiguities of Dependence in South Africa: Class, Nationalism and the State in Twentieth Century Natal*, Johannesburg: Ravan Press.

Marks, S. and S. Trapido (eds) (1987), *The Politics of Race, Class and Nationalism in Twentieth Century South Africa*, London: Longman.

Massey, D. (1984), *Spatial Divisions of Labour, Social Structures and the Geography of Production*, London: Macmillan.

Massey, D. (1994), *Space, Place and Gender*, Cambridge: Polity Press.

Max-Neef, M. A. (1992), *From the Outside Looking in: Experiences in 'Barefoot Economics'*, London: Zed Books.

Midgley, J. (1984), 'Introduction', in J. Midgley and D. Piachaud (eds), *The Fields and Methods of Social Planning*, London: Heinemann Educational Books.

Midgley, J. (1995), *Social Development*, London: Sage Publications.

Midgley, J. and D. Piachaud (eds) (1984), *The Fields and Methods of Social Planning*, London: Heinemann Educational.

Mitlin, D. and D. Satterthwaite (1996), 'Sustainable development and cities', in C. Pugh (ed.), *Sustainability, the Environment and Urbanization*, London: Earthscan, pp. 23–62.

Mitlin, D. and J. Thompson (1995), 'Participatory approaches in urban areas: strengthening civil society or reinforcing the status quo?', *Environment and Urbanization*, 7(1), April: 231–50.

Mohanty, C. T. (1988), 'Under Western eyes: feminist scholarship and colonial discourses', *Feminist Review*, 30: 61–88.

Mohanty, C. T. (1992), 'Feminist encounters: locating the politics of experience' in M. Barrett and A. Phillips (eds), *Destabilizing Theory, Contemporary Feminist Debates*, Cambridge: Polity Press.

Mohanty, C. T., A. Russo and L. Torres (eds) (1991), *Third World Women and the Politics of Feminism*, Bloomington: Indiana University Press.

Moore, H. (1994), *A Passion for Difference*, Cambridge: Polity Press.

Moser, C. (1987), 'Women, human settlements and housing: a conceptual framework for analysis and policy making', in Moser and Peake (eds), *Women, Human Settlements and Housing*, pp. 12–31.

Moser, C. (1993), *Gender Planning and Development: Theory, Practice and Training*, London: Routledge.

Moser, C. (1996), *Confronting Crisis: A Comparative Study of Household Responses to Poverty and Vulnerability in Four Poor Urban Communities*, Environmentally Sustainable Development Studies and Monographs Series No. 8, Washington DC: World Bank.

Moser, C. and L. Peake (eds) (1987), *Women, Human Settlements and Housing*, London: Tavistock.

Nicholson, L. (ed.) (1990), *Feminism/Postmodernism*, London: Routledge.

OECD (1995), *Women in the City, Housing, Services and the Urban Environment*, Paris: Organisation for Economic Cooperation and Development.

Parpart, J. (1993), 'Who is the "Other"?: a postmodern feminist critique of women and development theory and practice', *Development and Change*, 24: 439–64.

Pearse, A. and M. Stiefel (1979), *Inquiry into Participation: A Research Approach*, Popular Participation Programme, UNRISD/79/C/14, Geneva: UNRISD.

Phillips, A. (1993), *Democracy and Difference*, Cambridge: Polity Press.

Pickvance, C. (ed.) (1977), *Urban Sociology*, London: Tavistock.

Rakodi, C. (1991), 'Cities and people: towards a gender-aware urban planning process?', *Public Administration and Development*, 11(6): 541–60.

Ranger, T. (1983), 'The invention of tradition in colonial Africa', in E. Hobsbawm and T. Ranger (eds), *The Invention of Tradition*, Cambridge: Cambridge University Press.

Rees, W. (1992), 'Ecological footprints and appropriated carrying capacity: what urban economics leaves out', *Environment and Urbanization*, 4(2): 121–30.

Sachs, W. (1992), *The Development Dictionary: A Guide to Knowledge as Power*, London: Zed Books.

Sapire, H. and J. Beall (1995), 'Introduction: urban change and urban studies in Southern Africa', *Journal of Southern African Studies Special Issue: Urban Studies and Urban Change in Southern Africa*, 21(1): 3–18.

Satterthwaite, D. (1996), 'The scale and nature of urban change in the South', Paper of Human Settlements Programme, International Institute for Environment and Development, London, June.

Saunders, P. (1979), *Urban Politics: A Sociological Interpretation*, Harmondsworth: Penguin.

Scoones, I. and J. Thompson (eds) (1994), *Beyond Farmer First: Rural People's Knowledge, Agricultural Research and Extension Practice*, London: Intermediate Technology Publications.

Sen, A. (1990), 'Gender and cooperative conflicts', in I. Tinker (ed.), *Persistent Inequalities*, Oxford: Oxford University Press.

Shetty, S. (1991), 'The assessment of "empowerment" in development projects – an enquiry', M.Sc. dissertation in the Department of Social Policy and Administration, London School of Economics.

Sitas, A. (1996), 'The new tribalism: hostels and violence', *Journal of Southern African Studies*, 22(2): 235–48.

Stefano, C. di (1990), 'Dilemmas of difference: feminism, modernity and postmodernism', in L. Nicholson (ed.), *Feminism/Postmodernism*, London: Routledge.

Turner, J. (1976), *Housing by People: Towards Autonomy in Building Environments*, London: Marion Boyars.

UNCHS (Habitat) (1990), *Building-Related Income Generation for Women – Lessons from Experience*, Nairobi: UNCHS (Habitat),

UNCHS (Habitat) (1996), *An Urbanising World, Global Report on Human Settlements*, Oxford: Oxford University Press.

UNDP (1991), *Cities, People and Poverty: Urban Development Cooperation for the 1990s*, New York: United Nations Development Programme.

UNDP (1995), *Human Development Report*, Oxford: Oxford University Press.

Vail, L. (ed.) (1989), *The Creation of Tribalism in Southern Africa*, Berkeley: University of California Press.

Wilmsen, E. N. with S. Dubow and J. Sharp (1994), 'Ethnicity, identity and nationalism in Southern Africa', *Journal of Southern African Studies Special Issue: Ethnicity and Identity in Southern Africa*, 20(3): 347–54.

Wilson, E. (1991), *The Sphinx in the City: Urban Life, the Control of Disorder and Women*, London: Virago.

Wilson, G. (1991), 'Thoughts on the cooperative conflict model of the household in relation to economic method', *IDS Bulletin* 22(1): 31–6.

You, N. (1996), 'Habitat II in focus: towards a habitable future', *City*, 3–4.

Wuyts, M., M. Mackintosh and T. Hewitt (eds) (1992), *Development Policy and Public Action*, Oxford: Oxford University Press in association with the Open University.

CHAPTER 2

Participation in the City: A Gender Perspective

Jo Beall

Participation, like equity, is something we all support, and yet it is a word to which very different meanings can be given. As Nicci Nelson and Susan Wright put it, the term participation 'can be attached to very different sets of relations, often seemingly by its "warmness" distracting close attention from the nature of those relations' (Nelson and Wright, 1995). Thus, in writing about participation in the city, I want to be clear about how I use the term 'participation' and about the gender relations involved.

Participation is most commonly associated with political participation or activity. In the second half of this chapter I address this view of participation by reviewing some of the critical gender issues in urban governance, understood both as government responsibility and as civic engagement.[1] I focus on women's involvement in the organisational life of the city – in public office and in organisations of civil society – and the importance of both for incorporating a gender perspective into urban development planning and practice.

However, in order to understand participation in political or organisational terms, it is also necessary to explore the related issue of how women and men participate in the social and economic life of the city, how they benefit and contribute, as workers, carers, users, clients and as pleasure-seekers.

A useful distinction in developing my thinking has been that between *participation as entitlement* and *participation as empowerment* (Borner et al., 1995). 'Participation as entitlement' is used here to refer to how women and men command resources and contribute to and take responsibility for the well-being of their households, communities and the city. 'Participation as empowerment' is used here to refer to the processes by which organised groups in the city (and individuals within them) identify and articulate their interests, negotiate change with others and transform urban organisational life and their role within it.

This chapter starts by giving an overview of the 'gendered city',[2] historically designed by men and for men – but inhabited by both women and men, who have diverse interests and needs at different stages of their lives and in different family and community contexts. Through thinking about 'participation as entitlement', I examine how women and men benefit from and contribute to urban life, through examples of opportunities for making a living and for using urban resources and services.

This picture of the 'gendered city' provides a backdrop for discussing 'participation as empowerment'. Here I consider some of the problems faced by women in both public office and within grassroots organisations. The chapter concludes by arguing that a gender perspective will not inform urban policy and planning processes automatically. There is a need to transform City Hall from within, while continually holding it to account from outside.

Women and men use and experience cities in different ways, and not always in ways anticipated by planners. Elizabeth Wilson (1991) has pointed out that historically, gender stereotyping has profoundly affected urban planning and urban institutions. Cities are spatial and organisational expressions of social relations, which are based as much on power and conflict as on cooperation and consensus. This has meant that the needs of women have often been ignored.

Gender and poverty in the city

By the twenty-first century the majority of the world's poor people will be living in urban areas, most of them in cities of the Third World. While the development of human settlements has led to significant improvements in living conditions for many people across the globe, cities can also be places where opportunities are denied and the quality of life declines, particularly for the urban poor. Urban people in poverty are usually those without secure employment, savings or saleable assets. They are vulnerable to changes in demand in the labour market, and in prices of basic goods and services, and they cannot afford adequate housing.

Women predominate among urban people in poverty for three reasons: first, because those jobs they can obtain are poorly paid, part-time or insecure (even in contexts where there are high levels of male unemployment or where women workers are preferred); second, because of inequities in resource distribution and decision-making power within the household, so that women do not always control their own income; and third, because of the fact that women generally do not command equal resources or assets compared to men in their society. The increase in women-headed households in cities everywhere, and the growing phenomenon of women-maintained families, make it even more necessary to adopt a gender perspective in response to urban poverty.

Currently, in cities worldwide, there is evidence of 'new poverty' resulting from economic reform. Economic restructuring has made urban people insecure and vulnerable. For example, cuts in public sector jobs, reduction in subsidies on staple foods or services such as transport and the introduction of user charges and cost-sharing for basic services have increased urban poverty.

While the urban poor are bearing the brunt of structural adjustment, it is the women among them who are doing most to compensate for declining real incomes (Elson, 1989). There is evidence from Africa and Latin America (Chant, 1995; Kanji, 1995) that women are reducing their own consumption in the face of pressures on domestic budgets imposed by user charges or cost-sharing. In Europe, demands are being made on women's time, as a result of the withdrawal of state responsibility for welfare and the shift towards community care. In countries of the South, women are the ones who take responsibility for the management of their communities, organising for facilities and services in the face of inadequate provision. Women respond to urban problems in ways different from those of men. They have proved inventive and resilient in managing communities, maintaining social cohesion, and building homes and neighbourhoods under conditions of dislocation or disharmony. As urban management fails to deliver urban infrastructure and services, and as economic restructuring erodes the real incomes of poor people in cities, there is increased competition for affordable shelter, and for employment or income-earning opportunities, as well as for services as basic as drainage, sanitation, or meeting places. There is ample evidence of women organising to improve their surroundings and their security. In a review of the literature Moser cites examples of a range of low-income urban women's activities: health issues, childcare, water, waste recycling, self-help housing, and transport (Moser et al., 1993).

Making a living in the city

Millions of people in the cities of Africa, Asia and Latin America cannot find work in the formal sector and have to create work themselves or find it within the informal economy. Everywhere women are entering the labour market when household wages fall. It has been pointed out that increased responsibility as breadwinners does not always lead to greater status or decision-making power for women (Moser et al., 1993). From the perspective of participation as entitlement, women in the city do more, and command less.

Women are everywhere over-represented in the non-conventional labour force. There may be restricted demand for women's labour, and they might have inappropriate or inadequate skills for the formal wage employment available; wages in the formal sector may be lower than returns from the informal economy; or women may find it easier to balance income-earning activities with their other responsibilities in the more flexible environment of the informal economy. At the same time, in some places demand for women's labour has increased, resulting in a feminisation of the labour force, particularly where production is labour intensive.

Recognising the interaction between the organisation of work and other social relationships and responsibilities is crucial to the development of sustainable strategies towards promoting urban livelihoods. Women and men are never just workers but have other social responsibilities and relations in the household and community which impinge on the manner and extent to which they engage in income-earning activities and participate in the productive life of the city.

Urban planning as a gender issue

The fact that the buildings and structure of cities last for generations means that the architecture, urban design, land-use planning and infrastructure are legacies of past eras. Women's priorities have often been ignored in the design of human settlements, the location of housing, and the provision of urban services. Conventional urban planning has been characterised by cities being divided into zones intended for specific activities, with houses, markets and factories in separate locations. Today, cities designed along these lines no longer conform to the reality of the lives of women and men. Stereotypical notions of nuclear families – with male breadwinners journeying across town to work, and women as housewives caring for their children and elderly relatives in residential neighbourhoods – have never applied in some situations, and in others no longer apply. The separation of home, work and leisure is being challenged in the cities in both the North and the South, as women and men work to transform the urban environment.

A look at any number of informal settlements in the cities of the Third World tells us that many different activities go on within them; and that with or without planners, people create and organise their surroundings in a variety of ways. Women squatters in Africa build their shacks not in a grid pattern but around central spaces, to facilitate communication and communal childcare. A shopkeeper in India can call behind a curtain to his wife cooking and sewing in the back room. Their children can run between the two of them as well as their uncle in the motor-cycle repair business he conducts from the adjoining yard and the street in front of the shop. In the North, the rise in home-working and telecommuting means there is less separation between work, community and family lives than in the past.

Getting around the city

Functionally fragmented cities often make it difficult for people, and particularly women, to manage the tasks of daily life. Women often need to travel outside of rush hours, and to destinations different from those of men, for example to shops, schools and clinics. Yet cost-cutting inevitably involves a reduction in off-peak services, and private operators are reluctant to take on routes and times that are not so busy.

The problems women face are caused by the fact that transport systems have invariably been designed around the man's journey to work; and because the current focus of transport planning is on mobility rather than accessibility. As mothers and carers, women have to escort others; as working women engaged in informal sector activities, they often have to carry heavy loads. Yet public service vehicles are often designed without these requirements in mind. This results in women having to struggle with inconvenient public transport or to walk (Levy, 1992).

It is not only the gender roles of women which require consideration. As Patsy Healey (1995) argues, we also need to integrate the concept of social diversity into public policy, to make the built environment less like an assault course or a danger zone, and to make it more user-friendly, safe and secure for everybody – women and men, the healthy and robust as well as the frail and disabled, and for everybody at different stages of their lives.

Access to resources and services

There are countless ways in which income, status and patronage affect people's ability to use services and facilities. At one extreme it is access to the city itself that is restricted. Urban authorities have variously expelled migrants without residents' permits, bulldozed illegal settlements, arrested illegal workers, harassed street-traders and closed down unlicensed enterprises. Gender relations can also serve to restrict women's access and can intersect with other social relations to exclude women from participation.

The urban poor in general are denied land tenure, adequate housing, and necessary infrastructure and services. They are often confined to places that are unsuited to human settlement, such as hillsides, swampy areas and sites near sources of pollution such as industrial areas or garbage dumps. When housing programmes, upgrading schemes or infrastructure developments present opportunities for the improvement of human settlements, women are often excluded, because their incomes are too low, or they have no appropriate collateral or patronage, or they are illiterate and cannot read legal documents and fill in the required forms, or they do not have the time and skills to engage in self-build schemes. Women who are included in schemes as members of households are rarely consulted, despite the fact that women, as prime users of housing and human settlements, often have insights that can prevent failure and wastage.

Violence in the city

The issue of safety is one of growing urgency as cities in many countries are becoming more violent, restricting access and mobility in the city, particularly for women. Violence and public safety are gender issues. Young boys face different sorts of pressure from young girls, often wreaking havoc and creating fear themselves, while at the same time being vulnerable to physical assault and attack as a consequence of male gender roles and norms. Women too experience gender-specific forms of urban violence and sexual assault. Violence or the fear of it can prove just as effective as more direct forms of seclusion, such as purdah, in restricting women's mobility and keeping them in terror behind closed doors.

Fear and violence prevent participation, either as entitlement or as empowerment. As stated in the Canadian National Report to a recent OECD conference on women in the city (OECD, 1995), 'violence and the fear of violence prevent women from full and equal participation in the social life of their community and threaten our understanding of what should be the democratic functioning of our society'.

Women's participation in urban governance

Recent concern with governance in urban areas stems from a more general attention being paid to the issue of 'good governance' in development. There are two main approaches. One is 'essentially preoccupied with questions of financial accountability and administrative efficiency' and the other is more interested in political concerns related to democracy, human rights and participation (Robinson, 1995). Cities have particular governance problems of their own. They are not completely independent, with various tiers of government intervening in urban areas, and they are subject to national and international economic, environmental and social pressures. Urban governance used to be equated solely with urban management. More recently it has come to be understood both as government responsibility and as civic engagement involving a full range of participants, and thus making it more possible to integrate a gender perspective.

Women's representation in public office

There are a number of reasons why women should participate in public office. First, there are the demands of equality and democracy. Second, women need to demonstrate their capabilities if legislation for equality is to result in real social change. Third, women have particular experiences of and relationships to the urban environment and they have proved themselves to be effective change agents at the city or local levels on a range of issues. However, there continue to be a number of obstacles to women's participation in public life, such as lack of confidence, know-how, connections and courage to stand for office without support. In many developing countries, there are additional handicaps restricting women's participation, such as cultural constraints on women engaging in public life.

Even in countries with a good record on women's political representation there is no room for complacency. For example, in Australia five years ago, nearly half the mayors of the capital cities happened to be women. Now there is only one female mayor (OECD, 1995). Even when the proportion of women remains fairly constant, there is a high turnover of elected women. One conclusion to be drawn here is that women themselves run out of steam or burn out through trying to balance multiple responsibilities. Another is that if women elected representatives are to have a sustainable political career at any level, their multiple responsibilities have to be recognised and accommodated by government. In Sweden there has been considerable progress in increasing the participation of women in policy arenas as well as the labour market – the expansion of childcare facilities and parental insurance have made it possible for both women and men to combine productive and political life with family responsibilities. Thus there are legislative and material prerequisites for women to take part in public life.

Women are better represented at the local than the national level, for reasons such as proximity and convenience, although they still remain a minority (Gwagwa, 1991). Existing male-dominated interest groups are likely to be reluctant to give up the power and control of resources that are associated with local office and patron–client networks. Thus current trends towards political decentralisation of power may not necessarily increase the number of women elected to local office.

However, the fact that women hold public office does not guarantee that the interests of all women will be represented. Political responsibility to a women's constituency at metropolitan or municipal level does not come automatically to women representatives, and there is no point in heaping blame on individual women in public office. It is more important to ensure that there are institutional structures that enable the specific interests of women to be represented by local councils, and that councillors have transparent, accountable and open channels of consultation and communication with their constituencies. This is essential for participation as empowerment, and yet, in many countries and many cities, the political will is lacking.

Community organisation and advocacy

Community activism is an important avenue towards participation in city-level planning and policy-making processes and is necessary to keep politicians accountable. Issues reach the policy agenda when powerful or well-organised groups in society identify and press for solutions to their problems. Adopting a women's perspective in policy and planning would not have been possible without the sustained organised force of women over the last two decades. This has been forged through women organising separately, or in broad coalitions with men, or through inclusive networks in support of social justice and equitable policy change.

The importance of women's grassroots organisation is increasingly appreciated by governments, external agencies and NGOs. This is particularly the case when women organise services themselves, in the absence of adequate provision from other sources (Moser, 1987). In Peru, women organised self-help responses to the economic crisis. To provide for their own and their families' survival they started community kitchens and 'glass of milk' committees, some of which went on to become larger health and leadership training initiatives (Barrig, 1991).

There is a danger, however, if women confine themselves to organising self-help and survival strategies. This can result not only in other sectors and institutions being allowed to abdicate responsibility for provision and redistribution at the urban level, but in women being left to manage communities on their own, without resources or political and professional support. To ensure 'participation as empowerment', therefore, it is important that women in organisations of civil society, such as NGOs and community-based organisations, are not only involved in community management, self-help and service provision, but also have the opportunity for personal self-development, campaigning and advocacy.

The Society for Promotion of Area Resource Centres (SPARC) in Bombay recognises this problem and, while addressing the basic needs of women, also works with them to increase their political effectiveness. Two examples of SPARC's work are support for an organisation called Mobile Crèches, which provides childcare for women construction workers; and training in 'legal literacy' for women pavement-dwellers threatened by a demolition scheme, which enabled them to fight themselves for their right to shelter (SPARC, 1986). In Sweden new women's networks have recently been formed to campaign for better political responsiveness to women's issues. Women joined forces and threatened to register themselves as a women's party if the existing political parties did not take gender issues more seriously. This challenge, which received excellent media coverage, had the desired effect of making established political parties place women's issues higher on the political agenda (OECD, 1995). Thus it is primarily the organisational power of women that holds the 'mainstream' to account, ensuring that political parties, national and local governments, international agencies or NGOs involve women and take their interests seriously.

Planning with a gender perspective: men can do it too

Policy-makers, planners and activists, whether women or men, can fail to recognise the specific interests of women, and fail to consult them and to address their needs. When women are not vocal they become invisible. Thus the importance of women organising in civil society cannot be over-emphasised. However, it is also important to work within City Hall, for policy-makers and development professionals and practitioners to be made alert to the impact of their decisions on the lives of women and men. Policy and planning with a gender perspective *can be learned*. It is not the sex of the urban practitioner, but the perspective he or she adopts that matters. A gender perspective needs to become embedded in planning expertise and development action and recognised as best practice. Together with public action, this will begin combating a long history in which women's interests and needs as users of cities rarely feature in urban policy or investments.

Forging linkages through participation

To achieve entitlement and empowerment through participation it is necessary that policy-makers and planners are not left to transform cities alone. Increasingly there is a focus on urban partnerships in which the creative energies of the public, private and community sectors are combined to meet the growing demands of rapid urbanisation. All too frequently women are included in urban partnerships only at the implementation stage and remain excluded from the formulation, design and resource allocation stages of programmes and projects.

New forms of urban partnership, therefore, need to foster (on the part of all actors or groups involved) a commitment to developing genuinely participatory processes that include both women and men at all stages of development. Gender-sensitive urban partnerships have to recognise the different approaches that women and men adopt in organisation, negotiation and planning as a result of their socialisation and experience of public life, and to change their organisational practice accordingly. Strong links are needed between grassroots organisations, urban professionals and their organisations, and the decision-makers and planners responsible for policy-making and implementation. The more women are involved in all these arenas, the easier it will be to keep local activism robust, to make strong and empowering links and to fight for equal entitlement for women and men to participate fully in the life of the city.

Notes

I would like to thank Oxfam for their permission to reproduce this chapter, which first appeared as an article in *Gender and Development*, 4(1), February 1996.

1. The terms 'government responsibility' and 'civic engagement' are those used in 'The Habitat Agenda' or Global Plan of Action, which grew out of the preparatory process for the Habitat II Conference in Istanbul in June 1996.

2. This term was first used in a paper entitled 'Moving Towards the Gendered City', which I co-authored with Caren Levy and which was commissioned by the Women and Human Settlements Development Programme of the United Nations Centre for Human Settlements [UNCHS (Habitat)] for the First Prepcom for Habitat II, Geneva, April, 1994.

References

Barrig, M. (1991), 'Women and development in Peru: old models, new actors', *Environment and Urbanization*, 3(2): 66–70.

Beall, J. D. (1995), 'Social security and social networks among the urban poor in Pakistan', *Habitat International*, 19(4): 427–45.

Borner, S., A. Brunetti and B. Weder (1995), 'Political credibility and economic growth', Basel (mimeo), quoted in P. Nunnenkamp, 'What donors mean by good governance: heroic ends, limited means and traditional dilemmas of development cooperation', *IDS Bulletin*, 26(2): 9–16.

Chant, S. (1995), 'Gender aspects of urban economic growth and development', paper prepared for UNU/WIDER Conference on Human Settlements in the Changing Global Political and Economic Processes, Helsinki, 25–7 August.

Elson, D. (1989), 'The impact of structural adjustment on women: concepts and issues' in B. Onimode (ed.), *The IMF, the World Bank and African Debt, Vol. 2: The Social and Political Impact*, London: Zed Press, pp. 55–74.

Environment and Urbanization (1995), 7(1), April and 7(2), October (special issues on urban poverty).

Gwagwa, N. (1991), 'Women in local government: towards a future South Africa', *Environment and Urbanization*, 3(1): 70–8.

Healey, P. (1995), 'Integrating the concept of social diversity in public policy', in OECD, *Women in the City, Housing, Services and the Urban Environment*, Paris: OECD, pp. 50–8.

Kanji, N. (1995), 'Gender, poverty and economic adjustment in Harare, Zimbabwe', in *Environment and Urbanization*, 7(1): 37–56.

Levy, C. (1992), 'Transport', in L. Ostergaard (ed.), *Gender and Development: A Practical Guide*, London: Routledge, pp. 94–109.

Molyneux, M. (1985) 'Mobilisation without emancipation? women's interests in state and revolution in Nicaragua', *Feminist Studies*, 11(2): 227–54.

Moser, C. (1987), 'Mobilisation is women's work: struggles for infrastructure in Guayaquil, Ecuador', in C. Moser and L. Peake (eds), *Women, Human Settlements and Housing*, London: Tavistock, pp. 12–32.

Moser, C., A. J. Herbert and R. E. Makonnen (1993), 'Urban poverty in the context of structural adjustment: recent evidence and policy responses', World Bank TWU Discussion Paper No. 4, Washington, DC.

Nelson, N. and S. Wright (1995), *Power and Participatory Development*, London: IT Publications.

OECD (1995), *Women in the City: Housing, Services and the Urban Environment*, Paris: OECD.

Robinson, M. (1995), 'Introduction: towards democratic governance', *IDS Bulletin*, 26(2): 1–8.

Sen, A. (1981) *Poverty and Famines*, Oxford: Clarendon Press

SPARC (1986), *Annual Report*, Bombay: SPARC.

Wilson, E. (1991), *The Sphinx in the City*, London: Virago.

PART TWO

Living and Working in the City: Sustainable Homes and Livelihoods

CHAPTER 3

Women's Income-generating Activities in the Informal Sector

*Allison Freeman, Francine Pickup
and Lamia Rashid*

Women the world over are engaged in productive work both inside and outside the home. In the urban context, the majority of women involved in productive work conduct such work in the informal sector. Despite women's prevalence in this sector, policy-makers have consistently overlooked this important area for women's income generation. This chapter first argues for policy-makers' recognition of women's work in the urban informal sector, calling for a new, gender-sensitive definition of 'work'. It goes on to look at existing projects that successfully support women's income-generation activities, and from this delineates examples of 'best practice'. Finally, it draws some policy recommendations for supporting women's income-generating activities in the urban informal sector. In doing so it challenges urban planners to acknowledge the benefits of the informal sector for women and to create an urban environment more enabling to women's informal sector income generation.

Productive and reproductive work

Women the world over are engaged in productive work both inside and outside the home. Their contribution, however, has been consistently underestimated by both academics and planners. Elson (1995) argues that this 'gender blindness' must be addressed by looking at work and workers in a gender-disaggregated way. First, the myth that women are involved only in reproductive work[1] in the home must be questioned, and women's active participation in the economy, especially in the informal sector, must be acknowledged. Only then can development policy and practice benefit rather than worsen women's situations. There is also a close relationship between women in the household not directly involved in the economy and those who are. The former, usually adolescent girls or older women, take on additional domestic work to release other women for income generation. Second, in the workplace, women are paid less on average than men; they have less access to and control over resources and processes of production; and they are excluded from decision-making roles. This is accounted for by 'male bias' in societies in which seemingly neutral policies often serve to disfavour women (Elson, 1995). This in turn rebounds on their relationships within the household and the value placed on their labour and contribution.

Policy-makers need to recognise the perceived social value or worth of different types of work within a cultural context and to help make visible the work of women. The apparent invisibility of women's work is reinforced by the ethnocentric assumptions of researchers and policy-makers and by culture-specific gender ideologies (Moore, 1988: 43). If work is understood as 'paid work outside the home', then the value of women's subsistence and domestic work goes unrecognised and under-valued. Gender-sensitive policy should see the household not as immutable, but as a site not only of cooperation but also of conflicting interests (Kabeer, 1994). Additionally, by recognising diverse household forms, policy-makers can address the particular problems women-headed households face, such as trouble obtaining loans, credit, access to the formal work sector and title to land.

Women and the informal sector

The more widely accepted definitions of the informal economy assume that it is relatively easy to enter, it operates on a smaller scale than the formal sector, the resources utilised in the informal sector tend to be indigenous in origin, and the work done is labour intensive and usually accomplished by members of a household or family (UNCHS [Habitat]/ILO, 1995). Statistically this sector is hard to quantify because its activities occur outside of the watch of governments. Women's work in the informal sector is even more invisible as it often stems from and blends with their reproductive activities. From a policy perspective, this leaves women's economic activities unacknowledged, which in turn leads to the assumption that they have free time on their hands. However, it is not enough simply to make women visible in this sector. Gender differentiation cuts across the formal/informal distinction in such a way that the value placed on work comes to depend on whether it is perceived as 'women's work' or 'men's work', and not just on whether it is in the informal or formal sector (Elson, 1995: 21). The advantages of the informal economy for women are flexibility, being your own boss, combining productive and reproductive work and it being carried out 'at home' or 'on the street'. These go hand-in-hand with the disadvantages of lack of safety and security, illegality and risk. Urban planners can intervene by acknowledging the benefits of the informal sector for women and making it a more enabling and less risky work environment for them.

Policy-makers need to recognise that entrepreneurial behaviour and patterns of growth are gendered; men generally employ specialisation strategies, choosing to concentrate on improving one economic enterprise, while women, who are more security oriented because of their domestic responsibilities, tend to diversify their enterprises (Downing, 1991). Within the informal sector, income-generating activities include a wide range of waged and entrepreneurial work such as the preparation and/or sale of cooked food, seasonal fruits, sweets, beer, tourist items and repair services. A gender-sensitive approach to women's participation in small enterprises also means differentiating between the economic goals that women have. These goals vary depending on a woman's productive and reproductive situation, individual and household coping strategies, and available resources; the goals may be oriented to 'survival' for the most vulnerable, 'security' for those whose basic survival is ensured, or 'growth' for those who are better off and feel secure enough to take risks (Grown and Sebstad, 1989). The policy implication of this is for planners to understand and respond to the diverse nature of women's involvement and earnings, and their particular rationale for labour or business activities, in order to avoid underestimating women's business patterns or imposing on them inappropriate growth strategies.

Women and income generation in practice

This section shows how women are active participants in the informal sector, and employ various strategies in order to earn an income. The examples described have been selected because recommendations can be drawn from them to show how planners might better enable women working in the urban informal sector.

In India, where 94% of women are self-employed and not in formal employer–employee relationships, women are particularly susceptible to exploitation because of the unfriendly institutional arrangements they confront. The Self-Employed Women's Association (SEWA) is a collective grassroots organisation run by women and for women nationwide. It has set up 30 all-women production service and banking cooperatives in rural and urban areas, helping to stress the importance of women as workers and owners in a collective. It emphasises the need to bridge the gap between women working at the grassroots level and the formal planning system. SEWA produced a report from a nationwide study of self-employed women with recommendations to formalise a legitimate system for women in the informal sector; it suggested the setting up of decentralised protective boards, the incorporation of women into urban planning, improvements in women's health through training local women as health workers, and the establishing of autonomous umbrella organisations that hold groups accountable. Only by having a critical mass of leaders who represent the voices of these women in decision-making roles in planning can the importance of such a policy be demonstrated.

Two organisations in the Dominican Republic provide examples of credit reaching women through alternative collateral schemes. Collateral is one of the main drawbacks to women accessing credit as they often do not or cannot have assets, such as land, in their names. Alternative forms of collateral may include jewellery or other personal assets that women may have control over, or the use of loan co-signers (INSTRAW, 1990). The Asociacion Dominicana Para el Desarollo de la Microempresa (ADEMI) disburses credit (to both women and men) with little waiting time and minimal paperwork. Its innovation in collateral means borrowers may use machinery or managerial skills to support their loan requests. Repayment rates are very high, ensuring the programme's sustainability.

The Asociacion Dominicana Pro-Desarrollo de la Mujer (ADOPEM) is an urban branch of Women's World Banking, which provides training to its loan recipients in managerial skills and in basic accounting and banking procedures. The organisation provides credit to individual women or women in solidarity groups of three to five. Interest rates are differentiated between individual loan recipients, who are usually better off and therefore charged at higher rates, and group loan recipients, whose incomes and profits tend to be lower and who are therefore charged at lower rates. When women's credit needs surpass the organisation's limits, ADOPEM links women entrepreneurs to formal banks by acting as third-party guarantors, thereby overcoming the constraint of collateral (INSTRAW, 1990). The above examples demonstrate ways to open up access for women to gender-biased institutions such as banks and credit/loan schemes. When women's saving and consumption patterns and entrepreneurial behaviour are accounted for, such schemes find that a much higher percentage of women than men successfully pay back their loans. The schemes also take account of women's various economic survival needs, through smaller loans and appropriate training, and larger loans and technical training for women with security- or growth-oriented goals. However, credit programmes must be women-friendly in their delivery of credit and of support services in order to avoid increasing or doubling women's burdens. They must take account of the following considerations: the kinds of training women need given their existing skill and responsibilities; locations that are accessible to women; and follow-up that is supportive and flexible rather than penalising.

It must be recognised that, in some areas of the world, entrepreneurship is not new and traditional cultural practices may be advantageous to women's income-generating activities. The Asante women traders of Ghana (Clark, 1989) have a cultural tradition of women-headed households, and of women traders working independently from men. In this culture, women are responsible for acquiring the goods to be traded, trading these goods in the market, and managing all the money acquired in these transactions. Women traders often use a younger daughter or a hired helper to take over their domestic responsibilities, thus freeing themselves from having to work a double day and enabling them to focus on building up their trading businesses. Women who need help in business might train an older daughter in the skills required to take over the business eventually; older retired women will act as informal consultants to younger traders. This example shows us a cultural practice that alleviates women's dual burdens, thereby allowing them to focus on income generation. It also shows the valuable, advising role the elderly can have in a society. This practice of passing skills and knowledge from generation to generation should be recognised by policy-makers. An important point to note here is that those Asante women who can rely on consistent support for their children from their children's father(s) are better able to focus their time and money on building up their businesses. Women are, therefore, able to be growth-oriented rather than simply risk-reducing when their domestic responsibilities are less burdensome and worrisome (Downing, 1991).

Associated Businesswomen in Tanzania was founded in 1990 by middle-income women. These women were operators of small-scale businesses, such as bakeries, hair salons and dry-cleaners. They offer free advice and seminars to poor women around topics related to business skills. One of their goals is to become involved in mediating loan applications by women. Not surprisingly, the members of this group have realised that women can go only so far without representation at top levels; their overall agenda now includes political action. Through this example, we see that some policy-maker and NGO involvement might be of limited duration. Once women gain skills, confidence and recognition from those in the formal economy, they have an opportunity to help themselves and one another (Tripp, 1994).

In contrast to the above situations in Ghana and Tanzania, in which women's work outside the home is accepted – and perhaps even facilitated by conditions outside the home – is the situation of women working in their homes. In this case, where women are isolated in their homes and often unwilling to speak out about the problems they face because of the uncertain and/or illegal nature of their work, organising women poses considerable difficulties. For example, migrant women homeworkers in Tate's study are isolated in the sense that they often do not speak English, are separated from relatives, and are not familiar with their legal rights (Tate, 1994). The intensive nature of the work, coupled with their childcare responsibilities, also means that these women have few opportunities to make friends and engage in supportive networks. Tate describes the West Yorkshire Homeworking Group, which established contact with and con-sulted women homeworkers on their priorities and needs, created an information pack about rights and welfare benefits in several languages and set up an advice line and newsletter. Through this process, the women have become aware of their common struggle and have organised into local groups.

However, once women pull together in this way, they may face a new set of problems. For example, when women homeworkers pressure employers for better rates of pay there is greater risk that the employers who rely on their cheap labour will find a new pool of unorganised workers elsewhere who are willing to work for lower wages. Therefore, as in the example of the West Yorkshire women, organising may not be sufficient in itself to overcome exploitation. Policy around home-working must also change. 'The emphasis on working with homeworkers by involving them in campaigns and providing them with practical services has brought into focus different aspects of women's lives, in particular the interrelationship of class, race and gender on homeworkers in Britain today' (Tate, 1994: 196). The goal here should be not to eliminate the practice of home-working, as it is clear that in many situations it is the only means by which women can generate income, but to back up women's organising with policy that will increase their security.

The foundations of a 'best practice' process

This section draws together conclusions on how to plan an enabling urban environment for women that recognises gendered patterns of work and needs. There are difficulties in finding comprehensive best practice examples that both address women's immediate and practical needs and advance their strategic gender interests. Policy must aim to decrease women's reproductive burdens while increasing their ability to work either inside or outside the home. Policy to improve women's income-generating options must begin with the actual, lived experience of women (as it is often different from that of men), and recognise the intersection of factors that reflect the diversity of women's lives – age, race, income level, level of physical ability, level of education, marital status and number of dependants. Policy also needs to recognise the diversity of roles and goals women have in the informal sector, as highlighted by Grown and Sebstad (1989). 'Best practice' is that which aims towards being 'better practice': it is self-critical and recognises what policy-makers can and cannot do. This is especially important in the case of the informal sector, where often the absence of intervention or regulation is its life blood. 'Better practice' looks at the processes by which women empower themselves; it gears itself towards the specific context of women's lives; it does not attempt to force women into a predetermined framework, but stems from the reality of urban women's lives. Several guidelines are suggested below.

Acknowledging reproduction

The example from Ghana shows how women income-earners rely on the unpaid work of other female family members. Policy-makers can learn from this and recognise how responsibility for domestic tasks and childcare cannot be ignored when addressing the needs of women workers and entrepreneurs. The example from Ghana also shows that women who were able to rely on a steady income to cover their domestic costs were better able to focus on building up their businesses. Policy-makers can learn from this as well, designing loan schemes and repayment schedules that are geared toward the actualities of women's lives. Credit programmes should recognise that women are often forced to spend credit on consumption items for the home as well as on inputs for their businesses. Women are often involved in reciprocal obligations and networks and 'lend on' credit to mothers-in-law or neighbours. But they are repaid and can call on mutual assistance in turn. Thus, where loan schemes recognise these patterns and accommodate and allow for women's consumption and expenditure patterns, not only do women have an opportunity to build up their businesses, but loan repayment rates suffer. Planners must recognise the rationale for women who spread out risk by engaging in several activities rather than relying solely on one activity; loans must be made available in varying amounts to allow women to fund in advance their various activities.

Women into decision-making

The examples of SEWA in India and the West Yorkshire Homeworkers Group also illustrate how women can go beyond participation at the project level, which addresses their practical needs, towards intervening in the broader policy-making agenda. Women do not need to have assistance handed to them; rather, they need a opportunity to become involved in planning the longer-term policies that affect their lives. Such participation ultimately increases the efficiency of planned programmes. When women are included from the beginning in the decisions that affect their lives, they are able to inform policy-makers of the advantages and disadvantages of current situations and can ensure that solutions are tailored to meet their lived realities. Including local women in the making of policy means that people knowledgeable about the programmes implemented and who actually live in the communities concerned are able to monitor results. This ensures that if a policy is misdirected or brings about undesirable results, people within the community can sound the alert before valuable time and money are lost.

Successful organising

Both the SEWA example and that of the women in West Yorkshire demonstrate the importance of organisation and of consulting women about their priorities. However, the implications of organisation for a large association like SEWA and for a relatively small group of women homeworkers are very different. Additionally, in the British example, the policy context is such that a woman's immigration status makes it risky for her to identify herself or engage with others outside the home in a high-profile way. For those women who are able to take such risks, organising for better rates of pay combines economic needs with political interests. Working collectively allows women to benefit from calling on the knowledge of other workers, borrowers and businesswomen. This provides an opportunity not only to organise and utilise older women who have 'retired' from the informal sector as consultants. There is also a chance here for women of different economic backgrounds to work together to improve their opportunities, as shown in the Tanzanian example. Campaigning for rights of homeworkers can be an empowering process for the women involved. In this case they challenge policy-makers to address their interests. However, maximising their life chances and securing their livelihoods may mean that women choose silence or less strident means of organisation.

Providing flexible financial support

The examples from the Dominican Republic demonstrate that credit can be opened up for women through alternative collateral mechanisms, third-party guarantors, and NGO links with formal credit institutions. The size of loans and the complementary services involved must cater to the economic goals of different groups of women. Banks might also consider helping women improve their work environment by blending home improvement and business improvement loans. Ideally, women might prefer to work outside their homes. Where this is not an option, however, planners must acknowledge the fact that low-income women suffer from working in overcrowded, poorly lit and poorly ventilated home environments. When programme planners recognise that women are engaged in productive work within the home, they are able to think of innovative ways in which they might enable women to improve their work environment. As mentioned earlier, these programme planners must deal with the reality of women's lives and create borrowing schemes that require a minimum of paperwork and include reasonable and appropriately timed repayment rates.

Policy for diversity

When looking at the question of replicability of policy, planners at all levels (grassroots, regional and state) have to work out strategies of employment maximisation that fit with their specific cultural, historical and socio-economic context and benefit the diverse groups of women and men. As the example of the Asante women in Ghana showed, in some situations, policy-makers might be able to build on existing cultural practices that favour women's income-generating activities. In this culture, the existing emphasis on training young girls to be numerate and skilled in trading, and the practice of drawing knowledge from the elderly, help us see how two often overlooked groups – the young and the elderly – might be brought into policy-making to the benefit of all three age groups, young, middle-aged and old.

The case of Honduras amplifies the need for the recognition of diverse household types – women-headed households and sub-households – which are often overlooked in policy-making that assumes male headship of households. Within households, assumptions of 'complete pooling' and sharing of resources do not correspond to the empirical reality of 'incomplete pooling' (Elson, 1995) and conflicting interests. This has implications for wages, credit and income and profit from businesses. Therefore, women within male-headed households may need different support from that required by women-headed households although the latter too may be sub-households. More generally, the role of policy-makers should be to recognise women's diverse initiatives in income generation and to create an enabling environment that allows them to expand their choices and reduce their risks.

Note

1. It is somewhat artificial to separate 'reproductive' from 'productive' work, especially in many Third World contexts. However, for ease of reference, the term 'reproductive work' broadly refers to the activities associated with procreation, domestic labour and consumption by which people are reproduced on a day-to-day and generational basis, while 'productive work' refers to activities undertaken for income.

References

Clark, G. (1989), 'Separation between trading and home for Asante women in Kumasi Central Market, Ghana', in R. Wilk, *The Household Economy: Reconsidering the Domestic Mode of Production*, Boulder, CO: Westview Press.

Downing, J. (1991), 'Gender and growth of microenterprises', *Small Enterprise Development*, 2(1): 4–12.

Elson, D. (ed.) (1995), *Male Bias in the Development Process* (2nd edn), Manchester: Manchester University Press.

Grown, C. and C. Sebstad (1989), 'Beyond survival: expanding income-earning opportunities for women in developing countries', *World Development*, 17(7): 937–52.

INSTRAW (1990), 'Alternative credit programmes for women in the Dominican Republic', *INSTRAW News*, 15, Winter: 15–16.

Kabeer, N. (1994), *Reversed Realities*, London: Verso.

Moore, H. (1988), *Feminism and Anthropology*, Cambridge: Polity Press.

Rowbotham, S. and S. Mitter (eds) (1994), *Dignity and Daily Bread: New Forms of Economic Organising Among Poor Women of the Third World and the First*, London: Routledge.

Tate, J. (1994), 'Homework in West Yorkshire', in Rowbotham and Mitter, *Dignity and Daily Bread*, pp. 193–217.

Tripp, A. (1994), 'Deindustrialisation and the growth of women's economic associations and networks in urban Tanzania', in Rowbotham and Mitter, *Dignity and Daily Bread*, pp. 139–58.

UNCHS (Habitat)/ILO (1995), *Shelter Provision and Employment Generation*, Nairobi: UNCHS/Geneva: ILO.

CHAPTER 4

Women and Housing in the City

Loren B. Landau

Women in the urban areas of developing countries increasingly rely on domestic labour as a base for the 'productive' economic activity they must undertake to meet their families' financial needs. In a milieu in which the 'informal sector' accounts for more than half of the activity within many national economies, the 'house' has ceased to be merely private shelter (if it ever was) and is a site of both economic and political action. Working from the perspective that policy-makers and practitioners must consider the multiple responsibilities of women – both to themselves and to their children and adult dependants – this chapter advocates building housing that can simultaneously lessen the opportunity costs associated with domestic labour while improving the earning potential of income-generating activities located within a given shelter. Through an analysis of past policy successes and failures, the body of this chapter centres on a series of recommendations directed first towards giving women greater access to housing and then towards expanding the flexibility of existing and new housing to enhance women residents' economic and social opportunities.

It is now recognised that an accurate evaluation of housing cannot be based solely on the physical qualities of a structure but must be assessed on its ability to meet the economic, political and social needs of its users. As women have typically undertaken much of their activity within the private sphere of the house, they are particularly influenced by variances in a structure's characteristics (Moser, 1987: 17). In industrialised countries women compete in the formal workforce. This has influenced women's status or position within the home. Nevertheless, domestic responsibilities persist and many 'First World' women have had to work 'double shifts' or rely on paid help, a redivision of labour within the home or improved technology in order to compete in the labour market. Moreover, home-working is on the increase in the West. Within the developing world, different conditions and options exist in the informal economy. Co-operative childcare arrangements are often employed, or some women in the household take responsibility for domestic work to release others for income generation. Women strive to convert their gender-ascribed roles into productive activities and services such as selling cooked food or charging for childcare. The standard division between domestic and productive work has thus become blurred to such a degree that it may no longer be appropriate to speak of the two as separate entities. Housing is therefore an instrumental commodity, the adequate provision of which is essential if women are to live full and creative lives.

This chapter outlines the issues associated with housing and women's economic advancement and makes general recommendations for their possible incorporation into regionally specific proposals. The recommendations represent important guidelines for process and are not, in and of themselves, a guaranteed recipe for 'best practice'.

Domestic and productive labour

Friedrich Engels suggested that 'the emancipation of women will only be possible when woman can take part in production on a large, social scale, and domestic work no longer claims anything but an insignificant amount of her time' (Engels, 1986: 199). His message that the hours dedicated to domestic labour have consistently acted as a significant obstacle to women's ability to gain status has stood the test of time. His positing of domestic and productive labour as binary opposites has not. Engels' legacy had led many policy-makers and academics to assume a clear division between productive and domestic work in times and places where such a distinction may not exist. There is invariably a direct link between domestic and productive capacity. With growth of the informal economy often outpacing that in the formal sector and with changes in global production processes, the division between formal and informal activities has become blurred. This has also helped to dim the distinctions between domestic and productive labour.

In the search for positive models, one quickly confronts the remarkable paucity of absolute successes in housing policy. As Hardoy and Satterthwaite suggest, governments have tended to have more to do with creating housing problems than with solving them (Hardoy and Satterthwaite, 1989: 137) and housing policy is invariably informed by the objective of providing shelter rather than a productive asset, thus exhibiting a reproductive bias. The following list of recommendations represents a starting point for a housing policy that recognises the interrelationships between domestic and productive labour. Assuming the political will and the presence of a human development and woman-sensitive policy perspective, the recommendations are divided into two strongly interrelated categories: improving access to shelter and then examining what can be done to enhance the functionality and flexibility of low-cost housing for all inhabitants.

Improving access and increasing flexibility

The type of house and the activities that take place within it are of little importance to an individual who is not first able to acquire shelter. Actions should therefore be taken to improve women's access. The provision of housing can be a first step towards providing women with the means of incorporating livelihood strategies into or alongside their domestic labour and, in so doing, improving their status. Housing can then act as security or collateral for accessing credit and improving income-generation opportunities.

Government housing tends to be priced out of the range of urban people in poverty. Women's real wages tend to be lower than men's (when they are able to find employment) and they are thus even further disadvantaged. As appropriate shelter may be central to a woman's ability to earn an adequate income (Chant and Ward, 1987: 15; Moser, 1987: 25), allowing women the opportunity to 'get into' housing may enable them to pay for it. Creating areas with relaxed building standards (while maintaining adequate safety measures) will help lower cost but will not guarantee access for people in poverty. Lowering minimum income or entrance requirements are an additional enabling step to allow women to access publicly funded housing.

While men and women are often afforded equality before the law, such provisions are rarely translated into reality (Bunch, 1992: 7). For example, in many parts of Nairobi, customary law requires that a man be the official holder of any given property. Such protocol means that a woman (or women) with the funds to purchase land must rely on their husband, uncle, or brother to sign the deed. Once it is signed, the men are officially entitled to do what they wish with the property (Landau, 1994). Without *de facto* rights to land, women's ability to operate independently of men is greatly reduced, limiting their options for family structures and economic enterprises. Thus the *de jure* and *de facto* recognition of women's property rights should be promoted.

Women's reliance on paid labour to construct their houses in self-help housing projects has often made it too expensive for women. Training women in construction skills can be positive but should not be seen as a blueprint for house construction or income-earning strategies as it may challenge the existing gender division of labour. If it is to be successful, women also need to be included in institutional relationships such as apprenticeships.

Expanding flexibility

Flexibility means allowing people to use the space in the home for numerous domestic and productive purposes, as they deem appropriate.

If one wishes to promote women's ability to use the home in various ways, laws (such as zoning regulations, which are often ignored anyway) must not be created which prohibit economic activity from taking place within residential areas. Projects with flexible standards have been implemented with some success in Sudan and Colombia (Hardoy and Satterthwaite, 1989: 119). Women must be involved directly in the design of housing projects. 'Not only is a woman's domestic labour affected by the quality of housing, but also it is women who are most knowledgeable about the ways in which housing might be best improved to increase their efficiency' (Chant, 1987: 40).

Governments have often based their vision of housing on Western stereotypes of small nuclear families. Housing built on these assumptions is often inappropriate for Third World households, which can comprise single, woman-headed, extended or joint families. It also inhibits sub-division for renting or for accommodating small-scale enterprises conducted at home (Drakakis-Smith, 1981: 31; Moser, 1987: 22). However, 'the most important consequence of the male-headed nuclear family stereotype is the women who head households are frequently excluded from low-income housing projects because of a lack of gender awareness in the eligibility criteria' (Moser, 1987: 25). Providing an opportunity for a variety of traditional and non-traditional family forms often challenges existing laws and elite biases. Nevertheless flexibility is an important instrument for improving women's access to and gains from housing, and is a goal that should be pursued.

Housing is not just shelter, it is part of human settlements development and as such cannot be separated from services such as accessible water, adequate sewerage and electricity. The provision of such services provides a twofold benefit. The collection of water and fuel,[1] and the care of children made ill by exposure to water-borne contaminants or excreta, are labour-intensive tasks that increase the time a woman must dedicate to her domestic duties. Reducing such exposure not only improves the health of children but limits the time spent on their care, freeing a woman for other pursuits. However, such services are rarely provided to the poorest areas, especially informal or illegal settlements. Songsore and McGranahan's study in Accra, Ghana revealed that even in an accepted formal housing settlement, 28% of women had to rely on informal water vendors, 8% on communal standpipes, and 4% on 'open waterways, rainwater collection … and other private sources' (Songsore and McGranahan, 1995: 18). Services are also an economic issue, as access to water and electricity broadens the range of possible livelihood activities, possibly enhancing productivity and profits.

Peter Ward reports that '[w]hen squatters are asked about the most important community problems they face, they invariably cite those of land tenure and lack of services' (Ward, 1982: 203). Without legal rights to their holdings, squatters have no leverage to demand infrastructural improvements and have no legal recourse against landlords. Such a situation can lead not only to emotional insecurity, but to an unwillingness to improve housing beyond survival standards (Ward, 1982: 203). Throughout the developing world governments have regularly attacked squatter settlements, citing various plausible and implausible justifications (aesthetics, health, safety, anti-sedition campaigns).[2] Such policies have proved relatively ineffective at stopping settlements (Drakakis-Smith, 1981: 121), but these factors are successful in preventing inhabitants from converting their full potential into needed goods and services, and destroy the networks upon which so many women (and men) rely for their survival (Kobiah, 1985).

Conclusion

Engels and others suggest that the only way to advance the long-term, strategic goals of women is to move their operational sphere away from the home. This chapter has argued that it is perhaps more appropriate to recognise the apparent success of the alternatives devised by women themselves, at work and in the home. In the mid-1990s it remains a given that the primary responsibility for domestic labour continues to fall upon the shoulders of women. Social and economic policy-makers must therefore recognise that if they wish to improve the conditions of women and the society in which they live, they should work to limit the opportunity costs of domestic labour so that women may expand their roles in the 'productive' sphere. As Schlyter writes, 'the household itself, its formation and composition, is part of a woman's survival strategy' (1988: 21). The incorporation of women's interests into the design and provision of low-income housing can ease women's domestic tasks by offering a chance for cooperation and productive, income-generating activity while providing income and time for other pursuits.

Notes

1. Even within urban areas, women are often heavily dependent on such combustibles. Songsore and McGranahan's work in Accra, Ghana reveals that 88% of homes regularly used charcoal while 7% were known to burn wood; 68% relied on charcoal and 8% on wood as their principal fuels (Songsore and McGranahan, 1995: 22).

2. There are no universal solutions to tenure arrangements. Security needs vary by region and group, with some in need of permanent housing while others prefer to rent (Peil, 1976: 155). Nevertheless, security from random attack can safely be assumed to be a virtue.

References

Bunch, C. (1992), 'Women's rights as human rights', in C. Bunch and R. Carillo (eds), *Gender Violence: A Development Issue*, Dublin: Attic Press.

Chant, S. (1987), 'Domestic labour, decision making, and dwelling construction: the experience of women in Querataro, Mexico', in C. O. N Moser and L. Peake, (eds), *Women, Human Settlement and Housing*, London: Tavistock Publications, pp. 33–54.

Chant, S. and P. Ward (1987), 'Family structure and low-income housing policy', *Third World Planning Review*, 9(1): 5–19.

Drakakis-Smith, D. (1981), *Urbanisation, Housing and the Development Process*, London: Croom Helm.

Engels, F. (1986), *The Origin of the Family, Private Property and the State*, Introduction by M. Barrett, London: Penguin.

Hardoy, J. E. and D. Satterthwaite (1989), *Squatter Citizen*, London: Earthscan.

Kobiah, S. M. (1985), 'The origins of squatting and community organisation in Nairobi,' *African Urban Studies*, 19 and 20.

Landau, Loren B. (1994), Interview with Julia Mulaha, Dir. Women's Program of National Council of Churches of Kenya, 13 July, Washington, DC: Human Rights Watch-Africa.

Moser, C. O. N. (1987), 'Women, human settlement and housing: a conceptual framework for analysis and policy-making', in C. O. N. Moser and L. Peake (eds), *Women, Human Settlement and Housing*, London: Tavistock Publications.

Peil, M. (1976), 'African squatter settlements: a comparative study', *Urban Studies* 13: 155–66.

Schlyter, A. (1988), *Women Householder and Housing Strategies: The Case of George, Zambia*, Gävle: National Swedish Institute for Building Research.

Songsore, J. and G. McGranahan (1995) 'Environment, wealth, and health; towards an analysis of intra-urban differentials within Greater Accra Metropolitan Area, Ghana', *Environment and Urbanisation*, 5(2): 135–45.

Ward, P. (1982), *Self Help Housing: A Critique*, London: Mansell.

CHAPTER 5

Children Living, Learning and Working in the City

Margaret Curtin, Tazeen Hossain
and Alice Verghese-Choudhury

Any review of difference in the city would be incomplete without a discussion of children, who are among the most visible and most vulnerable of citizens. Because of rapid urbanisation, the number of urban children has been growing steadily over recent decades. With some regional variations, urban populations are becoming increasingly youthful, both through natural increase due to high fertility rates and through migration, an activity that often involves the young and more robust. Demographic trends are not the only reason for paying particular attention to urban children. The social deterioration in urban areas resulting from economic restructuring and cutbacks on social sector spending, inadequate and declining infrastructure and services, poor urban management and the increase in urban poverty and urban violence is devastating and impacts on children in particular ways. On the surface people in poverty in urban areas may appear economically privileged compared to those in the rural sector, but appearances conceal extreme inequities in resource distribution in cities and children are among those who face neglect and exploitation.

The lives and life chances of children in the city are shaped by the environment in which they live. For 70% of urban children in the developing world this environment means conditions of continuous poverty, inadequate housing and food, lack of basic services and an institutional and legislative framework that is rarely supportive of their diverse interests and needs and often hostile to them. Children adopt various strategies and mechanisms to cope with these conditions, both as individuals and as a part of families and households. Disadvantaged in terms of school attendance and performance, many children earn incomes for themselves and their families. Those whom we most often see are the (mostly) boys who work the streets, as rag-pickers, beggars or car attendants. Less visible are the boys and girls in the informal factories and sweatshops and the (mostly) girls who work as domestic workers in households.

This chapter begins from the position that it is inappropriate to define children or their problems too narrowly, by one particular aspect of their lives such as shelter, work or education. To do so leads to development which is uni-dimensional and compartmentalised and which does not reflect the experience of children themselves. A narrowly defined focus can lead to some groups of children becoming invisible to policy-makers. The same danger exists if a gender perspective is not retained. Boy children who work and live on the streets are more visible than girl children toiling in the kitchens and sculleries of the better off, and this can render the girl child invisible and therefore neglected by policy and social development practice.

The challenge is for policy-makers to address children on their own terms within multi-sectoral and participatory approaches to urban development. This requires coordination and cooperation among organisations working with children, within a broader understanding and vision of developments and in ways that incorporate the interests, views and insights of children. Those with access to power need to listen to what children have to say and allow them to present their own realities as part of an inclusive urban planning process. The chapter pays reference to two case studies that highlight some of the issues outlined in the conceptual discussion, and offer experience of different ways in which the issues facing urban children can be addressed. While the Bangladesh project focuses on identifying appropriate education alternatives for working children, the project run by GOAL in Addis Ababa approaches work with children from a more holistic perspective.

Policy for children

It is nearly thirty years since the General Assembly of the United Nations declared the Declaration of the Rights of the Child (Resolution 1386xiv, 1959). In 1989 the United Nations Convention on the Rights of the Child codified the rights of children in such a way that they could be elaborated to be acceptable across political boundaries and account for cultural differences. The policy approaches that have accompanied the articulation of the rights of children have varied, although children have long been a focus of development policy and the primary target group of the United Nations Children's Fund (UNICEF). During the 1960s and 1970s, UNICEF did not have a specifically urban focus, but assisted children in cities through general programmes such as support to maternal and child health and through health, nutrition and social services for children. By the late 1970s and in the context of a basic needs approach to development UNICEF had developed its 'urban basic services' strategy, which constituted a comprehensive approach that included:

- an emphasis on social services for the poor linked to infrastructure development;

- a multi-sectoral, multi-level approach which was area-based rather than sectoral and which was premised on participation by different levels of government;
- low-cost and appropriate technologies;
- the active involvement of residents in community development programmes, either as volunteers or paid workers; and
- a strong focus on women and children.

This programme support has been fairly effective and its problem-solving and participatory focus is an approach that has been widely adopted by other agencies working with children. It was given greater urgency during the 1980s as it became clearer that the structural adjustment programmes introduced in many countries were having negative social consequences. Accumulated evidence revealed that urban people in poverty were bearing the brunt of economic reform measures as prices rose, user charges were introduced, food and transport subsidies were cut and formal sector employment declined. All this impacted on urban children in low-income households as increasing numbers of women entered the labour force in response to declining real incomes, often followed by children themselves. The emergence of growing numbers of street and working children can be seen as a survival strategy amongst poor urban households, a response to declining real incomes and changes in the demand for labour.

In response, the 1980s saw a growing focus on advocacy work and asserting the rights of the child, as well as on addressing the specific needs of children in difficult circumstances, often urban older children in high-risk groups, tenuously linked to families and communities. In addition to poverty, it was recognised that globally, many children leaving home and living on the street are victims of tensions and violence at home, factors themselves not unrelated to social and economic deprivation. The advocacy movement was given tremendous impetus by the lessons that emerged from the experience of the Brazilian children's rights movement, facilitated by the linked organisational and lobbying skills of community-based organisations and NGOs. The lessons included the fact that the majority of street and working children are not threatening to public life, are not involved in illegal activities and are in fact in close touch with their families. Moreover, the Brazilian experience demonstrated that collectively, children can take responsibility for their own lives and, with the support of allies such as local NGOs and international agencies such as UNICEF, can influence policy. The experience of Brazil actively inspired the terms of reference for UNICEF's Urban Child Project, which has been under way during the 1990s (Szanton Blanc, 1994).

On a smaller scale in cities all over Latin America, Africa and Asia, organisations working with children struggle to encourage alternatives to the punitive police, judicial and social service systems, which ignore, penalise or institutionalise children. They attempt, by contrast, to work with children starting from where they are and where they feel secure, providing them with practical alternatives that are responsive to the realities of their lives. Their advocacy work urges policy-makers to respond to the real demands placed upon an urban child in poverty, so that unrealistic policy and legislation do not force children into situations where they live or work illegally in the most invisible recesses and exploitative excesses of urban life. It is our view that children can make a valid contribution to the city but that their priorities are all too often overlooked by those who design policies, including policies meant to be in their interests.

Living and working the streets

Urban children in poverty can live in a variety of circumstances: as part of a family, attached to a non-kin household, in groups or gangs on the street or in institutions. Categorising children according to where they live overlooks the fact that they often move between different settings. The reasons why children choose to do this include household structure, family relations and the need to earn an income in any way possible, either for the family or independently.

It is important to realise, therefore, that not all urban children live permanently in a family home and there are an estimated 23.4 million children worldwide who live on the street (Ennew and Milne, 1989). For these children, their experience of family is one of a domain of vulnerability and risk, and their experience within the home often leaves them little choice but to vacate the household. A recent study for UNICEF of urbanisation issues affecting children and women in Eastern and Southern Africa says that most children working on the streets still live with their families but the numbers who have lost contact are also rising. This is exacerbated by the problem of AIDS orphans (Kanji, 1996).

Street children feel isolated and seek security and a sense of belonging from individuals and groups outside the household. Referring to the global phenomenon of street gangs, Agnelli (1986), notes that young people organise easily along cooperative lines, and that what officialdom interprets as delinquency is a positive adjustment to the circumstances in which they find themselves. Children are resourceful and canny and know how to work and survive in the city. Anthony Swift poignantly demonstrates street children's vulnerability and resourcefulness in a recent article on Brazil:

> Home for many is a box, some metres square, up a long muddy track of similar boxes, far from the city centre. Street children separated from home do not lament the loss of the 'house'. Some celebrate the city, by contrast, as a mansion of many rooms in which they want for nothing, describing the restaurant district as their kitchen, the city park as their garden, its lakes or beach front as their

bathroom. And the adults whom they rob or serve in various ways they dignify as 'clients'. What pains them sharply is the loss of the caring they once had, or know they should have had, from their families before the final blows of poverty put paid to that (Swift, 1996: 14–15).

But street life can be fatal for urban children. There is a constant risk of accidents as children try to work in busy city centres, and the cost of food in the city is high. Swift (1991) uses the striking example of Brazil in the 1970s, when economic growth was rapid yet 53% of children were malnourished. Because of their underdeveloped bodies children are particularly susceptible to high levels of environmental pollution found in cities (Harpham, Lusty and Vaughan, 1988). Velis (1995) points to ill health as a major problem faced by all street children. Disease can spread quickly from one to the other and wipe out whole groups of children. Chronic skin conditions and infections are common. Children are usually denied access to health services if they are not accompanied by an adult, and the reception they receive from health personnel can often put them off attempting to attend a second time. With the spread of AIDS, urban children in poverty are a high-risk group but health education rarely reaches out to them. The street experience is often unsustainable without the assistance of drugs (Swift, 1991). Children use solvents, alcohol and other drugs to calm their nerves, respond to peer pressure or stave off hunger (Velis, 1995). This increases their vulnerability to disease and causes permanent damage to their livers and lungs.

Street girls (and often young boys as well) may be forced into prostitution. Out of two million people engaged in prostitution in India, three to four hundred thousand are children. The number of girls on the street is significantly underestimated because studies concentrate on traditional male occupations and prostitution is overlooked (Szanton Blanc, 1994). Young prostituted women are condemned because they are sexually active, but little consideration is given to their lack of choice of occupation. Even their status in the hierarchy of prostituted women is low. Lack of facilities means that they are dirty and desperate and are exploited by pimps. Rape and physical abuse are common, and they have very little power to protect themselves from sexually transmitted diseases. They risk becoming pregnant at a young age and then have to deal with motherhood on the street as well. When they are seen with a child the fact that they are children themselves is often overlooked. There appears to be a reluctance on the part of organisations involved with street children to address the problems faced by girls (Swift, 1991, Velis, 1995).

The environment in which children live is structured not only by physical characteristics but also by power relations, usually with adults. When an unsuitable environment is combined with an exploitative relationship with adults, the effects on children can be very detrimental. Those in authority with whom people in poverty have the most contact are the police (Wratten, 1995). Children are no exception. Police are often charged with keeping the streets 'clean', and the presence of children makes the place 'untidy'. 'Harsh repression of poor children, whose behaviour is seen as divergent from accepted standards' (Swift, 1991: 8) is widely accepted, with punishment meted out by anyone who feels threatened by them. Children live in constant fear of arrest. Agnelli (1986) argues that the number of arrests and detention in conditions totally unsuitable for children is more illustrative of the attitude of many governments than is any examination of national legislation. There is no protection from police brutality and when they are arrested they are often subject to abuse in adult prisons.

Closely linked to detention centres, and often indistinguishable from them, are the orphanages in which children deemed to be without a family are placed. These institutions, often relics of social policy approaches of the nineteenth century (Dalglish and Connolly, 1992), are under-staffed, under-equipped and offer little to the child, stifling their abilities and preventing the development of social skills. An alternative approach adopted by many agencies working with children in cities is to provide them with shelter and emotional support and resources of various kinds without removing them from what has become the familiar context of the street, yet offering them reprieve from what is often a harsh environment and, eventually, alternatives to it.

Child work and child labour

In the monetised economy of the city, children in poverty have no option but to work and a majority of them see this as a essential part of their lives. Many value the contributions they are able to make towards their families' well-being; policies that assume children are better off not working fail to address this reality. From the literature on why children go to work, it is clear that there is a range of push and pull factors. The household constitutes the major push factor. Where welfare support is absent and where incomes are low and irregular, the labour of children becomes crucial. This is especially the case when the household head is unemployed, or where the support structures of family, kin and community are considerably weakened. This is common in urban settings, particularly under conditions of economic stress. Evidence from the Philippines and Thailand, for example, shows that the earnings of children even help parents to pay their taxes, fund special events or cancel debts (UNICEF, 1995). It is not surprising, then, that parents see children as assets rather than as costs.

Although poverty is the primary factor that underpins children working, there are other factors at work. Sometimes parents push their children out to work just to keep them busy and out of bad habits (Swift, 1991). Parents have also stated that children are working because there are no schools or because schools are not pleasant places to be. The need to go along with a particular style of living may pull a child to work and in some communities it is difficult to imagine anything else (Niewenhuys, 1994). In some areas, particular communities are associated with certain kinds of work and this reinforces the exploitation of bonded labour of children. For example, brick-kiln workers in the Punjab in Pakistan are from the same social groups and are *de facto* if not *de jure* bonded as families to particular brick-kiln owners for life (Beall et al., 1993).

What children's work means to working children themselves has to be understood in relation to their context, the way children are defined and how work is understood. Concepts of childhood and work are embedded in contradictory frameworks that simultaneously admit the productive agency of children while denying they have real value. If the discriminatory treatment of children by adults in the workplace is to be prevented then the existence of child work has to be acknowledged. Legislation that excludes children from working drives child labour underground and makes it more difficult for them to be protected. Children's work operates outside the officially recognised formal sector channels and this reinforces its 'inferior' status. Inferior status translates into long working hours, low pay, and unacceptable working conditions that are socially isolating and harmful to health, education and safety. They deny childhood itself and in the long term are likely to inhibit physical and psychological well-being.

A common distinction is now made between child work, child labour and child slavery. Child work is work that is not exploitative and can accommodate education. It can be part of a child's socialisation and plays a positive part in a child's development. Child work becomes child labour if the child is working for long hours in difficult conditions that interfere with schooling, or are hazardous or otherwise injurious to the child's physical, mental, social or moral well-being. Child slavery is the most severe form of child labour where the child is taken from or handed over by parents or guardians and compelled to work for others in full or semi-bondage, their labour often paying off the debts of scores of adults.

Social acceptance of children's household labour has resulted in the household work of girl children being far less of a policy issue than children engaged in other forms of child labour, paid or unpaid (Niewenhuys, 1994). Within the household, irrespective of caste, class, marital status or education, girls are primarily responsible for tasks such as cooking, cleaning utensils, washing clothes, sibling care and fetching water. This may arrest the intellectual and psychological development of the girl chid. In many countries, the education of girls is seen as a lower priority than that of boys. In addition to girls being kept at home to perform domestic tasks they are also sent into paid work earlier than their brothers, who are kept in school for as long as income allows. Thus there are internal hierarchies based on age and gender within households as well as outside them, even when these households comprise only a woman and her children.

Addressing child work or child labour in policy terms is no simple matter. While we have concentrated on the supply side, the demand side cannot be ignored; this is not merely a local matter but is also linked to international demand for the products and prices of goods produced by child labour for global markets. Research shows that even in the 1990s, children are the cheapest labourers on the global assembly line and in the global plantation. Hence child labour is intricately linked to the socio-economic situation at both the micro and macro levels. Even though the United States, Germany and other countries advocate the banning of products made by child labour, the pressure on low-income countries to compete economically and for profits at a global level persists and it is often based on the comparative advantage provided by the low cost of child labour. Moreover, child labour is not only a feature of the South but is on the increase in the United States and around the world. Child labour can include children kidnapped from their homes to weave carpets in India as well as children stitching garments in the sweatshops of New York and the free trade zones of Honduras.

Case studies

The previous section has provided a brief overview of the variety of factors in the city that influence the lives of children. There has been a limited success in addressing these issues in many developing countries. In this section successful interventions will be outlined. These projects on their own do not meet the diverse needs of the broad spectrum of urban children. Their value lies in the approach they have taken to children. The lesson to be learned is that by empowering children with the right to decide their own priorities, their lives can be enhanced.

GOAL's programme for street children in Addis Ababa, Ethiopia Ethiopia has a population of 51.2 million, of whom 24.8 million are under 16 years of age (UNICEF, 1995). It has a rapidly growing urban population, an estimated 60% of whom live below the absolute poverty line (ibid.). As in many other countries, there is limited statistical information on street children. Estimates by those working with children in Addis Ababa put the number of children living rough in the city at 10,000. This is a relatively new phenomenon in Ethiopia with a much lesser degree of violence both by and towards the children here than in, for instance, Latin America. However, having emerged from 19 years of war in 1991 and now following a structural adjustment programme, Ethiopia has limited resources. Velis (1995) estimates that by the year 2000 there will be only enough school places for 50–59% enrolment in Ethiopia. Given these constraints it is not surprising that there is cause for concern over the specific needs of street children.

Programme background   There is considerable cooperation between the various NGOs assisting street and working children in Addis Ababa under the umbrella of the Forum for Street Children Ethiopia (FSCE). This allows for the exchange of ideas and a coordinated approach to advocacy work. One organisation is GOAL, which began working with homeless children in Addis Ababa in 1991 and today reaches up to five hundred children. The project reaches out to the children on their own territory, accepts them as they are, and includes them in the planning process. It also fulfils an advocacy role on behalf of the children and in this way has improved the lives of other street children in Addis.

The programme began as a small pilot project attached to another project in Addis and provided night shelter for 16 homeless boys. Swift (1991) states that one measure of the success of an approach is if the children spread the word, and there was much demand among the children to be part of the project. Presently, the project consists of a day drop-in centre, which provides advice and basic services, and four night shelters, three for boys and one for girls. Central to the success of this project is the relationship between the staff and the children. This is built on acceptance and trust, which took time to develop. Prior to the opening of the centre a great deal of time was spent with the children on the streets, getting to know them. Youth workers still spend at least one evening and two days per week out on the streets. They know where each child works, plays and, when not at the shelter, sleeps. This also gives the children the opportunity to show the staff members their 'place' and even invite them to eat or drink with them. This is an act that is central to Ethiopian culture and one of the many ways in which the children can express their cultural identity and social dignity.

The children are always made to feel that the centre is also their 'place'. They pay a small rent for the shelters and in this way feel not like the beneficiaries of charity but like a group sharing accommodation. It also means that they continue to support themselves. It is the children who decide on the house rules and organise all activities such as cooking and cleaning. The staff act as facilitators and listeners. Any adult working at the centre is available to any child who should want them. It is of particular importance that there are people available and that girls in particular feel they can confide in them without fear of judgement. Street girls are very defensive and, like most teenagers, are embarrassed about discussing their sexuality. However, they do need advice and this is available from trained female staff at the GOAL project.

Access to services A major problem faced by the children is lack of access to the services available to the rest of the city. The first thing that they need is an identity as part of a community. Through the location of the project in a suitable neighbourhood and through involvement of the local people in activities in the project, the children have gradually been accepted. The local *Kebele* (community or ward) leader has provided them with the necessary papers. Even though non-formal education is available at the project, contact with local schools has been made to facilitate the enrolment of street children. Opportunities for appropriate vocational training and apprenticeships are also sought out on behalf of older youths. The children are not forced or even expected to participate, and they choose the areas in which they are interested.

Sport activities play an important part in the programme. Games are organised between the street children and other local groups. This gives them the chance to interact with other children on an equal basis, and provides the much needed space in which these diverse groups of children can enjoy themselves in a safe environment. Lack of access to health facilities causes major problems for all street children in Addis, particularly in the rainy season when typhus and relapsing fever reach epidemic proportions on the street. The GOAL team has built up a good relationship with the staff of the local health centre and the social worker in the nearby hospital. These people are invited to visit the project and thereby many of the misconceptions they had about street children have been challenged. Given the chance, the children themselves will gladly show these professionals that they are not all delinquents. Services that cannot be found elsewhere are provided at the centre. These include showers and clothes-washing facilities, a safe place to keep belongings and money, first aid and affordable food.

Szanton Blanc (1994) says that any successful intervention on behalf of street children must improve their relationship with the police. In Addis Ababa, as in so many other cities, the street children are rounded up and locked in prison when there are dignitaries in town. Children who sell small items are considered to be hawking without a licence and have their goods confiscated by the police. The GOAL project has established a good relationship with the local police, who are willing to cooperate to some extent. Of greater benefit is the fact that project staff and children have been given the opportunity to attend police training and talk to them about how to relate to the children. Equally important is the relationship established with the juvenile remand centre, which allows project staff to continue to work with children in prison and to assist in their rehabilitation.

Even though improving relations with these key individuals is important, significant improvement will not take place unless the attitudes of society as a whole are changed. Through the FSCE advocacy work has continued in Addis. The media are used to educate the public on the reality of the children's lives. The various projects involved, including the GOAL project, invite key groups to come and meet the children. These groups include students from the university and teachers from local schools. Staff have found that very often these people are surprised at how well behaved the children are and will admit to never having acknowledged a street child previously. It also gives the children a chance to meet adults.

There are many barriers that need to be broken down before society and the street child can interact fully. Attitudes to homeless children need to be assessed. The problems they experience can be attributed largely to societies' lack of acceptance of them and their subsequent exclusion from services. Projects such as GOAL can make a huge difference to the lives of street children. They will not lead to the total elimination of the need to live on the street, or ever hope to reintegrate every child back into society, but through ongoing advocacy the adult world may become more accepting and supportive of them.

UCEP in Bangladesh   The Underprivileged Children's Education Programme (UCEP) now caters for some 10,000 children in Bangladesh and an additional 12,000 in Nepal. UCEP buildings are donated by government, local authorities, communities and private citizens from a number of countries. They are located in areas of the city where there are concentrations of working children. Teaching is organised in short shifts throughout the day and into the evening to enable the children to continue working. Pupils receive practical and theoretical training and also vocational training in one of eight trades, in addition to being taught hygiene, nutrition, bookkeeping and basic management. After six or seven years they are placed in the job market with resources and skills (UCEP Annual Report, 1990). UCEP does not fight for the rescue of child labourers so much as provide a service and offer alternatives. Moreover, it prepares them for work and places them in the labour market with better credentials, thus working with their reality and expanding their livelihood options.

A recent innovation of UCEP in Chittagong is a training programme that would establish an organic cooperative link between UCEP and entrepreneurs in the private sector. The basic rationale behind the programme has been that it brings together the demand for and supply of workers. UCEP will have a pool of workers and will prepare them in terms of their skills and the work standard expected of them. This assumption has been further accepted by a group of well-known industrialists, who have agreed to cooperate with the UCEP team in operating the proposed vocational training in Chittagong. This model is based on the concept that the profit to industries would come from providing for and benefiting from underprivileged children, not from exploiting their social disadvantage. Moreover, underprivileged children would be allowed to exploit their own economic potential. This marks a 'dynamic linkage' and is potentially a basis for partnership, although one that needs careful monitoring. The linkage is considered important because the mass of working children in the slums of Bangladesh have little or no opportunity to exploit their economic potential on their own. They cannot interface directly with industry and can benefit from the mediation and overseeing of an NGO like UNICEF. Hence the key to a successful training intervention is to give them the opportunity to exploit effectively this economic potential. This would require appropriate education, tailored to the circumstances, abilities and aspirations.

Although education is necessary for any child, working or not, it is not by itself the means of eliminating child labour. As illustrated above, child labour is intricately linked to the local and global markets and the demand for products that require the labour of children to be competitive. Hence policy-makers have to engage with the private sector, even though this may entail some economic costs or trade-offs in terms of loss of profit over market share. The UCEP model of 'dynamic linkage' between trained children and industries points to a way forward where partnership may reduce trade-offs on both sides of the partnership. Such a model not only reduces exploitation of child labourers, but also ensures their future income, and this is more realistic from the perspective of both children and their families. The UNCEP experience will test the premise that policy-makers need to be more holistic in their approach to the problems of child labourers, and that governments need to invest more in non-formal education and vocational education, in partnership with the private sector, for future jobs.

Conclusion

The reasons why children work, leave home and move to the street have their roots in the poverty and vulnerability of the low-income city-dwellers in developing countries. As long as these exist there will be street and working children. The projects outlined above demonstrate that an important way forward is through cooperation between adults and children. Children want not handouts or institutions, just a chance to be part of the city.

Children need access to decision-making. If society views children as capable of undertaking waged work, contributing positively to their families, or, at the opposite extreme, as capable of committing criminal offences, then should society not also accept that children are capable of contributing to decisions on policies that affect their lives? Participatory approaches towards poverty alleviation are gaining popularity. These emphasise that the poor are the experts on their own situation (Chambers, 1989). This approach needs to be broadened to include children. In cities where children have been listened to they have made a positive contribution to urban policy. A striking example of this is provided by Swift's (1991) description of the children's movement in Brazil. Its message is that children are 'human beings' not 'human belongings' and have the potential to contribute positively to the city.

References

Agnelli, S., S. Aga Khan, P. E. Arns, H. Beer, M. Lachs and L. Mojsov (1986), *Street Children: A Growing Urban Tragedy*, London: Weidenfeld and Nicolson.

Beall, J. D., N. Kanji, F. Faruqi, M. Mirani and C. Mohammed Hussain (1993), *Social Safety Nets and Social Networks: Their Role in Poverty Alleviation in Pakistan*, London: report for the Overseas Development Administration, UK.

Boyden, J. and P. Holden (1991), *Children of the Cities*, London: Zed Books.

Chambers, R. (1989) 'Vulnerability: how the poor cope', special issue, *IDS Bulletin*, 20(2): 1–9.

Dalglish, P. and M. Connolly (1992), *Too Much Time, Too Little Money*, New York: Street Kids International Toronto.

Ennew, J. and B. Milne (1989), *The Next Generation: Lives of Third World Children*, London: Zed Books.

Harpham, T., T. Lusty and P. Vaughan (1988), *In the Shadow of the City: Community Health and the Urban Poor*, Oxford: Oxford University Press.

Kanji, N. (1996), *Review of Urbanization Issues Affecting Children and Women in the Eastern and Southern African Region*, report for UNICEF, March.

Niewenhuys, O. (1994), *Children's Life Worlds: Gender, Welfare and Labour in the Developing World*, London: Routledge.

Swift, A. (1991), *Brazil: The Fight for Childhood in the City*, Florence: Innocenti Studies, UNICEF International Child Development Centre.

Swift, A. (1996), 'Scared of our own kids', *New Internationalist*, February: 14–18.

Szanton Blanc, C. S. (ed.) (1994), *Urban Children in Distress: Global Predicaments and Innovative Strategies*, New York: UNICEF.

UCEP (1990), *UCEP Annual Report*, Underprivileged Children's Education Programme, Bangladesh.

UNICEF (1995), *State of the World's Children*, New York: United Nations Children's Fund.

Velis, P. (1995), *Blossoms in the Dust: Street Children in Africa*, Paris: UNESCO.

Wratten, E. (1995), 'Conteptualizing urban poverty', *Environment and Urbanization*, 7(1): 11–36.

CHAPTER 6

Housing, Gender and Work in Dhaka

Elinor Jenkins

This chapter details the gendered process of urbanisation in Bangladesh with particular reference to the impact of the garment industry on the gender division of labour and housing needs. The availability of new waged employment in an exported-oriented industry with a stated preference for female workers has brought women out of the private and into the public domain. The combination of migration, changes in employment and a new urban lifestyle is creating a space between 'girlhood' and 'motherhood', so that the concept of adolescence is emerging as a new dimension of diversity in urban Bangladesh.

Many of the young single women migrating to the city live separately from their family and, for reasons that will be discussed, have broken ties with their kin groups. As young women, living without a male guardian, they are subject to suspicion, hostility and violence within a cultural context that respects seclusion. Thus the availability of safe, appropriate and affordable accommodation is central to the survival strategies of these young women. This chapter explores the reality of the housing situation in Dhaka city and questions the support it provides to urban adolescent women. It offers an interesting perspective on the way in which housing, as part of the urban environment, can facilitate or inhibit the involvement of diverse groups in city life.

The context

Bangladesh has a population of 122.2 million, of whom 52.5 million are presently under the age of 16 years. While the population is mainly rural it is estimated that 18% now live in urban centres and that the cities are growing at a rate of 6.3% per annum (UNICEF, 1995). With a GNP of $220 per capita many Bangladeshis live below an absolute poverty line and recent estimates place 86% of the urban population in this category (ibid.). Islam is the majority religion in the country, with 85% of the population Muslim. In June 1988 the 8th Amendment to the Constitution, making Islam the state religion, was passed. Feldman (1992) charts the growing influence of conservative fundamentalist groups such as Jamaati-i-Islam within both political and social spheres, a factor that is significant to the lives of young female workers.

Employment opportunities

Bangladesh has long been one of the most densely populated but least urbanised countries in the developing world. This began to change in the 1970s and the country is now urbanising rapidly, with estimated rates of 10% of absolute urban growth being recorded (Choguill, 1987). In the period between 1951 and 1988 the population of Dhaka city has increased 15 times (Islam, 1989). Many unskilled males migrated to the city in the hope of finding employment in the construction industry, an activity that offered better remuneration and was more constant than the alternative option of agricultural labour. The reality for many has been much less security, the majority only finding employment in the informal sector, many as rickshaw wallahs.

Since the early 1980s the garments industry in Bangladesh has expanded rapidly: in 1981 it earned £4 million, and by 1994–95 the export earnings were £1.2 billion, 57% of total foreign exchange earnings (Le Quesne, 1996: 29). Over 70% of investment in this industry came from Singapore, Hong Kong and South Korea (Feldman, 1992). As the newly industrialised countries (NICs) faced an increase in labour costs and the imposition of export quotas for the US and Europe, Bangladesh presented a possible location for sub-contracting, which offered low or no quota restrictions, minimal wages, generous tax holidays and liberal profit repatriation policies. The government of Bangladesh's New Industrial Policy of 1982 and the Revised Industrial Policy of 1986 outlined prescriptions that were to change significantly the gender division of labour within society: 'Female workers were defined a priori as the preferred labour force, following tradition and ideology established for garments and apparel manufacture in export-processing zones (EPZs) around the world' (Feldman, 1992: 118).

Tailoring skills, traditionally male dominated, experienced a sudden and significant gender shift, with 90% of export garment workers being female (Feldman, 1992). While female migration continued to be a matter of basic survival, women's urban employment opportunities were no longer limited to domestic service, begging or prostitution: the garments industry now offered an additional and preferable option (Kabeer, 1995). Both Feldman (1992) and Kabeer (1995) identify a proportion of middle-class, educated women seeking employment in this sector yet they conclude that the vast majority of employees are young, single, low-income women (also Le Quesne, 1996). This chapter focuses on the latter group, for whom work in the city has brought both risks and opportunities.

Family ties

For many young women the process of migration from village to city is negotiated through a village or kin contact, someone who has succeeded in the city and returns to share his success with his kin (Kibria, 1995). For some this is a secure and successful route, offering the young woman a safe and appropriate social context in the city, with a male guardian or accommodation with a family member. By using these structural supports, the family ensure their daughter's safety and fulfil their 'cultural contract' (Kabeer, 1995) to protect her until marriage. However, this process is not an option for all young women migrants, nor does it always ensure safety and support. In an Islamic culture, young women who fail to conform to *purdah* norms and live outside familial supervision are automatically sexually suspect and a threat to family honour (Kibria, 1995). In this event, it appears that the 'cultural contract' is broken, if the family fail to protect and provide for their daughter until marriage, or if the daughter fails to observe the behavioural norms of Islam. Kibria (1995) suggests that the failure of daughters in Bangladesh to send their wages to the village, common in many other Asian societies, may be indicative of this contractual breakdown and the weakening of kin ties. Despite the increasing visibility of young women in the streets and factories of Dhaka, there has been little relaxation in the attitude to young and single women living and working in an urban context. This in turn influences and affects the importance placed on access to safe, affordable and appropriate housing.

Gender relations and adolescence in Bangladesh

Travelling into Dhaka city from the airport, one is struck by two dramatic images. On one side of the road billboards emphasise the benefits of immunisation, breast-feeding and appropriate child nutrition. Opposite, thousands of young female factory workers walk to and from work. The contradiction between the affirmation of women's reproductive roles (supported by policy and provision) and the denial of women's productive roles (failing to command the provision of affordable and appropriate transport) is stark.

Bangladesh is one of a number of countries that displays a strong preference for sons in its population profile. Parents view a daughter as a burden, an investment that will never reap returns. Rearing a daughter is 'like watering a neighbour's tree' (Kabeer, seminar at London School of Economics, 1995). Poor families have limited resources and must make what they see as careful investments. As a result the girl child in Bangladesh is a bad investment, less likely to receive curative health care, adequate nutrition or formal education.

However, new employment opportunities in the garments industry have managed to effect a change in the position of girls and young women in Bangladesh where evolutionary change has largely failed. They have moved from the private to the public domain and from being an economic burden to being an economic asset. A woman's life-cycle, hitherto characterised by a transfer of dependence from father to husband to son, may now include a period of independence.

While paid work has provided greater economic security, this has been accompanied by a social threat described by Kabeer (1995: 32) as 'the fear that women have'. For young 'adolescent' women in Bangladesh the threat of sexual violence or attack on their virtue leads to fear and insecurity. Participation in the garments industry and enhanced economic power has also meant greater visibility and mobility. This has not been without its social costs, particularly in the eyes of some Bangladeshi males. In speaking of the garments workers, they say that 'their value has gone up but their reputations have gone down' (cited in Kabeer, 1995). As a result: 'A striking feature of gender subordination is the extent to which women rely on male protection as much as they rely on male provision' (Kabeer, 1995: 32).

This threat of violence is very real for many young women in Dhaka, and tales of trafficking, rape, sexual abuse and exploitation are common among young single migrants in the city who come without or who get separated from kin networks (unpublished case history material, CON-CERN). While some find secure employment and accommodation, others are either 'trafficked' – sold directly into the sex industry in Dhaka or abroad – or suffer abuse while working as domestic servants. Once 'spoilt' by this abuse the young women perceive themselves as 'bad', feel shame for themselves and their families and will not return to the village. With few other employment or accommodation options, they often enter the sex industry.

The availability of safe, appropriate and affordable housing must be central to any preventative and protective strategy for young adolescent women in 'A City for All'. The creation of a safe environment, one that seeks to reduce the vulnerability of young women and the event of sexual exploitation and fear, is as important as providing opportunities for income earning. Both are essential if these young women are to have social and economic security.

Housing and work in Dhaka

The supply and type of urban housing in Dhaka are affected by a number of factors, probably the most significant of which is the land being low lying and vulnerable to flooding. The shortage of suitable land and speculative investment has led to inflationary land prices. Fewer than 10% of the urban poor own any land (Islam, 1989), leaving a significant percentage renting, sharing or squatting. With minimal 'public' provision monopolised by civil servants, the poor of Dhaka are dependent on the market to find housing. Household strategies to reduce the percentage of income spent on housing and on travel mean that 70% of Dhaka's population live in poverty and occupy only 20% of the land (Shefali, 1995), while wealthier Dhakites move to the periphery of the city. Poor women are further constrained, within the context of their age, gender and culture, by the need for 'appropriate' housing, a factor that may weaken their other survival strategies. The experience of two NGOs working with the 'floating' population of recent migrants to Dhaka city illustrates both the vulnerability of young women and the social and economic value that they place on safe accommodation.

CONCERN Worldwide operates a project supporting young women, many of whom have migrated to the city in search of work. Some have been domestic workers, others have been dependent on begging or prostitution. The project offers women a number of services such as non-formal education, counselling, health care and skills training and through these seeks to equip the young women with the skills and confidence to cope with city life. For many of the young women who pass through the project a job in the garments industry is their hope for the future. Over a period of 18 months the project worked with three groups of 15–20 young women between 16 and 23 years old to secure employment and accommodation.

Although most of the young women had received training in industrial sewing, the factories in which they secured employment insisted that they start on a 'helper' grade with very low wages ($10–$15 per month). The project staff were concerned that with such low wages some of the young women may return to prostitution, which is potentially more lucrative. The staff therefore sought accommodation for the adolescent women that was close to the factory and at a price that would not command their total income.

In all cases the accommodation was rented, and the tenancy agreement had to be carefully negotiated by the NGO with the owner of the property as many were reluctant to lease to a group of young women. In part this reluctance stems from an awareness of possible problems associated with leasing to groups of women, for instance disapproval and questioning from neighbours, harassment from local young men and conflict with the police, who might suspect the young women of prostitution. Another possible reservation on the part of landlords may be an awareness of the irregularity of some factory work and therefore of their own income. When factories have a lot of orders, work and overtime is plentiful. If the orders or production stop for any reason[1] then workers have no income. For some workers who exist within a corporate household structure, it may be possible to negotiate and survive these periods. However, for many of the young single women, with little or no family support to fall back on, these times can mean an inevitable return to destitution.

Group 1 The first group that CONCERN Worldwide worked with secured employment and accommodation in a Dhaka suburb. They lived collectively in 'mess'[2] fashion, with 8–10 women per room and shared cooking facilities. The young women spent almost 50% of their basic wage, 250–300 taka, on their accommodation. It is important to note that similar types of 'mess' accommodation for men cost in the region of 50–100 taka per month. Such a discrepancy has inevitable implications for the physical and economic security of young women and their potential to participate equally in city life.

This group was intensively supported by staff members of the NGO and their progress was monitored. During this time many left both the accommodation and the employment. A number of factors were involved:

- Financial difficulties resulted from periods without work due to scarcity of orders or as a result of sickness with the added cost of medical care.
- The group reported harassment from local young men on their journey to and from the factory and also outside the flat.
- A combination of failing to pay the rent on time and disturbance by these young men made the group unpopular with both the landlord and neighbours.
- The neighbours were also suspicious of this group of young women living without a male guardian, and the group received attention from the police.

Once members left the group it was difficult to monitor their progress. However, reports from other group members suggest that some returned to prostitution, some got married and some secured new living arrangements with friends, often with an older woman, which suggests that this may be more socially acceptable than a young group. The few who remained were extremely dependent on the staff support, raising questions about the sustainability of such an arrangement but also emphasising the long-term nature of the investment needed to 'empower' vulnerable groups.

Group 2 Following this first experience a quite different strategy was adopted with group 2. Employment and accommodation were secured in a more rural area on the outskirts of Dhaka city. The assumption was that food and accommodation would be more affordable, travel to and from work safer and the community more accepting. The landlady appeared supportive, and food supplies were purchased by CONCERN to help while the group became established.

Despite various attempts to make sure that this group was both physically and financially secure, within a few days the project staff received reports that a 'broker' had arrived at the village and forced the women to return with him to Dhaka to work as prostitutes. Whilst there was some controversy as to how this broker became aware of the group's living arrangement, it is clear that the young women were vulnerable to exploitation and that the community was either unwilling or unable to protect them.

Group 3 By the time the third group were ready to find jobs, safe, appropriate accommodation was seen as essential if the project were to succeed. The possibilities of hostel accommodation were explored and CONCERN established a cooperative working relationship with another NGO, Nari Uddug Kendra (NUK; Centre for Women's Initiatives). This NGO was established in 1981 with the objective of promoting women's rights and gender equality in development through the integration of women as active agents and equal participants. NUK not only offered accommodation but also provided other support services for the young women, including ongoing education, day care for working mothers, health care services, and information on women's rights and labour laws. Over the course of the last five years NUK has conducted its own research into the lifestyles and living arrangements of young migrants in Dhaka, and this research has been supplemented by Katherine Denham's unpublished work (Fulbright scholar, Harvard University, personal communication, 1994). The main findings coincide with the project experience of CONCERN Worldwide.

Proximity to the factory is often the highest priority for young women in seeking accommodation. Two main reasons have been suggested: the need to minimise transport costs as part of a survival strategy and the threat of harassment while travelling to and from work. The second priority noted is the need for a secure living environment. The women are under constant threat of harassment, especially if they do not have the protection of their family living with them. The third priority is affordability.

Space was not found to be a priority for these women. They are willing to sacrifice space to be close to their work and have some degree of security at their residence. They work long hours and spend little time in the hostel, and NUK notes that the women often view the hostel as temporary, their permanent home being in the village or with a future husband (the need to support and maintain kin ties clearly being important).

NUK offers hostel accommodation that is clean, safe and secure. It also provides three meals a day, which reduces the domestic burden on women who are often working up to 14 hours a day. These services cost a total of 600 taka per month, often equal to the basic salary of a low-grade worker. While the service is relatively expensive, NUK argues, and supports this with evidence from its research, that these adolescent women were spending comparative amounts on very poor slum accommodation. Living in the slums they were vulnerable to abuse and exploitation from a number of sources, particularly landlords who realised that adolescent women have few housing options. Living in the hostel they are able to avail themselves of education and recreation facilities, and this type of accommodation also appears to support links with kin groups. Mashuda K. Shefali (1994) reports that many women in the hostels regularly send remittances to their village, in contrast with Kibria's (1995) findings for adolescent women living in other types of non-family accommodation.

It was assumed by CONCERN that group 3 would use the hostel place as a launch-pad from which to become established, but would move very quickly to cheaper accommodation. In the event what happened was that the young women appeared to value highly the opportunity to live in a secure, socially appropriate environment and were willing to pay a very high percentage of their wages to do so.

NUK has taken up the issues of housing young urban migrants not only on the level of provision but also through advocacy. In August 1994 it organised a conference, inviting interested parties such as garments manufacturers, private house owners, private sector developers, government and NGOs. The conference concluded with the recommendation that these groups work together to initiate solutions to low-income women's housing problems. While NUK stands out as an example of good practice, the organisation recognised that its operation was capital intensive and that any replication would depend on willing investment.

Conclusion

In 1996 people began to suggest that the Bangladesh garments industry may have seen its best times. The phasing out of the Multi Fibre Arrangement (MFA) over the period 1995–2005 removes the quota advantage once held and leaves Bangladesh at the mercy of the free market competing with neighbours such as Vietnam who are emerging as strong competitors (Le Quesne, 1996). In such an event the industry may manipulate its remaining comparative advantage and reduce wages. Within the current unregulated, private housing market the pressure of increased demand for security, coupled with its limited supply, is likely to result in a price increase for safe accommodation. Already women are spending a high proportion of their income on appropriate housing. Increased rents or reduced wages will leave adolescent women more vulnerable to trade-offs between physical and financial insecurity. The manifestation of either will reduce their capacity to participate.

The adolescent young women identified in this chapter who face the problems of poverty, insecure housing and weakened links with their family or kin are particularly vulnerable in the urban context. The emergence of the garments industry may present a real opportunity to change the position of the girl child in Bangladesh and empower women within society, but this potential will be realised only if risks are minimised through appropriate provision. Safe, affordable and appropriate housing could go far to achieve this.

Notes

1. In early 1996 there was a period of 'non-cooperation' called for by the opposition party of the government, which in effect brought the country to a standstill for over a month. During this time factory production would have been impossible and if there is no production then the workers have no wage.

2. The phenomenon of 'mess' accommodation is mentioned by both Feldman (1992) and Kabeer (1995). However, neither has focused on housing issues in detail.

References

Choguill, J. (1987), *New Communities for Urban Squatters: Lessons from the Plan that Failed in Dhaka Bangladesh*, Plenum.

Feldman, S. (1992), 'Crisis, Islam and gender in Bangladesh: the social construction of a female labour force', in S. Feldman and L. Beneria, *Unequal Burden: Economic Crisis, Persistent Poverty and Women's Work*, Boulder, CO: Westview Press, pp. 105–30.

Islam, N. (1989), 'Dhaka metropolitan fringe: land and housing development', Dhaka: Government of Bangladesh.

Kabeer, N. (1995), 'Necessary, sufficient or irrelevant? women, wages and intra-household power relations in urban Bangladesh', Working Paper 25, Institute of Development Studies, University of Sussex.

Kibria, N. (1995) 'Culture, social class and income control in the lives of women garment workers in Bangladesh', *Gender and Society*, 9(3): 289–309.

Le Quesne , C. (1996), *Reforming world trade: the social and environmental priorities*, Oxford: Oxfam.

Shefali, M. K. (1995), 'NUK information and internal reports', unpublished mimeo.

UNICEF (1995), *State of the World's Children*, New York: United Nations Children's Fund.

CHAPTER 7

The Woman Dweller: Public Space in Santiago

Olga Segovia

Women living in low-income areas in Chile, as well as in the rest of Latin America, play a vital role in *barrio* life. They have principal responsibility for the construction and maintenance of survival networks and reproductive tasks, actively participating in externally and internally generated initiatives to improve their immediate surroundings. Urban planning has, however, failed to consider and therefore failed to integrate the specific priorities and needs of women in relation to the space of the *barrios* around them. Different actors are always going to contest the way in which space is used, what meanings are accorded to it and the ways in which they motivate for different usage of space. In the accompanying conflict and consensus, gender relations are ever present. It is through the relationship between material and social dimensions that this chapter attempts to identify patterns of spatial appropriation and to distinguish those spatial domains that are influenced by gender roles within the *barrios*.

In the external spaces where the wider social life of the *barrios* is conducted, it is possible to observe spatially expressed behavioural patterns, reflecting the roles defined as feminine and masculine within the *barrios*. Women generally are involved in reproductive tasks within the private space of the home, while men, in travelling between the *barrios* and their place of employment, occupy a wider, public space. Interviews with women in the *barrios* reveal that they closely identify with this view: 'Men have great freedom of movement, they leave the house without giving any notice.' This situation of female permanence and male movement is linked to established gender norms and conduct. On average, there are 20% more men than women in the public spaces of the *barrios*, with variation at different periods of the day: during the morning, 12% more men than women; in the afternoon, 20%, at night time, 24%. This difference is due to the fact that public spaces used by women during the day become dangerous for them at night. The major difference is seen during Saturdays and Sundays, when men make between 25 and 30% more use of public space than do women. What elements affect women's presence in public space and interfere with the diversity of its use?

When women consider their opportunities in the public spaces of the *barrios*, they are commonly expressed in terms of their children's enjoyment rather than those of their own. Women's use of public space is closely related to their reproductive roles – shopping for family food, taking children to and from school, supervising children's play and accompanying them to the medical centre. This means that for certain periods in the day, the street becomes a sphere of 'feminine' activity. Other areas of public space that women use are related to work and training activities. In Villa O'Higgins and Estrecho de Magellanes, the two *barrios* on which this chapter concentrates, women have participated in support groups and training activities outside of the home. In Villa O'Higgins there is a Women's Community House where women meet to discuss ways of supporting each other and of improving the *barrios* in general. In 1992, women participated in influencing the physical improvement of the squares and alleyways of both *barrios*. At weekends women also often accompany their husbands to the soccer field near the *barrios*. Overall, women in the *barrios* recognise that their participation in daily activities related to reproductive roles, as mothers and housewives, is strongly oriented towards the home as a locus of activities. Thus for many women the home is their 'legitimate' space, their area of moral authority. In Estrecho de Magellanes, there is a common pattern of *allegados* – those relatives without a house of their own who then share with members of their extended family. This often contracts the private space available to women, who become involved in childcare for their nieces or grandchildren.

As most men in both *barrios* work outside the area and do not contribute to household reproductive tasks, their use of public space in the *barrios* is more strongly oriented towards external entertainment and social activity. Men meet on street corners to chat, drink beer and play *rayuela*, a common street game. At the weekend they meet at the soccer field or at the liquor store, an exclusively masculine space. Use of public space is also often related to the man's own definition of his social role. 'Now that I am getting married, I have responsibilities and I do not go out at night. Those who go out are much younger, those who are married do not go out in the street as much.' Most men in the *barrios* express desire for the rehabilitation of public space in terms of sports or recreational activities, as they consider sport to have a crucial role in alleviating the *barrios'* problems of drug abuse and delinquency. In common with the women of the area, they feel threatened by groups of drug users, *volados*, in the *barrios* and worry about the potential effect on their children.

Groups of young men are highly visible, making intensive use of the streets and consequently occupying a disproportionate amount of external space within the *barrios*. Their activities include gathering at games arcades, hanging out on street corners, listening to music and dancing. Different groups mark and identify certain areas as their own and women may find passing through these areas threatening. Dark alleyways, empty lots and groups of young men at street corners at night all promote a strong sense of insecurity for women who may have to use these areas; they are therefore avoided where possible. Use of space is also gendered within groups of young people. A young woman commented that it was not acceptable for a 'lady' to walk or stand alone in the street: 'We must always be accompanied, it is acceptable for us to talk with a friend in the doorway of our home at night.'

Spatial organisation is not, however, a fixed entity, set in concrete walls of design and specifically relating to one gender or the other, but rather is often defined in relation to its opposite. In the *barrios* the interior position – the private – is associated with the feminine and therefore the external – the public – becomes associated with the masculine. According to women and men in the *barrios*, external and internal space not only symbolise gender roles but also serve to reinforce them. Those men who spend a great deal of time within the home may be considered to be less masculine, while women occupying a great deal of external space risk social approbation in their use of public space. This extends to speech – the linking of 'woman' and 'street' is taboo in the *barrios*, bringing with it the same connotations of prostitution that are common across the world. Methods of social control also work to limit women's use of public space. As one woman commented: 'I do not like to go out too much, my husband says that there are jealous people out there ... that I'd better stay at home and on holidays I cannot go out alone.' Men in the *barrios* commented: 'Women should stay at home, the street is too dangerous for them, but not for men.' The time of day at which public space is used is also significant. One woman said: 'At night I feel excluded from every-where ... besides, they begin to gossip about me.' Spatial use also varies inter-generationally; an older woman in the area commented: 'Young women remain on the street more than we do, sometimes they meet at street corners ... they are allowed to go beyond the fence of the house to chat.'

One of the main uses of space outside the home by women and children is related to the design of houses within the *barrios*. Where homes meet, on the borders of plots or in the streets and alleys between homes, women regularly occupy this semi-public space for social interaction. A large percentage of surveyed women, more than 77%, stated that they hold the majority of their conversations with their neighbours. The combination of proximity and contact between inhabitants gives the neighbourhood or *vecindario* its identity. Neighbourhood in its spatial dimension is perceived by women as an intermediate territory between the reduced space of their homes and the greater space of the *barrio*

(Segovia, 1993). Here, women chat to their neighbours, keep an eye on children playing outside the house and observe the movement of the neighbourhood. The space around and within the home, shared between family and neighbours, is perceived by women as 'their' or their children's legitimate and valued space. As mentioned above, outside this space women risk differing degrees of conflict.

Use of physical space is often an articulation of a social environment, identifiable through the various uses of space by different members of a community. These activities in turn reinforce and affirm social relations and the two thus become intertwined. The meaning that individuals accord to the space they use and the way in which they then use that space, literally creating the space around them, is significant in conceptualising space as a wider socio-cultural entity, not only as a physically given area. Obviously the meaning and significance of space will therefore vary widely between older men and younger women, between children and young men and women in paid employment and women at home. Issues such as identity and sociability, priorities for safety and protection, the need for privacy and trust and the search for quality and beauty in surroundings (Segovia, 1993), all intersect with gender, age and income to create a particular set of spatial priorities for each individual in the *barrios*. The question, then, is how may we identify these criteria, particularly those influenced by a gendered use of space, in order to strengthen and promote priorities of women within *barrio* areas?

As discussed above, the residential neighbourhood is more closely identified with feminine than with masculine use of space. Women conceive of the relationship between house, neighbourhood and *barrio* as a linear one, predominantly taking the household as their starting point, expressing as it does the reality of their daily life patterns. In the two *barrios* studied, neighbourhoods as distinct areas within each *barrio* are characterised by a shared alleyway or common street within which inhabitants maintain contact with their immediate neighbours. In areas of very high density of housing, it is more difficult to define clearly the extent of one particular neighbourhood. Where blocks of housing are facing in opposite directions and walls are built around backyards, the common ground of the neighbourhood is often lost. Inhabitants ascribe both a social and a spatial dimension to neighbourhood. The frequency and intensity of inter-household contact in terms of reciprocal relationships and sharing of information is vital in this context: 'Sometimes we have problems with our family and we have to ask for help. We know we can always count on our neighbour. The point is that we've shared a lot of things and have known each other a long time.' Women in the *barrios* most often view their neighbourhood as an intermediate area or a negotiating space between the *barrio* as a whole and their household as an individual unit. When inhabitants are asked to define their neighbourhood there can be widely varying conceptions within one area. Often these are best represented through asking women, in their role as home managers, to draw a circle of their neighbourhood with their home at the centre. Within one small area, the sizes of these circles will vary dramatically according to each woman's concept of neighbourhood.

Relations between inhabitants in the *barrios* are often closer where houses are facing or adjacent to each other. It is these semi-public spaces, the alleyways at the sides of houses or frontyards, that women use most intensively. Within these areas women are free from some of the risks that participating in a more public space may bring. Neighbourhood relations are formed and reinforced here. Communal courtyards, mesh fences and windows all offer opportunities for social interaction, stretching the boundaries between public and private space. In Estrecho de Magellane, plots are a maximum of 7 metres wide and there are generally 3 metres between household fences and the buildings. In Villa O'Higgins, plots are wider, with some 6 metres between the dwelling and the edge of the plot. Within both these areas it is common for women to do their washing and children to play. The physical elements that facilitate contact between women of the area are the courtyards and fences. During the week women can be observed interacting from the porches of their houses. This changes on Sundays, which tend to be marked by both increased use of private space and, conversely, more intensive use of communal space. Elements that act as markers for public space becoming private are urban furniture or vegetation in the alleys, squares and streets. These stress the sense of belonging for people, particularly women. In this sense the reclamation of public space is also an indication or motivation for women to participate in physical improvements in the *barrios* and in dwellings (Haramoto, Moyano and Kliwadenko, 1992). Short distances and small proportions are important to women in their controlling of space. It is also important that the locus of many of their activities, such as schools and medical centres, are near to their dwellings. Women need protected urban spaces with places for children to play in.

Research in the *barrios* has shown that both in the actions and in the discourse of women and men the most recurrent themes are sociability and identity; reinforcing the sense of territorial belonging and social integrity, security and protection; avoiding threats of delinquency and drug abuse, minimising fears and prejudices; increasing privacy and trust; making the *barrio* a better and more beautiful place to live (Segovia, 1993). *Barrio* inhabitants need passages, streets, plazas and street corners with borders that encourage diverse collective activities; parks and windows, stairs, small businesses, schools, sports clubs, public telephones and open places in which to sit, walk and interact. Overall, they need a place that gives them a sense of identity and belonging.

The meaning of space is socially constructed and socially reinforced.

In the *barrios* it is possible to observe how the 'home-space' is for many women a border with the public world. Also within public space are areas that are intensively used for social activities, incorporating women and men. As planners we must strive towards both public and private spaces that accommodate and understand the gender-defined uses of space within specific contexts. This may go some way towards allowing people to define their own space in constructive, supportive and gender-sensitive ways.

References

Haramoto, E., E. Moyano and I. Kliwadenko (1992), 'Espacio y comportamiento en el entorno inmediato de la vivienda social', working paper, Santiago: CEDVI FABA, Universidad Central.

Segovia, O. (1993), *Public Space and Gender*, Copenhagen: Department of Human Settlements, Royal Danish Academy of Fine Arts.

Box 2.1

Comments on Urban Space from Participants at the Special Event 'A City for All'

I want to make a comment. My first comment is related to what Olga [Segovia] has established. It seems to be very common to be living in cities where there is a process of privatisation of public space. I do not believe this is accidental. Behind this process there is a model, there is a planner who is doing a terrible job. Insecurity and violence are the results of a lack of confidence in social order. But how can we recapture this confidence within our families and neighbours? We need to work hand in hand with men, especially in the most traditional societies.

I would like to make a comment on the situation in Germany. We have noticed that there has been an increase in the privatisation of public space and when this is combined with a feminisation of poverty poor women no longer have access to public space. Therefore we in Germany are committed to working to keep public space public. There has been a creation of public space that is not general to the needs of women and this should be challenged. Feminist planners in Germany are just discussing how to make policy that addresses those responsible for problems of public space – men.

PART THREE

Building a Liveable City: Secure Homes and Neighbourhoods

CHAPTER 8

Urban Violence: An Overview

Rajeev Patel

Violence has started to receive considerable attention as a significant urban phenomenon. Its recent acknowledgement as a cause for concern accompanies both its increasing severity and the increasing recourse to social development as a means of tackling its root causes (Pinheiro, 1993). Social development is a broad church which positively encourages the multi-disciplinary approach necessary to understand and tackle the causes of urban violence. In particular, methods such as incarceration are being re-evaluated in recognition of the fact that any durable solution to urban violence must involve the marginalised urban youth often responsible for its perpetration. This chapter examines the multi-dimensional nature of violence and initiatives to deal with the problem. Diverse experiences of violence are recognised. It is argued that a broader conception of violence than that of 'violence as criminal activity' is necessary so that attention is drawn to groups other than young urban men. The chapter concludes by noting that schemes which have successfully dealt with urban violence have included *all* members of a community.

Dictionary definitions tend to stress the physical nature of violence; the *Collins English Dictionary* defines violence as 'the exercise of physical force, usually effecting or intending to effect injuries, destruction, etc.' To the extent that violence is a physical phenomenon, this is a correct definition. Violence may be actual harm or damage, against either people or property. This harm may comprise either physical or sexual assault. However, policy initiatives that have been constructed around this definition have missed out other important dimensions of urban violence that are highlighted below.

Characteristics of urban violence

Acts of violence in the urban context have some characteristic features. First, from a purely statistical perspective, the *frequency* of violence is greater in urban than in rural areas. Consider, for instance, that urban violence in São Paulo is the single most common cause of death (Hardoy, Cairncross and Satterthwaite, 1990: 94), with homicide accounting for 5% of all deaths in that city in 1986, or that the most significant cause of death in Colombia in 1995 was violence (Vanderschueren, 1996).

Second, the *intensity* of violence is greater in cities than in rural areas. In the domestic context, particularly concerning violence against women and children (Friday, 1993), there are high levels of physical, sexual and non-physical violence. These are increased by the heightened incidence of urban alcoholism and drug abuse. At a neighbourhood level, violence tends not to escalate to the same extent in rural areas (Vanderschueren, 1996) because social structures exist to prevent and manage pathologies as and when they arise. Moser's (1996) work on social capital maintenance and erosion in cities illuminates this. Within urban communities, reciprocal relations and bonds of trust are particularly compromised by this intensity, to the point where social capital stocks have, in some urban areas, been entirely consumed.

Third, there exists the fundamentally urban phenomenon of *street violence*. In addition to 'individualist' physical or sexual urban violence where victim and perpetrator are not known to each other, this category includes rioting and gang or organised violence. The incidence of gang violence is increasing. The breakdown of family units makes the gang an attractive social support network, especially to young males – often, gangs provide a collective identity or 'street family'. Violence under such circumstances of anomie and marginalisation becomes a means of self-expression. Gangs themselves are not entirely negative phenomena. Through long-term community measures, gangs have been 'reintegrated' into communities. Successful urban regeneration schemes in Colombia and the United States have had gang cooperation as a prerequisite for success.

Significantly, it is poor families who disproportionately suffer the consequences of urban violence. It has been suggested that the existence of vast inequalities in wealth and their frequent juxtaposition in the urban context may be the cause of a decline in psycho-social health (Le Grand, 1985). If this is true, it is a further argument to buttress the already compelling case for a reduction in income disparities in the cities of developing countries. Within poor communities, it is men who suffer most direct harm from, and are most likely to be perpetrators of, urban violence. In the US, for instance, black men are more likely to die of homicide than of any other cause, and male life expectancy in the Bronx, New York, is 30 years (Novello, 1991) – far lower than that in low-income countries such as Bangladesh.

Responding to urban violence

Previous developmental paradigms held urban violence as a pathology to be dealt with by the police in the short term, and by social workers in the medium term. This view has been replaced by an understanding that the causes of urban violence are systemic and multidimensional. Examples of sectoral responses to urban violence can be found in respect of health, education, employment, the law, housing and urban design.

Recently violence has come to be seen as a health threat. A postmodern analysis of health has brought to the fore the issues of psychological and social health and well-being. The threats to health posed by urban violence have been incorporated into strategic public health initiatives in the US and South Africa, for example. Further, a link between psychosocial health, income and urban violence has recently been suggested (Zwi, 1993; Harpham and Blue, 1995).

Children in particularly poor families may often be prevented from attending school. The influences on children outside the education system are likely to be less benign than those within it. In the absence of parental supervision due to employment commitments, other influences such as street gangs (and television in more developed countries) loom large in formative education. For (predominantly male) adolescents, gangs provide the only opportunity for esteem-building and, to an extent, skill-building (where the skills may be antisocial ones such as burglary). Invariably, formal education programmes are not designed to cope with such problems, while successful alternatives include informal participatory approaches.

The existence of urban unemployment and the lack of opportunities for work create stresses to which poor people are particularly susceptible. For young men, this stress is often compounded by social norms which demand that they provide the main income for the household (Campbell, 1992). The social consequences of urban unemployment are well documented, and the failure of government to provide opportunities to harness these human resources is another factor contributing to urban violence (OJJDP, 1996). The lack of income lowers the opportunity cost of crime as a means to an end, and hence increases the incidence of violence in poor areas. A vicious circle then ensues as a region becomes known for violence. In Jamaica, for example, employers are unwilling to hire people from certain areas for fear of the violence they will bring with them.

The law, in certain communities, is seen as antagonistic to the interests of the community, as just another means by which the elite suppress the majority. This is not polemicism – these were the terms used by rioters in Los Angeles after the Rodney King incident in 1992, in which a young black man was gratuitously and severely beaten by police. This image of the judiciary and law enforcement agencies as an 'army' of a certain class (and often race) is not limited to the United States. There is abundant evidence that such a view is held by communities in India, Brazil and, most obviously, South Africa (Hardoy, Cairncross and Satterthwaite, 1990; Nbabandaba, 1987). Major reform of the methods of policing urban communities is necessary. But law enforcement agencies have argued that while it is true that they may need to reconsider their techniques, their duties are largely residual – they are forced to face and deal with the consequences of failures in other agencies in the urban context. In short, the police argue, with some justification, that they are the scapegoats for urban violence.

Housing and urban design can influence urban violence in two ways. First, the degree to which housing and work environments create comfortable environments to live in is a parameter of psycho-social health (Ekblad, 1993). Poorly designed buildings can contribute to poor health (consider 'sick building syndrome'), physical isolation and depression, the latter particularly affecting women. Moreover, the built environment can provide circumstances conducive to violence. The labyrinthine nature of urban housing areas, in both developed and developing countries, makes street crime (e.g. mugging, pickpocketing, etc.) easy and fosters fear (Ekblad, 1993).

Second, the degree to which a community is able to influence, plan and transform its environment is a measure of its ability to control itself. Violence is often a response to a lack of precisely this kind of autonomy. Evidence need be sought only in the relatively high levels of violence against property in poor urban areas. Writing graffiti, for instance, is an act predominantly carried out by marginalised young men and boys. A consideration of this action supports an interpretation in which the artists are disenfranchised from their environment and feel a need to shape it, and to achieve recognition for it.

In an attempt to respond to this, and to reduce the incidence of inner-city vandalism, a London city council made available several walls for graffiti artists to use. The walls were filled up quickly in an initiative involving artists and local schoolchildren in the production of several often beautiful murals. But despite a brief reduction in vandalism, the council did not provide similarly attractive follow-up opportunities. Within weeks, incidences of graffiti returned to their previous levels. This has been observed in parallel schemes in both developed and developing countries (*Passage*, 1995).

If physical violence is an assault on physical health, non-physical violence is an assault on psycho-social health and is an important component of urban violence. This sort of harm may include such phenomena as verbal harassment on the basis of sex, race or religion, and psychological stress resulting from environmental factors. Most countries acknowledge the existence of non-physical violence such as racial hatred, sexual harassment and harassment such as 'stalking'. However, it is not always acted on, while it is difficult to legislate against some aspects of non-physical violence, such as the *fear* of rape or of domestic violence.

Who are the victims of urban violence?

Women in particular bear the brunt of urban violence, both as victims, and as those forced to deal with the long-term consequences of it (as mothers whose sons kill or have been killed, for instance). Domestic violence is an important component of urban violence and is discussed in the following two chapters. Persistent sexual harassment is one of the long-term problems faced by women in developing country cities. Bombay, the centre of the Indian film industry, produces 800 films per year in which women are portrayed as sex objects. Rai (1993) reports that as a consequence there are increased sexual expectations of women, and non-fulfilment of sexual demands has even led to murder. Rinka Patel, for instance, did not want to marry immediately after her college graduation and was dubbed 'too modern' by young men in her neighbourhood (and indeed, subsequently by the media). The son of a community leader, together with other youths, gang-raped her before killing her and burning her body. Because of the perpetrators' status, the incident was initially registered as a suicide.

The gendered effect of urban violence has an impact on women's choice of housing, as illustrated in Chapter 6. Women are prepared to pay at least 50% over the market rate to live in accommodation that is secure.

Finally, evidence that the long-term stresses of violence rest disproportionately on the shoulders of women comes from the World Bank (1993). Psycho-social disorders are, according to the *World Development Report 1993*, among the top ten diseases in the disease profile of Third World cities. Further, within cities, women and the young seem to be more affected than men. The *elderly and disabled*, although statistically unlikely to suffer direct physical violence, face an increased fear of vulnerability to attack. This can often severely affect their quality of life.

In some areas, *ethnic, religious, sexual or other minorities* are subject to open targeted violence. South Africa has been the scene of institutionalised and targeted ethnic violence, but any city where minorities exist is liable to communal violence (Nbabandaba, 1987). The UNHCR estimates that there are currently around 30 million internally displaced people. In times of conflict, these people tend to head for the cities. This leads to tensions, and conflicts which increase the chance of escalating violence.

Street children face particular difficulties, in terms of both vulnerability to violence and exposure to the factors that normalise it. Exposure to violence in urban areas has also led to children accepting and promoting violence as acceptable behaviour. They risk death by vigilante groups 'cleaning the streets', as in Rio (Allsebrook and Swift, 1989). Both girls and boys face being forced into prostitution – in Nairobi, there have been instances of street girls as young as eight being involved (Vanderschueren, 1996). Children are also at risk in violent homes. Ekblad (1993) has detailed the particular difficulties that children face with respect to psychological and domestic violence.

Better practice

A common feature of the better practice solutions is that they all have a political empowerment component. It is often the case that the poorest members of a community are also among those least politically represented. Violence is not only a response to bad governance, however; it is a symptom of it, a sign that voices are not being heard and that groups of people are marginalised from the political process. Given the chance, communities worst affected by urban violence have shown themselves able to begin to tackle it at community and municipal levels, by trying to change the factors that are partly the result of, partly a contributing factor to, urban violence. An exceptional example of this is a scheme in Cali, Colombia (Guerro, 1993). In 1992, murder was the most frequent cause of death for the general population, and Cali had a murder rate of 87 per 100,000 per year. In June 1992, a public initiative called DESEPAZ (development, security and peace), involving local NGOs, CBOs and municipal authorities, began. It acknowledged the multidisciplinary nature of the problems, and responded in kind with a three-tier policy solution.

At the level of *law enforcement*, the court system was modernised to increase local involvement, protection for the police in dealing with violence was increased, and public safety councils were created to deal with community violence issues. At the intermediate level, *micro-enterprise schemes* were started and the creation of 25,000 sites and service plots was authorised. It was hoped that the security of tenure provided through these would decrease incentives for criminal income, and decrease psychosocial stress. At the long-term level, DESEPAZ had a strong *community education* component: young people, often in gangs, surrendered their weapons and persuaded children to give up their war toys in exchange for passes that allowed access to play areas citywide. This was mirrored by a gun amnesty for gang members, which resulted in the disarmament of four entire gangs. Similar moves, fundamentally from a community level, have been encouraged in the US (OJJDP, 1996).

Another example of successful urban violence management comes from Uganda. 'Resistance Councils', similar to the Public Safety Councils of Cali, have a range of responsibilities to the small urban populations that elect members to them. Councils must guarantee security and respect for the law within their jurisdiction. Significantly, they are also links between government and the community, and as such aim to promote community development within their constituency. By all accounts, they have proved successful. Not only have they contributed to the socio-economic status of their areas, but crime rates have been reduced, relations with the police improved and, most tellingly, the 'abuse of power by the military' has been avoided (Vanderschueren, 1996: 108). Their success has been based on an effective involvement of local residents, and on genuinely inclusive practice.

Conclusion

Urban violence has diverse causes and effects. Moves to include urban youth in programmes to combat urban violence, are, of course, to be welcomed, but urban violence is more than just street crime. The disempowering psychological and domestic dimensions tend to be underplayed in policy initiatives, and thus those people excluded from voicing their experiences are ignored. To remedy this, two courses of action suggest themselves. The first is to enhance municipal and government cooperation across the sectors mentioned above, in order that a coordinated solution might be brokered. But, as the DESEPAZ and Ugandan Council cases show, institutional multi-sectoralism is insufficient by itself. Inclusive community level involvement is also necessary. Resources also need to be directed at these community-level initiatives. The initial results from DESEPAZ appear promising, and if they continue perhaps governments can be persuaded that these measures are a cost-effective solution to an increasingly costly, isolating and dangerous problem.

References

Allsebrook, A. and A. Swift (1989), *Broken Promise: The World of Endangered Children*, London: Hodder & Stoughton.

Campbell, C. (1992), 'Learning to kill? masculinity, the family and violence in Natal', *Journal of Southern African Studies*, 18(3), September: 614–28.

Ekblad, S. (1993), 'Urban stress and its effects on children's lifestyles and health in industrialised countries', unpublished draft, Florence: UNICEF International Children's Development Centre.

Friday, J. (1993), 'Violence prevention from a public health perspective', *Urbanisation and Health Newsletter*, 9, December, Tygerberg, South Africa: 33–41.

Guerro, R. (1993), 'Cali's innovative approach to urban violence', *The Urban Age*, 1(4), Summer: 12.

Hardoy, J., S. Cairncross and D. Satterthwaite (eds) (1990), *The Poor Die Young: Housing and Health in Third World Cities*, London: Earthscan.

Harpham, T. and I. Blue (1995), *Urbanisation and Mental Health*, Avebury, Aldershot.

Le Grand, J. (1985), *Inequalities in Health: The Human Capital Approach*, London: Suntory-Toyota International Centre for Economics and Related Disciplines.

Moser, C. (1996), *Coping with Crisis*, Washington, DC: World Bank.

Nbabandaba, G. (1987), *Crimes of Violence in Black Townships*, Durban: Butterworth.

Novello, A. (1991), 'Violence is a greater killer of children than diseases', *Public Health Reports*, journal of the US Public Health Service, 106(3), May–June: 6–11.

Office of Juvenile Justice and Delinquency Prevention (OJJDP) (1996), *Gang Sup-*

pression and Intervention: Community Models, Washington, DC: US Department of Justice.

Passage (1995), 'Sane in St Paul – peace and violence in the hood', editorial, 4(1), December: 1–2.

Pinheiro, P. (1993), 'Reflections on urban violence', *The Urban Age*, 1(4), Summer: 3.

Rai, U. (1993), 'Escalating violence against girls in India', *The Urban Age*, 1(4), Summer: 10.

Vanderschueren, F. (1996), 'From violence to justice and security in cities' , *Environment and Urbanisation*, 8(1), April: 93–112.

World Bank (1993), *World Development Report 1993*, New York: Oxford University Press.

Zwi, A. (1993), 'Public health and the study of violence – are closer ties desirable?' *Urbanisation and Health Newsletter*, 9, December, Tygerberg, South Africa: 7–33.

CHAPTER 9

Violent Homes in Violent Cities: Experience from India

Meenu Vadera

Violence, in the home, in the community, society in general and by the state, can all combine to make a poor urban woman's life extremely insecure. As customary rural social norms break down, few alternative safe spaces or sanctioning mechanisms remain available in the homes, neighbourhoods and cities of women subject to urban violence. Homelessness as an effect of and a response to violence is a critical issue. Women belonging to either a minority race, ethnic group, religion or tribe often become visible targets in situations of heightened social conflict at the community level. Finally, institutional violence directly experienced by women through policies such as slum clearance and removal increases their vulnerability to police oppression and land mafias, adding to the indirect impact of gendered institutions that discriminate against women in areas of personal law relating to marriage, property and inheritance.

Organised women, both rural and urban, have struggled against this situation. On one hand they have pressed for changes in legislation (for instance, laws against rape, dowry and inheritance); on the other, grassroots women have themselves mobilised for their right to peace (for instance, the anti-liquor movements in Karnataka, Orissa and Manipur). These efforts have been complemented by efforts to provide alternative safe spaces, and counselling and support to women survivors of violence. This is a crucial element in combating violence, especially in a society where women own less than 1% of the property and thus have little command over resources.

This chapter discusses urban women's experience of violence (with a special focus on domestic violence) in their specific socio-spatial context. Although a causal relationship between urban violence and domestic violence is not being argued for, and in any case would be difficult to measure, it is proposed that an increasingly violent external environment is reflected in greater violence within 'private' spheres. It also leads to a greater tolerance by communities of the incidence of violence, in particular domestic violence.

Violence and women

Significant numbers of the world's population are routinely subject to torture, starvation, terrorism, humiliation, mutilation and even murder simply because they are female. Crimes such as these against any group other than women would be recognised as a civil and political emergency as well as a gross violation of the victim's humanity. Yet despite a clear record of deaths and demonstrable abuse, women's rights are not commonly classified as human rights. The narrow definition of human rights abuse, recognised by many in the West as solely a matter of state violation of civil and political liberties, is a major factor impeding the consideration of women's rights. Some important aspects of women's rights do fit into a civil liberties framework, but much of the abuse of women is part of a larger socio-economic web that entraps women, making them vulnerable to abuses that cannot be delineated as exclusively political or solely caused by states (Ashworth, 1985; Bunch and Carillo, 1992).

Sex discrimination is not just a matter of catcalls, whistling or even molesting (although even the smallest gesture of discrimination can make a woman feel humiliated). When this works along other axes of discrimination – those of caste, class, race, religion, etc. – it 'constitutes a deadly denial of women's rights to life and liberty on a large scale throughout the world' (Bunch and Carillo, 1992). However, the most pervasive violence against women is domestic violence in its many forms, including wife battery, incest, rape, dowry deaths, genital mutilation and sexual slavery. Even today most crimes within households go unreported. The scale, nature and extent of domestic violence has only recently begun to emerge, with crimes being reported because women have begun to protest and articulate their sorrows.

Wife beating is concealed in the many intimate, intricate layers of the relationship between husband and wife. However, apprehension about treading into personal, private territory is quickly dissipated when the nature and extent of this violence is investigated. Though few data exist, available evidence indicates a rising trend worldwide and dispels the myth that families are safe havens, that violence is largely restricted to lower classes and that men's violence is predominantly alcohol influenced. Not all men violate women, but every man benefits from the fear violence has generated in all women.

Understanding violence in an urban context

While on one hand cities bring to mind glittering images of high levels of consumption, they also carry the dark image of a high crime rate and a violent environment. Studies indicate that urban violence has risen by 3 to 5% a year over the past two decades across the world. At least once every five years, 60% of those living in cities with 100,000 or more inhabitants are victims of one form of crime or another. The pattern of crime differs across cities. Stadium violence may be more common in Eastern and Western Europe, armed robberies and car hijacking are a feature of urban life in Johannesburg or Nairobi, and drug-related incidents are associated with certain cities of Latin America. Cities in Asia, like most cities, suffer from crime against property (organised in the form of powerful land 'mafias' that exist in most big cities), the drug trade, ethnic/communal violence and a high level of domestic violence.

Violence in urban areas is increasingly explained as a phenomenon endemic in societies embedded in inequalities of class, caste, religion, race and gender. Rajan (1993) traces features of urban violence peculiar to post-colonial nations. She lists them as the central role of the state, inequalities in the social structure, the contrary pulls of nationalism and regionalism, and the conflict between tradition and modernity. Ironically and sadly the state has emerged as a major perpetrator of injustices, either directly (through its military and police power) or indirectly (by providing silent support to vested interests in maintaining a status quo in the dominant power relations). For instance, political support enjoyed by land mafias is very well known to people across the developing nations. Forceful evictions and illegal occupations – very often by extremely violent means – have led to urban people in poverty, especially women, living with a constant feeling of insecurity (Beall, 1995). Another major feature is communal/ethnic violence (especially in the cities of South Asia). Instigated by vested interests either for explicit political purposes (increasing votes) or for other manipulative reasons such as evicting poor people from high-value property, this kind of violence is often fed by fundamentalist feelings and religious passion. Communal violence leading to curfews and more violence by the police and the state is a nightmare for families affected by it. Violence in the external environment is reflected with greater intensity in violence within homes, where women and children are the principal victims. Despite or because of this, 'the pressure is on women to provide rootedness and a sense of community and continuity. The growing helplessness that men experience in a hostile environment is sought to be compensated by a reassertion of power and control over women within the family' (Kannabrian and Kannabrian, 1995).

The gendered nature of urban violence

Violence is in itself a gendered concept. It represents masculinity in its strongest, most powerful and glamorous form. And it is used to keep people in their place. 'Emasculating' men of another community (as in the Sikh riots in Delhi in 1982) is an ultimate humiliation, next perhaps only to the rape and torture of the women of these communities. The everyday experience of violence is reinforced by its presentation in the media. Films and advertisements glamorise the use of violence, almost legitimising it; newspaper and television reports sensationalise it. And where the youth learn to aspire to violence in real life, women learn to fear it. A violent urban environment keeps alive the feeling of fear or insecurity perpetually in a woman's mind. It becomes a day-to-day lived reality – violence at the public taps while collecting water; getting caught in street violence on the way to or from work; sexual harassment while using public transport; physical and sexual violence at the workplace; returning home through dark streets fearful of any noise/gesture/touch, of being molested or even raped. That some men are violent is enough to keep all women fearful of venturing out. Such is the nature of sexual terrorism, yet ironically most acts of individual violence against women are perpetrated by a man known to the victim, often inside the home (Ashworth, 1985).

The high levels of violence in urban external environments are reflected in families in the form of wife battery, dowry deaths and child abuse. The phenomenon of dowry deaths especially has long been a feature of city dwellers, a reflection of women's unhappy response to the further commodification of women's value in an increasingly commercialised society. In the ugliest form of the ritual the bride is burned to death by her husband's family for want of more dowry. This came to light in the early 1970s, when some deaths 'due to accident' were investigated by women's groups in Delhi. Statistics from the Government of India Department of Women and Child Welfare for 1991 indicate that there is a dowry death every two hours in India as a whole, a rape every hour and an act of cruelty against a woman every half-hour. It is estimated that only 2% of crimes against women are reported.

Responses to violence: the case of Shaktishalini

Gender oppression cuts across caste and class, making violence against women as political an issue as peace. Increasingly, debates have centred on violence against women as a human rights issue, as it denies basic freedom from fear and want (Ashworth, 1985).

The women's movement in India started taking up the issue in the mid-1970s. Having started with political aggression cases during the emergency period, it turned its attention to rape cases involving state and public officials (Shah and Gandhi, 1992). Around the end of the 1970s, investigation of deaths by 'burning' or by 'accident' brought to light the dowry deaths that had claimed the lives of several young married women in North India. Since then a wide range of issue have been taken up, such as amniocentesis (used to identify and abort female foetuses), explaining the 'missing millions' in India. Violence against women's bodies in the form of poor contraceptive and sterilisation projects is another issue, along with women's experience of social and communal violence and violence perpetrated by the state.

In addition to strategic calls for legal and attitudinal change, practical responses included providing women's shelters for the increasing number of women made homeless because they were victimised within families and had no alternative support structures to turn to. Though state-run shelters exist in some cities, they have been severely criticised for the high level of corruption and forced prostitution that women inhabitants are coerced into. Some NGOs have, on a self-help basis, intervened by providing shelters and other legal and counselling services to women in distress.

Shaktishalini is one such organisation. Based in Delhi, it was formed in 1987 by the parents (mothers) of dowry victims. Today Shaktishalini has expanded its functions. The short-stay home provides shelter for periods ranging from three months to two years. It can accommodate up to thirty women at a time and provides free board and lodging. Literacy and craft classes are also arranged (ACTIONAID India, 1994). It serves as a crisis intervention centre and a temporary refuge until the women resolve their problems. Most women who approach Shaktishalini are from the lower socio-economic strata and do not have the educational qualifications or skills to earn enough to pay for accommodation. Depressed and helpless, they need time to analyse their situation, gain confidence and think of their future. Many therefore stay longer than originally envisaged.

Shaktishalini spends a lot of its time on networking activities. Women who approach Shaktishalini seek assistance for a variety of problems – emotional, psychological, physical, medical and legal. In order to discharge its role effectively, the organisation maintains a network of contacts with other NGOs, police, lawyers, the media and doctors. Shaktishalini has also launched an education and awareness programme in the urban slums around Delhi. Through theatre workshops and discussion groups and campaigns, it tries to prevent atrocities against women.

Of the women who approached Shaktishalini for help, over 80% were in the 16–35 age group. Nearly 90% were married, with arranged marriages most common. Cruelty by husbands or in-laws was the major reason why women approached the shelter. They had been rejected because their families could not meet escalating dowry demands, because they were infertile or because they had not produced sons.

Issues ahead

Shelters play a critical role for women survivors. Women rarely have property rights and there is an absence of alternative support networks and structures and places of refuge in cities. Even where refuges do exist it is not always clear whether women from all ethnic and religious minorities have equal access to their facilities. However, the most critical problem in the practical management of such shelters is the shortage of funds and the inadequate infrastructure. The struggle of women who have questioned violence and left their homes is often not looked upon as struggle. Women get termed victims instead of survivors, and any support extended to them is seen as 'welfare' rather than 'empowerment-oriented' help. Within the existing development strategies there has been a damaging implicit hierarchy of approaches, which often rates welfare goals as being less important than empowerment goals. An empowerment perspective needs to inform all approaches and welfare initiatives remain vital to the process of empowering women (Beall, 1995). In the absence of this understanding most shelters for women are chronically short of funds. This leads to a high burnout level in the women responsible for managing them, and diminishes the effectiveness of the services provided.

At a more general level, the issue of cities being physically unsafe also needs to be squarely addressed. Almost all public spaces are experienced as 'gendered' spaces by women: parks, streets, public transport, cinemas, etc. need to be looked at from the point of view of women's safety and convenience. The involvement of women's organisations and feminist subject specialists is crucial, and they should work alongside city planners and architects in planning urban services and sectors.

It is vital to bring violence in the cities on to the agenda of planners and policy-makers. A violent environment within and outside the home threatens the lives of one-half of the population and keeps women from participating actively in development processes, depriving women of security and denying cities the benefit of their creative energy and different insights.

References

ACTIONAID India (1994), *Violent Homes: A Study of Shaktishalini's Experience with Victims of Domestic Violence*, New Delhi: Learning from Experience Series.

Ashworth, G. (1985), *Of Violence and Violation*, London: Change Think Books.

Beall, J. (1995), 'Social security and social networks among the urban poor in Pakistan', *Habitat International*, 19(4): 427–45.

Bunch, C. and R. Carillo (1992), *Gender Violence: A Development and Human Rights Issue*, Dublin: Attic Press.

Kannabrian, V. and K. Kannabrian (1995), 'The frying pan or the fire? Endangered identities, gendered institutions and women's survival', in Sarkar and Butalia, pp. 121–35.

Rajan, R. (1993), *Real and Imagined Women: Gender, Culture and Postcolonialism*, London: Routledge.

Sarkar, T. and U. Butalia (eds) (1995), *Women and Right Wing Movements: Indian Experiences*, New Delhi: Kali for Women.

Shah, N. and N. Gandhi (1992), *The Issues at Stake: Theory and Practice in the Contemporary Women's Movement in India*, New Delhi: Kali for Women.

CHAPTER 10

Safe Spaces for Battered Women

Antonia Kirkland

This chapter seeks out best-practice examples of policy and projects confronting domestic violence in the urban context and urbanisation process. It analyses the various economic, social and spatial factors that contribute to the incidence of domestic violence in the city. It promotes safe spaces for battered women as a way of meeting domestic violence survivors' immediate needs with a view to wider sustainable human development. It considers domestic violence to be as harmful, if not more so, than 'public' violence, necessitating gender-aware law enforcement. Listening to what urban women want in pursuing their strategic interests to end domestic violence is the key in cities of both the North and the South.

The need for domestic violence shelters: refuges

Women's greatest risk of violence is at the hands of men they know. In the United States, for example, '21–34% of all women will be physically assaulted by an intimate male during adulthood' (Koss et al., 1994: 42). Men perpetrate against women overwhelmingly more aggressive actions such as punching, kicking, choking, beating up, using a knife or gun, than women perpetrate against men. Furthermore, women in the US are more likely to be killed by their male partners than by all other categories of persons combined (Koss et al., 1994). This bleak picture is much the same across the globe. In countries such as India and Papua New Guinea domestic violence has been identified with other cultural factors, such as dowry and polygamy respectively. In many contexts domestic violence is explained away by 'culture'. Thus culture provides a ready excuse for not getting involved, for resisting tackling domestic violence as a development issue.

Ghana is an example of a country where no study of domestic violence was carried out until 1991, thereby perpetuating the myth that the problem did not exist. In 1991, R. O. Ofei-Aboagya, a Ghanaian working in Canada, returned to Ghana to interview 50 women at the Legal Aid Clinic of the International Federation of Female Lawyers (FIDA). Her research examined the 'traditional' aspects of Ghanaian life that contribute to the fact that domestic violence remains unacknowledged. She also identified existing organisations and structures that could expose and help reduce domestic violence. She stated that: 'the very fact that these women had gone to FIDA at all was an act of determination and courage. It indicates a shift, at least among the urban women, in perceptions about what women feel they can or should do within the culture.' Most of the women in her study finally broke their silence out of fear for their mental and physical health, even though their resources were limited. It is important to bear in mind Ofei-Aboagya's assertion that:

> Tradition must not be allowed to be used as defense for such a situation … Nor does the eradication of domestic violence from a society mean transforming the culture as a whole. It only means the removal of the unsatisfactory societal mores for a 'better' society, a society free of domestic violence (Ofei-Aboagya, 1994: 931).

Domestic violence in the urban context

Many factors can contribute to the incidence of domestic violence in urban settings. Indeed, the UN went as far as to describe violence as 'almost a way of life' in situations of poor housing and economic vulnerability (UN, 1989: 29). Economic crises and declining real incomes associated with economic restructuring; increasing male unemployment and growing reliance on women as breadwinners; insecurity of tenure; overcrowding; poor services and social tensions all lead to urban life becoming increasingly volatile and violent. This does not explain, however, why some poverty-stricken men do not behave violently to their wives and why other, better-off men are wife-batterers. Domestic violence traverses class boundaries and economic brackets. The economic, social and environmental reasons particular to the urban context that may influence the forms and levels of domestic violence will therefore be examined without implying direct and causal relationships.

Nevertheless, families involved in domestic abuse are often living at absolute subsistence levels or going through household economic crises (UN, 1989). In Latin America,

> One of the effects which recent macro-social changes have had on poor urban households is that men have lost their position as the sole or principal bread-winner and this, in turn, has weakened their identity and their authority … Emotional insecurity and the undermining of their authority as father and husband prompt them to try to impose their will upon the rest of the family by violent and authoritarian means (ECLAC, 1992: 12).

Interestingly, less violence was found to occur in women-headed households (ibid.: 13).

Crucially, 'In many developing countries, traditional social norms and practices, which may have once served to restrain wife abuse, are in the process of disintegration' (UN, 1989: 29). This may be particularly so in the process of urbanisation. Overcrowding or close living quarters, which are linked to poverty, can perpetuate domestic violence. Unfortunately, 'in large urban settings, where it may be easier for women to leave abusive relationships, there is often nowhere to go as illustrated by the links between domestic violence and homelessness' (Bunch and Carillo, 1992: 18).

Why they stay

In discussing domestic violence it is important not to perpetuate the attitude that women are helpless, dependent, passive or submissive. Many stand up to abusive men, defend themselves and protect their children. But why do women remain with their abusive partners? Women stay in abusive relationships for a range of reasons: fear of reprisal, social isolation, having nowhere to go, financial dependence, social stigma, emotional dependence, poor self-esteem, and because of *unhelpful responses from family, friends, and community agencies*' (Queensland Domestic Violence Task Force, 1988: 7; emphasis added). A woman's kin group, even if it is located in the urban centre, will not always provide her refuge and may even encourage her to go back to her partner if they can not afford to keep her or if they believe it would bring shame upon the family.

In Thorbek's study of slum culture in Ratmalana, Sri Lanka, it is clear that a woman's position is dependent on her marital status and gender struggles are exacerbated by the urbanisation process. To begin with, women are strictly guarded by their families in order to keep their virginity intact before marriage; they then become wholly dependent on their husbands' families after their marriage. As one woman explained, 'If you're in Sri Lanka, you have to marry in order to live in society' (Thorbek, 1994: 95). Unfortunately, drunkenness amongst men often leads to violence, which is generally accepted and justified because the wife must learn how to behave properly. It is considered acceptable behaviour because 'men are perceived as a trifle childish, unable to control their instincts and their anger and liable to go wild and drunk. Women, on the contrary, are responsible for their own good behaviour and that of their husbands or sons' (ibid.: 38). This is not confined to low-income countries: a 1987 survey in Queensland, Australia, revealed that some women are so socially conditioned by patriarchal attitudes that they deemed it 'justifiable to shove, kick or hit a wife if she did not obey him, wasted money, was a sloppy housekeeper or refused him sex' (Queensland Domestic Violence Task Force, 1988: 6).

Mutual help among Sri Lankan women in the slums is unusual, because women accept violence in the home as a disciplinary technique. However, when one young woman was beaten badly enough to need hospitalisation the women declared: 'As women we must help other women when they are in difficulties' (Thorbek, 1994: 37). Even if a woman in the slums of Ratmalana wanted to leave her husband, which would diminish her own status, a divorce is difficult to obtain. The behaviour of the police, legal difficulties and costs and, most importantly, severe social sanctions all work to discourage women from seeking a divorce. If a woman does bring the case to court, publicly stating that she no longer wants to live with her husband, she will not receive any alimony and the father will have custody of the children.

In 'illegal' slums there is often a fear of repression or discrimination by state authorities, which may further contribute to a domestic violence survivor's reluctance to seek external assistance. In general, the state–individual relationship can be viewed in terms of a hierarchial power relation in which individual women are at the very bottom. This is illustrated by the fact that domestic violence is often still perceived to be a private matter and not one that merits much in the way of public resources or attention. As a result women think they are alone in their experiences and are further isolated.

Minorities and the decision to stay

Central to any discussion on safe spaces for women is the pivotal nature of race or ethnicity and the way it intersects with gender and power relations in wider society. It affects a woman's decision to seek help and the nature of that assistance. Black women within a predominantly white society who make public their domestic violence, 'risk exacerbating the racism directed at both men and women in their communities' (Razack, 1994: 89), and violence in immigrant communities is often viewed as a 'cultural attribute' (ibid.). As a result, black women are even more reluctant to call the police for fear of the racism they may encounter.

In general, 'community support systems do a poor job of serving certain groups of battered women, including minorities, immigrants (both documented and undocumented), lesbians, and women with mental and physical disabilities' (Loseke, 1992: 96). There has been some progress, though, as the first ever refuge for women with learning disabilities was recently opened in London. This came about from a partnership between the East Thames Housing Group and Powerhouse, which is an organisation of women with learning disabilities. In addition, a London refuge catering to women from Latin America, Spain and Portugal has just celebrated its tenth anniversary (*Everywoman*, 1996).

Providing support and addressing immediate needs

The first known facilities to house abused women were developed by women's organisations in the early 1970s in North America and the UK. They were designed to provide temporary homes, free food and clothing, social support, legal and social advocacy services and a secret location. Most emphasised the value of consensus decision-making, individual empowerment and self-help. In general: 'Refuges provide escape from the immediate dangers of assault and the anxieties of waiting for another assault. For some women a refuge is an avenue for a new life, for others it provides a respite from violence' (Hancock, 1979: 17). One American shelter's overall organisational goal was 'to help women develop a sense of worth while they are achieving independence and self-sufficiency' (Loseke, 1992: 59). It must be emphasised, however, that refuges or shelters, though crucial to battered women's immediate needs, are only a temporary measure for dealing with domestic violence.

Physical evidence of abuse should not be required and women should be accepted on their own terms, since emotional or psychological abuse is 'invisible' and physical injuries may have healed by the time a woman is able to apply for housing. There is also a problem with stipulations of county or local residence, because a shelter may not exist in a woman's area or her partner may have found out where she is and may threaten her. Addresses of refuges are often revealed through court proceedings, by children on their way to or from school and even through statutory services. Furthermore, the location of the support network, which could include family and friends, may be an important factor in seeking refuge.

Alternatives to shelters, such as bed and breakfast accommodation, do not offer any supporting social or legal resources, are less secure and are often more expensive than refuges or shelters. Northern Ireland's Women's Aid found two-thirds of their clients were satisfied with refuge accommodation despite the communal living arrangements and occasional over-crowding (McWilliams and McKiernan, 1993: 108). The English Women's Aid Federation report also stated that despite the lack of privacy and bad conditions, many found the communal living experience a positive one (Binney, Harkell and Nixon, 1988: 41). Often the realisation that one is not alone in such an adverse situation is pivotal to healing and will greatly improve a woman's psychological well-being. Despite great differences of culture and background, a shared identity is fostered because of the centrality of violence in the women's lives.

The design of a model shelter would be based on a sensitive mix of privacy for family units and communal areas for interaction and support. The shelter would also need to be physically secure, provide access to legal and other resources and be adequately staffed. Unfortunately such 'ideal' shelters were not in evidence in the case studies examined. Most were described as being poor-quality accommodation that could be rented cheaply. Clearly it is important not to spend more time on fund-raising than on helping the women themselves, and funding should be long-term and reliable so that the asylum provided to women is secure and guaranteed. This is why local authority or state support is so crucial. For example, the South Coast Shelter in California, USA, is charged a pepper-corn rent of $1 a year rent by the local authority, allowing them to concentrate on funding support services.

Community programmes for violent men

Traditionally, refuges and shelters have focused on women and on providing them with respite or new beginnings. However, more recently there has been a focus on causes of domestic violence, which has meant addressing men. In Victoria, Australia, programmes targeting violent men were first set up in 1985. It is important to note that the men voluntarily attend these programmes, in contrast to those such as CHANGE or Lothian Domestic Violence Probation Programme in Scotland, which are criminal justice responses to domestic violence and are not informed by a gender relations perspective. In Victoria, men's houses operate under the belief that 'men should take responsibility for their violence and its consequences and that *women and children should not have to move out of their own home on account of men's violence/abuse*' (Francis, 1995: 401; emphasis added). It is vitally important to offer women the option of remaining in place so that their social networks are not further denuded of support. Most women will only accept this option if they feel that their security is guaranteed, and this requires a strong institutional commitment.

Men staying at the houses are also required to attend an attitude- and behaviour-change group. The majority of violent men and their partners agreed that the groups had a positive effect, with violence altogether ceasing or the rate of incidence significantly diminished. Further, there is no evidence to suggest that the groups in community health centres undermined the agencies' capacity to provide support services for women (Francis, 1995). This Australian programme could be considered an example of best practice for both the survivor and the perpetrator in that it is a step towards preventing domestic violence, and not just punishing men.

Advocating change and promoting the interests of battered women

There is only so much that women's organisations can do in the fight against domestic violence without the cooperation of state legislative

bodies, legal resources and police departments. By making domestic violence a public issue, organisations can effectively lobby law-makers into
recognising it as a social problem. In the US, criminal law may be invoked
against a violent spouse for all forms of assault. However, 'Until the late
1970s, assaults against wives (including marital rape) were considered
misdemeanors in most states, even when the same actions would have
been considered felonies if perpetrated against strangers or acquaintances'
(Koss et al., 1994: 101). Under criminal law, the United Kingdom Offences
Against the Person Act 1861, the Sexual Offences Act 1976 and the Police
and Criminal Act 1984 have all been used to protect married women from
their violent husbands. Significantly, however, much law and legislation
does not protect unmarried partners. As late as the autumn of 1995 the
Family Law, Homes and Domestic Violence Bill was stopped short because
it would have undermined the institution of marriage. There has been
progress in some countries, such as India and Bangladesh, which have
outlawed dowry-related violence, but without adequate enforcement they
remain meaningless. In the US, a Senate judiciary committee found nearly
three times as many animal shelters in the United States as shelters for
abused women (Koss et al., 1994). This is despite the fact that the Family
Violence Prevention and Services Act of 1984 provides states with grants
to establish, maintain and expand shelters, childcare programmes and
related services for domestic violence victims and their children. International law, including the 1979 Convention on the Elimination of All
Forms of Discrimination Against Women, does not directly address the
issue of domestic or 'private' violence.

Even though existing legislation, such as court injunctions, may not go
far enough in helping battered women, there is widespread recognition
that domestic violence is a problem that must be dealt with publicly.
Obviously this is not always the case. For instance, 'Since most Latin
American countries traditionally do not have legislation that considers
domestic violence an offense, intra-family aggression is not considered a
crime or a punishable act except in extreme cases, such as death or serious
injury' (ECLAC, 1992: 22).

The role of the police

Unfortunately, police forces themselves are often to blame for the inaction
against wife-batterers and for perpetuating the idea that domestic violence
is not a public issue. In 1976, the New York City Police Department had
a class action suit[1] brought against them as a result of this attitude. They
were charged with 'making a distinction between wives and other victims
of violence and failing to provide for their protection' (Dobash and
Dobash, 1979). They won their case and in 1978 the NYC Police Department agreed to significant changes in procedure, including arresting a

violent husband, enforcing injunctions, and helping the battered woman obtain medical care when needed. These are the steps necessary in police procedure if a private matter is to be treated in a public and socially responsible manner, which is important as evidence suggests that arrest is an effective deterrent in domestic violence cases (Dobash et al., 1995). A Chilean study 'showed positive results in 72.5% of all cases, where aggressors, shaken by being summoned and investigated by police and judicial authorities, stopped their aggressive behavior with the realization that it would no longer go unpunished' (ECLAC, 1992: 24).

In Latin America 'women's police stations' in countries such as Argentina, Colombia, Costa Rica, Peru, Uruguay and Venezuela operate from the assumption that violence against women is a specific problem requiring special treatment (ibid.). The Women's Defence Offices set up in 1985 in capital and major cities of each state in Brazil are an example of best practice in this area. This initiative included an all-female police force, with social workers and psychologists, as well as a 24-hour phone service. In São Paulo alone there were 7,000 reported incidents in 1988. According to the ECLAC report:

> The success of these police posts consists not only in their full coverage of reports by abused women, but also in the systematization of statistics compiled, which has made it possible to pinpoint the groups most affected and specific forms of violence, and in their role as consciousness-raising vehicle for the rest of the population on the extent and the nature of the problem (ibid.: 30).

It is clear that cooperation between police, social services, housing authorities, courts and shelters is the most effective curative solution. For example, refuges in New Zealand at Napier, Nelson and Christchurch were autonomously organised, operated and controlled by centre members but had extensive links to outside organisations, which helped women find their way to the shelter and then find permanent housing more quickly (Hancock, 1979: 22). Cooperation is also important so that women do not have to keep repeating their painful stories.

Conclusion

Gender struggles are often intensified in the process of urbanisation because of dislocation, wage work and poverty (Thorbek, 1994). This often results in domestic violence. Proactive city planning that incorporates safe spaces for battered women with an aim to ending domestic violence is a worthy and necessary goal for human development. Clearly there is a need for shelters, particularly in urban areas, because women often feel isolated; they may be great distances from their own kin or symbolically cut off in the sense that they are forced to be dependent on their husbands' families. Shelters can be an agent for social change as well as providing the much-needed 'safe space' for abused women and their children. They can function to educate the public about the social context of violence against women and its roots in patriarchy (Koss et al., 1994). Providing the conditions for promoting the interests of battered women in the form of legal resources such as just divorce laws, homelessness and housing legislation, programmes that target violent men, and cooperative police units that arrest batterers and work with social agencies is equally important.

However, 'Long-term community education is seen as the primary means of bringing about a significant reduction in family violence and violence towards women' (Francis, 1995: 405). Only when domestic violence is recognised internationally as a public rather than a private matter, and when marital violence, including rape, is prosecuted on the same terms as violence perpetrated by a stranger, will women be safer in their own homes. Only when the oppression of women is eradicated in all forms will the need for shelters or refuges gradually disappear. For the time being, an inclusive and supportive city means one that recognises the need to support and be responsible for those within the city, including battered women, by working towards a truly universal freedom from violence.

Note

1. A 'class action suit' refers to a legal action being taken by a 'class' or group of people with a common characteristic and a common legal cause of action. They can be the plaintiffs (e.g. a group of women with defective breast implants suing the manufacturer) or the defendants (e.g. in the case of someone bringing a lawsuit against all pharmaceutical companies selling a defective drug), or both parties can be 'classes'.

References

Binney, V., G. Harkell and J. Nixon (1988), *Leaving Violent Men – A Study of Refuges and Housing for Abused Women*, Dept of the Environment, London: Women's Aid Federation England.

Bunch, C. and R. Carillo (1992), *Gender Violence: A Development and Human Rights Approach*, Dublin: Attic Press.

Dobash, R. and R. E. Dobash (1979), *Violence Against Wives – A Case Against Patriarachy*, New York: Free Press.

Dobash, R., R. E. Dobash, K. Cavanagh and R. Lewis (1995), 'Evaluating criminal justice programs for violent men', in R. Dobash, R. E. Dobash and Noaks, *Gender and Crime*, Cardiff: University of Wales Press.

Economic Commission for Latin America and the Caribbean (ECLAC) (1992), *Domestic Violence Against Women in Latin America and the Caribbean, Proposals for Discussion*, Santiago, Chile: United Nations.

Everywoman (1996), 124, April: 8.

Francis, R. (1995), 'An overview of community-based intervention programmes for men who are violent or abusive in the home', in Dobash et al., *Gender and Crime*.

Hancock, M. (1979), *Battered Women: An Analysis of Women and Domestic Violence, and the Development of Women's Refuges*, Wellington, NZ: New Zealand Committee on Women.

Koss et al. (1994), *No Safe Haven – Male Violence Against Women at Home, at Work, and in the Community*, Washington, DC: American Psychological Association.

Loseke, D. R. (1992), *The Battered Woman and Shelters*, Albany, NY: SUNY Press.

McWilliams, M. and J. McKiernan (1993), *Bringing it Out in the Open, Domestic Violence in Northern Ireland*, Belfast: HMSO.

Ofei-Aboagye, R. O. (1994), 'Altering the strands of the fabric: a preliminary look at domestic violence in Ghana', *Signs*, 19(4): 931–6.

Queensland Domestic Violence Task Force (1988), *Beyond These Walls*, Brisbane, Australia.

Razack, S. (1994), 'What is to be faced by looking white people in the eye? Culture, race and gender in cases of sexual violence', *Signs*, 19(4): 896.

Thorbek, S. (1994), *Gender and Slum Culture in Urban Asia*, London and New Jersey: Zed Books.

Toft, S. (ed.) (1985), *Domestic Violence in Papua New Guinea*, Law Reform Commission of Papua New Guinea.

Toft, S. (ed.) (1992) *Final Report on Domestic Violence in Papua New Guinea*.

United Nations (1989), *Violence Against Women in the Family*, New York: UN.

CHAPTER 11

Housing for Diversity: Roma-Gypsies in Madrid

Amor Vieira

This chapter discusses a resettlement programme provided by a Spanish government agency for a group of 300 Roma-Gypsies in Madrid. The case study follows the process by which social planners recognised difference but constructed it as deviance, thus failing to work with social diversity. This resulted in the stigmatising of and virtual exile from the city for a group of Roma-Gypsies. The way housing was allocated and provided meant that this group was marginalised at two levels: spatially and socially. As a result, these Spanish citizens were denied their right to participation in the city and its development.

Infra-housing for Roma-Gypsies in Spain

Since the late 1960s the Spanish economy has rapidly expanded, and Spain is now regarded as a major partner within the European Community. Central to this process of economic transformation has been the cultivation of an image of cohesive national identity and a homogeneous nation. As a result, the specific rights and needs of groups who for various reasons have fallen outside this concept have been severely neglected. The inevitable conclusion is that significant numbers of the Spanish population remain in a disadvantaged position. The Spanish Roma-Gypsies form one of the groups that have become invisible in this highly homogenised social map. The neglect that this group suffers is based on a construction of 'the other' as bearing characteristics different from or opposite to the ideal of the normal Spanish citizen. 'The other' is then allied with negative connotations and seen to present a threat to the 'normal'. In this context, those responsible for local and national policy treat groups not meeting the image of the ideal Spanish citizen as deviant and uncooperative. Within this discourse Roma-Gypsies are being denied their right to cultivate and re-create their existence as a group with shared history, memories, cultures and traditions.

At the same time, recent changes in patterns of employment have seen their traditional occupations, such as agricultural labour, rapidly diminish while low standards of education and training have denied them movement into more modern sectors. Increased policing of street vendors has led to a *de facto* criminalisation of peddling and hawking which has further increased the economic vulnerability of Roma-Gypsies. A subsequent shift into more high-risk ventures such as the drug trade has served only to reinforce their negative public image. This marginalisation extends to housing. In 1987, it was estimated that a quarter of the Roma-Gypsies in Spain, that is around 130,000 individuals, made up as much as 95% of the population of shanty towns (Hayward, 1996).

Consorcio, Madrid

In 1986 a joint initiative between local, regional and national government led to the creation of Consorcio, the Consortium for the Rehousing of Marginalised Populations. The overall aim of the Consorcio was to clear the shanty towns on the outskirts of Madrid by 1993. The Consorcio treated the shanty town dwellers as a homogeneous group and failed to consider diversity *within* the shanty towns. In terms of rehousing this meant that a blanket policy was applied in allocating housing, with no consideration of differences in ethnic background or livelihood patterns and culture.

The starting point of the programme was a census aimed at assessing the real extent of homelessness in Madrid. At the end of 1986 this census identified 2,672 huts. Health standards, educational levels, income-generating activities, housing expectations and approximate earnings were recorded. This census, and the subsequent assessment of households, proved to discriminate against Roma-Gypsies in the following ways.

First, the census formed a cut-off point whereby any hut built after the census was deemed to be 'illegal', therefore disqualifying it for rights to housing within the programme. In effect, the Consorcio's decision to deny access to the housing programme to huts built after the census constituted an attack on highly mobile groups such as the Roma-Gypsies.

The census recorded numbers of huts there in 1986, ignoring those away from the area at the time and those constructed subsequently. Each individual hut was treated as a separate household and this was used as the unit of targeting by the Consorcio. The assessment procedure was also flawed in its inflexible definition of a household. Each hut was seen as consisting of a male-headed, nuclear household, and its employment status was based on that of the male head. This rating system placed all work traditionally falling within the Roma-Gypsy sector at the bottom of the scale. An employment hierarchy was constructed and the closer the job was to a monthly waged, stable ideal, the higher the household was placed in the rating system. This effectively placed Roma-Gypsy households at the bottom of the Consorcio's assessment structure. The first house-holds to be housed were the last few 'white' Spanish families still homeless in 1986 (Presencia Gitana, 1994). These households were rehoused in completed, formal accommodation. Special *barrios* and camps planned to house those households lower on the rating scale were not completed for two years. Moreover, when these were provided, they fell far short of meeting the projected standards of services and infrastructure promised by the Consorcio.

The programme aimed to eradicate shanty towns by providing each hut with rental housing in flats or in single-storey detached houses in special-typology *barrios*, or in sites and services camps.

An agreement with the Social Housing Department stated that 10% of all new flats offered by the department with no more than two units per individual block were to be reserved for the Consorcio's programme. It should be noted that the provision of social housing by this department is presently extremely low and unlikely to rise. These flats were to house families thought guaranteed to adapt successfully to this type of living and to make a positive contribution to the surrounding community. The single-storey detached houses were provided in groups of a maximum of 80 units, which were to form fully serviced neighbourhoods in special *barrios*. These were for households that, according to the assessment, were deemed to have particular difficulties in adapting to living in a flat.

Within the programme, there were 80 units of site and services camps, each consisting of a prefabricated house provided with electricity, water and sewerage. Each 'camp' would be provided with asphalted roads and road lighting. This type of housing was intended for semi-nomadic house-holds with mobile jobs or for families who had not previously made satisfactory use of accommodation in the other two categories. The Consorcio treated these camps as a provisional arrangement for a couple of years, after which households would be eligible for accommodation elsewhere within the scheme.

The Consorcio's 10% quota was aimed at respecting the host com-munity's sense of community and well-being and the preservation of a peaceful environment by not overwhelming the 'white' community with large numbers of Roma-Gypsies. However, this quota system has been described by Presencia Gitana, an NGO working with Roma-Gypsy com-munities in Spain, as contravening the spirit of the UN Commission of Human Rights (cited in Presencia Gitana, 1994: 20). These declarations state that when members of an ethnic group live in a concentrated (not isolated) manner, they have more opportunities to preserve and develop their culture (Declarations on the Rights of Persons belonging to National or Ethnic, Religious and Linguistic Minorities, cited in Liegeois and Gheorghe, 1995: 4).

Although ostensibly sensitive to diverse lifestyles, the allocation criteria employed by the Consorcio deliberately constructed a hierarchy of cultures and livelihoods. The closer to a given cultural ideal a household found itself, the greater the benefits that household received. It can also be said that the practice of education and training in community living provided to groups of shanty town dwellers, without an equal emphasis on educating 'host' communities, represents a policy of cultural assimilation, a view cogently argued by Liegeois and Gheorghe (1995) in their pan-European study of Roma-Gypsies. From a gender perspective, an unwelcoming and non-responsive host white community impacts most strongly on those members of the family who spend most time in the house and its surrounding spaces, the majority of whom are inevitably women.

The Consorcio's programme has shown a significant lack of institutional mechanisms to deal and work with conflict creatively at any level. Even though the Consorcio's monitoring department reports a positive self-assessment of the work done up to 1995, there is concern regarding further funding and the general future of the programme. The Consorcio itself acknowledges that having different political parties at the different levels of governance involved in the Consorcio has made things run rather slowly. Hostile reactions from the white Spanish communities in whose areas Roma-Gypsies were to be rehoused has also contributed to this slowness. As a result of this incapacity to encompass difference and work with conflict in the social planning process, the Consorcio's response to the various demonstrations by 'white' neighbourhood associations rejecting the placement of Roma-Gypsies close to their homes was to cede to their demands. This led to a reduction in the number of households rehoused in flats. It also meant a relocation of the special-typology *barrios* and the camps to a more distant location (Presencia Gitana, 1994; Montoya, 1987: 27), further marginalising the Roma-Gypsy population, spatially as well as socially, in remote sites with scarce or no public transport and infrastructure (Montes, 1986).

The application stage of the programme: the case of an illegal shanty town created by the Consorcio   To illustrate the above critique of the Consorcio's resettlement programme, this section follows the progress of a particular case in Los Focos, a shanty town with 268 'legal' and 150 'illegal' huts. The land had been sold for private development and therefore needed to be cleared of huts as swiftly as possible, starting from June 1993. Out of the 268 'legal' households only 18 were eligible, according to the assessment criteria, to be housed in flats in Vicalvaro, a neighbourhood in Southern Madrid.

On 9 May 1994 Los Focos' last 56 'legal' households, comprising 300 individuals, were resettled in a new site, designated by the Consorcio as a special-typology *barrio*. No prior information on its location was disclosed to the individuals to be resettled, reflecting the power inequality between planners and the community involved. On their arrival in Valdemingomez, a remote site with no public transport links with the city, this group found that the 'special-typology *barrio*' was open land where the only sign of the promised housing was units marked with white squares painted on the earth. The infrastructure provision had been reduced to plywood sheets and corrugated roofing donated by Caritas (a social agency of the Catholic Church). With those they were expected to build new huts. There was no provision of basic services such as water or electricity. The official description of the *barrio* provided by the Consorcio bore no resemblance to the reality experienced by the community. The site was the centre of a large rubbish tip. To one side of the site lay the largest incinerator facility in Spain, which disposes of Madrid's waste and which has been widely criticised for unacceptable levels of environmental pollution. Lorries bring waste past the site at the rate of three per minute, causing extremely high levels of noise pollution. There is also an illegal dumpsite adjacent to the unit where illicit dumping of contaminating products is regularly practised. To the other side of the site there is a pig farm from which animal sewage spills on to housing land (Presencia Gitana, 1994).

The Madrid Water Supplies Department refused to connect the area to the general supply system for fear of contaminating the city's water system, so the Consorcio opened two illegal and contaminated communal taps. Lack of electricity prevented the use of fridges during the summer of 1994, which led to the consumption of food rendered inedible by the extreme summer heat while the surrounding environment combined to produce acute problems from vermin and mosquitoes. In the months following their initial occupation the Roma-Gypsies suffered a dramatic decline in their health, with intestinal and skin diseases spreading rapidly.

Declines in health standards have been more acute among children and women, as their specific biological vulnerabilities have been coupled with longer hours spent at the site. Women have also suffered a considerable increase in hours and energy spent in household maintenance because of the lack of services and the longer distances to shops and hospitals. The convergence of poor health and increased caring for the ill have seen women's capacity for participation in the city undermined. Another long-term and irreversible effect of this isolation is that children have been denied their right to formal education in schools. This will inevitably place them in the less privileged loci of society, perpetuating the marginalisation suffered by their ethnic group.

Conclusion and lessons for the future

The above case study attempts to show that social planning that is blind to diversity, or measures it against some majority or dominant perception of 'normal', actively reinforces existing inequalities. Planners working with dichotomies and hierarchies based upon images of the 'normal' and the 'other' actively constructed policies that brought 300 Roma-Gypsies to the outskirts of the city and to a highly unsafe and isolated site. This has diminished their capacity for participation in the city on two levels: first, and most visibly, they have been physically robbed of their means to participate by being placed in an isolated and unhealthy ghetto. This has led to decreasing levels of health, leisure time and income. On another more subtle and pervasive level, they have been denied their social space, rights and collective identity.

To enable people to enjoy fully their rights to participation and to a safe and healthy environment, housing provision needs to be sensitive to the specific economic, political and social needs and rights of all groups in the city. A shift in the focus in housing discourse from production to consumption (Little, 1994) and a concern for secure homes and liveable environments, provides the framework to enable social planners to promote this goal. Housing for diversity is a means to facilitate participation for all in the city.

If the Consorcio had shifted the focus of planning to the users of housing and had employed planning processes to reach diverse groups, then different needs and demands would have rendered the housing programme more sensitive to difference and provided mechanisms to deal with competing interests and conflict. This approach creates urban spaces where different communities can coexist with mutual respect rather than conflict. Social planning that encompasses diversity therefore has the potential to transform existing structures and inequalities as well as the planning processes themselves.

References

Hayward, V. (1996), 'Spanish shame', *The Big Issue*, 170, 26 February–3 March: 27.

Liegeois, J. P. and N. Gheorghe (1995), *Roma/Gypsies: A European Minority*, London: Minority Rights Group International.

Little, J. (1994), *Gender, Planning and Development*, Oxford: Pergamon.

Montes, J. (1986), 'Sobre el realojamiento de los Gitanos', in T. San Roman, (ed.), *Entre la Marginacion y el Racismo*, Alianza Universidad, pp. 155–70.

Montoya, J. M. (1987), 'Problematica de la vivienda para minorias etnicas. Aproximacion al caso del Pueblo Gitano', in *Los Movimientos Sociales ante el Problema de la Vivienda, II, El Nudo de la Red*, Madrid, pp. 22–7.

Presencia Gitana (1994), *Nuestra Ruanda mas cercana, un informe-denuncia*, Madrid: Asociacion Nacional Presencia Gitana.

Box 3.1

Violence in the Urban Context: Apartado, Colombia

Gloria Cuartas[1]

Many voices have been heard in this north-western corner of Colombia, where I come from. Three states, Antioquia, Corooba and Choc, lie within the Uraba Basin region on the Caribbean seashore. The region's wealth in natural resources contributes to the region's development and benefits the productive population, currently living in an armed conflict zone. This is where the city of Apartado lies, with its 97,000 inhabitants. It has grown without urban development policies; with almost no state participation and with a lack of business investment or welfare programmes, resulting in irregular human settlements in high-risk areas, persistent unemployment rates and low-quality access to education, health and public services. This has led to social and political unrest, which has encouraged an armed conflict that is seemingly endless and has an absolute disregard for human life. Selective and indiscriminate killing, 'disappearances', massive rural migration to the city, institutional decay and harassment focusing on political and civil rights have entangled civilians in this silent war. Families, and particularly women, have carried the burden of the war. Women have been forced into situations that have corroded the community's social structure.

People from the most diverse origins live under these circumstances. The possibility of building a collective history, one that respects everyone's identity and acknowledges regional, national and international development spaces, lies within the strength of their rich ethnic and cultural backgrounds.

People from Apartado think peace should be achieved through a daily working process that seeks the improvement of the living standards of its population. In 1994, 14 political, social and civil organisations, including the Catholic Church, began working under the slogan 'Consensus and Governability', thus opening the way to a process strengthened and guided by consensus. After in-depth analysis, a candidate was chosen and working methods were established. The consensus is made up of a diverse range of organisations including the Indigenous Movement of Businessmen and Sportsmen; Patriotic League Racamandaca; Hope, Peace and Liberty Generation XXI; the Christian Movement Communist Party; Catholic Church

---

1. Gloria Cuartas is mayor of Apartado.

BOX 3.1   127

Christian Community Commitment; the Black People's Movement Liberal Party; and the Civil Movement Conservative Party. Together they decided on a number of guidelines, which included respect for life and human rights; free political participation; agreement to a municipal development peace plan; social development policies that particularly address the needs of women; cooperation between NGOs and the public and private sectors to achieve local competitiveness and skills; and national and international investment in facilities and infrastructure. A political factor with great influence in the region has been the peace process that began in 1991, involving the national government and a faction of the Popular Liberation Army currently known as the Hope, Peace and Liberty Movement, as well as negotiations undertaken with the Socialist Renovation Movement.

Amid all these voices … a process is under way

Men and women have been working towards the achievement of better living conditions. They have learned about the past and have acknowledged that these experiences will enable them to build in the present and the future. These are some quotes from participants of the process we have been building in Uraba [the region of which Apartado is capital]:

'With a cord we measured the small squared terrain in which we were going to make the small ranch stand, in each corner we plotted a pole to hold a tent; it didn't matter if it was plastic, anything we could use to cover from the sun or from rain. People are already paying for their small plots. I want to go on living, I don't feel tired being 71. I think we've left moral principles, culture and the meaning a human being, a human life has, along the way. Thanks to the *consoy* [the consensus] we have some unity.'

'I fight for the sake of my daughter. In this region you can find very valuable people who give everything for the sake of the community; this is not known in the rest of the country because we don't have money to tell our story.'

'We began forgetting how to live, how to concede, how to respect ethnic and cultural diversity, how to be respectful in dissent, how to see in conflict an opportunity for growth, to see how it brings an answer, not verbal or physical intolerance towards others. With this transitional government, and based on the experiences that we are building, we are trying to humanise the processes we are involved in.'

'Where there's no respect, there's nothing. Here, we are all joined into a single unit, we learn from each other, from each race, in any field and fight discrimination.'

'From every corner in Uraba there is a clamour for peace ... Peace will not arrive unless we pause in our way and think about ourselves, think about differences, about mutual respect, about tolerance and peaceful social life. The most difficult task we have had is to keep supporting a violence-free struggle when people all around us are being killed.'

'To my understanding, Uraba is a very special zone, it is beautiful. It has positive things even though we live immersed in violence. Sometimes, negative things get much more attention; if something bad happens, its importance is greatly exaggerated. In Uraba, if you starve to death it's because you chose to – we have bananas, plantains, so if you work you're sure to find something. I think we have to encourage other things, bring other things, good things to the zone; we have to retake the good things we have here and put them to work; we have to work together a little harder and stop thinking about how we are destroying ourselves.'

'I've always thought about people who threaten, he's got a gun to shoot people, that he is bad. But no, maybe he is good, maybe he's had a hard life. God gave us the faculty to talk, to understand, to be able to agree and I think that's the point we are missing. We have to try to speak with others because every person has their own culture, we must try to open up spaces and new possibilities for everyone.'

PART FOUR

Creating the Inclusive City: Urban Design and Decision-making

CHAPTER 12

Disability and Diversity in the City

David Jones and Anita Payne

This chapter outlines the issues related to disabled people in urban environments and the importance of inclusive planning and diversity for social development. It focuses upon the much-neglected area of social and political inclusion as opposed to the complementary, but more widely covered, areas of preventative health strategies and rehabilitation programmes. Thus the underlying societal assumptions about and attitudes to disabled people and their influence on planning and provision are discussed. Consideration is given to the importance of the self-advocacy movement and the action for social change in urban society undertaken by disabled people themselves. The potential for greater collaboration between governments, NGOs and disabled people's organisations is outlined. Finally, it is suggested that the aims, approaches and actions of the disability movement provide useful lessons for the wider issues of successful inclusive urban planning.

Historically, urban and state planning have tended to reflect the interests of politically powerful interest groups. They have generally failed to allocate resources on the basis of fairness and equality, often militating against the interests of weaker and less powerful social stakeholders. The concept of planning for diversity, however, necessitates an embracing of difference and individuality and should be based upon principles of social inclusion rather than exclusion and marginalisation. Nowhere is this concept more starkly applicable than in relation to the historical exclusion and marginalisation of disabled people from mainstream social planning.

Generally speaking, 'it is rare to find disability being considered systematically within developmental attitudes by development planners at the level of governments or international agencies' (Coleridge, 1993). Disabled people have typically been excluded from both national and international development efforts and are often among the poorest and most socially deprived members of society. There are numerous reasons why this has occurred but the most dominant factor would appear to be the general social attitudes of non-disabled people, whose 'prejudicial beliefs, attitudes and behaviour have largely determined the quality of life and fate of disabled people' (Helander, 1993).

If the position in which disabled people find themselves is to change, then the attitudes of planners and policy-makers will also have to change. Planners need to embrace human difference and diversity and to recognise individuality as opposed to simplistic concepts of standardised 'normality'. If the cities of tomorrow are to reflect the diversity of society, the needs of all social stakeholders will have to be addressed through an inclusive, flexible approach to urban planning. The appropriateness and success of inclusive planning approaches will be determined largely by the level of support and involvement of the people such policies are designed to assist.

It is our firm belief that any notion of planning for difference and diversity necessitates the inclusion of a disability perspective. This chapter outlines the general situation currently faced by disabled people in developing countries and presents the case for inclusive planning approaches in meeting the needs of disabled citizens within urban environments.

Disability: an overview

In 1976 the WHO estimated that 10% of the world's population experienced some form of disability. Subsequent studies, however, have tended to be more specific in their categorisation of disability, suggesting a global operative rate of around 5.2% of the world's population with moderate to severe disabilities.

By the 1980s there were 34 million disabled people in Latin America, more than 50 million in Africa and 250 million in Asia/Pacific (Driedger, 1989). Many suffer discrimination and lack of access to resources and services. The WHO claimed that in the Asia/Pacific region fewer than 2% had access to any kind of services (DPI, 1992a). In addition the 1988 UNESCO consultation on special education revealed that out of 51 countries surveyed, 34 acknowledged that they had met the educational needs of fewer than 1% of their disabled citizens (UNESCO, 1988).

The residualistic nature of services has largely been the result of the low priority given to disability issues by governments and international development agencies. Service developments have tended to be initiated by non-governmental agencies motivated through a desire to provide charitable assistance to more vulnerable members of society. According to Lynch, 'the initiators of specialised services in nearly all countries in Asia have been religious, mostly Christian, missionaries during the late 1800s and early 1900s' (Lynch, 1995). This is a trend also noted within other regions, such as West Africa (Jones and Kalley, 1994).

Typical responses to disability service provision have been shaped and 'seduced by the modernisation mirage which has fostered the illusion that western skills, knowledge and attitudes should be diffused to developing countries' (O'Toole, 1991). This has meant that the majority of disability services in developing countries have tended to be based around imported models of segregated, institutional care. Such approaches tend to reflect 'social Darwinism' and the medical and charitable interpretations of disability that have perceived disabled people as the victims of personal tragedy and loss, or as the 'permanent patient' in need of institutionalised care and support.

Over more recent years such approaches have been increasingly challenged and rejected by the growing international disability movement in favour of what is now commonly referred to as the 'social model' of disability. This perspective is based on a rejection of the 'victim-blaming' approach (Barnes and Mercer, 1995) and on an assertion of disability as a 'socially imposed restriction' (Oliver, 1983). As Joshua Malinga, chairperson of Disabled People's International, has said:

> Charity has entrenched negative attitudes; it has made the position of disabled people worse ... It is not part of national socio-economic development. Disabled people want to be treated as normal citizens, with rights. They want to be treated equally and participate as equal citizens in their own communities. To achieve this, you need political and social action to change society (Coleridge, 1993: 54).

This change in emphasis is quite clearly illustrated in the following contrasting definitions of disability:

> Disability is any restriction or lack (resulting from an impairment) of ability to perform an activity in the manner or within the range considered normal for a human being (WHO, 1980).

> Disability is the disadvantage or restriction in the organisation of society, which prevents an individual with a functional limitation or impairment from fully participating (DPI, 1992b).

The influence of professional and societal attitudes

The dominance of institutional forms of service provision has been strongly influenced by general social and professional attitudes to disabled people. In many developing countries disability is often associated with traditional beliefs and attitudes that tend to associate disability with spiritual disapprobation. Traditional responses to disabled people have ranged from infanticide and social ostracisation through to manipulation and exploitation, with many disabled people being forced into begging through a lack of alternative means of support.

Disabled people are often assumed to have been judged or cursed and frequently experience prejudice and discrimination in their daily lives. Overt examples of governmental/official prejudice are common and include practices such as 'clean-ups' in tourist areas and the rounding up of disabled beggars, informal sector workers, street children and prostitutes prior to major events or state visits.

Disabled people have largely been denied the right to self-determination and social inclusion. They have had to face both societal and professional discrimination, and have generally had to accept paternalistic charity or institutional segregation. There is an increasing rejection of 'the inappropriateness of so much of the work done by disability professionals, their attitudes and their seeking to represent disabled people' (Du Toit, 1993). The frustration, anger and dissatisfaction among disabled people fuelled the growth of the international disability movement, and led to the foundation in 1980 of the umbrella organisation Disabled People's International (DPI). Initially DPI was criticised for its underrepresentation of young people and women, deaf people, and those with learning difficulties and mental disabilities; inequalities still need to be addressed. Nevertheless, the granting of consultative status to DPI by a number of international development agencies including the UN, UNESCO and the ILO indicates the power of cooperation in international self-advocacy (Barnes and Mercer, 1995).

Gender and disability

Gender and disability are both social constructs predicated upon physical characteristics. Although gender and disability operate as structures of oppression for both disabled men and women, they experience this oppression in different ways (Morris, 1993). 'Women with disabilities face double discrimination. We not only have to establish our rights as female citizens but also to convince society that we are human beings with feelings and needs and capable of carrying out tasks like any other women' (Sosefo, 1992). In some societies a woman's value is assessed by marriage and motherhood, but these social roles are often denied to disabled women. In the tough marriage markets of India, for example, disabled men invariably find wives but the reverse is not the case and certainly not without a handsome dowry. The rights of disabled women to express their sexuality and to reproduction, motherhood, social life and employment are often severely restricted. Young disabled women are particularly vulnerable to sexual harassment and abuse (Ashton, 1994). The economic and cultural pressures on some families with disabled children are such that many babies, especially females, do not survive (Coleridge, 1993). The expectations placed on men in urban society influence the discrimination experienced by disabled men, especially regarding access to resources such as land, housing, education, training, employment and credit.

Disability and diversity in the urban experience

Changing patterns in population growth and movement have resulted in a growing proportion of the world's poor living in cities. Poverty is an increasing feature of urban life, aggravated by structural adjustment programmes. Poverty, malnutrition and aspects of urban life such as environmental pollution and degradation are significant contributory causes of disability. Coleridge (1993) believes that the increasing number of disabled people in urban settings is possibly exacerbated by the greater risk of injury in road and industrial accidents. There are also the attractions of services and institutions, better medical care, the greater likelihood of finding sedentary jobs and the possibility of an income through begging.

It is reasonable to assume that with an average 5% of the population being disabled, one in four urban households will be affected by disability. This is a significant factor when planning for diversity. The cities are home to people with a variety of roles and responsibilities within the home, workplace and community. Disabled children and adults are part of this diversity, with a range of survival strategies based on the opportunities and constraints that result from contributory factors such as age, gender, social status or ethnic background.

Planners need to be aware that disabled people cannot be considered a homogeneous group. Disabilities vary in type and extent, and some are present from birth, while others are acquired through poverty, work, war, accident or old age. There is also a wide socio-economic diversity within the urban disabled population itself – people have varying skills and access to resources, and varying needs and aspirations. Disabled children are among the most marginalised and their coping strategies are often constrained and determined by adults. Disabled people from wealthier homes may have access to education and 'white-collar' employment, and some former independence fighters may be rewarded with government positions. Poorer disabled people are doubly marginalised, lacking status, education, employment or access to basic amenities such as food, sanitation, better housing, and other basic needs (Asindua, 1995). However, both are often equally affected when it comes to the main issues and the attitudinal barriers of non-disabled people and a non-disabled urban environment.

Spatial organisation and access

Cities are physical spaces where people interact with the built environment. Accessibility is therefore a vital key in such interaction. Disabled people in urban environments face considerable discrimination regarding mobility and accessing infrastructure and services. Consideration needs to be given by planners to the physical differences between people and the distribution and control over resources. Changes in accessibility can come through a range of initiatives, including national government legislation, as in America, local government initiatives, as in some inner-London boroughs (UK), or self-help initiatives by disability groups, as in Bulawayo, Zimbabwe.

Information is a key consideration. Centres of Independent Living (CILs), established in an increasing number of cities, provide disabled people with information regarding their citizenship rights in campaigning for an accessible public environment and for suitable housing, transport, educational, employment and leisure opportunities (Finkelstein, 1993). The Fiji Disabled People's Association (FDPA) is a self-advocacy group that lobbies for increased access and runs an urban resource centre in Suva. Lobbying by the National Council for Disabled People of Zimbabwe (NCDPZ) has helped raise awareness of the need for greater accessibility. Appropriate cheap accessible transport is essential, and individual transport such as rickshaws needs to be encouraged. Subsidised transport services (such as Dial-a-Ride) have proved useful in some developed countries. Self-help mobility aids are increasingly being produced by disabled people in developing countries from locally available materials. These include wheeled sledges, locally made wheelchairs, ramps, walking aids and artificial limbs.

Urban schools often exclude disabled children, either because they cannot reach the school or because of inappropriate attitudes of staff and parents and the lack of inclusional training for teachers. In Kampala, Uganda, the Kyambogo Teacher Training Centre provides pre- and in-service training in integrated education. Early diagnosis and intervention strategies for pre-school children have also been developed by ministries of social welfare or by community-based rehabilitation (CBR) programmes in urban areas in developing countries, including Malaysia and Guyana.

Access to urban health care can be increased by the multi-sectoral approach. The Resistance Council representation system in Uganda has been linked with the training of community health and rehabilitation workers to improve the effectiveness of health promotion, disease diagnosis, treatment and disability rehabilitation. The inclusion of mental health issues into the training of community health workers in the Kampala urban area is an innovative scheme which, with appropriate referral support, offers care in a much-neglected area of disability.

Access to secure land rights and housing is often denied to disabled people. Where provision has been made it has often taken the form of segregated residential housing. There is greater need for attitudinal changes related to inclusion and integration. Self-managed accessible independent living schemes are becoming established in developed countries as 'care in the community' becomes more acceptable. In Bangalore, India, the Association of the Physically Handicapped has encouraged disabled women to gain independence through income-generation skills and independent living schemes. The inclusion of disabled people (especially women) in cooperative committees for self-help sites and services or core housing projects would minimise exclusion and benefit other vulnerable members of the community such as children and elderly persons, whose access is also often restricted by standard designs.

People with learning difficulties are often hidden in their own homes for cultural, social or religious reasons. They are amongst the most marginalised of urban communities. 'People First' is a self-advocacy organisation which has gained sufficient influence in some developed countries that they have been able to influence social service provision away from segregated, institutionalised homes towards independent living and inclusion in local communities. Examples of inclusive strategies are becoming more common, and such approaches are at their most effective when disabled people and the wider community are directly involved in combined efforts to combat societal prejudice. An often-quoted strategy for social and educational inclusion is that of the various 'child to child' programmes[1] implemented in an number of developing countries. These programmes are an accurate representation of the potential community resources available to disabled people in their struggle for recognition and social inclusion, and may indicate a way forward in a climate of financial austerity.

Inclusion in socio-economic organisation

Women play a specific role in the organisation and management of poor neighbourhoods and communities and in the labour market. The rise of Disabled People's Organisations (DPOs) and community-based rehabilitation programmes have enabled disabled women to contribute positively in these areas. Disabled women are also increasingly playing a productive role in the informal sector.

Income generation and employment are high priorities in the monetised economy of urban life. Access to education, training and employment is, however, greatly restricted for the majority of disabled urban dwellers. Those who do gain employment are often to be found in the low-skilled, low-status, low-paid jobs. Some governments in developed countries operate anti-discriminatory legislation encouraging the employment of disabled people. However, there is considerable resistance to the employment of disabled people despite the fact that International Labour Organisation (ILO) research has shown that disabled workers tend to have higher productivity than non-disabled workers (quoted in Coleridge, 1993). In a UK government survey it was found that disabled people are six times more likely to receive a negative response to job applications and that 91% of employers said they would have problems employing a disabled person (Morrell, 1990). However, research in the US has shown that anti-discrimination legislation is largely cost-effective as it enables disabled people to become more economically active and independent (RADAR,

1994). Some companies have found that making themselves more accessible has dramatically increased their profitability (NCCL, 1994).

In many developing countries the reality of state assistance in urban employment is relatively low. NGOs and DPOs tend to be the more influential actors. DPOs are investing not only in vocational training but also in quality assurance, business management and marketing skills. The Uganda Crafts Organisation runs a successful craft shop and restaurant in central Kampala. Goods and services are supplied by disabled and non-disabled people. Friends of the Handicapped (FoH) in Lebanon initiated the first telephone-request taxi fleet in Tripoli (1990). In Malawi the Disabled People's Association of Malawi (DIPAM) has undertaken the necessary market research and improvement in quality control to market its goods internationally through the OXFAM international catalogue. The NCDPZ has opened a successful supermarket in Bulawayo which employs disabled people. The Nairobi Family Support Services (NFSS) is a CBR approach to urban disability managed by a local committee of parents, community leaders, disabled people and professionals.

Politics, power and participation

Disability is not only a socio-economic struggle but also a political issue; the 'last civil rights movement' as Driedger claimed (Driedger, 1989). UK governments have rejected 15 attempts, to date, to outlaw discrimination against disabled people (Hale, 1996). However, the Americans with Disabilities Act (ADA) became law in 1990. The recent history of social protest and consciousness-raising by disabled activists, the Black Civil Rights movement and other groups including Vietnam war veterans may have played some contributory part.

In countries that have gained independence through war or conflict, disabled civilians and war veterans have raised the status of disabled people and influenced anti-discriminatory practices or legislation, as in Nicaragua and Namibia. Disability is often very common, particularly after wars that have either directly or indirectly targeted civilian populations through land-mine use. In such cases disabled people often become a more visible and substantial part of the population. In Namibia, following independence, the government incorporated disability issues into the formal government structure through the Department of Rehabilitation within the Ministry of Land Resettlement and Rehabilitation (Payne, 1992).

Planning for diversity

Concerning the need to plan for difference and diversity in recognition of the rights of disabled people within national development plans, the most significant document to date has been the UN Standard Rules on the

Equalisation of Opportunities for People with Disabilities (UN, 1994). The Standard Rules categorically reject segregated approaches to disability service provision within urban environments.

The Rules strongly emphasise the need for planners and policy-makers to 'consult' and 'involve' disabled people in the planning and implementation of general development programmes from the initial planning stages when public projects are being designed. The overall message from all target areas is the need for states to develop 'standards' and 'guidelines', and to 'enact legislation to ensure accessibility to various areas in society, such as housing, buildings, public transport and other means of transportation, streets and other outdoor environments'. In addition to these physical planning components are recommendations for the passing of laws to ensure the wider rights of disabled people in relation to accessible and integrated education, training and employment programmes, and their recognition and participation within the general social and cultural activities of society.

Virtually all these Rules emphasise the need for policy-makers and planners to develop inclusive planning strategies in close collaboration with disabled people's organisations. It is recommended that DPOs should have considerable influence in programme design and coordination, and should participate in the development of government policy.

Instances of collaboration between governments and DPOs are still rare. However, in Zimbabwe the government has collaborated with the NCDPZ in supporting a new consciousness regarding disability issues. The NCDPZ has been involved in the training of government rehabilitation assistants. Access to buildings has improved in the last ten years and public transport now makes some provision for disabled people. Integration in schools is a reality now for many children, and pro-disability legislation is on the agenda (Coleridge, 1993). Despite differing agendas, collaboration and participation can effect positive change.

Conclusion

If cities are to be planned in celebration of difference and diversity then planners and policy-makers have a responsibility to recognise the needs and rights of disabled people and to develop programmes that lead to an inclusive, enabling environment. Examples of such inclusive, holistic strategies are currently sparse. The efforts by some NGOs and DPOs to adapt and improve existing sectoral services have rarely been supported by concerted governmental efforts to develop broader inclusive programmes. However, the UN Standard Rules represent an attempt to rectify this situation and provide planners and policy-makers with some general guidelines for the development of inclusive planning programmes.

The aims of the disability movement coincide in many instances with investment in civil society. The rebuilding of civil society in Lebanon is a case in point. The disability movement in Lebanon is committed to rebuilding an inclusive society: 'The situation of disabled people and the disability movement provides a visible and tangible model that can illuminate the problems and act as a laboratory for doing things differently' (Coleridge, 1993). Not only has the Lebanese disability movement successfully lobbied for the end of inappropriate institutional care for disabled people, but it has also worked for the wider issues of peace and the reconstruction of society. In 1985 there was the first demonstration by disabled people against the war in Beirut. This was followed by the Peace March from Tripoli to Tyre in 1987 and the Tripoli Festival of 1988. Political participation on the streets of cities and direct action are becoming the agents of change in urban and national life.

Celebration of difference and planning for diversity are at the heart of the disability movement. Increasingly, urban life is becoming more vulnerable and unsustainable. The 'brown' agenda of environmental issues such as clean water and sanitation, and the expanding ecological 'footprints' of the cities are of increasing international concern. The potential for social disaffection and disintegration, and the threat of social and political unrest, are issues that were debated at Habitat II and that will be discussed throughout the world. Improvements in services for disabled people bring improvements to wider society. It will become even more vital for the future of sustainable urban livelihoods that community involvement in planning be embraced. The future is uncertain and the challenge is considerable. However, the disability movement's underlying aims of inclusion and diversity and their role as a catalyst for action and social change may have much to contribute to the issues of urban sustainable development.

Note

1. The child-to-child programme is a non-formal educational programme that began in 1979 during the International Year of the Child. It aims to equip children with ways to protect and improve the general health and lives of other children by teaching them curative and preventive measures that can be passed on to other children and family members.

References

Ashton, B. (1994), 'Children, disability and development: achievement and challenge', SCF Conference Report, 42, London: Save the Children Fund.

Asindua, S. (1995), 'Comparing urban and rural CBR', *CBR News*, 19, January–April: 6–7.

Barnes, C. and G. Mercer (1995) 'Disability: emancipation and community participation and disabled people', in G. Craig and M. Mayo (eds), *Community Empowerment*, London: Zed Books.

Coleridge, P. (1993), *Disability, Liberation, and Development*, Oxford: Oxfam Publications.

DPI (1985), 'DPI constitution', Disabled People's International Development Office Files, Winnipeg.

DPI (1992a), 'Economic and Social Commission for Asia and the Pacific regional programme on disability concerns', 2, DPI Development Office Files, Winnipeg.

DPI (1992b), 'Definition of Disability', *Vox Nostra*, 5(4), December: 1.

Driedger, D. (1989), *The Last Civil Rights Movement*, London: C. Hurst.

Du Toit, M. (1993), cited in Coleridge, *Disability, Liberation and Development.*

Finkelstein, V. (1993), 'Disability: a social challenge or an administrative responsibility?' in J. Swain et al., *Disabling Barriers*, pp. 34–43.

Hale, G. (1996), *Beyond Disability*, London: Sage.

Helander, E. (1993), *Prejudice and Dignity*, New York: UNDP Publications.

Jones, D. and A. Kalley (1994), *International Conference on Community Based Rehabilitation*, Banjul: Gambia Ministry of Social Welfare.

Lynch, J. (1995), 'Provision for children with special educational needs in the Asia region', Washington, DC: World Bank Technical Paper No. 261.

Morrell, J. (1990), *The Employment of Persons with Disabilities: Research into the Policies and Practices of Employers*, London: Department of Employment.

Morris, J. (1993), 'Gender and disability', in J. Swain et al., *Disabling Barriers*, pp. 85–92.

National Council for Civil Liberties (NCCL) (1994), *Access Denied: Human Rights and Disabled People*, No. 9, London: NCCL.

Oliver, M. (1983), *Social Work with Disabled People*, London: Macmillan.

O'Toole, B. (1991), 'Guide to community based rehabilitation services', Guide for Special Education No. 8, Paris: UNESCO.

Payne, A. (1992), 'Health Desk Tour to Namibia', unpublished report, London: Voluntary Service Overseas.

Royal Association for Disability and Rehabilitation (RADAR) (1994), *Lessons from America: A Study of the Americans with Disability Act*, London: RADAR.

Sosefo, K. (1992), 'FDPA (Fiji Disabled People's Association)', in *Challenging a Disabling World*, Milton Keynes: World Development Education Centre.

Swain, J. et al. (eds) (1993), *Disabling Barriers: Enabling Environments*, Buckingham: Open University Press.

UN (1994), *The Standard Rules on the Equalisation of Opportunities for Persons with Disabilities*, New York: UN Department of Public Information.

UNESCO (1988), *UNESCO Consultation on Special Education*, Paris: UNESCO Publications.

WHO (1980), *International Classification of Impairments, Disabilities and Handicaps*, Geneva: WHO.

CHAPTER 13

Ageing as an Urban Experience

*Chitta Bunchandranon, Gerard Howe
and Anita S. Payumo*

The theme of this book is how social planners embrace difference and work creatively with diversity, and nowhere is this difference more apparent than within an elderly urban population. Gender, class, income and ethnicity in varying degrees intersect and define urban life for elders. This chapter therefore does not attempt to offer definitive solutions but draws from a range of experiences, case studies and the interplay between commonalities and diversities to illustrate the experience of older life in the city. From a social development perspective it is vital to be clear about how ageing, as both a social and an economic process, coincides and impacts with urban life, denies or supports access to social and economic resources and influences the 'voice' of older people in the city. Overall we must search for 'ways and means of integrating the elderly into [urban] communities characterized by diversification rather than segregation' (INSTRAW, 1993: 5). Referring to cities of the North and South, but paying particular attention to the Third World context, this chapter argues that often the needs of elderly urban citizens have been ignored by urban planners who have not recognised that the integration and recognition of elders in the city has a positive part to play in creating an inclusive city.

The definition of who is or is not elderly is contextually and culturally specific. It may be based simply on the need to determine a point of official retirement from employment, eligibility for various services made available to older people, physical frailty or, when defined by ordinary people, the presence of grandchildren (Beall et al., 1993). Butler and Lewis (1982: 5) note that the choice of age is an arbitrary one and can fluctuate with political pressure. Tinker (1992) similarly warns against any preoccupation with chronologically defined population groups, arguing that older people are merely those who have reached a certain age and that they do not constitute a homogeneous section of a given population. Indeed, it can be argued that ageing has social, political and economic connotations, all of which seek to define who may or may not be considered 'elderly', and that uncritical use of the term further confuses the issues that older people may face in urban environments. A social benefit system may require a certain age to be reached before funding can be accessed, whereas a social concept of older people may not correspond with that chronological point. In Venezuela, for example, the official retirement age of 55 for women and 60 for men was set some 40 years ago and has failed to react to changing life expectancy rates and the wish of those people to continue working (Margolies, 1993).

Ageing in the cities of the South

In cities of the South, those people defined as older constitute an increasing proportion of the population. Whilst the West already faces a rapidly ageing population, the South has yet to witness the large-scale demographic shifts in their urban populations. Traditionally, the history of urban migration in Third World cities was one of younger people leaving rural areas to gain urban employment, leaving older people in rural areas. Over the last two decades, factors such as internal displacement and population growth within cities have led to an increase in older urban residents. Indeed, the predominantly youthful demography of many cities in the South at the present indicates the dramatic extent of change that will occur in demographic profiles over the next 35 years (Alvarez, 1993). One in every two of the world's senior citizens currently lives in Asia (INSTRAW, 1993), and population ageing in developing countries is estimated to surpass rapidly the rate that has so far occurred in developed nations. Projections by HelpAge International, an international NGO working with and for older people worldwide, estimate that by 2025 seven of the ten countries with the largest absolute population of older people will be among those countries presently classified as 'developing' (Tamang et al., 1996). The crucial point is that this demographic shift is taking place against a background of minimal welfare provision, no formal social security, dwindling public resources and significant gaps in infrastructure provision. Whereas developed countries have been able, by and large, to accommodate the needs of their older people in terms of financial support and services, this appears beyond the reach of countries unable to meet the basic needs of the majority of their citizens. Developing countries will address the issues presented by 'old' demographic profiles at much lower levels of per capita income than industrial nations and this will inevitably cause problems in terms of providing for their older people. However, even a small pension can enable older people to maintain their livelihoods successfully and this issue remains fundamentally the political one of resource distribution.

Research

There is a paucity of research on older people in urban areas. Traditionally, as detailed below, urban social policy research has focused on processes of poverty and poverty alleviation such as income-generation strategies and housing. To the extent that there has been a disaggregation of need within households, the emphasis has been on gender and basic urban services. These debates are only just being widened to include the experience of ageing. While there is a great deal of project-related literature on working with older people, usually in the context of small-scale projects, this has yet to be collated to give a clearer idea of the issues that older people in cities confront on a daily basis and to inform policy. It must also be stressed that any discussion has to be firmly contextualised – research findings cannot be generalised. Whereas older people may be politically active in Latin America, this is less often the case in West Africa, for example. Cultural traditions – joint and extended families, remittance payments from migrants, customary kinship arrangements and organisation and practices of reciprocity – all play their part in defining the different experiences of older people in cities across the globe. Issues for urban elders cut across social, economic and political boundaries and attempts to categorise them neatly are inevitably flawed. However, some common themes become apparent.

The urban situation

As Rakodi (1994) states, figures on urban growth have become almost a cliché of the scaremongering predictions about urban growth swamping the capacity of nations. Hardoy and Satterthwaite (1989) warn against the uncritical acceptance of figures for urbanisation, particularly long-term predictions, as statistics are dependent upon a range of unreliable variables such as differing national definitions of urban areas and highly inaccurate census information. They are also critical of urbanisation being portrayed as negative. Although the figures draw attention to the scale of growth, the overall characteristic of the 'urban problem' is not simply the rise in the urban population but the 'scale of the mismatch between demographic and institutional change' (Arrossi et al., 1994: 3). Although Arrossi et al. were not referring specifically to older people, their argument has significance in relation to issues facing older urban residents.

Diversity in the city among older people

The older urban population is obviously not homogeneous: the great differences in income, gender, ethnicity and political power will also be reflected among older people. Differing access to income has great significance in defining any aspect of life for older people. Those with sufficient incomes may be able to protect themselves from the shocks and strains of urban life that more impoverished people may experience. For the urban poor, often on daily wages, their main asset is their body. For older people this asset is continually decreasing in its effectiveness both physically and within a social process that denies the contributions older people can make in the workforce. Understanding vulnerability as defencelessness, insecurity and exposure to risk and as the inability to cope with change and shocks enables us to realise that for older people the process of ageing is one of acute change, affecting almost every sphere of their lives. In this sense to be poor is to be vulnerable, and to be poor and in the later stages of ageing is to be doubly vulnerable. This prism of a wider conception of poverty as a process as well as a condition is useful in analysing the position of older urban residents. It encompasses their access to household and social resources and to social and psychological support, their opportunities for income earning, and the impact on them of infrastructural deficiencies within urban environments. Understanding the mechanisms of entitlement and the ways in which individuals command resources (Wratten, 1995) is extremely important in order to comprehend the capabilities and vulnerability of older people. This is particularly the case with regard to *social* entitlement, to customary methods of supporting older people. Ethnicity is another obvious area in which older people will be different, and often poverty and vulnerability are the fate of older people in ethnic minority communities. There is little literature on ethnic difference among older urban dwellers although it may be fair to say that where ethnic minorities or particular castes are discriminated against socially or economically, then this experience will continue when they are older. Holmes and Holmes (1995) argue that cultural or ethnically related differences play a significant part in varying patterns of care and support of older people. A study in South Africa showed that in Cape Town there was only one small residential home for Muslims, although they constituted some 16% of the population (Burman, 1994). Burman argues that this is because South African Muslims have a strong tradition of caring for elderly relatives in the household. There was significantly more residential accommodation catering for other groups of older people. Lee Samuel, the founder of the Carib Housing Association, which caters for the needs of older people of West Indian origin in Britain, makes the point that: 'The basic issues we face are the same for all older people. However, if providing sheltered housing to a specific group, in this case elders from the Caribbean, enriches their lives, then the spin off is the enriching of the community in which they live, and in Britain as a whole' (Older Women's Network, 1996: 6).

Another aspect of diversity within older populations is that based around physical capability. The vast majority of older people are 'active elderly', engaging in aspects of income generation, social networks and household life. The minority are those often referred to as the 'frail elderly', those older people requiring increasing amounts of physical or medical care and who, because of age-related disability, play a lesser part in their surrounding economic or social life. Any urban policy must recognise this difference and acknowledge also that older people may move between these categories at different stages of their lives. Policy must be sensitive to the needs of older people and their carers in transition stages. Where relatives move from inner-city areas, older people may be left without immediate support networks. Likewise, in more developed countries urban elder migration to non-metropolitan areas has been a consistent feature. These 'amenity movers' are normally the better off who wish to escape the pressures of urban life. There is also evidence of inward urban migration by 'support movers' who have moved away but return to metropolitan areas to access family-based support or medical facilities.

Social aspects of ageing in the city

As already noted, older people face very different circumstances and futures depending on the family structures and kinship networks on which they can rely. Ageing is a combination of economic, physical and social processes and an analysis of social ageing allows a deeper understanding of the intersections of the processes of vulnerability and ageing. Livi-Bacci (1992: 111) defines social ageing as 'the process of relinquishing meaningful social functions, with the ensuing increased risk for each individual, of becoming prematurely obsolete ... and estranged from society'. While acknowledging that this gives a pathological slant to the process of ageing, it is also possible to understand ageing as being about role change. Where extended or joint households have been seen as the main source of social support for older people, when these break down older people's vulnerability will be extended. In South Africa, the residential segregation of generations is an effect both of the ambitions of young people to live within urban societies and of the built environment itself, with the priority it gives to nuclear accommodation (Bozzoli, 1991). In South Asia, the joint family now shows signs of cracking very fast, with the advent of industrialisation and urbanisation (Andrews et al., 1986). In other parts of the world, persons who were born and raised in urban places often find it hard to secure employment in the same urban area in which their older parents may reside. This leads to a weighing up of travel opportunity cost versus retaining traditional household structures and the support of ageing parents. Gilbert and Gugler (1992) describes the pronounced selectivity of urban relationships and how this can mean nuclear units cutting ties with dependants. It is a case, however, of examining not simply *where* older people live, but *how* they live and what disaggregating process is taking place *within* the household. Do they receive support and how do they maintain their entitlement? In what circumstances do households depend upon older people for support, and how can urban planning enable and promote supportive strategies from or towards older people? Survival strategies for the urban poor and new-poor have meant that many married women, traditionally providers of intra-household care, have now joined the labour force and have less time to devote to caring for older relatives (INSTRAW, 1993). Under structural adjustment policies in Zimbabwe, changes have been noted in household structures. Kanji (1995) found that households had expanded in size over a one-year period but, importantly, that this expansion was due to dependants rather than income-earners joining households. This placed further pressure on the core household and conflict within households had risen, causing 'irreparable damage to kinship relations' (ibid.: 51).

Bozzoli (1991) points to another trend, that of older women returning alone to rural areas after years of working in the city because their children are unable or unwilling to support them in their old age. Older people are more likely to be dependants and, as such, they may well bear the brunt of household conflict. In the *katchi abadis* (low-income areas) of Karachi, Pakistan, 75% of older people live with their families in a society where joint and extended families are the norm. However, for 30% of these people this means only a physical share of the house; little or no social, economic or psychological support is offered (Tamang et al., 1996). Burman (1994), working in Cape Town, South Africa, discovered that of 100 older African people interviewed, only one-third reported that they received any support from direct descendants. Of these, only half reported that they received any regular assistance in terms of goods in kind or occasional cash payments. Yet 70 of the 100 interviewed lived in the same accommodation as their children. (It should be noted that there are universal pension rights in South Africa and that in 1993 the goal of parity of pensions between black and white people was brought in. However, owing to lack of awareness and illiteracy, etc., this does not mean to say that all those entitled receive pensions. Often it is the older people who are looked to for their regular pension cash income rather than the other way round.) Further interviews conducted by Burman with religious and community leaders revealed that there was 'unanimity on the low number of children who supported their aged parents' (1994: 5). Indeed, when asked where they turned to for social or economic support, older people listed, in decreasing order, neighbours, friends, sons, daughters and other relatives (ibid.). Gorman (1996) argues that there is a link between the social status of older people and their economic power; where that power is lessened, there is a parallel loss of status within social networks and if older people become rapidly marginalised from economic opportunity within urban areas then this will also affect their status within households. Indeed, Gorman argues that it is poverty, as opposed to 'modernising forces', often seen as the driving force in urban areas, that lies at the root of much inter-household conflict.

In addition to family stress and changing household structures, less cohesiveness in urban areas and the concomitant loss of community identity may mean a reduction in the sense of community responsibility and reciprocity in terms of support for older people. This can lead to older people feeling socially and culturally isolated in, for example, areas that have been subject to gentrification in the North or transformed by big influxes of incomers in the South. However, much also stays the same. For example, 'tribal' social organisation is very much in existence in many African urban communities (Rosenmayr, 1993). Bonds of kinship, of neighbourliness, and personal relationships are nevertheless likely to come under great pressure in urban areas. The 'intense individualism' (Moser, 1989) of urban poverty, expressed in terms of access to housing and to income and of vulnerability, takes its toll on reciprocal relationships, which are often a major survival strategy for older people. Kanji, working in Harare, found that:

> Older women, usually widows and main householders, had the least resources and opportunities and were heavily dependent on adult offspring. Much therefore depended upon their relationships, especially with sons, who tended to have more available resources than daughters to support the family. When sons did not meet their obligations, conflict was exacerbated by economic hardship, and where daughters were not able to help, the effect on the household was particularly severe (1995: 53).

Positive aspects of ageing in the household

While the issues outlined above are clearly pertinent to older urban dwellers, it is important not to build an overwhelmingly negative picture of ageing in the city, as policy then becomes supportive rather than promotive in outlook. Gorman (1996: 43) uses this distinction in the analysis of development that seeks to enable the poor to *have* more or to *be* more. Where older people are perceived uni-dimensionally as a burden, services, where they do exist, will be welfaristic in approach. However, older people, particularly women, often offer cultural reference points to their families when marital relationships are vulnerable or under stress. Others recognise that older people provide childcare, releasing other household members for paid employment. In those cities devastated by recent wars older people often take up the role of the 'missing generation' in terms of childcare and income earning (see Chapter 17). A similar pattern can be observed in parts of Africa, where high rates of HIV or AIDS have led to a 'literal decimation of the middle generation in some communities' (Gorman, 1996: 42), leaving older people to offer childcare and economic support to orphaned children. Older people are a repository of culture and skills, and these are often under-utilised.

In Buenos Aires, Argentina, CEPEV (Centro de Promocion y Estudio de la Vejez) runs a Retired People's Centre with over three hundred members. In 1994 the centre set up a health post to provide nursing and chiropody care for older people, to develop preventive care strategies and to promote self-care in everyday life. The health post is supported by a team made up of older volunteers from the centre. The volunteers collate medical information about older people in the area, maintain a database, organise talks by specialists and assist other members of the centre in negotiating the complicated public health system in Buenos Aires.

In Lima, Peru, APROUTED (Asociacion Promotora Universidad de la Tercera Edad) has established a herb production programme and pharmacy. The older people involved in the programme use their knowledge to grow, harvest and process the herbs to produce a variety of syrups, tonics, embrocations and basic products for medicinal use. One of the group's main objectives is to compete commercially and to reach the most frail and vulnerable groups with their low-cost medicines. Thirty community health promoters chosen from among older members of the community will be trained by traditional healers and doctors. As training continues, the promoters will begin to work with target families, teaching the correct use of herbal remedies and collecting health information from the population.[1]

Crime, security and well-being

Violence as an urban issue is examined elsewhere in this volume, but its specific implications for older people have still not been fully analysed in the context of the South. One exception is the *Revista Dominicana de Psiquiatria* (1996), which has published research into the frequency of verbal, sexual and physical violence among a sample population of 300 people over the age of 60 years in the Dominican Republic. Although the incidence of abuse is often not registered, the research has found that verbal and emotional aggression towards older people is the most common, followed by physical and sexual abuse. Women between the ages of 60 and 69 are the most vulnerable, particularly those from lower-income groups. Domestic violence reaches high levels against older people, with the home being the main place where violence is exercised. Older men and women are beaten, murdered and robbed; according to reported cases, the majority of attacks are premeditated and the aggressor is most likely to be a relative, neighbour or friend of the victim. One of HelpAge International's partners, Movimiento Manuel Ramos, offers advice to older people on abuse and legal issues. In the cities of the North links are made between ageing and vulnerability to violence and crime, especially for older women. However, many argue that it is fear of crime, as distinct from the actual incidence of crime, that is the most pressing issue facing older people in cities (Fattah and Sacco, 1989). This fear affects behaviour by reducing mobility and limiting daily activities often related to and linking with social support networks or income generation. This fear then contributes to the further isolation and loneliness of elders and is compounded when financial decline in old age forces elders to live in the poorer districts of the city, which have relatively high rates of crime.

A gendered experience of ageing

Gorman (1996) singles out the situation of older women as one of 'accumulating disadvantage'. Where lifetime nutrition rates show a gender bias, and women undergo multiple pregnancies and are involved in reproductive as well as productive tasks throughout their lives, women approach old age rapidly. Because of different ageing patterns, single-headed female households in cities outnumber male equivalents and this is set to rise as life expectancy increases at a faster rate among women than among men. For example, the percentage of older people living alone was 13.5% for women and 1.9% for men in Indonesia in 1986 (INSTRAW, 1993: 12) and it is clear that single-person households are more vulnerable to shock and change than multiple-occupant households. At present, women make up almost three-quarters of all older Americans living in poverty. Older women are thus almost twice as likely as older men to be poor, which means they are more likely to need public benefits. Although public programmes may provide cash benefits as well as assistance in paying for food, housing, health care and home energy costs, many eligible women do not apply (AARP, 1996). In certain contexts older women may become impoverished after the death of their husband, when their property is distributed amongst male children. Women may also suffer more than elderly men from a fear of crime, and thus have a more restricted lifestyle. Although fear of crime can imprison older women in their own homes, statistics show that they are far less likely than men actually to experience violence first-hand. They are, however, more vulnerable to certain kinds of crime. In America, for example, older women are the biggest target for telemarketing fraud and other consumer crime, and they are more than twice as likely as men to be victims of elder abuse (AARP, 1996). Some research has shown that vestiges of gerontocracy continue in urban areas (Rosenmayr, 1993), but where these do exist it is often through older men rather than women that external organisations negotiate programmes or access to the wider community. The problem facing older men is that they are more likely than women to lose contact with wider family structures, often because they do not maintain or contribute to sustaining reciprocal relations.

American women have longer life expectancies than American men, but life expectancy does not equal better health. Women are more likely than men to develop chronic conditions that can restrict everyday life. Until recently, most health researchers rarely acknowledged women's issues like breast cancer and menopause. When it came to shared problems like heart disease, researchers simply applied results from male subjects to women. However, health conditions do affect women differently. For example, heart attacks are more often fatal for women than for men and some diseases, such as osteoporosis, strike women four times as often as men.

Where user charges have been applied to health care, mainly in urban areas, there has been little effort to understand the intergenerational or gendered impacts on the utilisation of health care. Because retirement income is tied to earnings and time spent in the workforce, inequalities persist even after women retire from paid employment. Men receive on average incomes 37% higher than women through state and occupational pensions in the United Kingdom (Older Women's Network, 1996). Women in jobs covered by pension plans, for example, are more likely than men to leave their jobs before qualifying for or investing in their plans, and lower wages mean that many women are unable to save enough for a comfortable retirement. However, women are more likely than men to be able to gain employment in both the formal and informal sectors and often maintain closer ties with families.

Economic aspects of ageing in the city

The situation of older people in urban areas is less flexible than that of their rural counterparts, as they may have to shift their economic activities in response to social, cultural or economic pressures. The fact that the economy of the city is almost totally monetised increases the vulnerability of those who are unable to convert their labour into capital. Structural adjustment policies and the subsequent 'downward' pressure on urban employment patterns where retrenched workers have moved into the informal sector have often displaced more vulnerable workers, such as older people. Whereas self-employment and employment in family-related activities tend to be greater in rural areas, allowing elders to switch job assignments or to reduce their hours, this flexibility may not be so possible in urban areas. Moreover, unlike traditional societies where personal relations can be the basis of transactions, in the city the purchase of services and goods must normally be done on a monetary basis.

In the majority of cities of the South a substantial proportion of income-earning opportunities are defined as 'informal'. Official retirement age and its concomitant benefits affect only a small proportion of the population. Indeed, in most developing countries, pension systems are virtually non-existent and cover only a relatively privileged minority, such as public sector workers. In South Asia, for example, these pensions are seen as part of a survival strategy in themselves, with public sector jobs being 'bought' and closely guarded by workers who realise that their pension will allow them to cope with expenses later in life such as secure housing, dowry payments or illnesses (Beall, 1997). In more developed nations, in the face of a receding welfare state, the increased use of private pension schemes plays an ever increasing role in providing income for elders; this will depend on previous employment and will vary substantially between men and women or skilled and unskilled workers.

In terms of household income, Burman (1994) found that a pension was seen as contributing to household income, sometimes against the wishes of the person in receipt of the payment. The other side of this argument is that a dependence on pension income aided their incorporation into a family structure and their status within it. Household and individual survival strategies in the face of changing economic circumstances mean that most elderly people continue to do some form of income work in order to purchase food and essential goods (Tout, 1993). In Eastern, Middle, and Western Africa, over two-thirds of men aged 65 and over remain in the labour force (INSTRAW, 1993), a statistic that contradicts many stereotypes. A recent study cited by Tamang et al. (1996) estimated that 64% of older people actively earn a living in Karnataka State, South India. A large proportion of older women are engaged in work, although often it is discontinuous, part-time or seasonal, and frequently invisible and difficult to distinguish from domestic activities performed within the traditional sector of the economy or in family enterprises (Recchini de Lattes and Wainerman, 1986). Kanji (1995) found that in Harare, contrary to studies in Latin America, women were unable to expand their income-generating activities as a response to economic hardship, because of market saturation. All women reported that in order to maintain their income at present levels they were forced to work harder for longer hours than previously. The effect of this on older people's participation in an informal economy is clear. They have to work longer hours with diminishing energy for smaller returns. Unfortunately information on employment patterns of older people is often poor, as in the example of surveys in Latin America, where census-takers were instructed to register older people automatically as economically inactive (INSTRAW, 1993).

There are many examples of people cushioning themselves from vulnerability through access to credit for small-scale enterprises. Credit is accessed mostly through 'informal' money-lenders and, over the past decade, through NGOs or other community organisations. Older people have difficulty securing credit as they are perceived as being more of a risk than younger people, particularly by money-lenders who provide the poor with the main source of credit for income generation and who reap the returns over the long term. In Manila, the Coalition of Services for the Elderly provides income-generation opportunities, recognising that many older people have significant skills that can be regenerated through credit schemes. They have found that 80% of older people are capable of earning an income, with only the 20% of 'frail' elderly being incapable of income generation (Phillips, 1992). The Andrus Center of the University of Southern California estimates that a minimum of 8 million Americans over 65 want to continue working, and a Harris Poll showed that 70% of pre-retirees hope to work after retirement (AARP, 1996).

Public action can go some way to promoting 'older employment': German firms hiring people of 45 or older are eligible for grants of up to 80% of the new employee's wage costs for two years. In Japan, the government subsidises three-fifths of the elderly person's wage for six months and one-half of their wage for the next six months; a benefit for continuous employment is given to employers who employ an individual beyond the age of 60 for at least one year. These initiatives are, however, dependent on the state of the labour market and may become threatened where unemployment is rising.

Ageing in human settlements

As noted above, a large proportion of older people in Southern cities live with children. However, it is important to acknowledge the diversity of older people's urban housing situations. For example, studies have shown a predominance of nuclear elder households in both Brazilian and Egyptian urban communities (INSTRAW, 1993: 15). Self-help housing initiatives may well be inappropriate for older people, although there is some evidence to challenge this (Tamang et al, 1996). Badshah (1996) suggests co-housing, based on Danish models of separate units with communal areas for a full range of generations, as an integrated housing policy for older people in cities. In response to a perceived breakdown in the extended family system, the Singapore government has put into action a programme to support family care for older people in their own homes (Tout, 1993). This includes inter-generational co-residence whereby married children and their parents are allowed to apply for adjoining public authority apartments. Income tax relief is available to someone caring for an elderly dependant and practical support services to carers have been introduced or improved. These have included services for domicile, day-care and respite opportunities and encouragement to local communities to increase their efforts to support their elders. The programme has two main objectives: to keep elders fit and active and able to participate in the mainstream of community life, and to ensure that the frail elderly can access adequate and appropriate services or family and community support to enable them to continue residing at home rather than be admitted to an institution (Tout, 1993).

The issue of housing is as much about affordability as about appropriate design, and the major urban issue of insecurity of tenure will impact upon older people in different ways. Housing as an area of concern is not just about how planners design and manage housing for older people but also, vitally, about how planners view households and the ability to plan housing for 'life' rather than for nuclear families. It is also important to realise that even where older people may have some form of housing it may be inadequate for their needs and may not offer the support they require within it. As noted above, because women become increasingly likely to live alone the older they get and have a lower average income, many women have difficulty finding affordable housing that will allow them to live independently well into their later years. Eviction is often a major problem for elderly people faced with declining incomes. The issue of residential care for frail or abandoned older people in cities is one that has yet to be examined in any detail in the South. However, according to project workers, residential care is increasing within urban areas, often through charitable organisations or church-based projects. The issues facing older people in residential care – for instance, the preservation of dignity and adequate social interaction – cut across national boundaries.

In colder cities, older people often suffer greatly from lack of heating, exacerbated by a lack of income to supplement their heating costs. An example from Glasgow shows how planners can meet wider needs. The young and the old have the greatest need for warm accommodation, but older people may suffer more from the cold due to a reluctance to spend extra income on heating during particularly cold weather.

Action for warm houses, Glasgow, Scotland, UK Glasgow, a northern city with a rich heritage, has, for some decades, been suffering the effects of unemployment and poverty. To counter health problems caused by the inadequate heating of homes, Glasgow has developed the 'Action for Warm Housing Programme' to improve energy efficiency in municipal housing and to provide whole-house heating and electricity for not more than 10% of net household income. This has required a mass energy audit, the implementation and monitoring of demonstration projects, the application of advanced heating technology, and a major investment shift towards heating and energy efficiency. New relationships with tenants have been forged to give them confidence in using advanced heating systems. Thousands of city council homes have now received a combination of insulation, new windows and central heating (Best Practices Programme, UNCHS, Nairobi, Internet). The needs of older people and younger families have then been catered for within a sectorally based programme.

Facilities and infrastructure within the city must allow for the needs of elders. A common strategy to increase mobility among elders is to provide reduced fares on public transport. Sweden has developed several projects to aid older people in moving around cities. For example, for those with severe mobility problems, there are special buses that must be booked one day in advance. It is important to realise that reduced fares can be operational only where there is a functioning public sector transport system. Where services have been privatised or where most public transport is 'informal', there is little ground for public action to reduce costs for elders. Joyce Malombe's comments in Box 4.1 on the difficulty of public travel in Nairobi for disabled people have equal pertinence for older people with mobility problems.

Any discussion about health must be concerned with the utilisation of health facilities. In the past debate has been concentrated around the fact that, per capita, urban residents have far greater access to health facilities than their rural counterparts. This is being increasingly challenged, however, as studies have attempted to illustrate that the utilisation of health facilities is skewed towards the better-off or the mobile in the city. Hospital-based care tends to prevail in urban areas, often requiring significant travel between home and service. Where more appropriate community-based services have been initiated, they have rarely included older people as a priority (Gorman, 1996). The introduction of user charges for health services has been concentrated primarily in urban areas and may have a significant impact on older people's use of health facilities, but this has been another under-researched topic in Southern urban research. It may be that household survival strategies mean keeping the main income-earners in better health and not using scarce resources on older, less economically productive, members. As an older man in Kasur, Pakistan, interviewed by Beall et al. (1993: 73) commented, with money: 'The doctor's fee can be paid without fear of dying because one does not have the money for treatment'. Where incomes are lower, related factors such as quality of housing, nutrition, sanitation and solid waste management have a positive effect on reducing health-related expenditure for older people.

Political organisation

If the voices and priorities of older people in cities are to be heard and the prioritisation of other concerns is not to become the justification for inaction over older people's concerns (Badshah, 1996), then a political process may well offer this opportunity. Governments can no longer presume that older people's needs will be met within family units, and political pressure may be one avenue to incorporating the needs of older urban residents in integrated planning strategies. While North America at present still leads the way in the political organisation of older people (AARP, 1996), the examples below show instances in the South where older people have striven to have their concerns listened to and acted upon in the city.

During the 1996 presidential election campaign in the Dominican Republic a local NGO, Centro de Apoyo Aquelarre, organised a seminar to publicise the proposals for social security and older people, contained in the manifestos of the various political parties. The aim was to encourage debate about and recognition of the needs of older people with a view to establishing commitments for the country's older population. The result of this seminar was the inclusion of the theme of ageing in the national political agenda. The presidential candidates from all parties were explicit in their commitment to the older population, whereas some had previously failed to mention ageing as a political issue (HelpAge International, 1996).

In Bolivia, a working group of more than twenty organisations, including HelpAge International, Pro Vida Bolivia and the Department of Intergenerational Affairs, set up a commission in La Paz to produce and present a draft Supreme Decree for the legal protection of older people in Bolivia. The draft was presented to the president of the republic in August 1995 and was ratified by the president on Bolivia's National Day of Older People in August 1996 (ibid.).

In Argentina, President Menem will be presenting a National Plan on ageing as a result of the work of the Department of Intergenerational Affairs and FAIAF, a member organisation of HelpAge International which has been lobbying the government to take up the issue of older people (ibid.).

In Sweden, formalised participation by older people in decision-making processes is the result of prolonged efforts by pensioners' organisations to increase the say of elders in policies that affect their lives (Sydow, 1981).

In Germany, pressures for participation came primarily from policy-makers and professionals serving the ageing, rather than from elders themselves (Nusberg, 1980). The resulting Hannover Model, however, has been very successful in supporting older people and city administrators in working together. This has led to reductions in public transportation costs, improving housing facilities for the elderly and reducing staff/patient ratios.

In Australia, the Older Women's Own Network (OWN) is an autonomous, self-generated agency springing from older women's own initiatives. It aims to challenge the stereotypes of ageism and sexism through groups focusing on health, housing, retirement income and self-protection (Onyx et al., 1992). Its four principal objectives relate to the development of older women's skills, the strengthening of support networks, the involvement of older women in assessing their own specific needs and the dispelling of the 'invisibility of older women'. OWN also joined the Human Rights Equal Opportunities Commission to set up a forum on the theme 'Security and dignity for older women: developing action'.

The American Association for Retired Persons (AARP) currently has a membership of 33 million people and as such is the largest non-politically affiliated lobby in the United States. One-third of its members are currently in the workforce and it represents a significant political lobby in terms of occupationally related rights. The fact that President Clinton attended the most recent AARP National Convention bears testament to the broad base of political power that AARP currently holds.

Aspects of diversity

Acknowledging the diversity inherent within older urban populations and the processes of poverty, vulnerability and social ageing allows a wider conception of the experience of urban ageing. However, it is important not to overstress the negative aspects of urban life for older people. As the examples above have shown, older urban residents are a resource and a source of support for many low-income urban households. Documenting problematic urban issues for older people is intended not to further a negative social conception of ageing but to illustrate the extent to which urban planning and social development have so far failed to address the specific and general requirements of older residents. A perspective that embraces difference and recognises the fact that older people's needs cannot be neatly compartmentalised can only serve to enrich further the contribution that older people already make to urban living.

Note

1. The authors would like to thank Susanna Connor at HelpAge International for providing case study material and suggestions for the paper.

References

AARP (1996), unpublished paper given at Habitat II workshop, Istanbul, July.

Alvarez, J. (1993), 'The prospects for a greying world', in K. Tout (ed.), *Elderly Care: A World Perspective*, London: Chapman and Hall.

Arrossi, S., F. Bombarolo, J. Hardoy, D. Mitlin, D. Satterthwaite and L. Coscio (1994), *Funding Community Initiatives*, London: Earthscan.

Badshah, A. (1996), *Our Urban Future: New Paradigms for Equity and Sustainability*, London: Zed Books.

Beall, J. D., N. Kanji, F. Faruqi, M. Mirani and C. Mohammad Hussain (1993), *Social Saftey Nets and Social Networks, Their Role in Poverty Alleviation in Pakistan*, report for the Oversesas Development Administration, UK, towards the World Bank Pakistan Poverty Assessment.

Beall, J. (1997), 'Households, livelihoods and the urban environment: social develop-ment perspectives on solid waste management in Faisalabad, Pakistan', Ph.D. thesis in preparation, London: London School of Economics.

Bozzoli, B. (1991), *Women of Phokeng, Consciousness, Life Strategy and Migrancy in South Africa 1900–1983*, Johannesburg: Ravan Press.

Brillon, Y. (1987), *Victimization and Fear of Crime Among the Elderly*, Toronto: Butterworth.

Burman, S. (1994), 'Intergenerational family care: legacy of the past, implications for the future', paper presented at Journal of Southern African Studies Conference, York, September 1994.

Butler, R. and M. Lewis (1982), *Aging and Mental Health*, Toronto: C.V. Mosby.

Costa, J. (1985), *Abuse of the Elderly: A Guide to Resources and Services*, Massachusetts: Lexington Books.

Dominican Bulletin of Psychiatry (1996), *Revista Dominicana de Psiquiatria*, 7, February.

Edwards, E. (1983), 'Native-American elders: current issues and social policy', in R. McNeely and J. Colen (eds), *Aging in Minority Groups*, London: Sage.

Fattah, E. and V. Sacco (1989), *Crime and Victimization of the Elderly*, London: Springer-Verlag.

Gibson, M. (1984), 'Educational opportunities', in C. Nusberg (ed.), *Innovative Aging Programs Abroad: Implications for the United States*, London: Greenwood Press.

Gorman, M. (1996), 'Older people and development: the last minority?' in M. Anderson (ed.), *Development and Social Diversity*, Oxford: Oxfam.

Gilbert, A. and J. Gugler (1992), *Cities, Poverty and Development: Urbanization in the Third World*, 2nd edn, Oxford: Oxford University Press.

Hardoy, J. and D. Satterthwaite (1989), *Squatter Citizen: Life in the Urban Third World*, London: Earthscan.

Herbert, A. (1983), 'Enhancing housing opportunities for the black elderly', in R. McNeely and J. Colen (eds), *Aging in Minority Groups*, London: Sage.

Holmes, E. and L. Holmes (1995), *Other Cultures, Elder Years*, London: Sage.

INSTRAW (1993), *The Situation of Elderly Women, Available Statistics and Indicators*, Santo Domingo: INSTRAW.

Kanji, N. (1995), 'Gender, poverty and economic adjustment in Harare, Zimbabwe', in *Environment and Urbanization*, 7(1), April: 37–56.

Karp, D., G. Stone and W. Yoels (1991), *Being Urban: A Sociology of City Life*, New York: Praeger Publishers.

Krishnan, P. and K. Mahadevan (1992), *The Elderly Population in the Developed and Developing World: Policies, Problems and Perspectives*, New Dehli: B.R. Publishing.

Livi-Bacci, M. (1992), 'Social and biological ageing: conradictions of development', in *Population and Development Review*, 8(4).

Margolies, L. (1993), 'A crisis of perceptions', in K. Tout (ed.), *Elderly Care: A World Perspective*, London: Chapman and Hall.

McNeely, R. and J. Colen (1983), *Aging in Minority Groups*, London: Sage.

Milgram, S. (1973), 'The experience of living in cities: a psychological analysis', in J. Helmer and N. Eddington (eds), *Urbanman: The Psychological of Urban Survival*, London: Collier-Macmillan.

Moser, C. (1989), 'Community participation in urban projects in the Third World', in *Progress in Planning*, 32(2): 70–130.

Niebanck, P. (1965), *The Elderly in Older Urban Areas*, Pennsylvania: Institute of Environmental Studies.

Norman, A. (1977), *Transport and The Elderly: Problems and Possible Action*, London: Anchor Press.

Nusberg, C. with M. Gibson and S. Peace (1984), *Innovative Aging Programs Abroad: Implications for the United States*, London: Greenwood Press.

Older Women's Network (1996), *Older Women in Lewisham Speak Out*, Newsletter, March, London Borough of Lewisham.

Onyx, J., P. Benton and J. Bradfield (1992), 'Aged services in Australia – community development and government response', *Community Development Journal*, 27(2): 166–74.

Phillips, D. (1992), *Ageing in East and South-East Asia*, London: Edward Arnold.

Rakodi, C. (1994), *Urban Poverty in Zimbabwe*, Department of City and Regional Planning, University of Wales.

Rosenmayr, L. (1993), 'The family undisturbed', in K. Tout (ed.), E*lderly Care: A World Perspective*, London: Chapman and Hall.

Sauer, W. and R. Coward (1985), *Social Support Network and the Care for the Elderly*, New York: Springer.

Scharf, T. and G. Wenger (1995), *International Perspectives on Community Care for Older People*, Vermont: Ashgate Publishing Company.

Schlessinger, B. and R. Schlesinger (1984), *Abuse of the Elderly*, London: University of Toronto Press.

Sekiguchi, S. (1980), 'How Japanese business treats its older worker', *Management Review*, October.

Simpson, I. and J. McKinney (1966), *Social Aspects of Ageing*, North Carolina: Duke University Press.

Sydow, T. (1981), 'Self-determination by the elderly in Sweden', in C. Nusberg (ed.), *Self-Determination by the Elderly*, Washington, DC.: International Federation on Ageing.

Tamang, D., A. Sharman, S. Conner and K. Peachey (1996), 'Working with older people in urban areas', in N. Hall, R. Hart and D. Mitlin (eds), *The Urban Opportunity*, London: Intermediate Technology Publications.

Tinker, A. (1992), *Elderly People in Modern Society*, London: Longman.

Tout, K. (1989), *Ageing In Developing Countries*, Oxford: Oxford University Press.

Tout, K. (ed.) (1993), *Elderly Care : A World Perspective*, London: Chapman and Hall.

Wratten, E. (1995), 'Conceptualizing urban poverty', *Environment and Urbanization*, 7(1), April: 11–36.

CHAPTER 14

City Transport for All

*Gareth Ward, Sydney Smith
and Jeffrey Barron*

While city transport – defined broadly as the methods people use to move into, within and out of urban areas – has traditionally fallen within the planning domain of economists, engineers and technicians, social planners also have an important contribution to make. If the 'City for All' is to enable diverse social groups to participate fully in urban life, then planning for effective and equitable transport plays a crucial role. The need for city transport is universal; however, the unique problems that transport users and planners face in Southern cities must be understood as requiring context-sensitive solutions. This chapter discusses an example of such a solution, using a 'best practice' model of city transport planning from Brazil. Without suggesting that this specific solution can be directly transferred to other cities, some general, useful guidelines emerge. In particular, the need to strengthen connections between transport planning and social planning is shown to be particularly important in Southern cities.

Key issues in city transport planning

It is well documented that groups such as people in poverty, women, elderly people, people with disabilities, and children are disadvantaged in the city, and are therefore the most directly affected by a lack of appropriate social planning. From a transport planning perspective, this disadvantage is manifest in their lack of mobility. This may impact on their potential income-generation opportunities, their access to medical and recreational facilities, and their participation in political or public gatherings; they are affected by the disproportionate time-lags endured while travelling on infrequent services and the physical impediments to travel. All these disadvantages contribute to exclusion from urban life. If transport is seen as a device for enabling mobility, which in turn enables citizens to participate in the institutions and benefit from the amenities of the 'City for All', then effective transport systems must be seen as a fundamental goal of social planning.

A clear example of how inadequate transport planning leads to reduced mobility and reinforced exclusion is that of apartheid South Africa, where policies of racial segregation were partly enforced by transport restrictions on mixed race and black groups. A heavy economic burden was placed on blacks from the rural Bantustans and the townships on the fringes of urban areas, who were required to commute long distances to work. They were the social group with least money and time to spare and yet the longest journeys to face. In addition, the politicisation of public transport was evident in both the draconian state regulations and the popular responses of bus boycotts, attacks on state vehicles and taxi wars (Pirie, 1992: 177). Transport acted as a site for both top-down political control and bottom-up resistance. Post-apartheid, the emergence of the 'black taxi industry' has been acclaimed as a small business success story and a crucial aspect of black empowerment (Khosa, 1992: 182), but the less malleable settlement patterns that necessitate commuting continue to exclude people from an equitable transport system.

Social inclusion of diverse social groups into urban life is thus intricately linked to mobility between the multiple and often widespread centres that are the focus of activities – for example shopping areas, such as arcades or markets, sites of recreation, such as leisure centres or the home of family or friends across town, or services such as health centres or schools. But the need to provide effective transport for mobility does not explain the particular problems of diverse groups with regard to access. If access to transport is not equitable then some citizens will be less able than others to take advantage of and contribute to the 'City for All'. In cities of developing countries, where the public transport system provides a high proportion of journeys, the issues of access and affordability are apparent in a clear spatial way. Transport infrastructure for shanty towns on the outskirts of Third World cities is usually lacking, and if it is available, for example through private operators, it invariably absorbs a large proportion of poor people's income. Yet social concern is conspicuously absent in much orthodox transport planning. Following a critique of previous approaches to transport planning in the city, this chapter presents a critical discussion of the Curitiba model and its implications for replicability or adaptability. To conclude, a series of guidelines are proposed that incorporate an awareness of how to cater for diverse social groups, and how to offer them transport choices.

Approaches to transport planning

In everyday usage the word 'transport' is often limited to the simplistic definition of how people, goods and services can be moved from point A to point B, and 'planning' is governments' attempts to ensure that those adequate flows are maintained. 'Transport planning' in this sense exists as a purely utilitarian concept. Indeed, this everyday meaning is often the starting point for top-down transport plans intended to achieve certain well-defined, predominantly economic, goals. Cost–benefit analysis, efficiency measures and 'urban transport planning' (UTP) are all examples of this instrumental approach.

In the 'City for All', 'transport' is given a far wider meaning. Starting from the idea that transport is about enabling mobility, affordability and access, it is argued that transport planning has more than a purely instrumental role to play in ensuring the well-being of the people it serves. In particular, it is argued that in the complex spatial environment of the city, transport is as significant a social planning issue as are more obviously 'social' sectors such as education and health care. Without an adequate, basic provision of transport to city inhabitants, full participation in society may be impossible. Thus, when the city is seen as a 'dynamic interface machine of movement channels' (Dimitriou, 1992), there are serious implications for those people who are denied sufficient access to the channels, and the provision of better transport facilities becomes an end in itself.

Much transport planning emerges from a theoretical analysis of the functions transport plays in 'modern' economy and society. It is rightly asserted that the growth of commerce and industry in national and international contexts relies heavily on transport to move raw and manufactured materials to points of production and consumption. Similarly, mobile labour is crucial to the economic performance of industrialised society (Giddens, 1989). By providing linkages between points of residence and employment, transport contributes to economies of scale and allows specialisation to exploit comparative economic advantages. By extending these principles from 'modern' society to the contemporary city, it follows that not only are the external links of a city to emergent resources and fast-changing markets important, but so too is the internal mobility of individual economic actors. However, people are not mobile units of labour, are not exclusively economic actors, but have multiple roles and diverse responsibilities. Yet many transport systems are organised primarily around the main breadwinners' journey to work. Within the diverse labour markets of the city, where short-term flexible contracting is becoming the norm and there are no more 'jobs for life' with nearby accommodation provided, the need for changes in the approach to transport rises in significance (Standing, 1989), even when viewed from a primarily economic viewpoint.

In the urban areas of developing countries, where economic growth is seen as a first step to development, it follows that transport systems that function effectively are a basic prerequisite of a healthy economy and efficient society. Northern orthodoxies such as UTP, designed in and for US cities, have attempted with varying degrees of success to put this theoretical analysis into practice. However, serious questions remain about the sustainability of this top-down form of transport planning in developing country cities. Until indigenous transport practices are given proper attention, transport planning will continue to cater to a select sector of the population while excluding the diverse social groups who make up the majority of users, or will continue to be ignored by private and informal operators. Although indigenous methods are affordable, without some regulation they can increase the level of danger, congestion and pollution on the roads of Third World cities.

Context-specific transport planning is needed in Southern cities. Rapid urban growth and increasing levels of motorisation have led to increased pressure on indigenous transport systems. First, the physical growth of cities has meant longer trips for most citizens, and the rising population of car drivers, bus passengers and other road users has led the growth of transport volume to outstrip growth of infrastructure. The availability of maintenance and management skills for sustainable transport thus becomes a problem (Dimitriou, 1990). Between 1975 and 1985, 17 transport projects and 32 projects with a transport element were funded by the World Bank at a cost of US$1,040 million. These projects were often focused on quantitative transport goals, financial viability and technology transfer, including highly sophisticated 'people-mover' systems such as light rail or subway systems as a way to ease the load on overburdened roads, seen as essential for economic transport. However, this transfer of technology has been threatened by austere economic regimes and cuts in government spending, further increasing the importance of appropriate planning as a way to improve the effectiveness and equity of resource-limited transport systems.

It is also important to disaggregate the category of transport. Even a superficial comparative investigation into Southern cities reveals that diverse groups use diverse modes of transport. 'Modern' or 'formal' modes of transport such as cars, buses and metros coexist with 'traditional' or 'informal' modes such as walking, rickshaws and animal-drawn carts. These two categories are not discrete, for informal ways of running formal transport are devised. 'Paratransit' systems are home-grown, makeshift or adapted solutions to the unavailability of modern modes of transport and the inadequacies of informal systems. They include the *tro-tro* in The Gambia, *colectivo* in Guatemala and *mama-wagon* in Ghana (Armstrong-Wright, 1990) and constitute a high proportion of transport in cities in developing countries. The tendency of transport planners to ignore informal solutions to problems often leads to unworkable policy prescriptions.

Thus appropriate transport planning can emerge only from an understanding of existing forms of transport and the diverse social groups that use them. A flexible, bottom-up approach complements the technical analysis of transport problems and enables effective and equitable solutions to be found. It is not a trade-off between equity and growth, since only with appropriate planning can a transport system continue to contribute to the economy in the long term. Equity in transport also functions to promote equity as a part of wider social development goals. More traditional analysis of the intersection between transport and social development has focused on the significant proportion of income that the poorer groups spend on transport. This means that 'the ways in which public authorities choose to obtain or encourage investment in transport and allocate the costs can effect a significant redistribution of income' (Mitlin and Sattherthwaite, 1994: 49).

By adopting a less rigidly functional analysis of transport, its importance can also be shown as a primary input when planning such social initiatives as education, environmental protection, sanitation and health, and employment generation. Effective and equitable transport thus has a multiplier effect on other social sectors. In addition, a more gender-sensitive approach to transport, away from the stereotyped model of the male, car-driving head of household, would take into account the fact that women need to use transport out of peak hours (Levy, 1992: 100). The gender issues associated with transport are covered in more detail in Chapter 2 of this book and will not be elaborated further here. The best-practice case study discussed in this chapter not only demonstrates the way that transport planning can benefit diverse social groups, but also stresses the importance of transport as a crucial factor in the success of other social policies.

Diversity and the Curitiba model

Curitiba is a city in Southern Brazil that has gained a reputation for progressive urban planning, particularly in the field of transport. At the Habitat II summit in Istanbul in 1996, a replica of one of the raised tubular bus stations was placed as a 'best practice' exhibit outside the main conference centre. In stark contrast to Northern-type UTP models of transport planning, which are also dependent on Northern loan money and technical expertise, Curitiba provides an example of an independent, Southern-based approach. The transport system and planning process presented here not only address the direct problems of planning for diverse social groups and choices, but also absorb transport into broader social planning goals to create an integrated development effort for the city as a whole.

The main *technical features* of the Curitiba system, as described by one of its principal planners, Jonas Rabinovitch (1992), are as follows:

- Choice of buses as the city's 'anchor' system of human transport, as a practical and affordable solution to public transport for a Third World medium-sized city.
- Design of a city road system based on two structural axes running

north and south into the city, complemented by a hierarchy of four types of feeder or interconnecting roads.

* The axes themselves consist of a central road with two express bus lanes in the middle flanked by two local roads. Along each side of the central road, one block away, there is a high-capacity, free-flowing one-way road, one into and the other out of the city.
* Inter-district bus lines include new connections between the city centre and an industrial city on the outskirts.
* Rapid Bus System uses special raised tubular stations to cut down boarding times.

The main *social features* of the new system include:

* Social fare: a standard fare paid by all bus users results in major benefits for bus users living on the city periphery, predominantly poorer groups, as shorter journeys subsidise longer ones.
* Full fare integration between express buses, inter-district buses and conventional (feeder) buses; a single fare is valid for all buses.
* Pedestrian-only zones in the central city.
* A system of braille markings on lamposts to indicate stops and locations for visually impaired users.

Planning for diversity is a process that extends beyond designing appropriate systems to integrate social groups into the process. The planning process adopted by Curitiba's Urban Planning Group (UPG) gives priority to the social features and also includes consultation with communities. This community-based planning has led to the support of local people, and to high project use. Popular support for the project is evident from the fact that Jaime Lerner, the Mayor of Curitiba who initiated the project, has been elected to the post of provincial governor. *Successes* of the Curitiba planning process include the following:

* Two-thirds of the population now use Curitiba's public transport system (more than 1.3 million passengers per day).
* Of present direct-route bus users 28% previously travelled in their cars. This has helped secure savings of up to 25% of fuel consumption city-wide.
* The city has one of the lowest rates of ambient air pollution in Brazil, despite having more cars per capita than any other major Brazilian city.
* Residents spend only about 10% of their income on transport, which is a relatively low proportion by Brazilian standards.
* The whole public transport system operates with no direct financial subsidy, since the system itself is managed by a mixed capital company, and the buses are privately owned and operated under contract to the municipal government.

Various aspects of the Curitiba planning process need further attention.

For instance, social groups are not sufficiently disaggregated in Rabinovitch's description (1992) and thus the main focus of our case study based on his account is difference based on class, although the particular needs of some disabled people are also recognised. The fact that people in shanty towns on the city outskirts use bicycles or walk to the nearest bus route means that those who are unable to do so for whatever reason are excluded. In addition there is little reference to the informal transport networks and operators, and little suggestion as to how they are affected by the new system. If the planning process is to achieve further successes, these issues need resolution.

An integrated approach

It is important to realise that the success of Curitiba's transport system also rests on its integration with other urban development policies, including land use legislation and municipal land purchasing programmes. These have allowed the city to zone for higher-density development along roads served by the public transport system. This zoning and development not only took commercial pressure off the central city by encouraging new commercial developments outside the central city, along each structural axis, but also permitted the government to organise high-density housing programmes close to the transport axes; in all, some 17,000 lower-income families were located close to these (Rabinovitch, 1992: 65). Curitiba's effective integration of public housing policy with public transport planning demonstrates the creative role that integrated social planning can play in improving the quality of life for all urban dwellers.

Curitiba's UPG has creatively integrated the city's transport system into other social policies and programmes that have had a significant impact on the city's quality of life and commitment to social equity. While the details of the programmes themselves lie outside the scope of this chapter, the ways in which they intersect with Curitiba's transport system demonstrate the importance of taking a holistic approach to urban social development. Curitiba's transport policy intersects with policies on sanitation, environment, education and employment.

Sanitation *Favela* (shanty town) residents sell garbage in return for bus tickets. This sanitation programme ultimately stems from a transport problem, as *favelas* lack adequate access roads that trucks can use to remove garbage. Rather than invest in expensive road infrastructure, however, the city recognised *favela* residents' ability to walk or cycle to nearby roads where they could access public buses using their sanitation tickets. At the same time, the low-income areas' rubbish removal problem was solved.

Environment Green areas were set aside for park use and environmental education, and the city instituted special bus routes and fares to encourage weekend access to and use of these green areas' environmental programmes. The fuel savings also have an important and positive impact on pollution levels, suggesting that sustainability in an ecological case is compatible with including diverse groups in transport.

Education   Mobile classrooms using retired buses bring basic education programmes into low-income areas where residents' access to education has been a problem due to financial and time constraints, as well as prohibitive distances to mainstream educational sites. The potential exists for these classrooms to act as learning resources for diverse groups who are denied access to facilities such as libraries and information centres.

Employment   Not only does Curitiba's transport system improve workers' access to jobs in other areas of the city, but the road network itself allows formal and informal transport systems to flourish, thus generating transport-based employment in both sectors. The knock-on effects of improved access to transport can be particularly important for the many women who work at home and need to move their products to market for sale.

Through a transport planning process that recognised and incorporated diversity amongst social groups, it has been shown that the Curitiba system includes features that contribute directly to efficiency and equity. These include a focus on buses, the social fare and provision for the visually impaired, and features that make secondary contributions such as sanitation, income generation through 'garbage for tickets programmes' and improved education.

Implications for socially inclusive transport planning

It must be remembered that Curitiba is a relatively wealthy city. The problems faced by transport planners in Southern cities vary, and there is a need to set achievable and context-specific goals. However, this should not mean decreased commitment to including diverse social groups. The guidelines that emerge from Curitiba 'best practice' can be categorised as follows. These guidelines are intended to be flexible according to context and are also critical of the Curitiba model where it is lacking.

City transport for all   Effective and equitable transport systems must differentiate mobility from equitable access, since quantitative measures of transport coverage do not account for the ability of diverse social groups to take advantage of them (Levy, 1992). The factors that determine this inequitable access are complex and intertwined. For example, the price of services and the marginalisation of poor groups caused by inconvenient public transport routes combines with services that are not attractive to women because of the lack of seating for them or young children and fear of violence at stations. The result is that poor women with children, elderly people, and disabled people are doubly disadvantaged. Curitiba's equity programme centres on the social fare and the integration of public transport with low-income housing programmes to facilitate access for diverse groups. The success of these measures should not divert attention away from the need to increase the provision of infrastructure to those areas where it is lacking. In addition the safety issue for women must be looked at more closely, as should the issues surrounding people with disabilities other than visual impairment. In this way city transport can be for all citizens.

Participatory transport planning Participatory planning is a vital support for 'City Transport for All'. Use should be made of community input and indigenous systems, so that top-down intervention meets with bottom-up participation. There is no point in a new formal initiative that conflicts with established and important informal patterns of transport. Decentralisation, allied with improved administrative responsiveness, can lead to user-friendly services, accountability and appropriateness. Curitiba's sanitation programme was devised jointly by the municipality and *favela* residents. The cooperative solution encouraged sanitation disposal while facilitating residents' access to public transport, without incurring significant extra costs to the city. This is an example of the synergistic effect of participatory planning, but there is always room for consultation to reach effectively those diverse groups who have the least access to transport decision-making.

Integration of formal and informal transport As suggested above, if too much focus is placed upon the 'modernisation' of transport then there is a danger of applying UTP plans – developed in the North with reference to car-owning cultures – where they are not relevant. Equally, it is not sufficient to suggest that the ways in which people have been travelling for centuries are the only appropriate ones in a growing city. In Curitiba the choice of a flexible, surface solution of road networks over a more self-contained, controllable system such as light rail or subway, suggests an interest in facilitating existing informal transport systems while paving the way for eventual formalisation. Specifically, the free-flowing access roads parallel to the restricted express bus lanes allow informal transport providers such as 'gypsy' vans and carpools access to the city's transport market. More inventive solutions would be needed in other cities where informal transport traditionally plays a greater role.

Transport and the environment   A coherent transport system must balance many demands, including the growing problem of long-term environmental damage caused by fossil-fuel combustion. In cities in developing countries environmental problems are often created when the pedestrian or the cyclist is not provided for, public transport is under-resourced, or there is ineffective traffic management. Curitiba's combination of a pedestrian-only zone, express bus transport for short journeys, and an integrated interregional and intra-city bus system for longer journeys actively discourages the use of private cars. In addition, the municipality's creative use of public transport to encourage education in and use of environmentally protected areas is a model applicable to urban areas in developed and developing countries alike.

The primacy of context   Context-specific transport packages that take into account a diversity of needs and specifications are required. In this way economic and social repercussions can be tailored to benefit target groups. This involves adopting more than just a 'basic needs' approach to transport targeted at helping the poor get out of their poverty, such as improving the spatial distribution of infrastructure, rerouting services or providing subsidies. It means promoting flexible and adaptable transport systems that will evolve with cities by regulating for many different modes of transport, and not excluding small private operators or public provision. Thus diverse social goups are given transport choices through which they can have increased access to the 'City for All'. The Curitiba example shows how planning beyond the 'basic needs' of the community can be possible.

Conclusion

One idea behind the Curitiba model is that a 'sustainable city is one that spends the minimum and spares the maximum' (Rabinovitch, 1992: 72). Curitiba has shown that pragmatic solutions can be found and implemented to achieve this goal. From the perspective of 'City Transport for All', however, another important step taken in Curitiba was to recognise transport planning as an inherently social, as well as technical, exercise. Following this recognition, social planners were able to enable diverse social groups to participate in designing and integrating the transport system into broader equity goals. Thus the Curitiba model reinforces the importance of reflexive and appropriate transport planning with an emphasis on diversity.

References

Armstrong-Wright, A. (1990), *Public Transport in Third World Cities*, London: HMSO.
Dimitriou, H. (1990), *Transport Planning for Third World Cities*, London: Routledge.

Dimitriou, H. (1992), *Urban Transport Planning: a Developmental Approach*, London: Routledge.

Giddens, A. (1989), *Sociology*, Cambridge: Polity.

Khosa, M. (1992), 'Changing state policy and the black taxi industry in Soweto', in D. Smith (ed.), *The Apartheid City and Beyond*, London: Routledge.

Levy, C. (1992), 'Transport', in L. Ostergaard (ed.), *Gender and Development: a Practical Guide*, London: Routledge.

Mitlin, D. and D. Satterthwaite (1994), 'Transport and communications', in *Cities and Sustainable Development*, Global Forum '94, Manchester (background paper), London: Human Settlements Programme, International Institute for Environment and Development.

Pirie, G. (1992), 'Travelling under apartheid', in D. Smith (ed.), *The Apartheid City and Beyond*, London: Routledge.

Rabinovitch, J. (1992), 'Curitiba: towards sustainable urban development', *Environment and Urbanization*, 4(2), October.

Standing, G. (1989), 'Global feminization through flexible labour', in *World Development*, 17(7).

CHAPTER 15

Community Food Growing in the Inner City

Joanna Depledge

By the year 2000, over half the global population will live in urban areas – in the United Kingdom, along with most of the industrialised North, this transition has long since taken place. The emergence of an urbanised world is directing the attention of social policy-makers worldwide towards the worrying trends of rising urban environmental degradation and social deprivation. These problems are, of course, interlinked – dirty air, over-crowding and noise pollution in cities are as much social concerns as they are environmental. In the United Kingdom, the meeting of the environ-mental and social agendas is at its most vivid in the inner cities of older urban areas – particularly those affected by industrial decline – where a degraded environment is just one dimension of a complex pattern of economic and social deprivation. Growing awareness of the human impact of urban environmental problems has in turn catalysed the incorporation of projects with an environmental focus into the primarily socially oriented work of some of the many community-based organisations (CBOs) operating in the United Kingdom's inner cities. The case of Ashram Acres, an urban food-growing project in the inner-city ward of Sparkbrook in Birmingham, the United Kingdom's second largest city, provides an in-structive demonstration of how a project with explicit environmental goals – in this case urban food growing – can also be used as a vehicle to promote wider social objectives.

Sparkbrook: social and environmental challenges

Birmingham's development was based primarily in manufacturing industry, so that city's economy suffered greatly from the general trend of industrial decline experienced in the 1980s throughout Western Europe. Recently, Birmingham has begun to reinvent itself as a conference and special events centre, directing resources towards a number of 'prestige projects' – such as the new International Convention Centre – designed to attract visitors and investment to the area. Whilst the success of such projects in raising the profile of Birmingham and regenerating the Central Business District is widely acknowledged, there is some concern that the benefits have been unevenly spread and have not reached inner-city wards such as Sparkbrook where levels of social deprivation are highest.

Sparkbrook, a mainly residential and commercial area, is home to nearly twenty-six thousand people (Office of Population Censuses and Surveys, 1991).[1] Even compared to the multicultural population of Birmingham itself, Sparkbrook is an area distinguished by its ethnic diversity. Within this diversity there is differentiation between long-term residents and new arrivals, mostly from Bangladesh. Associated with this mix is linguistic and religious diversity – Arabic, Urdu, Gujarati and a variety of regional dialects are common first languages in Sparkbrook, while mosques, churches and Hindu and Sikh temples coexist in the area (Birmingham City Council, 1991). Sparkbrook is a youthful ward – one-third of its residents are aged 15 or under – and is characterised by large families: 18% of households have three or more dependent children under 18, compared to fewer than 8% in Birmingham as a whole.

One of the greatest problems facing Sparkbrook is unemployment – about one-third of residents are unemployed, rising to nearly 40% among Asian men and up to 50% in the 16–29 age group. Sparkbrook was hit hard by the dramatic fall in manual and unskilled jobs associated with Birmingham's industrial decline – over half the economically active population is defined as manual, partly skilled or unskilled. These figures conceal a flourishing informal economy, particularly in the garment industry, providing very low-paid part-time work for women. Wages as low as £2 an hour or £6 a garment – where two per day are produced – were commonly quoted by interviewees, whereas the average daily wage a cleaner would expect to earn is approximately £36 (Central Statistical Office, 1996).

Sparkbrook exhibits many social and environmental problems typical of inner-city areas, including infrastructural decay, poor housing and a lack of amenities. The ward is, for example, the most overcrowded in Birmingham in terms of persons per room. Almost 14% of households live in dwellings with more than one person per room, compared to only 4% in the city as a whole. Although 60% of Birmingham's homes are owner-occupied, in Sparkbrook 60% of residents live in rented, mostly council, housing. Sixty-nine per cent of households do not have access to a car and over 40% lack central heating. While Birmingham as a whole has 16% of its surface area devoted to leisure or recreational open space, an equivalent of 3.26 hectares per 1,000 people, in Sparkbrook this falls to 7%, or 1.53 hectares per 1,000 people.[2] Ironically, Sparkbrook also has some of the largest expanses of wasteland in Birmingham (Birmingham City Council, 1992).

Ashram Acres: background and objectives

It is in this context of social diversity within a setting of high rates of social and environmental deprivation that the work of Ashram Acres must be seen. The Ashram Acres urban food-growing project operates as a branch of the Ashram Community Services Project (ACSP), a CBO that has been active in Sparkbrook since 1976. The Ashram Acres food-growing project was started in 1981 in the derelict back gardens of the terraced-house premises of ACSP. Ashram Acres is staffed by a single paid worker and a contingent of volunteers and trainees. Funding comes mostly from the sale of produce and membership subscriptions – members pay £11 a month, which entitles them to pick crops freely from the gardens. Ashram Acres guards its independence fiercely. With the exception of support for the 'play schemes' discussed below, links between the Ashram Acres and the municipal authorities are restricted to routine environmental health checks on the premises and farm animals. Ashram Acres has a set of clearly defined organisational goals that reflect the project's specific attempt to link the meeting of social objectives with explicit environmental aims:

- growing European, Asian and Afro-Caribbean vegetables organically;
- reviving unused skills and enabling people to learn new skills by doing;
- reclaiming derelict land as a community garden and resource;
- creating meaningful work on local land; and
- providing a place for people to meet and work together, regardless of background.

Ashram Acres: linking social and environmental objectives

In order to meet its environmental and social goals, Ashram Acres engages in a multidimensional programme of work, engaging in a variety of formal and informal projects. Its key activities are detailed below.

Creating a 'liveable space' for all   Ashram Acres provides Sparkbrook with 0.3 hectares of open space over six back gardens, freely accessible for use by the community. While the majority of the area is laid out to vegetable beds, herb gardens and soft fruit, one of the gardens houses a wildlife reserve, including a pond and native flowers, bushes and tree species that in turn attract birds, butterflies and urban animals such as foxes and squirrels. In the context of Sparkbrook's dense built environment where access to recreational open space is limited, Ashram Acres acts as a valuable 'liveable space' for people, particularly children, women and the elderly, to have some contact with 'nature'. A key dimension here is safety – while Sparkbrook does have two parks, a number of female and elderly interviewees expressed fear at spending time there alone. The goal of environmental conservation is therefore intimately linked to the meeting of the practical needs of residents for an urban 'green oasis'.

Working with the elderly and young people   This facilitation of access to nature is extended by Ashram Acres through the organisation of free visits for children and residents of care centres for the elderly to country parks on the outskirts of Birmingham. Ashram Acres has also set up free 'play schemes' during the school holidays for over a hundred local children aged between 8 and 11. Unlike the rest of Ashram Acres' activities, these play schemes are supported financially by the local council. The activities of the play schemes reflect how Ashram Acres engages with Sparkbrook's cultural diversity through the medium of the environment. One planned project involves the collection of images of dragons from different cultures in order to construct dragon costumes to be worn by children in a litter collection project in a nearby park. These play schemes can be seen as responding to multiple local needs. The burden of childcare on women is eased in a context of large families and small housing units, while children are given the opportunity of engaging in constructive activities in a secure environment in an area where facilities for youth recreation are scarce. Perhaps most importantly, communication between children of diverse cultural, ethnic and linguistic backgrounds is promoted.

Cultivating for diversity   The produce grown by Ashram Acres further reflects how the project views the cultural diversity of Sparkbrook as a valuable resource and endeavours to respond to the different needs of the community. Ashram Acres explicitly aims to cultivate foodstuffs relevant to Asian and Afro-Caribbean diets – such as coriander, callaloo and fenugreek – and meets requests for new crops to be grown wherever possible. Customers – overwhelmingly women – can choose, pick and weigh their own produce from the gardens and haggle over the prices. The multiple motivations expressed for 'shopping' at Ashram Acres reflect the diversity of needs of the community. Pakistani and Bangladeshi women originating from rural backgrounds, for example, have a preference for choosing and picking themselves the food their household will consume. Many women come to Ashram Acres to obtain produce, particularly herbs, important to their diets but unavailable in mainstream shops, while others are attracted to the organic cultivation methods of Ashram Acres and the consequent positive health implications. The deliberately low prices charged are also important for low-income households.

Reclaiming wasted resources   Another interface between environmental and social goals at Ashram Acres is the project's explicit objective of making use of idle urban resources. The food-growing project was set up in neglected back gardens and represents a reclamation of the productive and aesthetic potential of land as a resource. This is especially significant in view of the prevalence of waste and derelict land in Sparkbrook. Ashram Acres also engages with the principle of sustainable resource consumption, operating low-energy cultivation techniques and a comprehensive waste recycling system. Organic waste is reclaimed as natural fertiliser while inorganic waste is systematically re-used, for example as construction material. Similarly, Ashram Acres deliberately aims to make use of wasted human resources, of particular relevance in the context of Sparkbrook's high unemployment. It attempts to go beyond the identification of unemployment as a problem. Rather it recognises the unused time and skills of people as a resource to be developed and adapted in a constructive and positive way. Many of Sparkbrook's residents, for example, possess a diversity of agricultural and craft skills developed in their country of origin which are capitalised on at Ashram Acres. In addition to organised 'work-ins' on Saturday mornings and formal volunteer and traineeship schemes, Sparkbrook's residents are free to participate in gardening at Ashram Acres at any time. Advice on cultivation techniques of non-European vegetables is sought by Ashram Acres workers and freely given by the local community. As well as representing a more efficient use of resources, Ashram Acres' valuing of the skills of Sparkbrook's residents is explicitly seen by the project as an important vehicle for the raising of self-esteem.

Community building In addition to its official food-growing project, Ashram Acres undertakes a variety of related socially oriented activities through its links with ACSP. One of its most valuable functions lies in building up links between the diverse cultural communities of Sparkbrook through acting as an informal meeting place and focal point for the exchange of local information. High unemployment, language barriers and traditional cultural practices mean that isolation is a common problem, particularly among women, and the gardens and buildings of Ashram Acres provide a safe environment for informal meetings. In conjunction with ACSP, Ashram Acres organises a variety of more formal events to celebrate special occasions such as religious festivals – a party is organised annually to celebrate the Muslim festival of Eid, for example, with separate rooms provided for women and men in response to the requirements of the Muslim community. In 1996, a series of special events was held in partnership with the local council and other CBOs operating in Sparkbrook to celebrate International Women's Day. As well as representing an important opportunity for social interaction, the celebration was used as a vehicle to address the particular health needs of women through presentations, information and advice sessions and group discussion.

Addressing diverse needs A particular strength of Ashram Acres lies in its flexibility of response to the diverse and changing needs of the local community. The structure of the project as a small-scale CBO operating on a long-term permanent basis at the most local level means that it has built up strong networks of trust within Sparkbrook. The project therefore plays a key role as an informal advice and information centre, of particular importance in a context where many residents are wary of official structures and fear racism and discrimination. There is, for example, a legal team offering free advice, in particular on immigration and welfare matters. The staff and volunteers at both Ashram Acres and ACSP also provide a free interpretation and translation service in many of the languages spoken in Sparkbrook, which is widely used for help in writing official letters, filling in forms and for translation assistance during medical appointments. This service is particularly valuable for women as cultural restrictions tend to reduce their opportunities for learning formal English, while traditional childcare responsibilities mean that they come into more frequent contact with such official structures as the education, welfare and medical authorities. In addition, the projects deal with a constant flow of requests for help to meet practical needs – the Ashram Acres van, for example, is regularly used as a free taxi service to transport families without cars to special events such as wedding and funerals, while heaters were distributed to households without central heating during the winter.

Obstacles and challenges

In spite of Ashram Acres' long-term involvement in the community and its deliberate aim of engaging with Sparkbrook's diversity, the project is aware that some sections of the population are not being reached. Most significant among these are certain groups of Muslim women for whom the cultural and religious traditions practised by their households mean that it is not possible for them to attend public places. The needs of some of these women are addressed by Ashram Acres and ACSP – female workers will visit women at home, to help fill in forms, for example, although even this can attract disapproval. However, workers acknowledge that there is an unknown number of 'hidden' Muslim women with whom they have no contact. In order to reach these, it would be necessary to have more trained female – preferably Muslim – community workers. Another group not fully integrated into Ashram Acres is the disabled – to reach the gardens, narrow corridors and flights of stairs must be negotiated.

Ashram Acres and ACSP suffer from the ever-present problem of lack of resources. Workers at Ashram Acres expressed frustration over the inability of the project to expand and diversify its activities to meet more of the needs of Sparkbrook. The coordinator, for example, noted how Sparkbrook has many derelict open spaces that could be used to extend

the food-growing project, but she does not have the time, staff or resources to investigate how these could be acquired for Ashram Acres.
Following on from this, the impact of Ashram Acres on the problems of
Sparkbrook is necessarily limited. The local scale and community-based
nature of its work – while a strength in allowing flexibility and responsiveness – is also a weakness in confining the project's impact to a small area.
The problems faced by Sparkbrook are largely a function of wider national
and international forces. Although the work of CBOs such as Ashram
Acres does contribute to improving the quality of life of Sparkbrook's
residents, the long-term structural problems of unemployment, racial
discrimination and environmental degradation remain.

The future

Despite the problems identified above, Ashram Acres and ACSP have
ambitious plans for the future scaling up of their work. They are making
a bid to obtain a share of a European Development Fund grant recently
earmarked for community development with ethnic minorities in the area.
Together, Ashram Acres and ACSP plan to acquire and redevelop an
abandoned neighbouring house in order to expand their activities and to
equip their buildings and gardens to make them accessible to the disabled.

From an organisational perspective, Ashram Acres and ACSP are currently in a period of transformation. Ashram Acres is presently attempting
to strengthen its links with other community-based environmental projects
in the area and to investigate the potential for partnership. This is particularly positive as there are a large number of CBOs operating independently
in Sparkbrook with little contact between them, despite their broadly shared
goals. A more coordinated approach and the pooling of knowledge and
resources could lead to a greater impact on Sparkbrook's problems. In
addition, Ashram Acres and ACSP are in the process of operationalising
more explicitly their stated commitment to local democracy and participation. The projects plan to establish a more formal management and
policy-making structure to go beyond the present *ad hoc* and reactive nature
of decision-making. This structure would include more participatory
mechanisms to allow all individuals involved in Ashram Acres and ACSP
– paid staff, volunteers, trainees, clients and the community as a whole –
to contribute to decisions on the running of the organisations.

Conclusion

There are important lessons to be learnt from this exploration of the
work of Ashram Acres in Sparkbrook. By integrating its environmental
and social objectives, Ashram Acres provides an instructive example of
how the elusive concept of 'sustainable development' can work in practice

at the local scale. Furthermore, its engagement with Sparkbrook's diversity – particularly gender, age and ethnicity – in every aspect of its work reveals the importance of recognising the multiplicity of different needs in inner-city areas. Diversity must be seen positively as a valuable resource and dimension of vitality within a community. The experience of Ashram Acres also highlights the importance for CBOs working in inner cities to build up trust through a long-term commitment to the area by operating at the most grassroots level, and through flexibility and responsiveness to the diversity of needs of the community. By enabling Sparkbrook's residents to take control of a small piece of their own environment, Ashram Acres has created an oasis of environmental and social regeneration within an otherwise bleak inner-city landscape. The challenge is to find ways of replicating and extending this 'best practice' example as part of the process of building 'A City for All'.

Notes

1. All figures, unless otherwise stated, are from the national Population Census 1991.
2. Personal communication, Department of Planning and Architecture, Birmingham City Council.

References

Birmingham City Council (1991), *Ethnic Groups, Census Topic Report.*
Birmingham City Council (1992), *The Environment in Birmingham, Green Action Plan.*
Central Statistical Office (1996), *Social Trends*, London: HMSO.
Office of Population Censuses and Surveys (1991), *Small Area Statistics*, Sparkbrook.

Box 4.1

Experiencing Disability in the City

Joyce Malombe

There are physical barriers to my participation in the city. I will illustrate how these exclude me and impede my effectiveness in what I do, even though these ideas are commonly rejected. Comments such as 'recognising the difficulties of disabled people is common sense' deny the problems we face and professionals are as guilty of this as are others.

If you are disabled you are physically and socially excluded by physical obstacles. This gives rise to the feeling that *you* are the problem. For instance, offices in Nairobi, Kenya, where I'm from, are often inaccessible – this includes almost all government offices. If they do have lifts there are often stairs leading to the lifts. This means that people using wheelchairs can't get into the building. In order to gain access they may have to suffer the indignities of being carried into the building or having to crawl into the building. Why should we allow ourselves to be treated like this? If I make a noise then I may lose my job. This results in an effective silencing of disabled people. Disabled people are seen as trouble. In the university where I work there are no ramps and I work on the third floor. I have been asked several times: 'What is the issue?'

If you have a job then it can be difficult. The health services in the university have seven stairs and they were designed by people from my own Department of Architecture and Planning, people who work with me every day. The consultation room for health services is on the first floor, again making it difficult for people like me to reach it. Lack of access to office space excludes disabled people. Where there are ramps, they are often too steep and chairs are impossible to control on the slope. These ramps are meant for carrying goods and show how planners are not thinking about people.

I have noticed how in some developing countries it is fashionable to have steps leading up to the entrance to a building. It looks better and higher but makes access very difficult for us. Talking of conferences, I always have to worry about what it'll be like at times like this! Will I be able to get in? This can lead to a situation where you don't want to go, to even move in case you can't get there. I have been stuck in lifts several times. Even in the NGO forum here, people have had to be carried in and that is really embarrassing for them.

BOX 4.1   179

Access to housing in Kenya is most often determined by the ability to pay, and that determines the type of housing you will have. Newly built housing such as flats and bungalows, which may be more appropriate to our needs, is the most expensive, putting it out of the reach of disabled people. I myself have been in a temporary flat since 1990 as there is nothing more suitable and affordable for me. We need to ask: 'What happens to disabled people who don't have a voice in the city?' I am aware that I am one of the lucky ones.

In public transportation, there is no consideration for people with disabilities. In Kenya they have just raised the levels of all the buses because of the deep potholes in the roads which cause daily damage. This has made buses inaccessible to me and to others. Now if I want to catch a bus I have to find someone to help me on with a push. At a recent conference in Kenya in 1992, there was an accessible bus but it was withdrawn from service after the conference was over, a clear illustration that it is often a case of words and not of action.

If we are lucky enough to have private transport, parking in the city is a real problem as disabled people may need more space to leave or enter a car. I have left the office and then missed meetings as I can't find anywhere to park. There should be parking for disabled people but it just doesn't exist. Even at the UN HQ in Nairobi, the closest parking to the building is reserved for diplomats. Public parking is much further away and people get very tired with the walk. When I ask the guard if I can park closer, although there are spaces, he will not let me in. Pavements are irregular and this results in me falling most times I try to walk anywhere. I have a motorised wheelchair, but in reality it is a monument, it sits inside my house. I never use it as you have to drive in the road and this is very dangerous indeed in Nairobi.

I travel by air very often and so far have used at least twenty-five airlines and they are almost all a nightmare. It starts at the entrance to the airport with the attitude of people dealing with wheelchairs. In Africa we have to identify our luggage before flying and no one will go down the stairs on to the tarmac to identify your luggage for you. Then you have to climb the stairs to get to the plane. There is an attitude of 'What are you doing here if you are disabled?' Some of the staff quarrel with me, throwing the blame back at me. This shows the insensitivity of people who feel that as disabled people, we shouldn't travel. Some airlines are better for people with disabilities but people arranging travel don't often recognise the need for disabled people to be flexible in their travelling arrangements.

There are social barriers as well, such as rejection by parents in the African context. Disability is seen as a malfunction, that something that went wrong. People often panic when you move into a housing set-up. Why are people so scared of me? No one will believe that you can actually do something. Many disabled children end up not attending school because of the ensuing physical and social pressures there. Discrimination in employment is rampant. People seem to think that if you come to work for an organisation or firm you will cause problems for them. Outside of the university in which I work, life is far more difficult for disabled people. You have to cope or find a way of dealing with it. In the medical service we have to finance our own physical aids. It even says in the Kenyan Constitution that if you are disabled you cannot become president of our country!

In conclusion, we need to reorient our thinking. Accessibility is a right, not a privilege. We need to have a say in what needs to be done, to live independently. We need different initiatives to reach disabled people. Organisations are used to talking for disabled people and it's about time we got a voice and spoke for ourselves. International organisations and donors should set a good example. There is double trouble being a woman and disabled. We need role models. We need the UN to employ more disabled people. Where are the disabled people in the UN system? International agencies should push national governments to further equality for disabled people. Above all, we have a right to be in the city.

PART FIVE

Sustaining Urban Environments, Health and Well-being

CHAPTER 16

Water Supply and Sanitation

Julie Jarman

I go to collect water four times a day, in a 20-litre clay jar. It's hard work! When I first started collecting water I was about 7 and I used to do it with another girl, we carried a bucket between us on a stick. In those days we used to have to walk over a mile to fetch water. Now there is a tapstand about ten minutes from my home, which has made life easier. I've never been to school as I have to help my mother with her washing work so we can earn enough money. Our house doesn't have a bathroom. I wash myself in the kitchen once a week, on Sunday. At the same time I change my clothes and wash the dirty ones. When I need the toilet I have to go down to the river in the gully behind my house: I usually go with my friends as we're only supposed to go after dark when people can't see us. In the daytime I use a tin inside the house and empty it out later. I like playing hopscotch with my friends, but we have very little time to play (Elmas Kassa, a 13-year-old girl from the IHAUDP project area of Addis Ababa. Quotation provided by Catherine Johnson, WaterAid).

This chapter argues that water supply and sanitation provision have an important role to play in poverty reduction in urban areas of the Third World. There is widespread criticism of highly engineered systems based on expensive imported technology which is difficult to maintain. The need for more appropriate and participatory solutions has long been accepted but not often implemented. The urban services approach based on the belief that water is a human right has not led to the majority of the urban poor receiving an adequate service. The water and sanitation sector can benefit from new understandings of urban poverty, which see vulnerability and diversity as key concepts and which recognise the heterogeneous nature of urban poverty; the need for an integrated and intersectoral approach; and the need for qualitative methodologies and the need to involve the poor in projects. What such understandings may give rise to in practice is illustrated by the work of the Integrated Holistic Approach Urban Development Project (IHAUDP) from Addis Ababa, evaluated in the case study below. The chapter concludes with implications for future policy and suggestions for further research.

Water in the city

In the cities of the Third World rapid urbanisation is causing an increased demand for water, but as a resource, water is decreasing in both quantity and quality. Mexico City, having over-pumped the Mexico Valley aquifer, pumps its water from the Cutzamala river at massive economic and environmental cost. Increased pollution by industrial effluent, domestic waste water and storm runoff is affecting water quality, while the city faces the prospect of exhausting its supply by the year 2000 (Black, 1994).

In 1985 the World Health Organisation estimated that 25% of the developing world's urban population had no access to a safe water supply. A little over half have access to adequate sanitation and an even greater number lack adequate means to dispose of waste water (Hardoy, Cairncross and Satterthwaite, 1990). Even these statistics are often based on inaccurate government estimates. Detailed research in slum and squatter settlements presents a much worse picture. Amongst slum dwellers in São Paulo only 2% have any form of sanitation (ibid.). In Jakarta less than a quarter of the city's population has direct connections to a piped water system and 30% depend solely on water vendors. In Lima, Peru, a poor family pays a vendor 21 times the amount paid by a middle-class family with a household connection (Briscoe, 1986). Money spent on buying water can take up to 40% of household income (UNICEF, 1994). Much of the population has to use drainage canals for bathing, laundering and defecation. Around 30% of solid waste is not collected. Thus garbage ends up in canals and rivers and clogs drainage channels, causing flooding during the rainy season (ibid.).

This chapter adopts the broad definition of urban water supply and sanitation suggested by Harpham, Lusty and Vaughan (1988), covering water supply, rainwater drainage, solid waste disposal, grey water (sullage) disposal and excreta disposal. As the example of Jakarta shows, these elements are inextricably linked in the urban environment. For example, an improved water supply alone can actually create public health problems by increasing sullage and exacerbating waste water disposal problems.

Two main physical elements distinguish the urban and rural environments and make water disposal and sanitation in urban areas a particular problem. First, shortage of space coupled with high population density is a problem for sullage and human waste disposal: latrines quickly fill and overflow. Second, poor slum and squatter settlements are commonly found on low-lying, flood-prone or low-infiltration capacity land with a high water table. This means water cannot drain quickly into the earth and lies around in stagnant pools, which become breeding grounds for mosquitos. Most latrines are inappropriate in this situation as they quickly fill and flood and there is no seepage from the pit into the surrounding soils (Harpham, Lusty and Vaughan, 1988).

Water as an urban service

The traditional approach to water supply and sanitation provision in Third World cities is the urban services approach. Related to the basic needs approach to development, the urban services approach identifies lack of access to basic services such as water, health care and education as both a cause and a symptom of poverty. Services should therefore be provided as a basic need and right.

Lack of water and sanitation also causes problems that impact on the wider society of which the poor are a part. The fear of infectious diseases such as cholera, combined with the fact that water is a natural monopoly, provides the rationale for a state-subsidised, centralised water and sanitation supply based around mains water and sewers. Such public health engineering solutions, based on nineteenth-century European precepts, have been severely criticised as inappropriate. The operation and maintenance of highly engineered systems, based on expensive imported technology, is beyond the ability of many municipalities. As a result water and sanitation facilities are often not functioning to capacity (Tabibzadeh, Maxwell and Rossi-Espagnet, 1989). For example, in Manila 58% of the water expensively channelled into city pipes is unaccounted for (Black, 1994). The lack of an integrated approach to sanitation creates further problems, with the impact of water supply schemes on drainage and sanitation rarely considered (Kirke and Arthur, 1984).

Such centralised systems reach only a minority of city dwellers, as mains water and sewerage are concentrated in middle-class and better-off areas. In addition, new investment tends to be in existing serviced areas and therefore continues to ignore the needs of people in poverty (ibid.). In developing countries the receivers of services are estimated by the World Bank to pay an average of 35% of the costs. In effect, governments heavily subsidise the urban elite (Black, 1994), especially as cost sharing and user charges increasingly characterise investment in low-income areas.

Kirke and Arthur (1984) make the following suggestions for policy: the minimum basic needs of low-income areas should be met before demands for increased service of middle- and high-income areas; water tariffs should be set so that there is no government subsidy; appropriate, low-cost and local technologies that the poor can operate and maintain should be used; and water supply should be considered together with drainage and sanitation. They argue that by increasing revenue from cost-covering tariffs, and by reducing water wastage, the existing supply could be redistributed to reach all sectors of the urban population. Others have highlighted the importance of community participation to ensure both long-term sustainability and the suitability of projects for the needs of beneficiaries (Harpham, Lusty and Vaughan, 1988).

Such criticisms and policy prescriptions are widely accepted by both governments and donors, and some urban basic services programmes have shown affordable and appropriate solutions (Black, 1994). Despite this, new, highly engineered construction is often still favoured (Tabibzadeh, Maxwell and Rossi-Espagnet, 1989). There is frequently a gap between official rhetoric and reality. Eighty per cent of investments in the sector are still allocated to high-cost systems, while less than 5% of donor aid is spent on low-cost solutions (UNICEF, quoted in Black, 1994).

The urban services approach gives water and sanitation an important role in urban poverty reduction, but the conceptualisation of water as a human right has not led to the majority of the urban poor receiving an adequate service. On the contrary, the urban poor have remained largely unserved. The problem continues to be the way in which such projects are implemented. Despite a widespread understanding of the importance of involving beneficiaries and of affordable and appropriate technology, many projects are still implemented in a top-down way, using high-cost and sophisticated technologies. These criticisms are among the issues addressed by new understandings of urban poverty.

Poverty as a process

New approaches to urban poverty can be broadly characterised as qualitative and participative. They accept a wide, non-material, social definition of poverty related to a concept of well-being (Wratten, 1995). Moreover, poverty is seen as important primarily for moral and ethical reasons, with a stress on social justice. Poverty is viewed as a process, not a state. As poverty is subjective the poor should establish their own qualitative indicators for its measurement, with a focus on how people move in and out of poverty on the basis of their vulnerabilities, capabilities and exposure to risk. By taking the priorities and perspectives of the poor as a basis for policy and planning they cease to be the problem and become part of the solution.

Robert Chambers (1989, 1995) has challenged the parameters of the debate around poverty. He stresses the importance of moving away from an income-based view of poverty towards an understanding of vulnerability and lack of security as key concepts. Chambers argues that in order to survive and participate in their society, poor people manage a complex portfolio of tangible and intangible assets. They create complex and diverse livelihoods based on their assets. They are, however, vulnerable to shocks and crises, which may be external, such as war or drought, or internal, such as an accident or illness. Poor people emphasise the importance of security, self-respect and independence as well as material sufficiency, thus challenging economists' exclusive focus on income as a measure of poverty (ibid.).

Beall (1993, 1995) and Wratten (1995) relate Chambers' approach directly to the urban poor. Five main concepts can be identified as being of particular relevance to the role of water and sanitation in urban poverty reduction: access to assets and vulnerability to risk; the heterogeneous nature of urban poverty; the need for an integrated and intersectoral approach; participation of poor people in projects; and the qualitative nature of poverty. The following case study illustrates what these concepts may look like when translated into practice in relation to water and sanitation.

The Integrated Holistic Approach Urban Development Project (IHAUDP), Addis Ababa

IHAUDP was set up in its present form in 1989, but is based on a project that was supported by the international Norwegian NGO, Redd Barna, and ran from 1981 to 1986. The project has received funding from 48 donors since its inception, the main ones being Caritas, a consortium of English NGOs, ODA, Swedish Save the Children, GOAL and Catholic Relief Services (CRS). The project uses an integrated approach to target the poor in one of the most deprived areas of Addis Ababa. It has many components, one of which is the provision of water and sanitation. The project has operated in the context of a deteriorating economic situation and political instability and yet has made significant achievements.

IHAUDP works in Teklehaimanot Wereda, an area of the city that includes *kebeles* 30, 41, 42 and 43. (A *kebele* is a subdivision of the city equivalent to a ward.) The four *kebeles* have a total population of 36,373, of whom more than 35% are below 15 years of age. A majority of households are female-headed as a result of years of armed conflict. In 1989 92% of households had no water point inside the compound and relied on communal water points, which were often not working. Seventy-two per cent of residents shared latrines, with 40–50 people to each pit latrine. Diarrhoea was common in all children: one survey showed that 48% had suffered an episode of diarrhoea within the space of one week.

The project started by carrying out a three-month consultation process, identifying the needs of the community. The community prioritised their needs, with housing, environmental health and improved roads and alleys coming first. In response to the survey the project sought funding and employed five staff members to start implementation work; this number had increased to 44 in 1996.

The project divides each *kebele* into ten zones, which are in turn divided into neighbourhood groups of about twenty-five households (approximately one hundred and fifty people) who elect 15 people to form a neighbourhood committee. This means that around 10% of the population are directly involved in decision-making, implementation and management of the project through committee membership. The committees have subgroups, which take responsibility for each of the three main components of the project: community development, physical upgrading and primary health care.

Project staff work together with community members, who are sometimes paid for work on building houses or making the alleys and sometimes volunteer. The activities are as diverse as a feeding programme for malnourished children, vaccinating dogs against rabies, providing a library and an income-generation unit, and provision of transit kitchens and houses while new ones are built. The water, sanitation and environmental health part of the project has been identified as a priority by the community throughout, and has proved successful in both implementation and management terms.

Achievements of the project

The achievements of the main activities relating directly to water and sanitation over the six-year period January 1990–December 1995 are:

1. Excreta disposal:

- 88 communal latrines constructed.
- 18 communal latrines repaired. These latrines have between 2 and 10 cubicles and each cubicle is assigned to 3 families. The project aimed to construct more latrines but there is a problem of not enough land.
- Suction truck for emptying latrines provided. It emptied 4,263 latrines (710 per year on average). There is a small charge levied for this service, which covers 39% of the cost.

2. Water supply:

- 5 water posts constructed, each with 6 taps.
- Clothes-washing stands are provided.
- 3 public shower buildings constructed, each with several cubicles.
- 4,700 jerrycans for carrying water provided.

3. Solid waste disposal:

- 676 solid waste bins (each shared by 4 households).
- 8 skips provided and emptied.

4. Rainwater and sullage drainage:

- 6,297 metres of roads constructed.
- 2,057 metres of footpaths constructed. These include drainage ditches and are constructed using the labour of the poorest, often demobilised soldiers.
- 288 households recycle at least 10% of their sullage for vegetable growing.

5. Hygiene education:

• The project has a dynamic group of 30 education extension workers or 'yellow girls' who carry out hygiene education as well as other community mobilisation work. As a result of part of their efforts, an average of 6,300 people participated in 22 cleaning campaigns per year.

This project illustrates the way five main concepts identified above as part of the new approaches to poverty can be identified and addressed by the water and sanitation sector.

Water as an asset

Water is an important asset for the poor, both because it is essential for living and because it has productive potential as a raw material. Provision of water releases the money, time and energy of urban poor people: important assets that can be reallocated to more productive or creative activities. IHAUDP has several income-generating projects, including a block-making unit that is dependent on access to water. People also cultivate vegetable gardens with waste water. Employment as tapstand attendants and sanitary guards has been created. Projects should consider the adverse impact of water provision on water sellers and where possible involve them as tapstand or bath attendants.

Water and sanitation are important preconditions for good health, and protecting the health of the poor helps to reduce their vulnerability. Chambers (1989) has identified a healthy body as one of the most important assets of poor people: a sick adult moves from being an asset to being a heavy liability needing to be fed, clothed and housed. Cairncross and Feachem (1983) argue convincingly that in terms of health benefits, water quantity is more important than quality. The urban poor are therefore forced to make a trade-off between health on the one hand and money and time spent on obtaining a sufficient quantity of water on the other. Provision by IHAUDP of sufficient water close to people's homes has resulted in health improvements. Of the 61 deaths reported in the quarter October–December 1995, none was from water- and sanitation-related disease.

The direct impact on disease and death rates of water or sanitation in isolation has been hard to prove. It is clear, however, that to maximise the health benefits of improved water supply and sanitation their provision should be accompanied by hygiene education (Black, 1994). The project provides a good level of hygiene education through the 'yellow girls' at a household level and through community meetings and health staff at clinics.

Urban poverty is heterogeneous

Beall (1993, 1995) argues that a concentration on the urban household obscures differences among household members. Lack of water and sanitation impacts differentially on individuals according to factors such as gender and age. Women are generally responsible for the collection of water and the domestic tasks that need adequate supplies of water, such as laundry, cooking and cleaning. Women also care for family members who become sick from water- and sanitation-related diseases and become debilitated themselves: finding enough water to wash clothes poses a real problem when children are continually suffering from diarrhoea. It is therefore women who suffer the most when water is difficult to obtain (Mitlin and Satterthwaite, 1994). The time women use for collecting water could be released for income generation, for childcare or for participation in social or organisational activities. Briscoe (1986) argues that increasing women's available time by reducing domestic burdens is the most important factor in improving children's welfare. As a result of the civil war many women have been left to deal with the burden of providing for the family alone: the majority of households in the IHAUDP project area are headed by women. The project therefore has a stated aim of ensuring that women are a major focus and are involved in decision-making. This includes decisions over the siting and management of water, bathing and sanitation facilities.

Water and sanitation have important impacts on children's welfare by affecting their health, nutrition and access to education. Children are particularly vulnerable to diarrhoea and dehydration caused by insufficient or dirty water and their health also suffers from the burden of carrying water, which damages the head, neck and spine (Curtis, 1986). Children's nutritional status is affected by the incapacitation of adult earners from water- and sanitation-related disease, and such incapacitation is common. Cairncross (1990) and Pryer (1989) have shown from research in an urban slum that households where an adult earner has been sick during the previous month are two and a half times more likely than others to have a severely malnourished child. Collecting water and other domestic work often results in girl children being absent from school, or dropping out altogether, with implications for their future work prospects. The welfare and health of children are major focuses for IHAUDP. Improving the welfare of children is a central aim of all their work, including the water and sanitation elements.

The heterogeneous nature of poverty means that there may be certain groups, such as street children or the disabled, who have particular needs. For example, the plight of street children is worsened by the difficulty they have in finding places in which to wash and defecate and in obtaining clean drinking water (Mitlin and Satterthwaite, 1994). The disabled may need extra resources for a private latrine. The project works with many different groups and has an extensive programme offering services, including income generation, to elderly people, prostitutes, people with disabilities, and mentally ill children and their mothers. One of the main aims of this side of the work is to establish community awareness of the issues that such people face and to give them a sense of belonging, respect and dignity. The word 'holistic' in the title of the project carries with it the implication not only that all a person's needs and problems must be addressed, but also that all people within the community must define development priorities and participate in achieving them.

Partners in the city

Beall (1993) stresses the importance of listening to the views of urban people in poverty in devising policies to address the problem of poverty in Third World cities. She therefore identifies the importance of capacity building in order for people in poverty to participate in interactions between the state and civil society and for policy-making to move into the realm of public action. The poor can be active partners in the design, delivery and management of water and sanitation services and thus ensure their sustainability.

IHAUDP was established as a community-based, bottom-up and participatory project. The project began with a large survey to establish community priorities, within which environmental health, including latrines, showers and water, was second only to housing. Although these priorities differed from those of the professionals who conducted the survey (for example, the professionals did not identify lanes and alleys), the project based its objectives and planning on the priorities of the community. The extent to which the community has a sense of ownership is apparent in the fact that, during Mengistu's regime when there were riots in the area, all other public or community buildings were destroyed but the project offices were left standing. The skills in participatory techniques and the commitment of the 'yellow girls', who have a recognised status, working at the interface between the project and the community, have enabled the beneficiaries to be involved throughout the project. They have helped to train elected zonal coordinators and established the grassroots neighbourhood groups, which coordinate community involvement in the different activities.

The water taps, communal latrines, showers and drainage ditches provided are proving to be sustainable in terms of operation and maintenance as a result of good community management. For example, user fees have been locally established and are waived for the poorest who cannot pay (such as the very old or sick who are living without support). The project is in the process of handing over complete control of all aspects to a board elected by the community. The community leaders, grassroots neighbourhood groups and project workers have represented the views of the community in meetings and seminars with government officials and policy-makers.

An integrated and intersectoral approach

Beall (1993, 1995) and Wratten (1995) both advocate an integrated and intersectoral approach to urban poverty reduction. The concept of vulnerability highlights the fact that poverty cannot be solved by one intervention alone. The above discussion has touched on how water and sanitation are relevant to consumption and production, health, education, time and energy, income and a sense of dignity. Other sectors such as health, housing and employment have an equally broad relationship to poverty. Ill health and lack of access to basic services increase the likelihood of getting into debt, leaving the poor very vulnerable. A woman may have access to water, giving her the time and raw material for a beer-brewing business, but she still lacks access to credit for buying brewing drums and she still needs childcare. The problems of the poor are interwoven to create a fabric of poverty and the solutions must therefore tackle many issues at the same time.

As the title of the project highlights, this is precisely the approach IHAUDP has adopted. There is a broad spectrum of activities within which poor people decide what priority to give to water and sanitation. In addition, the project has given importance to solid waste disposal and sullage drainage as part of an integrated approach to sanitation, areas which many urban services schemes ignore.

Qualitative poverty

One of the two major objectives of the project is to change the quality of life of the community. The project identified poverty, leading to a poor quality of life, as the main cause of the fatalistic attitude common amongst the community. The bins and skips, latrines and suction truck, roads, alleys and ditches that are in place have resulted in a major improvement in the quality of the environment. This in itself motivates people to keep their surroundings clean, and there is now safer and cleaner space for children to play in. Privacy for defecation and bathing has added considerably to the quality of life of the community. For instance, women no longer suffer a high incidence of kidney infections caused by urine retention due to lack of access to a private place to relieve themselves.

Conclusion

The qualitative approach to urban poverty highlights the importance of involving the poor in integrated approaches to poverty reduction. A focus on the heterogeneous nature of poverty requires holistic responses that involve the diverse groups and individuals that go to make up a city. When this approach is applied to the water and sanitation sector it has implications for policy and lessons for project implementation.

Water and sanitation projects should be implemented as part of an integrated approach to poverty reduction. In order to reduce poverty it is necessary to work in bottom-up and empowering ways with poor urban communities. Such methods will lead to full community participation which, together with appropriate, low-cost and local technologies, will ensure the sustainability of water and sanitation projects. Water-related diseases are an important cause of illness, and hence vulnerability, of both adults and children. Water and sanitation projects should therefore maximise their health benefits by always including hygiene education and by ensuring that communities have access to enough water. In designing water supply projects the use of water as a productive asset should be borne in mind. Women, as the main collectors and users of water, should be involved in the design and management of projects but constraints on their time should be allowed for.

Areas for further research

As well as these immediate implications there is need for further research to be carried out in the following areas:

- the specific water and sanitation needs of vulnerable groups such as the elderly and disabled;
- the amount of time and energy women save in urban areas when water is provided, and how that time is reallocated by them;
- how the community regards the more qualitative benefits of water and sanitation, such as privacy and its spiritual value;
- whether there is competition between domestic and commercial use of water that impacts badly on women's access, and whether commercial use of water is gendered;
- the effect of water projects on water sellers; and
- the impact of withdrawal of agency involvement on the long-term operation and maintenance of project activities.

The Integrated Holistic Approach Urban Development Project shows that many of these policies can work in practice. It is important, therefore, to analyse how the project can be replicated, and to look at what factors are essential for such an approach to succeed in other contexts.

Note

I would like to thank IHAUDP for allowing me to use their project as a case study. All the information on IHAUDP has come directly from their project documents.

References

Beall J. (1993), 'Focus on urban poverty', *DPU News*, 29, August: 2–3.

Beall, J. (1995), 'Social security and social networks among the urban poor in Pakistan', *Habitat International*, 19(4): 427–45.

Black, M. (1994), *Mega-Slums: The Coming Sanitary Crisis*, London: WaterAid.

Briscoe, J. (1986), 'Water supply and health in developing countries: selective primary health care revisited', in J. Tulchin (ed.), *Health, Habitat and Development*, Boulder, CO: Lynne Rienner, pp. 105–21.

Chambers, R. (1989), 'Vulnerability: how the poor cope', *IDS Bulletin*, 20(2): 1–9.

Chambers, R. (1995), 'Poverty and livelihoods: whose reality counts?', *Environment and Urbanization*, 7(1): 173–204.

Curtis, V. (1986), *Women and the Transport of Water*, London: IT Publications.

Hardoy, J., S. Cairncross and D. Satterthwaite (1990), *The Poor Die Young: Housing and Health in Third World Cities*, London: Earthscan.

Harpham, T., T. Lusty and P. Vaughan (eds) (1988), *In the Shadow of the City: Community Health and the Urban Poor*, Oxford: Oxford University Press.

Kirke, J. and J. Arthur (1984), 'Water supply issues' in P. J. Richards and A. M. Thompson (eds), *Basic Needs and the Urban Poor*, London: Croom Helm, pp. 123–50.

Mitlin, D. and D. Satterthwaite (1994), *Cities and Sustainable Development*, background paper for Global Forum '94, Manchester, London: Human Settlements Programme, International Institute for Environment and Development.

Pryer, J. (1989), 'When breadwinners fall ill: preliminary findings from a case study in Bangladesh', *IDS Bulletin*, 20(2): 49–57.

Tabibzadeh, I., R. Maxwell and A. Rossi-Espagnet (eds) (1989), *Spotlight on the Cities*, Geneva: World Health Organisation.

UNICEF (1994), *The State of the World's Children 1994*, New York: UNICEF.

Wratten, E. (1995), 'Conceptualizing urban poverty', *Environment and Urbanization*, 7(1), April: 1–36.

CHAPTER 17

The Impact of Modern Warfare: The Case of Iraq

Gautam Banarji

Modern warfare is characterised by the destruction of infrastructure such as electrical power installations, telecommunications facilities, major roadways and bridges. Urban social sectors are hit by the incapacitation of water sewerage systems that are dependent on electrical supply, leading to a spiralling chain of health hazards. The situation is worsened by the disruption of transport and communications systems and its effect on food production, distribution and consumption. In the case of Iraq, we witness a classic case of a depressed economy caused by the combined effect of the Gulf war and the economic sanctions still in force. The principal sufferers are urban people in poverty, especially women and children. The country seems to have been relegated to a pre-industrial age, but with all the characteristics of post-industrial dependency. This contrasts starkly with the peace of economic development and welfare witnessed in the decade immediately preceding the war. This chapter aims to broaden our horizon to an understanding of the complex and ever-changing definition of conflict. At the same time it raises questions about a new imperialistic design in a destabilising role assumed by the international community. Even if this is justified as an effort to restructure regional systems so as to align them to a global economy, it has to be pointed out that somewhere in the process the interests of the individual get relegated to the background, and that those who suffer most remain the poor and the vulnerable, especially, as witnessed here, women and children in urban sectors.

A United Nations report issued on conclusion of a mission visit to Iraq in July 1991 stated that the 'effects of the Gulf War are risking a humanitarian crisis whose eventual dimensions would dwarf today's difficulties' (UN, 1991b). Almost five years later, Iraq continues to be in the grip of a severe economic crisis, threatening the lives of vulnerable population groups. Despite some general infrastructural improvement, the huge majority of the population subsists in a state of extreme hardship, where health care, nutrition, water, sanitation and other basic services are minimal. In urban centres, where close to 74% of the estimated 18 million population of Iraq live, overcrowding, poverty and malnutrition add to the risks posed by a fragile environment that bore the major brunt of the war and its aftermath. In March 1993, a United Nations assessment mission to Iraq confirmed that the living conditions of the population in general, and of the urban poor in particular, continued to worsen. In the intervening period, conditions are seen to have deteriorated further. The Gulf war for Iraq has been, in many respects, a major urban catastrophe.

Infrastructual damage

It is noteworthy that the first targets during the 42-day Gulf war were 20 electrical power generation systems, which sustained a modern network of infrastructural facilities extending across the length and breadth of Iraq. The magnitude of the destruction caused to electrical power grids in the war was drawn up in the Harvard University International Study Team report on public health (1991a). It reported that by the end of the war, only two of the country's power stations, generating less than 4% of Iraq's pre-war output of 9,000 megawatts, were in operation. Many generating facilities were destroyed beyond repair. Other damaged facilities could be repaired only through cannibalisation of parts from other electric power plants, since the economic embargo in force prevented the import of spare parts. Electrical power output could be restored to only around 22% of the pre-war level, despite the priority accorded by the government in its post-war restoration work (ibid.).

During the first few days of the war, Iraq's telecommunications system also suffered heavy damage. The ITU reported that as late as July 1991, 'no reliable telecommunications exist[ed] in Iraq' (ITU, 1991). Iraq's agriculture and food processing, storage and distribution system was also destroyed extensively in the war, and all the irrigation systems – including storage dams, barrages, pumping stations and drainage projects – came under attack during the bombing (Clark, 1994).

Whether by design or by intent, the crippling of the power grid had a devastating effect on water-treatment plants and sewerage works. Urban health facilities, which were heavily dependent on government subsidies to meet basic needs under a welfare system, continue to suffer under a depressed economy.

Rise in mortality and morbidity

This destruction led to a phenomenal rise in civilian mortality and morbidity in the aftermath of the war, affecting in particular the vulnerable urban population groups of women and children (Hoskins, 1993). Severe malnutrition appeared to affect around 14% of children under 5 and 10% of children under one (UNICEF, 1992).

The Harvard environmental and agricultural study (Harvard University International Study Team, 1991b) concluded that most of Iraq's population of 18 million were directly exposed to water-borne diseases in their potable water supply. It attributed the cause to the breakdown of water and waste water treatment plants, which were heavily dependent on electrical power supply for their operation. This created a cycle of contamination whereby untreated waste water flowed into the rivers that supplied an area's drinking water. This in turn led to high levels of water- and waste-borne diseases caused by organisms that were eventually returned to the river in untreated human waste.

In Basra, a city of close to 3 million inhabitants, a UNICEF team visit in January 1993 revealed that of 135 sewage pumps, only 25 were operational. Of the 27,000 litres of sewage pumped into the Tigris every second, 17,000 litres were discharged untreated. The team found that garbage collection services had virtually collapsed because of the lack of spare parts and vehicles. Overflow of raw sewage caused flooding in many residential areas. In other cities, including Samawa and Naririyah, streets and residential areas were often flooded while pumps and motors were not operational. In Amara, sewage was allowed to drain into open fields surrounding pumping stations and residential areas (UNICEF, 1993).

Following a breakdown in the system of garbage collection, huge piles of garbage accumulated in streets and urban residential areas throughout Iraq. In the three governorates, only 18 out of 52 garbage-collection vehicles were reported to be in service in 1993. It is estimated that Iraq's solid waste collection and disposal system is operating at less than 25% of its pre-war capacity. Lack of spare parts and the destruction of specialised equipment owned by the municipalities has paralysed efforts at garbage collection (Hoskins, 1993).

As the water supply remained deficient and with the near collapse of sewage- and garbage-disposal systems in major urban areas, the country experienced an increased incidence of water-borne communicable diseases like cholera and typhoid. For typhoid, the total figures for 1990 and 1991 were 98 and 230 respectively (UNICEF, 1992). The 1991 figures no doubt represent only a fraction of the actual disease incidence, since reporting and surveillance systems remained disrupted. Diarrhoea-related mortality in under-fives increased to three times the levels measured in 1989 (UNICEF, 1992).

Effect on development: a new dependency syndrome

The pre-war physical infrastructure in Iraq was modern and growing. Before the war, the country was in the midst of a rapid social and economic transformation, the pace of which had seldom been equalled in its recent history (UNICEF, 1992). The massive destruction inflicted on the country's infrastructure had a devastating effect on the economy. Martti Ahtisarri, under-secretary general of the United Nations, in his report to the secretary-general in March 1991, concluded: 'Iraq has, for some time to come, been relegated to a pre-industrial age, but with all the disabilities of post-industrial dependency on an intensive use of energy and techno-logy' (UN, 1991a). The Gulf war and its aftermath has put Iraq on a level with the poorest countries of the world today. Per capita income in 1992 was estimated to be US$44, which is far below the international poverty line of US$100 established by the World Bank. Dreze and Gazdar (1991) found that, in terms of private income, poverty is now greater in Iraq than in India, with the majority of Iraqi households earning incomes below the Indian poverty line.

Although the physical damage caused in the war was devastating enough, the ultimate collapse of the Iraqi economy can be traced to the effect of the sanctions in force since August 1990. For a country with a near 65% oil-based GDP and which depended for more than 90% of its foreign exchange earnings on oil exports, the oil embargo has had a crippling effect on almost every aspect of civilian life. The total loss of oil revenues (estimated at more than US$15 million annually) and the freezing of overseas financial assets, mainly in the UK and the USA, curtailed Iraq's capacity to finance and maintain its strongly centralised economy. The sanctions have been in many respects an extension of the war, and have been described as a 'major instrument used to wage a total war against the Iraqi people' (Clark, 1994).

The bombing deprived large sections of the urban population of the most basic supports of modern life, stripping the country not only of electric power, communications and other life-sustaining facilities, but of food, clean water and medical services. The destruction caused obvious difficulties in carrying out relief activities in the immediate aftermath of the war. However, the continuing embargo poses greater problems in planning and implementing long-term rehabilitation and developmental measures.

Urban poverty and vulnerability

The embargo has increased the vulnerability of marginalised urban popu-lation groups and pushed increasing numbers into poverty and hunger. The ability of households to satisfy their basic needs depends on what they can acquire through private purchases and through public provision-ing. War and sanctions in Iraq have threatened both private and public channels of acquisition for a whole range of nutrition-related commodities, leading to under-nutrition (Dreze and Gazdar, 1991).

The war and the resultant economic crisis have also led to a sharp deterioration in formal employment. In such a situation, female employees are vulnerable to losing jobs in the face of competition from males. While the war forced women to adopt roles and responsibilities traditionally assigned to men, it has also made their traditional roles harder to fulfil. The most serious consequence of this crisis is the greatly reduced food security at the household level. Hunger is the 'foremost preoccupation of low income groups in Iraq today' (Dreze and Gazdar, 1991). Households are known to have sold their assets, beginning with women's jewellery, thus increasing women's dependence and vulnerability. Women are also known to have been driven to prostitution and begging in extreme cases. Women's physical well-being and that of their families have been further reduced by an urban environment that poses serious health hazards (Bhatia, Kawar and Shahin, 1992).

In reviewing the effects of war, the psycho-social dimensions are often overlooked. Psycho-social effects of war are more pronounced in the urban sector because of increased stress, worsened by the effects of poverty and deprivation. Women in such situations are particularly vulnerable. They suffer from the loss of their husbands, sons and brothers in the conflict and from the considerable stress of providing for the household. Daily chores such as purchasing and preparing food take much longer and are more costly than before the crises. Men's frustration at their inability to find employment often leads to family conflict. Because of the increased prevalence of disease, women spend more time caring for their ill children (Hoskins, 1993). Sixty per cent of women interviewed by the Harvard University International Study Team (1991a) indicated that they suffered from psychological problems including depression, anxiety, headache and insomnia. Often anxieties manifested themselves as physical problems including weight loss, menstrual irregularity, difficulty in breast-feeding and other illnesses (Dreze and Gazdar, 1991).

Children in poverty also remain extremely vulnerable in the depressed economic situation following a war. It is worth emphasising that all urban children in Iraq today would be considered 'children in especially difficult circumstances', according to UNICEF's definition. The current economic crisis has forced more and more parents to send their children to work. This brings home additional family income that could mean the difference between survival and the economic collapse of the household. Girl children often drop out of school to work in the home, especially in cases where the head of the household is a female single parent. Young boys generally work in the informal sector selling items like vegetables or cigarettes. Also, especially in busy urban centres, one notices a marked increase in the number of children (both boys and girls) begging. This phenomenon, relatively unknown in pre-war Iraq, is a direct result of the increasing hardship faced by families (Hoskins, 1993).

Conclusion

Modern warfare has a potent capacity to relegate highly evolved economies, dependent on high levels of technological advancement, to a 'pre-industrial stage'. The present study broadens our understanding of the complex and ever-changing definitions of conflict and many of the levels at which it operates, in this case illustrating a global–local axis. An analysis of the political dimensions of the war and its aftermath reveals that the international community, in emphasising the authoritarian nature of the one-party state in Iraq, is frequently found guilty of erasing the welfare achievements of the regime and is doing little to address the problems of the poor and vulnerable victims of global warfare.

References

Bhatia, B., M. Kawar and M. Shahin (1992), *Unheard Voices: Iraqi Women on War and Sanctions*, London: Change Women and Society and Calvert Press.

Clark, R. (1994), *The Fire This Time: U.S. War Crimes in the Gulf*, New York: Thunder's Mouth Press.

Dreze, J. and H. Gazdar (1991), *Hunger and Poverty in Iraq*, London: Development Economics Research Programme, London School of Economics.

Government of Iraq (1994), *Impact of Sanctions on Health, Nutrition and Environment in Iraq, Baghdad*: Ministry of Culture and Information.

Harvard University International Study Team (1991a), *Health and Nutrition Assessment Report*, prepared for UNICEF, Cambridge, MA: Harvard University Press.

Harvard University International Study Team (1991b), *Environmental and Agricultural Study Report*, prepared for UNICEF, Cambridge, MA: Harvard University Press.

Harvard University International Study Team (1992), *Iraq Child Mortality Survey Report*, prepared for UNICEF, Cambridge, MA: Harvard University Press.

Hoskins, E. (1993), 'Children, war and sanctions', discussion paper prepared for UNICEF, Baghdad.

ITU, (1991a), 'Summary of International Telecommunications Union (ITU) mission findings on telecommunications in Iraq', Annex 10 in UN (1991a).

UNICEF (1992), *Children and Women in Iraq: A Situation Analysis*, Baghdad: UNICEF Iraq.

UNICEF (1993), *Executive Summary of Field Reports*, Baghdad: UNICEF Iraq.

United Nations (1991a), *Report to the Secretary-General on the Humanitarian Needs in Kuwait and Iraq in the Immediate Post-Crisis Environment by a Mission to the Area led by Mr. Martti Ahtissari, Under-Secretary-General for Administration and Management, dated 20 March 1991*, New York: Security Council Document S/2236.

United Nations (1991b), *Report to the Secretary-General on Humanitarian Needs in Iraq by a Mission led by Sadruddin Aga Khan, Executive Delegate of the Secretary-General, dated 15 July 1991*, New York: Security Council Document.

CHAPTER 18

Urban Disaster Management: Lessons from Bhopal

Rajeev Patel

This chapter takes the example of industrial hazard management as a background for examining exactly what happens when exclusionary planning procedures prevent concerns being voiced, and attempts to outline institutional areas through which social planning might lead to safer, better practice. Community involvement in industrial hazard management is still considered esoteric, at the very least. Schemes designed to integrate community, government and industrial objectives are almost non-existent, especially in developing countries. Those that do exist are relatively new and have yet to be fully accepted in mainstream policy debate in even the most progressive countries.

The chapter argues that good social policy and attention to diversity are crucial for best practice in disaster management, in both the short and longer terms. The case of Bhopal is chosen not because it is an example of best practice, but rather because it is an object lesson in how *not* to proceed. In the short term, the way in which the disaster was managed was exclusionary, with powerful groups and voices monopolising control over decisions; with a broader focus one can see this as part of a systematic exclusion of various disempowered social groups, not only within Bhopal, but in a wider political arena. This exclusion has continued long after international interest in the accident has waned. The conclusion deals with suggestions for improvements in the process of non-natural urban disaster management, both technical and political, and provides guidelines for better practice through a process of urban partnership involving the community, government and industry.

The events

On 2 December 1984 a chemical reaction started at the Union Carbide factory in Bhopal, Madhya Pradhesh, which resulted in the deaths of at least 1,754 people. In fact, estimates vary from 1,500 to 10,000 deaths, with as many as 300,000 others suffering long-term effects (Morehouse and Subramaniam, 1986: vii; Shrivastava, 1992: 55). The actual chain of events – failures, faults, back-up systems in disuse, safety procedures being ignored, and component and human errors – seems to demand a verdict of wilful neglect. Indeed, Union Carbide 'ruled out everything but sabotage', although their claim remains unproven. It seems that the real cause of the disaster was not sabotage but systematic and institutionalised negligence, on the part not only of Union Carbide, but also of the state.

The events themselves are technically complex. They began with a valve failure in a pressure tank. Management responded by switching to a tank containing methyl isocyanate (MIC) into which water was inadvertently poured, causing a chemical reaction that led to a tank rupture and the release of a large quantity of highly toxic MIC gas. A flare system designed to burn off dangerous gases was out of order, and in any case would not have helped because MIC is denser than air. A water sprinkler system to wash chemicals out of the air was out of operation, as was a vent gas scrubber. Attempts to operate the scrubber after the release of the MIC were wholly inadequate (Hazarika, 1987: 68). At the time of the accident, the emergency services were not informed. The plant did not admit anything was wrong until all the contents of the tank were in the air.

Union Carbide's safety record before the accident had not been good. There were instances of injury and fatalities in many of its plants, even in developed countries (*Rachel's Hazardous Waste News*, 1990). The plant at Bhopal, prior to the disaster, was no exception. The alarms sounded so often that they were not treated with any urgency by those living immediately outside the plant, and in 1982 they were disconnected so that warning could be given to workmen without 'unnecessarily' causing panic in surrounding areas (Morehouse and Subramaniam, 1986: 21). One person had died in an accident in 1981 and the Indian Labour Department had investigated and recommended a series of improvements, which were not implemented.

Such is the 'micro circumstance' of the tragedy. But larger, ultimately political questions must also be asked of the rationale in using MIC in the production process. The International Programme on Chemical Safety (the international coordination body dealing with information covering all known production chemicals) admits a paucity of experience concerning MIC. It is registered as a highly toxic gas for which there is no specific antidote (UNEP, 1985).

Why, then, was it used in India? Some (Banerjee, 1986) argue that it was an attempt by Union Carbide to take advantage of poorer environmental regulation in India to produce cheap low-quality agro-chemicals at high profit. Whilst it is certainly true that the level of environmental regulation is lower in India and other developing countries than in more developed ones, two pieces of evidence suggest that this cannot be a complete explanation. First, the *persistence* of lower levels of regulation by the Indian government suggests a degree of state sanction for Union Carbide's behaviour. In order to gain certificates to emit effluent into the air and water under the Indian Air and Water Acts, Union Carbide had to file a detailed description of the plant's activities with central government. The government would then have had the option to deny it a licence to operate, which it did not do. Second, the Bhopal plant also ran at a persistent economic loss and, as Bogard (1989) notes, the government had been far keener than Union Carbide to construct the plant. The Green Revolution in India required cheap agro-chemicals, which Union Carbide had experience in making. Union Carbide itself was keener on other areas of the Indian market, primarily in the disposable battery area, which it dominated with its 'Ever Ready' brand.

Although Union Carbide is *prima facie* at fault over the actual disaster, then, the state – despite not being legally at fault – would seem to share some of the responsibility for the circumstances leading up to it. It is argued below that much more could have been made of the opportunities for state/industry collaboration.

The urban dimensions of industrial hazard management

The particular characteristics of urban settlements have a significant bearing on the hazard management process for a number of reasons. Dense population distribution implies a number of factors for urban industrial disaster management. First, as a function of physical and human geography, the area under the control of industrial actors is smaller than that in rural areas or industrial parks. Thus a greater degree of flexibility, including the involvement of a range of institutional actors, is required in urban disaster management planning. Second, the number and nature of institutional linkages themselves are greater and more diverse than in other contexts. Urban settlements exist under particular constraints, such as a high degree of competition for land and government resources. As a response to this, many organisations exist, either because of government commitment or through non-governmental organisation, to cater to the needs of urban populations and to voice their interests in these domains. Third, and most importantly, the relatively high concentration of people in urban areas means that an accident which may directly affect a limited number of people in the first instance has the potential to become a disaster affecting thousands.

The diversity implications of industrial hazard management

As well as possessing a diversity of institutional actors, the urban context also possesses a diversity of human actors. Often, however, this diversity is ignored. The existence of variation in people – by religion, ethnic and geographical origin, location within the city, class, health status, education, gender, profession, age, sexuality and income – points to particularly different needs and circumstances, which need to be addressed in hazard management. Predictably, it is the invisible, those without real voices in the city, who are excluded from these processes: the poor, the landless, women, children and the elderly.

Different actors have different needs, and those involved in urban hazard management would do well to note that precisely the same event can have massively different effects on different people. The Bhopal case demonstrates this well. Bhopal is the capital city of the state of Madhya Pradesh in India, and has a population of approximately three-quarters of a million people. It is estimated that at least 10% of these people (Basu, 1994) live in slums. Immediately facing the Union Carbide plant was the slum colony of Jayaprakash Nagar. As one moves further south from the factory, land values and the wealth of the inhabitants increase. The poison gas cloud released on 2 December drifted in a south-south-westerly direction, which resulted in people being affected almost in inverse proportion to their income. Below, some of the groups affected by the gas leak are examined in more detail. Note that this schema concentrates examination of diversity on those most adversely affected and marginalised by the accident, since this is necessarily a chapter concerned with the human dimension of hazard management.

Impact on the poor in general

The area immediately surrounding the factory was populated by the poorest inhabitants of Bhopal. Most of the slums are in the 36 wards that the government declared gas-affected in 1984. Of these, Jayaprakash (JP) Nagar was one of the most heavily populated and the worst affected, being just outside the plant itself. The concentration of poor people in urban industrial areas is no accident. The economics of low land costs, limited alternative land uses, high external costs of living opposite an industrial plant (noise, risk of pollution, etc.) mean that the poor are often relegated to live in such areas.

Since the disaster, gas casualties have, despite their best efforts, been unable to mobilise themselves as an effective voice within Bhopal (although the Citizen's Commissions have skilfully raised their voices to the international community). Their lack of success in achieving a remedy might be explained through invocation of a 'multinational conspiracy' (Banerjee, 1986), whereby Union Carbide and the government have collaborated to minimise the legal and political impact of the poor. Although there is some evidence that this might be the case, such an explanation ignores other significant domestic factors (Basu 1994), discussed below.

Further, there has been no coordinated means for redress after the accident. The Indian government initially asked for $3 billion and filed against ten Union Carbide officials under the charge of culpable homicide. In November 1987 Carbide offered between $500 and $650 million, with payment to be spread out over ten years (Montague, 1988). By February 1989 the Indian government had agreed to drop all charges in return for a phased *ex gratia* payment of $470 million (Basu, 1994). The people affected by the gas were given some compensation, but the means for disbursal of this compensation have since been questioned as unjust and biased in favour of the Hindu community. Evidence that there are still unresolved grievances is to be found in the fact that there have been a number of riots involving slum-dwellers since the disaster (ibid.).

Impact on the Muslim population

The inhabitants of the slums in Bhopal were not only poor, but largely Muslim in a predominantly Hindu city. While race was not an overt issue in Bhopali politics in 1984, Basu (1994) argues that electoral and race considerations have always to some extent conspired against the Muslim community. Since the nationalist Hindu Bharatiya Janata Party (BJP) came to power in 1990 there has been clearer evidence of racial marginalisation. The BJP has not delivered on promises made to the gas survivors, despite an election manifesto commitment to a proactive stance on reparations. The BJP's traditional political base of Hindu shopkeepers has little to gain from such activities and, since its election, there seems to have been much discrimination against the Muslim poor. In a large slum-clearing programme many families were forcibly relocated. In one instance 400 families were sent to an area some four miles outside Bhopal to a patch of land in between a Hindu cremation ground and a Muslim burial ground, barely serviced by public transport and lacking basic infrastructure (ibid.).

Impact on women

The gender dimensions of disasters and disaster management have been relatively under-researched, but it is clear from the case of Bhopal that women have suffered disproportionately as a result of the tragedy. Women have been affected by the gas itself to a greater extent than men, since they not only suffer the cardio-respiratory effects, but have faced often severe reproductive impairment. A survey of 2,500 women pregnant at the time of the disaster found a spontaneous abortion rate of 14.8%, twice the average rate in India (Morehouse and Subramaniam, 1986).

The number of birth abnormalities among those exposed to the gas has soared and there are children being born without vital organs 12 years after the accident. Apart from the misery this causes for the mother, the high value of fertility and reproduction in Indian society has reportedly led to infertile women being divorced or left by their husbands. Support networks for divorced women and women without male children in Indian society are virtually non-existent. In partial reaction to this, the women affected by the disaster have organised themselves into a strong pressure group. The Bhopal Gas Peedit Mahila Udyog Sangathana (BGPMUS – Organisation of Bhopal Women Worker Victims) is composed primarily of Muslim women affected by the disaster. They have lobbied the Indian government and protested against their treatment. Sometimes, this has led to retaliation – on one occasion 220 women were beaten when they tried to enter the plant during a protest action (ibid.). Not only do they engage strongly in advocacy activities, but they maintain a strong grassroots presence, assisting in the day-to-day survival of fellow women gas victims in Bhopal.

One survivor has noted, however, that the NGO activity organised by the women has been subverted unintentionally by the actions of well-meaning external agents, 'non-Bhopalis' (Hazarika, 1987) whose concentration on the multinational legal implications of the disaster has drawn attention away from the plight of Bhopalis. In this respect, although BPGMUS is an important collective response to the effects of the disaster, the efforts of the women involved have been overshadowed by other agendas. Furthermore, the absence of an effective political voice has meant that, despite their best efforts, these women have been forced to remain marginal to the political processes shaping their lives.

Impact on children

Children suffered the most at the time of the gas leak itself; if they managed to avoid being trampled by the stampede away from the plant, they were subsequently more affected by the gas simply because of their lung/weight ratio. Those who have survived have suffered chronic medical problems, primarily affecting the eyes and lungs. Symptoms include shallowness of breath, chronic tiredness and varying degrees of blindness.

The social consequence of this is that there are many children who are unable to work to help to support their families. The vulnerability of those families that traditionally rely on child contribution is then increased. This legacy of disability has been virtually ignored by local authorities.

Impact on physical environment and animals

Over four thousand animals were killed by MIC poisoning. Vegetation was also destroyed by the gas, and there is some evidence of soil damage (Shrivastava, 1992). Again, the poor are most likely to be affected by this simply because their herbivorous livestock represent a far larger proportion of their assets than for the rich, and consequently the death of their animals is a major blow to their wealth, security and independence. There is little information about the long-term persistence of MIC in the environment, or the effects it has had at an ecosystemic level. Although MIC is not thought to be mutagenic, the large number of human and non-human reproductive abnormalities is serious cause for concern.

Responses at different levels

It seems to be the case that the poor, and women in particular, have suffered disproportionately, both from the direct effects of the disaster and from its aftermath. In searching for an explanation, it is necessary to disaggregate the interactions and players. The initial responses to the accident are outlined at the local and regional/national levels below.

When the first casualties started to arrive at local medical facilities, local doctors did not know what the people had been poisoned with, and could only provide limited symptomatic relief until the toxin was identified. Even when it was identified, they had little or no idea how to treat the victims of MIC poisoning. Here, then, is the first instance where actors other than the industry concerned, specifically the medical emergency services, should have been involved in hazard management.

In another case, Dr A. K. Sarkar, a medical officer for Indian Railways, ran against a tide of people to the railway control room where he gave orders that no trains were to be allowed into Bhopal. His exposure to the MIC has left him debilitated. The 'immediate threat to life' level of MIC exposure is 20 parts per million and at the time of Dr Sarkar's action, the highly concentrated MIC plume was still pouring out of the plant as two packed trains were scheduled to pass outside the factory (Morehouse and Subramaniam, 1986: 27). Through his action, many additional exposures were prevented. Again, this points to another area in which institutional mechanisms could have been coordinated in advance: the industry should have had pre-existing arrangements with the rail services, to be followed in the event of an emergency. It should not have been left to chance, and to the quick thinking of one of the railway employees. This example is included because, although its origin is institutional, it is often forgotten that institutional failure has a human cost. It also serves to illustrate the point that a number of actors are involved in disaster management, and that they all need to be included in the process for it to function successfully.

Critical to successful functioning of these processes is contextual awareness. But those institutions more directly concerned, including regulatory and administrative governmental organisations, have manifested a distinct lack of sensitivity towards their social environment – both at the

time of the disaster and during events since 1984. There is much quantitative and qualitative evidence (Shastri, 1985; Kapoor, 1992) to suggest
that the problems of many gas casualties are chronic and derive from
institutional as well as medical reasons. The people most exposed to this
insensitivity have been the poor.

As suggested above, there are reasons for thinking that political factors
influenced, and continue to affect, events at Bhopal. It has been argued that
the government took the decision that it was in India's wider interests
that a small part of the Indian community would bear the risk associated
with the manufacture of the lower-cost fertilisers necessary for economic
progress (Banerjee, 1986).

There follow two questions. First, should any community have been
asked to shoulder such a burden? In short, were the risks tolerable? This
question is one that developing countries face more acutely, for both
domestic and international reasons. The need for economic growth weighs
more strongly in the calculus of cost and benefit than in developed
countries. In economic terms, the marginal benefit (in terms of economic
growth) of resources devoted to industrialisation is greater in developing
than developed countries. This is simply because most developing countries
have an initially smaller industrial base, and the full effect of diminishing
marginal utility has yet profoundly to affect any major industrialisation.

The calculus is also weighted in favour of accepting risk by external
influences. MIC is a high-risk chemical, although its ultimate pesticide
product is considered beneficial to agricultural production. Developing
countries are faced with a choice as to whether to accept the high-risk
technology offered (at comparatively low cost) by developed country
corporations, to pay significantly more for a relatively less hazardous
technology, or to forgo the technology altogether.

Significantly, this decision is taken by governments, not individual
communities. Many factors play a part in the decision-making process.
The actual risks and benefits of the technology are dimensions in a
decision that might also include considerations of long-term industrial
and political goals: international relations with the foreign corporation's
country, employment considerations and issues of skills transfer, to name
a few. It is important to note that this process is natural within liberal
democracy, and involves the recognition that there are different and
sometimes conflicting interests at different levels of government.

Given that a decision to adopt a high-risk technology has been taken,
there follows the second question of location – where should the technology be sited? The decision to accept the *generalised* economic benefits of,
say, cheap agro-chemicals has to be accompanied by a decision as to who
should bear the highly *localised* costs and risk; in the resolution of conflicting national and local interests, the costs are often borne by those
least able to avoid them. In Bhopal, there is evidence to suggest that

middle-class campaigning had some effect on the location of the Union Carbide plant, although proximity to transport services and cheap land were also factors. The MIC unit (as distinct from the rest of the plant) should, according to the 1975 Bhopal development plan, have been situated away from the city centre, in the north-east of the city, downwind from heavily congested areas. It seems that Union Carbide's initial application to site the MIC part of the plant was rejected by municipal authorities, only to be approved by central government. Further, the areas worst affected by the gas were squatter settlements long before the plant was constructed (Basu, 1994). As Perrow observes, in calculations such as these 'the issue is not risk but power' (Perrow, 1984: 12).

This illustrates an important link between diversity and power. There is a failure of democracy in a system that allows a politically effective minority to impose its will on an ostensibly enfranchised but effectively disempowered group. The consequences of this for the poor in Bhopal were that the high levels of risk of the Union Carbide plant were forced upon them. The existence of this democratic failure hints at the potentially radical nature of the changes that are needed in order that a city be a genuine 'City for All'. In Bhopal, the right of all citizens to have an effective voice in planning issues was denied. It is a prerequisite for the implementation of the partnership plans suggested below, but also as part of a wider programme for turning cities into 'Cities for All'. It is necessary for successful inclusive social policy and planning that *all* sectors and members of the urban community be able to articulate their needs and wants.

Linkages: the sustainable solution

The production of a hazard is, above all, a multi-player process (Bogard, 1989). Although it is easiest to blame disasters such as the one that occurred at Bhopal on single individuals, it is more reasonable to see them as caused by a process within which human intervention can greatly magnify or mitigate the eventual outcome (Perrow, 1984). It is for this reason that a genuine partnership requires the involvement not just of the government and corporations, but of the community as well, *which means all the diverse and often conflicting parts of the community*. It is a common mistake to consider any of these public, private or community sectors as homogeneous entities. Governments and corporations have conflicting priorities within their departments (ministries of environment and transport may be opposed, for instance, as may public relations and research departments within corporations).

There are a number of difficulties in the implementation of such urban partnerships, and these vary according to context. Demonstrating them with reference to Bhopal will, I hope, show the kinds of obstacles that face the implementation of this particular social policy, given the existence of diverse urban governments, industries and, of course, communities. There are a number of difficulties with the implementation of such an urban partnership in any context. I shall attempt to illustrate these with reference to Bhopal.

Socio-political problems

Certain interest groups within Bhopal society would have been negatively affected by the introduction of urban partnership approaches to hazard management. In particular, local elites might have opposed it on several grounds. Those concerned with the actual maintenance of the plant would have considered the input of an NGO that represents slum-dwellers as an unwarranted intrusion into their domain. This is a constant problem with any sort of empowering programme. The first law of thermodynamics seems to apply to political power as well as energy – it cannot be created or destroyed, but can merely be transferred.

Although it is the general aim of empowerment programmes and urban partnerships to distribute power more equitably, it cannot be done without secession of power from elite groups. Some schemes have tried to compensate these groups through reference to increased security, community solidarity, etc. (Houghton and Williams, 1995). In Bhopal these benefits would probably not seem sufficient to compensate for the loss of power of elites brought up in a society organised around power inequalities. The caste system in India, despite government assurances and legislation, maintains a strong social presence. In the case of Bhopal, the minority group of 'untouchables' is supplanted, or rather augmented, by landless Muslims.

Further, local politicians whose cooperation and goodwill is necessary for the success of the scheme would have been extremely disinclined to participate. This is a critical issue. The poor in Bhopal had been organised into vote banks strategically placed in key electoral wards to ensure that the incumbent politician maintained power. In order for a change in power relations to take place, not only would local politicians have to hand over power to the poor, but the majority of them would be of an opposing religious group. There is little that might be conceived under this sort of political circumstance that would induce politicians to cooperate whole-heartedly. Here the role of networking, international opinion and the important role that can be played by the media can be used to effect.

Before the accident at Bhopal, there were attempts in the local press to expose the potential health and safety risks at the plant. A local Hindi-language newspaper had campaigned for some time over the lack of adequately enforced regulations in the plant. There had been many accidents at the plant and the paper was concerned that these incidents remained unaddressed (Banerjee, 1986). These protests were not, however, picked up by the mainstream media.

Industry

In Northern countries, where there is often competition for skilled labour, private corporations have shown enthusiasm for urban partnerships in the hope that they can benefit from 'increased recruitment and retention associated with schemes for pre-recruitment training for disadvantaged groups' (Christie, 1991: 3). This incentive does not necessarily translate to Southern contexts. For example, although training in fertiliser manufacture is a long and costly procedure, in countries such as India, which has the highest number of unemployed Ph.D. graduates per capita in the world, promoting urban partnerships on these grounds is hardly likely to be a process from which Union Carbide would benefit. While there are many benefits associated with urban partnerships, the problem remains that benefits accrue not to *individual* corporations, but rather to business *communities*. There is, consequently, an incentive for a business to 'free ride' – to appear to be an effective member of an urban partnership while not actually fulfilling its requirements.

It has been suggested that legislation has been the most effective inducement for industrial change in recent times (*Guardian*, 1996). Two problems present themselves, however, in a consideration of legislation for urban partnership. First, legal compulsion into partnership goes against the sprit of partnership, which carries with it connotations of mutual benefit and trust. Second, the environmental laws that have been passed in the North as a result of consumer pressure were initially very strongly opposed by the industries concerned. Co-optive regulation is likely to be a slow route to partnership.

Recent changes in large corporations' attitudes to environmental legislation give cause for hope, however. There has been an increasing realisation on the part of big business that the introduction of new legislation can be an opportunity, rather than a threat. If a corporation is able to adapt to a new law better than its competitors, it will find itself better able to compete in a market where others are falling foul of litigation (and hence incurring fines, poor publicity, etc.). These attitude changes are, however, a recent Northern phenomenon, restricted to the domain of environmental legislation, where high infrastructural costs of compliance with new legislation provide better opportunities for larger corporations to out-manoeuvre their competitors. In order for this to be attractive to industries in the South, solutions other than the 'stick' of litigation are required. These carrots might include:

- more dissemination of guidelines on good practice for companies in relation to organisation, budgets and policy development for investment in the community, thus reducing corporate ignorance about high compliance costs;

- development of 'Per Cent' clubs, where companies pledge a certain proportion of profits to the community in return for tax breaks;
- more resources to publicise the initiatives, with action by committed business to encourage suppliers and customers to participate, and hence provide a disincentive for companies to break away from partnerships; and
- government grants to smaller firms in order to develop a community investment policy (Christie, 1991).

A sensitive but effective carrot and stick approach to corporate participation seems, then, to provide a route towards better practice.

Governmental problems

Government needs to hear the voices in the city, and so must change, at both the national and municipal levels. In addition to the centralised disaster control unit, it is important to have a local government component closer to the site. In Bhopal, such a change in governmental style is difficult to envisage. As mentioned above, there are strong vested interests in the maintenance of hierarchical managerial government. Local politicians do very well out of the current situation, and there would seem to be little incentive for them to change. The tragedy is that local government provides the best chance for a link between centralised 'top-down' government and grassroots 'bottom-up' subsidiarity. It could broker between these two interests, to the benefit of both, and could integrate wider local and national concerns.

The outlook, however, is not entirely bleak. Urban partnership can offer the opportunity of reduced governance expenditure, so government might have an incentive to involve industry in this type of partnership from a cost-sharing point of view. The first step on this road is a change in the culture of government. The change would need to be a change in the government's perception of itself as well as people's perception of government. The change required is for government to transform itself from a managerial organisation to an enabling one. Cynicism and the experience of the majority of the poor who continue to be victimised by the state in Bhopal mean that this is difficult to imagine.

Conclusion

It is not pleasant to end on a downbeat note. Urban partnership offers a real and long-term opportunity for, among other things, industrial hazard management. A process of consultation and the involvement of *all* concerned at all stages of planning, construction and maintenance seem to promise better hazard management in the future.

In the event of a catastrophe, the involvement of all those affected should provide the most just outcome. The overwhelming majority of the dead and those suffering the long-term effects of the Bhopal disaster come from the Muslim slum around the plant. The marginalisation of these people at every stage of the Bhopal tragedy can be seen as the most significant injustice of the entire affair. There is a democratic imperative to involve and empower all stakeholders in the process of industrial risk management. This is a political problem without any particular geographical limit. The slum-dwellers of Bhopal were ostracised from any real democracy, and were used only as vote banks (Basu, 1994). The Hindi newspaper that tried to alert the residents by pointing out the dangers of the plant was ignored. It is this process of giving a voice to marginalised stakeholders that looks like being the most challenging part of any durable strategy of dealing with industrial hazards.

This chapter has tried to demonstrate a number of things. First, that through systematic and institutionalised exclusion, the poor have borne a disproportionate cost of a broader national strategy in terms of their risk burden. Second, the community has attempted to respond to this situation but, through its lack of access to power, has been unsuccessful in getting its concerns operationalised at higher levels. Third, 'diversity' is not restricted in its predication of social groups and communities. Governments and industries are not homogeneous entities either, and inevitably have different and conflicting priorities. Fourth, an awareness of this can lead to more successful inclusive partnerships, which work towards improved industrial hazard management. But, fifth, this involves a need to devolve both responsibility *and power* from those who have it. This final part is the challenge that inclusive policy represents. For, in the final analysis, inclusion is part of a radical popular democratic tradition. In talking about including people, we are talking about the challenge to ensure that *all* voices of a polity are heard, and this inevitably means that some groups who currently enjoy pre-eminence on a democratic stage must learn to share the limelight. It remains to be seen whether the challenge to implement this change effectively is taken; the challenge to provide, in this and other fields, a genuine City for All.

References

Banerjee, B. N. (1986), *Bhopal Gas Tragedy – Accident or Experiment?*, New Delhi: Paribus Publishers and Distributors.

Banerjee, B. N. (1987), *Environmental Pollution and Bhopal Killings*, Delhi: Gian Publication House.

Basu, A. (1994), 'Bhopal revisited: the view from below', *Bulletin of Concerned Asian Scholars*, 26(1), January: 3–19.

Bogard, W. (1989), *The Bhopal Tragedy – Language, Logic and Politics in the Production of a Hazard*, London: Westview Press.

Christie, I. (1991), *Profitable Partnerships: A Report on Business Investment in the Community*, London: Policy Studies Institute.

Guardian (1996), '20–20 Vision', 16 April.

Hazarika, S. (1987), *Bhopal: The Lessons of a Tragedy*, New Delhi: Penguin Books.

Houghton, G. and C. C. Williams (1995), *Corporate City? Partnerships, Participation and Partitions in Urban Development in Leeds*, Aldershot: Avebury.

Kapoor, R. (1992), 'The psychological consequences of an environmental disaster – selected case studies of the Bhopal disaster', *Population and Environment* 13 (3): 209–15.

Montague, R. (1988), 'Carbide officials face homicide charges', *Rachel's Hazardous Waste News* 58, Annapolis, MD.

Morehouse, W. and M. Subramaniam (1986), *The Bhopal Tragedy: What Really Happened and What it Means for US Workers and Communities at Risk – A Preliminary Report for the Citizens' Commission on Bhopal*, New York: Council on International and Public Affairs.

Perrow, C. (1984), *Normal Accident: Living with High Risk Technologies*, New York: Basic Books.

Rachel's Hazardous Waste News (1990), 'From Bhopal with love', 170, February, Annapolis, MD.

Shastri, L. (1985), *Bhopal Disaster: An Eyewitness Account*, New Delhi: Criterion Publications.

Shrivastava, P. (1992) *Bhopal: Anatomy of a Crisis* (2nd edn), London: Paul Chapman.

Shrivastava, P. (1995), 'Democratic control of technological risks in developing countries', *Ecological Economics* 14(3): 195–208.

UNEP (1985), 'Aware', *Industry and Environment*, 32, April/May/June: 32.

CHAPTER 19

Access to Health in Urban Areas

Andrea Lampis

> The Urban Poor are at the interface between underdevelopment and industrialization and their disease patterns reflect the problems of both. From the first they carry a heavy burden of infectious diseases and malnutrition, while from the second they suffer the typical spectrum of chronic and social diseases (Rossi-Espagnet, 1984).

The above citation was written 12 years ago. However, it remains a powerful articulation of the reality that the urban poor presently face in their struggle for good health. This chapter addresses this long-standing issue, and analyses whether current approaches to urban health care are appropriate in reaching the majority of poor urban dwellers. It then aims to stimulate discussion as to why the level and quality of the access to health in urban areas has not significantly improved over the last decade, and to identify factors that have prevented this improvement from being achieved. These ideas are explored through case studies representing the most commonly implemented approaches towards health for all.

Background

From a perspective embracing urban diversity, it must be noted that many issues concerned with inequalities in the access of the urban poor to health care are apparent in urban areas across developing as well as developed nations. Migration, low income, poor health status, high inequalities in service provision, social marginalisation, physical violence, vulnerability and insecurity all affect the poor of Paris, New York and London as well as those of Delhi, Lagos, Rio and Manila, albeit with different intensity and modalities. Allowing for differences in absolute incidence, the problems listed above represent a daily experience for all those who are poor and marginalised within the city. Thus 'urban health issues bring the developing and the developed world closer together' (WHO, 1992: 7). In particular women, children, elders, disabled people, those who are chronically ill, and ethnic and linguistic minorities are those who find the greatest difficulties in gaining access to health care and are therefore those most affected by low levels of health.

The health of the urban poor

In developing countries the level of urbanisation is expected to increase to 39.5% by the end of the century and to 56.9% by 2025 (Harpham and Stephens, 1991). This tremendous growth puts a great strain on the present and future resources of developing countries and on the capacity of both the public and the private sectors to provide infrastructure and services for an increasing mass of population (Feachem et al., 1992).

Taking into account the socio-economic determinants of health, three main groups of health hazards synergetically affect the poor in urban areas:

- hazards that ultimately have an economic origin, such as low income, limited education, labour exploitation, insufficient diet, overcrowding and insanitary conditions;
- hazards related to urban man-made environments, such as those related to industrialisation, traffic, stress and alienation; and
- hazards resulting from social instability, and insecurity such as alcohol, tobacco and drug abuse, prostitution and child labour.[1]

Most specifically, the most direct factors affecting poorer groups are the presence in the environment (especially inside and around the home) of pathogenic micro-organisms and housing conditions that are crowded, cramped and injurious to health.

For every single determinant of health the relationship of direct causation between health and poverty is very difficult to demonstrate in statistical terms[2] (ibid.). However, in the 1980s and 1990s a growing body of research has clearly shown the strong likelihood of a relationship between those factors and the conditions of ill health and poverty (Harpham, Vaughan and Rifkin, 1985; Harpham and Stephens, 1991). Thus, although not all those with a low health status are poor and not all the poor have a low health status, the poor and the most vulnerable groups do suffer disproportionately from the consequences of economic hardship and ill health (Whitehead, 1992).

In urban areas this situation is characterised by the existence of striking intra-urban differentials in health: the poor have a consistently lower health profile than do other groups. The levels of health and education in areas of extreme poverty and marginalisation are commonly three or even four times lower than those reported for the city as a whole or for the nation (Harpham, Lusty and Vaughan, 1988; Harpham and Stephens, 1991; Rossi-Espagnet, 1984).

The most direct determinants of ill health are the extremely low levels in the provision of water supply, sanitation and adequate housing. For example, in Bogota only 52% of the city's low-income households have easy access to a safe water supply and only 35% have access to adequate facilities for the disposal of liquid waste (Tabibzadeh, Maxwell and Rossi-Espagnet, 1989: 28). Many similar studies point to intra-urban differentials in morbidity and mortality. Throughout all of them it is possible to trace two main areas of concern: the first represented by the environmental conditions affecting health and the health of the poor in particular; the second consisting of the socio-economic determinants of health (Hardoy and Satterthwaite, 1991; Harpham and Tanner, 1995; Satterthwaite, 1993; Tabibzadeh, Maxwell and Rossi-Espagnet, 1989; Songsore and McGranahan, 1993; Stephens, 1995).

People in poverty are those who have the least access to non-hazardous environments, sanitation and clean water and, at the same time, are those whose economic constraints prevent them from gaining access to adequate education, shelter, and balanced and healthy nutrients. Unlike other groups they lack any freedom of choice (Whitehead, 1992) with regard to the above direct and indirect determinants of health.

In a recent book published by the World Bank, Mead, Randall, Joyce and Orville underline how the consequences of ill health often result in the household being 'forced to sell its productive assets or sacrifice the health of its other members by undernourishing and overworking them' (Mead et al., 1992: 190). In so doing, they cross a threshold of poverty from which the household cannot escape. The main assets of the poor are their bodies, as Pryer and Evans have sharply illustrated (Evans, 1989; Pryer, 1993). Economic and life-event shocks, such as illness in the family breadwinner, deplete those assets and are the main causes of a process that often ends in chronic deprivation.

Beyond the socio-economic determinants of health, both individuals and households play a role that cannot be overestimated in the shaping of poverty, health and their intertwining. Within the framework of a globalising world in which health and well-being are increasingly marketed as commodities, the ability of individuals and communities to adapt and actively contribute to the creation of new social and ecological niches assumes an increasingly greater importance. Individuals do have the chance to improve many aspects of their health dramatically, as is the case with smoking and drinking habits, or the responsible use of infrastructure and facilities.

However, the role of individuals has to be contextualised. A healthier lifestyle is not only a matter of choice but a question of access to health care, adequate nutrients, clean water supply, sanitation, education, and a full range of opportunities. Command over resources is shaped by power, gender, class and group relations within the household and society. A vast literature exists documenting how the poor in general – and more speci-

fically women, children, the elderly, the disabled and the marginalised –
are discriminated against in the allocation of resources from the general
level of governmental budgets down to the division of food quotas or to
the painful choice over who survives between a male or a female child in
the event of illness (Beall, 1995; Chant, 1991; Dréze and Sen, 1989;
Gonzaléz de la Rocha, 1994; among others).

The point made above has to be emphasised, since it has great ethical
and practical implication for policy. It is misleading, in fact, as for instance
in the World Bank position, to present the individual on the one hand,
and the household and the overall societal dynamic on the other, as having
the same influence on the dynamic that determines health and poverty
(World Bank, 1993). Rather, if the potentialities and contribution of
diversity and difference are to be recognised in a more just and equal
context such as the one the human development perspective struggles to
achieve, it is of the utmost importance to recognise how individuals and
households, albeit equally responsible, do not have the same power as
institutions within the spatial, social, economic and political organisation
of society in general and of the city in particular (see Chapter 1).

Concern over the question of access to health in urban areas is of
great relevance on several grounds – first in terms of ethics and social
justice, for the suffering that the lack of access to health generates, and
second in economic terms, for the high cost that ill health imposes on
individuals, households and societies.

The main approaches to the question of access to health in urban
areas are illustrated here by case studies. They represent the application
of the principles of the different approaches and are evaluated in these
terms.

Access to health: the holistic and the selective approaches

From the perspective of the future city as 'A City for All', access to
health is mainly an issue of equity. As noted above, literature on intra-
urban differentials in health and inequalities clearly demonstrates that
disadvantaged groups suffer not only from more illness than others, but
also from the onset of chronic illness and disability at younger ages
(Townsend, 1993). Improving equity thus means creating equal opportunities for health within society and within the city, seen, like the Greek
pólis, as a 'living, breathing, growing, changing complex organism that has
too often been considered as only an economic entity' (Tsauros, 1992:
145). Creating equity is to recognise that healthier behaviour is not always
a choice and that therefore action has to be taken against avoidable and
unjust inequalities and uneven access to health resources and services
(Whitehead, 1992). Whitehead (ibid.) categorises such positive action into

three main areas, which guide the analysis of the case studies below. Equity in health is defined as:

- equal access to available care for equal needs;
- equal utilisation for equal needs; and
- equal quality of care for all.

In order to define the concept of 'access to health' we need to distinguish between health and health care. Although the two necessarily overlap, the former embraces the whole range of human activities and determinants of well-being. The latter is generally employed in referring to the health care services and medical treatments directed at the prevention and cure of disease and ill health.

The holistic approach

The definition of health not only as the absence of disease but as a state of complete physical, psychological and social well-being has been at the centre of the World Health Organisation (WHO) arguments since the Alma Ata conference in 1978. This definition of health lies at the centre of the 'Healthy Cities' project. The project had its inception in 1986 and, since then, has been implemented in many European cities. Based on the definition of health put forward by WHO, the conceptual framework of the project centres on a holistic idea of health, taking into account all determining factors: biological, physical, environmental, economic, social and cultural. The shift from the previous concept of health as the absence of disease reflects the introduction of a positive concept in which health is seen as being socially constructed. This implies the development of a new 'salutogenic' epidemiology, which considers not only the factors that cause disease but also, and principally, those factors that cause good health. Going beyond the basic needs approach, the Healthy Cities perspective is oriented towards the importance of additional factors such as self-esteem, power and control over life events, and the need for sustainable ecosystems and liveable environments (Davies and Kelly, 1993). The overall aim of the initiative is to 'put health on the agenda of decision-makers in the cities of Europe and to build a strong lobby for public health at the local level. Ultimately the project seeks to enhance the physical, mental, social and environmental well-being of the people who live and work in Europe's cities' (Tsauros, 1992: 11). In order to achieve this goal, focal points for action are the pursuit of equity, the development of community action and individual skills, the creation of supportive environments, and the reorganisation of health services. Important landmarks of the project are the focus on groups, not on isolated individuals, and the belief that a solution to the urban health issue can come only from integrated collaboration across a broad range of disciplines.

Health in Glasgow[3]

In June 1992, the Women's Health Working Group of the Glasgow City Project launched the Glasgow Women's Health Policy initiative with the overall aim of improving the health and well-being of the women in Glasgow. The goals of the project were to be achieved by:

- raising awareness of women's health needs and promoting an understanding of the women's health perspective;
- introducing an awareness of women's health needs into the policy and planning processes of statutory and voluntary organisations;
- ensuring that women's health needs and a woman's health perspective are incorporated into the delivery of general health care; and
- ensuring the provision of services and support specifically for women.

In Glasgow 40% of women with children under the age of 5 and 48% of those with children under the age of 15 are in paid employment. Half of the local authority housing stock in the city of Glasgow shows signs of dampness or condensation, factors that have been demonstrated to be associated with a high incidence of respiratory diseases. The premature death rate among Glaswegian women is 19% higher than for Scotland as a whole. It is estimated that as many as 20,000 Glaswegian women may be victims of severe domestic violence, out of a population of 483,201. Lung cancer has overtaken breast cancer as the leading cause of cancer death among Glasgow women. In a Glasgow survey 70% of women placed 'improving emotional and mental health' as their first priority for improving women's health (Hair, 1994). These statistics are representative of the negative effect exercised on the health of women by their social and economic roles.

In order to improve the health of women in the areas of emotional and mental heath, reproductive care, the provision of support for women as carers, the reduction of the incidence of diseases, and health and safety at home and at work, several initiatives were undertaken.

An information campaign, supported by the publication of a magazine, was initiated to disseminate information on health-related issues and access to resources such as counselling services. Particular attention was concentrated on the problem of emotional support for specific problems such as smoking, drinking and fitness. The campaign was paralleled by the establishment of counselling services for different groups, such as black and ethnic minority women, lesbians, women with disabilities and women from areas requiring priority treatment.

Lobbying action was then undertaken to develop inter-sectoral linkages with the municipality, the professionals and the private sector. The outcome of this action was the establishment of new health centres and of particular facilities in those already in place. This enhanced the access of women to services providing care for mental and emotional needs as well as to specific medical and diagnostic care.

The Glasgow Healthy Cities project shares its achievements and its shortcomings with many other cities where the project has also been initiated (Curtice, 1993; Healthy Toronto 2000, 1988; Whitehead, 1993). On the positive side the Healthy Cities project shows that it is possible to break with the traditional disease-centred approach to health issues. In bringing together different professionals and institutional agents to discuss the health implications of their own areas of expertise, the basis has been created for an integrated and multi-sectoral approach to health. This has proved capable of taking into account not only epidemiological and environmental data, but also the importance of other social and economic determinants of health. There are other examples too of where these sorts of objectives have been achieved with non-standard and participatory methods. For example, in Toronto, children were asked to redesign the city according to their need for spaces, infrastructures and activities. This initiative brought to the fore the previously underestimated issue of security and safety and served to overcome different political and professional barriers. The example of the women's group in the Glasgow Healthy Cities project is also a strong endorsement for advocating and establishing initiatives for diverse and minority groups.

On the other hand, there certainly are many constraints and short-comings: first of all the size and financial resources of the projects have been small. Often the office in charge of the project has been run by too few members of staff to make an operative reality of a very ambitious vision of the future city. Second, the outcomes of the Healthy Cities projects suffer from the lack of short-term visibility and, possibly, long-term sustainability. Bringing together different interests and disciplines is a highly time-consuming task, which highlights the difficulties of reaching the city and its social components as a whole.

Evaluation carried on in Glasgow has also illustrated the difficulties found in getting constant and sufficient levels of participation from people. People may not often see any specific advantage accruing to them in terms of better hospital service or better access to services from a project that tackles health in what they might consider to be an abstract fashion. In this regard, Curtice's critique of the Healthy Cities project has to be taken on board: it is seen as 'too closely tied to the interests of an international bureaucracy and various professional groups' (Curtice, 1993: 47).

The selective approach

In its conceptualisation of health, the selective approach acknowledges the scarcity of available resources and seeks the most cost-effective medical interventions to improve health. It is characterised by a disease-centred conceptualisation of health. In line with modern scientific tradition it assumes that if sufficient resources and time are concentrated on a specific problem, then a solution can be reached (Davies and Kelly, 1993). The classic example of the selective approach is that of vertically organised immunisation programmes. Alternatively a selective approach might target a high-risk group, at risk themselves or to others. Or the approach might focus on particularly vulnerable populations or groups, such as women at certain stages of their life, or children. A second feature is the identification of the health problem with a problem of health care, even when the intervention focuses on basic needs such as water, sanitation, shelter and PHC.

There is an important difference between the holistic and the selective approach in terms of the role they see for community participation in health. The former, arguing from a position that holds social development and equality as central, supports the comprehensive participation of the community towards the social construction of health and well-being. This requires the social action of individuals as participant stakeholders in the making of health. The latter approach sees health as a status to be achieved through the intervention of an external beneficiary on the grounds of a specific knowledge of the situation at the local level. In the selective approach the community plays a more passive role. Although it accepts the involvement of the community it is considered to be unproductive without the involvement of medical professionals.

Ministries of health, international agencies and NGOs are all concerned with maximising the impact and coverage of scarce resources. Moreover they have long identified health mainly with the absence of disease and have therefore concentrated their resources on curative programmes, although more recently there has been increased attention paid to preventive action. Despite the efforts to promote primary health care (PHC) in developing countries, 'few countries manage to spend less then half of their budgets on hospitals and many spend up to two thirds' (Mead et al., 1992) and PHC in execution and practice has exhibited more of a selective approach than its origins and formulation in the goals of holistic health might have suggested or anticipated.

The Urban Basic Programme implemented by UNICEF and illustrated in the second case study is a 'best practice' example of PHC. However, it remains selective rather than holistic in approach inasmuch as the aim is always to prevent or reduce the consequences of diseases. Although the improvement of the general living conditions is given emphasis, there is no explicit concern with an idea of health as a state of comprehensive and holistic well-being. The first case study illustrates a selective approach which targets a high-risk group: people who are HIV positive or who have developed AIDS and their dependants and carers. Although deriving from a selective approach, the project attempts to adopt a more holistic conceptualisation of health.

'Project Hope': help for people with HIV/AIDS[4]

São Paulo is Brazil's largest state and the largest in the whole of South America. It has one of the highest rate of urbanisation (92.8%), a figure that outpaces Venezuela (91%) and the United Kingdom (89.2%) (CAFOD, 1995b).

The project was set up in 1989 in São Paulo Paulista, a district in eastern São Paulo, and is part of a broader range of partnership initiatives implemented in different areas of Brazil by the London-based NGO, CAFOD. The city has a population of 17 million of whom 3.5 million live in São Paulo Paulista. Living conditions are extremely hard and poverty widespread, and the area has a 14% rate of illiteracy against the 9.1% for the whole of São Paulo. East Zone 2, in which São Paulo Paulista is located, is the poorest area in the city and 'acts as a sort of dormitory town in that there are few jobs available to meet the demands of the population, which obliges inhabitants to work in other parts of the city' (ibid.: 3). The area happens to be host to half of the Brazilian HIV-positive population. Women emerge as the group most vulnerable to the epidemic: 'in 1983, the proportion of cases affecting males and females in the state of São Paulo was 25/1, while by 1993 this had risen to 4/1' (ibid.: 4). Against this background there is a situation in which statutory provision reserves only 170 beds for people with AIDS. With three nurses, a social worker and the help of over a hundred volunteers, the project provides support for people with AIDS in their own homes, for children who have been orphaned and for elderly women, who are often those left to take care of the children following the loss of their parents. Over a six-month period (November 1993–April 1994) personnel from the project visited 115 people with HIV to provide them with medication and support, and conselling visits were made to 292 people with HIV (ibid.: 9). A strong parallel component of the project is the educative campaign aimed at improving awareness and HIV prevention and at reducing prejudice and isolation, which add further suffering to the lives of those affected by the illness (CAFOD, 1995a).

The above is a very valuable project in terms of enhanced access to health in the city. By focusing on groups marginalised by HIV it contributes to a more equitable access to health in terms of equal quality of care for all, while at the same time it addresses the issue of externalities or risk to the wider population and does not ignore the issue of dependants or carers. From a diversity perspective this is crucial as it is often children who are left without support and elderly people, usually women, who are the carers. On the negative side, however, the project is small-scale, geographically limited and lacks multi-sectoral coordination, thus failing to address the issue on a wider scale. As the project case study report states, despite a 165% increase in the number of the beneficiaries and a doubling of the volunteers team, the project is still insufficient to meet demands: 'The major challenge we are facing is to maintain the quality of our service provision in the face of inevitable growth' (CAFOD, 1995b: 8). Although NGO projects can be the practical tool to enhance health and access to it in the city, this case study is particularly illustrative of the abysmal task faced by this type of initiative in the face of lack of cooperation and care by governmental institutions. The vacuum left by the state in this and so many other areas of social concern cannot be filled with scarce means and the goodwill of people to participate to the construction of a better future.

UNICEF Urban Basic Services Programme: the case of illegal settlements in Guatemala City.[5] In 1987 UNICEF initiated a programme for the creation of a community health care system in El Mezquital, a squatter settlement formed by 9,400 families on the outskirts of Guatemala City. The opportunity for the programme arose with the creation of a commission to address the problems of residents of squatter settlements (COINAP – Committee for Attention to the Population of Precarious Areas in Guatemala City). This agency became UNICEF's governmental counterpart for the provision of financial and technical advice through their Urban Basic Services (UBS) programme.

The project is one of the best examples of cooperation between an international agency and the local community in responding to the health needs of poor people. Through a process of democratic consultation, the community elected 50 *reproinsas*[6] (community health workers) who began detailed physical surveying of the settlement. The promotion and implementation of a PHC plan for action greatly benefited from the acquired knowledge of the specific health needs of the community.

Over the three-year period 1987–90 the programme achieved significant results, such as an increase in immunisation coverage of children aged under 1 from 16% to 59%, and from 51% to 85% for those aged between 1 and 4. The infant mortality rate (IMR) dropped by 9% each year, compared with a decrease of 3% for the entire city. The rate of morbidity due to diarrhoeal diseases dropped annually by 11%. Throughout the project, the core activities carried out in the area of PHC contributed to the identification of further areas in need of intervention, such as education, sanitation and services. 'Discouraged from thinking that help from outside agencies would be available or would provide answers to change local conditions' (Espinosa and López Rivera, 1994: 12), local people from within the community took action to create and maintain a school and a pharmacy. For more complex initiatives such as the provision of a better water supply system and the creation of a piped sewerage system, the community obtained the technical and financial collaboration from the municipality and UNICEF.

The El Mezquital programme is a clear case, then, of the successful application of tailored solutions against universal top-down paradigmatic models of intervention. Particularly significant is the gender component of the entire project: women play a key role as promoters and implementers as well as being one of the main groups to benefit. As the statistical data show, access to health for children is another point on which the project scores highly in terms of results. Although children are obviously the central focus of all UNICEF's activities, this is a point that deserves to be stressed since children represent a particularly vulnerable group that encompasses diverse and particular needs.

However, when considering equity in terms of enhanced access to health as a main criterion for the evaluation of a project, there are issues that remain. In terms of long-term sustainability, it is still unclear how poor communities will manage to maintain equal utilisation for equal needs once the support of UNICEF is withdrawn. In this sense, community participation and empowerment risk becoming euphemisms for a *de facto* abdication of responsibility on the part of the implementing institutions, as described in this case study.

Although in the El Mezquital case the degree of integration of diverse expertise is noteworthy, more needs to be done. Specific actions must provide for the needs of those – such as the elderly or the disabled – who are not specifically addressed in the project. These actions then need to be integrated on a wider basis to maximise their effectiveness in terms of resources.

Conclusions and policy recommendations

Both the holistic and the selective approaches highlight the importance of fostering community participation as a fundamental pillar for the achievement of significant results. The main lesson arising from the holistic approach is that health is a variable heavily affected by the human, social and physical components of the city, seen as a metaphor of society as a whole. Therefore, improving access to health for the poor and the marginalised means acting on the broader determinants of inequality within society, and as such requires a high degree of political commitment.

The selective approach shows that tremendous improvement can be achieved in terms of health indicators and living conditions if community participation is sustained by governments and institutions in terms of full financial and political commitment. However, it leaves unanswered the critical question of sustainability over the long term: the problem of what will happen to people's health once support is withdrawn if the conditions that determine poverty remain unchanged.

Sustaining access to health for all in urban areas necessitates an important shift: this has to be informed by the adoption of a human development perspective in which health is seen as a human right, and as such is defended and pursued within a market-oriented system. This implies a great effort in order to empower the different groups, in the acknowledgement of the fact that power and capabilities are unevenly distributed across society. In turn, this means that action by government and institutions is required to sustain the potentialities of the diverse communities and individuals in order to allow for greater social justice and more equal command over resources.

Notes

1. It is true that child labour has an economic origin. However, it also originates from family breakdown and high insecurity affecting the livelihood of parents. This has important implications for the nutritional level and for the psychological integrity and well-being of children. As such it is here singled out in a different group of health hazards from those originated by economic factors, of which this chapter fully acknowledges the importance.

2. This is due to the complex multiple and synergetic action of several variables at the same time. For example, it is very difficult to prove the relationship between income and health. Although overall levels of mortality decrease with the increase of the income variable, at the micro level it is almost impossible to disentangle the income effect on health from that exercised by other variables such as sanitation, nutrition and education, to mention only those most commonly studied.

3. From among the many cities where the Healthy Cities project has been implemented, this chapter has chosen Glasgow and in particular the 'Glasgow Women's Health Policy' initiative for two reasons: the availability of material and the concern of this chapter with diversity, which makes the gender perspective particularly relevant to the topic of access to health.

4. This case study draws on material kindly provided by the office of CAFOD in London. CAFOD, Romero Close, Stockwell Road, London SW9 9TY, UK.

5. This section draws largely from the study conducted by Espinosa and López Rivera (1994).

6. Literally the term means 'representatives'. However their function was the equivalent of what in English are called community health workers.

References

Beall, J. (1994), 'In sickness and in health: engendering health policy for development', *Third World Planning Review*, 12(2), May: 213–22.

CAFOD (1995a), 'Working in partnership – Brazil', London: CAFOD.

CAFOD (1995b), 'Projecto Esperança (Project Hope) case study', London: CAFOD, October.

Chant, S. (1991), *Women and Survival in Mexican Cities*, Manchester and New York: Manchester University Press.

Curtice, L. (1993), 'Research and the WHO healthy cities in Europe', in Davies and Kelly, *Healthy Cities: Research and Practice*: 34–54.

Davies, J. K. and M. P. Kelly (1993), *Healthy Cities: Research and Practice*, London and New York: Routledge.

Dréze, J. and A. K. Sen (1989), *Hunger and Public Action*, Oxford: Clarendon Press.

Espinosa, L. and O. A. López Rivera (1994), 'UNICEF's urban basic services programme in illegal settlements in Guatemala City', *Environment and Urbanization*, 6(2): 9–29.

Evans, T. (1989), 'The impact of permanent disability on rural households: river blindness in Guinea', *IDS Bulletin*, 2(20), April: 41–8.

Feachem, R. G. A., T. Kjellstrom, C. J. I. Murray, M. Over and M. A. Phillips (eds) (1992), *The Health of Adults in the Developing Countries*, Washington, DC and New York: Oxford University Press for the World Bank.

Gonzaléz de la Rocha, M. G. (1994), *The Resources of Poverty: Women and Survival in a Mexican City*, Cambridge, MA and Oxford: Blackwell.

Hair, S. (ed) (1994), 'Glasgow's health women count', Glasgow: Healthy City Project Women's Health Working Group.

Hardoy, J. E. and D. Satterthwaite (eds) (1991), *The Poor Die Young: Housing and Health in Third World Cities*, London: Earthscan.

Harpham, T., T. Lusty and P. Vaughan (eds) (1988), *In the Shadow of the City*, New York: Oxford University Press.

Harpham, T. and C. Stephens (1991), 'Urbanization and health in developing countries', Geneva: WHO.

Harpham, T. and M. Tanner (eds) (1995), *Urban Health in Developing Countries: Progress and Prospects*, London: Earthscan.

Harpham, T., P. Vaughan and S. Rifkin (1985), 'Health and the urban poor in developing countries', London: London School of Hygiene and Tropical Medicine, Spring.

Healthy Toronto 2000 (1988), 'Healthy Toronto 2000', Healthy Toronto 2000 Subcommittee, Toronto: City of Toronto Board of Health, September.

Mead, O., Randall, Joyce and Orville (1992), 'The consequences of adult ill health', in Feachem et al., *The Health of Adults in the Developing World*.

Pryer, J. (1993), 'The impact of adult ill health on household income and nutrition in Khulna, Bangladesh', *Environment and Urbanization*, 5(2), October: 35–49.

Rossi-Espagnet, A. (1984), 'Primary health care in urban areas: reaching the urban poor in developing countries. A state-of-the-art report by UNICEF and WHO', Geneva: UNICEF and WHO.

Satterthwaite, D. (1993), 'The impact on health of urban environments', *Environment and Urbanization*, 5(2), October: 87–111.

Songsore, J., and G. McGranahan (1993), 'Environment, wealth, and health: towards an analysis of intra-urban differentials within the Greater Accra Metropolitan Area, Ghana', *Environment and Urbanization*, 5(2), October: 10–34.

Stephens, C. (1995), 'The urban environment, poverty and health in developing countries', *Health Policy and Planning*, Oxford: Oxford University Press, 10(2): 109–21.

Tabibzadeh, J., R. Maxwell and A. Rossi-Espagnet (eds) (1989), *Spotlight on the Cities*, Geneva: WHO.

Townsend, P. (1993), *The International Analysis of Poverty*, Hemel Hempstead: Harvester Wheatsheaf.

Tsauros, A. D. (ed.) (1992), 'World Health Organization Healthy Cities Project: a project becomes a movement', review of progress 1987 to 1990, Copenhagen: WHO Healthy Cities Project Office/FADL Publishers.

Whitehead, M. (1992), 'The concepts and principles of equity and health', *International Journal of Health Services*, 22(3): 429–45.

Whitehead, M. (1993), 'The ownership of research', in *Healthy Cities: Research and Practice*, London and New York: Routledge.

WHO (1992), 'Report on the panel on urbanization', Geneva: WHO.

World Bank (1993), *World Development Report 1993: Investing in Health*, New York: Oxford University Press.

CHAPTER 20

Volunteers in Health and Family Planning in Dhaka

Catherine Arnold

Traditionally, Bangladesh has been thought of as having a rural population, with 85–90% of the population living in the countryside and villages (Pyle, 1991). As a result, almost all the attention of the government and of NGOs has been directed at rural development. Although the government of Bangladesh has a structured health and family planning service delivery system for the rural population, it does not have a comparable infrastructure for the urban poor (Jamil, Baqui and Paljor, 1993a). It is only recently that policy-makers have come to appreciate that the urban population is growing at an extremely rapid pace and demands serious attention. This chapter will briefly review the environment and health problems linked to urbanisation in Bangladesh before describing the work of the Urban Health Extension Project (UHEP) in Dhaka. Through the recruitment and training of community volunteers, UHEP has sought to address the imbalance in health and family planning services for the urban poor. From a perspective of urban diversity, the project illustrates the intersection between service delivery and cultural diversity, and highlights the contribution of female volunteers to improving the access of the poor to services.

The environmental and health problems of Dhaka's urban poor

Dhaka was the thirty-first largest city in the world in 1985, and is expected to become the fifteenth largest by the year 2000 (United Nations, 1987). With an estimated population of 7 million in 1991, it is projected to have nearly 10 million inhabitants by the year 2000 (Mahbub and Islam, 1990). While the problems associated with rapid urbanisation are felt throughout Bangladesh, Dhaka has emerged as the worst affected. Dhaka is ranked by the Population Crisis Committee as being among the five worst metropolises in the world for general living conditions and among the three lowest for public health services (Pyle, 1991).

Approximately one-third of Dhaka's population live in slums and squatter settlements (Jamil, Baqui and Paljor, 1993a). As the slums are scattered throughout the city and are growing very fast, Dhaka faces an immense environmental and health crisis (Mahbub and Islam, 1990). The urban slums are characterised by very high population density, poor housing structures, inadequate water supplies and sanitation, and almost no drainage or garbage disposal facilities. Many of the slums are located in low-lying areas which are prone to devastation by monsoons and floods. Only very recently have the government and NGOs turned their attention towards poverty alleviation and slum improvement programmes, though the scale is still too small (Islam, 1993).

Half of Dhaka's slum population are classified as 'hard-core' poor, or those who are on the borderline of starvation (Pyle, 1991). The urban poor population is characterised by high crude birth rates (as high as 39 per 1,000) and fairly high crude death rates (as high as 43 per 1,000). Infant mortality rates of 134 per 1,000 births greatly exceed the rural average of 93 per 1,000 (Islam, 1991). The incidence of environmentally related diseases and malnutrition is high. Diarrhoeal disease is the leading cause of death among one- to four-year-olds, and one study found that 63% of the children of lower-income groups suffered from nutritional stunting or chronic malnutrition (Pyle, 1991).

To date, the Ministry of Health's efforts to establish a primary health care (PHC) system have been devoted entirely to the rural areas. Government urban health facilities provide primarily curative services and these are not easily accessible to the vast majority of slum-dwellers, who are discouraged by overcrowding, lack of attention, time and cost of transportation, and treatment charges. International and local NGOs have been the primary health and family planning service providers for urban slum populations. However, their resources are limited, services are often selective and less than optimum, and coverage incomplete (Jamil, Baqui and Paljor, 1993a).

The Urban Health Extension Project

In response to the recognition that existing health facilities could not adequately reach poorer sections of Dhaka city, the International Centre for Diarrhoeal Diseases Research, Bangladesh (ICDDR,B) initiated an urban health project in 1981, with funding from USAID and technical assistance from the Johns Hopkins University School of Hygiene and Public Health. The ICDDR,B is an autonomous, international non-profit organisation performing research and providing education, training and clinical services. The project was formerly known as the Urban Volunteer Programme (UVP), and was later renamed the Urban Health Extension Project (UHEP).

The development of UHEP

UHEP was conceived as an operations research and service delivery pilot project to test the feasibility, effectiveness and impact of women volunteers from slum areas of Dhaka providing preventative health care and referral services for their communities (ibid.). Originally, the focus of the programme was on diarrhoeal disease prevention and management through health education and the distribution of oral rehydration solution (ORS). Over the years, the programme's focus has expanded to include immunisation, nutrition education and family planning, with the development of an urban surveillance system for health and demographic data collection. The overall objective of UHEP is to help develop a cost-effective and sustainable maternal and child health and family planning (MCH-FP) service delivery system that can be broadly replicable for urban populations.

The urban volunteer model

The Dhaka metropolitan area comprises 14 *thanas* or sub-districts. The project's service delivery is restricted to slum communities in five target *thanas*. Field operations are controlled by three field offices, each directed by a community health coordinator (CHC). Under the CHCs, there are a total of 18 field supervisors (FS) assigned to the field offices. Each FS is responsible for approximately twenty-five volunteers and visits them every fortnight to reinforce training, maintain morale, identify and solve problems, collect data, and distribute supplies (Khatoon and Paljor, 1993). In 1993 UHEP supervised the work of 383 volunteers, recruited from the project's catchment areas. The UHEP model has been based on the following assumptions: a) illiterate and semi-literate slum mothers can be recruited and trained as health volunteers; b) the volunteers can increase the community's awareness and create a demand for family planning and health services; and c) the volunteers can link the slum residents to government and NGO service points.

Potential volunteers are identified by community leaders, field supervisors and community health coordinators (ibid.). The criteria for selection of volunteers include:

- self-motivatation;
- respect from the community;
- willingness and ability to learn and teach others;
- willingness and ability to collect basic service data;
- minimum one-year residence in UHEP target slums;
- preferably a female over 18 years of age; and
- preferably a housewife with no more than two children.

Profile of volunteers

In 1991, data were collected to compare the socio-demographic character-istics of volunteers with the women in the slums (Khatun and Nazrul, 1993). Twenty-five per cent of the volunteers were widowed, divorced or separated, compared to only 13% of the slum women who fell into these categories. The volunteers are a sub-group of women with a higher level of education than their female neighbours. Thirty-eight per cent of the volunteers had no formal education, whereas 87% of slum women had no formal education. Volunteers were also more likely to be employed com-pared to the women in the slum communities. Hence the volunteers differ from women in the communities in general. The data on the length of service of the volunteers were particularly noteworthy. Drop-out rates were negligible, and the average length of service was 5.7 years (Pyle, 1991). The motivation of the volunteers when money was not an inducement, and the perception of the community towards them, are described below.

Following recruitment, the volunteers receive two weeks of basic health training on the four PHC interventions (diarrhoea prevention and man-agement, nutrition, immunisation and family planning), with a four-day refresher course every four months. Each volunteer is responsible for about thirty households in her 'cluster', and is expected to visit these households at least once a month. The target population is mothers and children below 5 years of age. For family planning, the target sub-popula-tion is currently married women aged 13 to 49. The volunteers provide health education, make referrals, accompany clients to health and family planning centres, and distribute ORS (Laston, Baqui and Paljor, 1993).

The impact of volunteers

In 1991, a four-cell study was undertaken in a sample of the target communities in order to evaluate the effectiveness of the volunteer service delivery system (Baqui and Paljor, 1993). The sample population was divided into the following four service cells for comparison: 1) UHEP activity only; 2) NGO outreach only; 3) joint UHEP and NGO outreach activity and 4) no outreach activity (comparison area). The analyses in-dicated that the volunteers effectively influenced mothers' knowledge of diarrhoea prevention and the ORS utilisation rate. Based on this finding, UHEP concluded that it was possible confidently to delegate certain health service delivery responsibilities to volunteers. The four-cell study also found that the residents of slums where UHEP was implemented demonstrated somewhat higher knowledge and practice of family planning and immunisa-tion, two interventions that relied on referrals. It was hypothesised that the volunteers were responsible for this performance, as they functioned as 'gate-keepers', helping the women to overcome their reticence about and barriers to using the facilities (Pyle, 1991). In all cases, the most successful areas were the ones served jointly by volunteers and NGO field workers (Baqui and Paljor, 1993).

Perceptions of volunteer services

One question that has been continually raised in the running of the programme has been why economically disadvantaged slum women should continue to work as community volunteers. In 1992, UHEP held 28 focus groups with volunteers and slum mothers in order to gain insights into their service within the community (Laston, Baqui and Paljor, 1993). The most common motivation for women to work as volunteers was to gain knowledge, help others in their community and, in particular, to help in the treatment of sick children. Most of the volunteers also hoped that they would eventually gain salaried employment. Indeed, the experience has helped some volunteers gain employment with other NGOs or clinics in slum areas. In addition, increased prestige and respect within their community through their work and association with ICDDR,B was a strong motivating factor. One volunteer said: 'People salute us (*salam*) and call us doctor.' Before becoming volunteers, many women had been virtually confined within the home. Volunteer work allows them to move freely within the community and develop relationships with members of the urban communities. This activity is critical in the slums, where social networks and support are weak compared to the extended family relationships in the rural areas of Bangladesh. In addition, in rural areas, women have well-defined roles in fetching water, collecting firewood and agricultural work. In the slums, however, women from migrant families typically lose their traditional responsibilities and feel underemployed and undervalued. Volunteers said that they have gained a new sense of identity and purpose, and feel empowered within both their family and the community. Focus groups with released volunteers indicated that they continue to practise the lessons they learned from their training, and retain their position in the community.

Volunteers perceive their work as important to the community and their families. Many said that through their efforts patients were recovering from diarrhoea, and there were fewer deaths. The volunteers were also proud that most mothers now know how to prepare low-cost, nutritionally balanced meals, and the majority of children in their communities are immunised. All the focus groups mentioned that family members and neighbours were initially suspicious, but now they feel that a volunteer accomplishes good work for the community and her family. However, a few volunteers said that their husband or mother-in-law objected, as they work without remuneration.

Volunteers saw their ability to refer families from their catchment areas to centres where they can receive help as being crucial to their credibility. This underscores the importance of maintaining a supported and integrated approach. Besides weekly door-to-door visits, some volunteers mentioned that mothers visit them at home when the need arises. This passive delivery of volunteer services seems effective since mothers know there is someone in the community they can go to for emergency advice at night, when other facilities are closed.

The volunteers' work appears to be well accepted by the community mothers and most volunteers have been able to develop close relationships with community members, benefiting all concerned. According to community mothers, most volunteers spent from one to two hours with them every week. The majority of mothers expressed an interest in becoming volunteers. One mother said: 'We want to be educated like the volunteers and educate others in our community.'

UHEP's increased focus on family planning

Family planning has been identified as an area of top priority by the government and by donor agencies. In response to the imbalance of both research and government service provision between rural and urban areas, a recent development in the activities of UHEP is research into the family planning and contraceptive use dynamics of the urban poor of Dhaka (Jamil, Baqui and Paljor, 1993b). Despite evidence of high awareness of contraception in Dhaka's slums, contraceptive use remains relatively low (Jamil, Baqui and Paljor, 1993a). To maximise access to family planning, the rural service delivery model has through necessity emphasised domiciliary provision of contraceptives by outreach family planning workers. However, in the urban areas, little is known about the need for similar labour-intensive service approaches to meet the needs of the urban poor. The more cost-effective and sustainable approach would be based on static clinics. Therefore, research focuses on the potential for encouraging active instead of passive family planning-seeking behaviour.

In the project, however, the issue of family planning has been treated with sensitivity and caution. No attempt was ever made to ask the volunteers to distribute contraceptive methods. This was primarily because the NGO Concerned Women for Family Planning (CWFP) was active in most catchment areas and had an active community-based distribution programme (Pyle, 1991). Moreover, there has been a conscious effort since the inception of UHEP not to overload the volunteers.

The role of volunteers in family planning

A small-scale study was conducted in August 1993 to learn about family planning issues in slum areas, through information gained from in-depth interviews with UHEP volunteers in three target *thanas* (Arnold, 1994). In the course of the wider study, further insights were gained on the role of volunteers in family planning. According to the volunteers, community women approached them more often for family planning than for any other service. Thus education, motivation and referral for family planning services were assuming greater importance in their work. It also emerged that women frequently approached volunteers for advice when suffering side-effects from contraception. Further training on the advantages and disadvantages of different methods, and basic advice on side-effect management, would enable the volunteers to provide accurate information and address the concerns of their clients. This is especially important in the slums, where the physical proximity of dwellings facilitates the rapid spread of rumours and misconceptions about different methods. The volunteers mentioned that local women particularly wanted a volunteer to take them to family planning clinics, because they did not know when or where to go, or their husbands would not allow them to go alone, or they were ashamed to talk about family planning with strangers. In this way, the volunteers facilitate active rather than passive family planning-seeking behaviour.

Findings from the study indicated that by mobilising demand for family planning and alleviating fears of an alien technology and delivery system, the volunteers contribute to contraceptive use in their communities. The volunteers may be described as agents of diffusion and ideational change, operating at the intersection of supply and demand for family planning. Changing family planning behaviour is a challenging task, particularly amongst uneducated couples and populations where superstitions often persist. In these circumstances, person-to-person counselling is vital. Volunteers are considered as 'insiders' in the slum community and they are more aware of local problems, and service-seekers may feel more comfortable discussing family planning with somebody they know and trust. For example, volunteers reported that they were often approached by unmarried and newly married women, who were too embarrassed to discuss family planning with fieldworkers.

Overall, the study showed that the volunteers' role goes well beyond their 'job description'. They have a role as a community's trusted friend and empower women to discuss the subject of family planning with their husbands. In addition, some interviewees had taken the initiative to procure their own supplies of the oral pill and condoms, which they provided to clients on demand. A few volunteers also provided services to women from outside their catchment area, and encouraged diffusion in their communities by asking clients to tell their friends about them. An unexpected finding was that several respondents motivate and educate men, and men sometimes come to seek their advice. However, this is by no means satisfactory since some women volunteers reported feeling uncomfortable talking to men, particularly those unknown to them. Yet this does indicate that traditional gender barriers may be breaking down in the slum societies and reveals the potential for developing a gender-informed approach that enhances and supplements the primary focus on women to date.

The findings also showed that volunteers may be an important source of ideas for family planning programme design and implementation. They know their communities' limitations and what is reasonable or feasible within the constraints. Opportunities should therefore be created for the greater participation of volunteers in programme design, perhaps as 'spokespersons' for their communities' health and family planning needs.

The volunteers pointed out that men often present a barrier to contraceptive adoption, and that without male volunteers or fieldworkers, it is not possible to educate and motivate men. To date, almost all family planning programmes and research have been directed at women and, as volunteers identified, there is a glaring need to involve men more. Respondents emphasised that any family planning education for men would have to take place outside working hours. In addition, it was suggested that the integration of basic health services with family planning would greatly help the slum communities and increase the number of acceptors.

Discussions with this representative group of volunteers revealed that they were on the whole eager to add oral pill distribution to their responsibilities. This could be a particularly important service in under-served areas. In addition, it was apparent that some volunteers were under pressure from mothers to supply oral pills. Research by UHEP has raised the issue of alternative channels of method supply such as community depot holders (Jamil, Baqui and Paljor, 1993b). Further research could investigate the possibility of using willing and competent volunteers to distribute pills, and remunerating them for this extra service, perhaps by keeping part of the profits. Many of the volunteers appeared ready, willing and probably able to assume more service delivery responsibilities.

Conclusion

The work of UHEP in Dhaka has been instrumental in raising awareness of the plight of the urban poor and the need to develop urban health and family planning interventions and community-based delivery systems, using local capacities and participation. UHEP has succeeded in developing an effective demonstration model for the delivery of simple PHC interventions by female volunteers. The low drop-out rates of volunteers contrasts with the experience of rural volunteers in Bangladesh, and suggests that volunteerism in the urban context can provide a valuable reservoir of talent (Pyle, 1991). Evaluation of the volunteer system indicates that it is not realistic to have a fully fledged primary service delivery system based only on volunteers. However, it shows that including a volunteer component in a structured urban health and family planning service delivery system can improve the acceptance and usage of the services provided, extend some basic services to the community level, and improve the overall effectiveness of the system (Baqui et al., 1993). This creative approach has broken down the barriers between service provider and receiver, reached those who may have been excluded by fieldworkers, and incorporated MCH-FP systems into the local culture. Importantly, the work has had an empowering effect on the volunteers, through changing their spatial mobility and transforming their societal status.

Since 1994, UHEP has evolved into a new operations research initiative for urban MCH-FP, and subsequently service provision through the project has been phased out. UHEP has provided technical assistance to a number of Dhaka-based NGOs to integrate the existing UHEP volunteers in their service delivery systems (ICDDR,B, 1994). Therefore a 'scaling up' of impact is being achieved by direct multiplication of the approach to a greater diversity of organisations.

Furthermore, the wealth of information and lessons learned has been disseminated through scientific reports, seminars and forums to assist other agencies operating or planning to initiate health and family planning service delivery in the urban slums of Dhaka. The work of UHEP has resulted in new and more robust collaborations between the Ministry of Health and Family Welfare, the Dhaka City Corporation, NGOs and the private sector. With the growing knowledge and maturity of the research, formal mechanisms to transfer capabilities and apply systems within existing public and private sector frameworks are being developed (Silimperi, 1995). Such successful partnerships between research institutions, government health systems, NGOs and the private sector merit close examination for application in other cities.

References

Arnold, C. F. (1994), 'Family planning issues in the slums of Dhaka, Bangladesh: views and experiences of urban volunteer women', undergraduate dissertation, University of Southampton, UK.

Baqui, A. H. and N. Paljor (1993), 'Urban volunteer program (UVP): an introduction', paper presented at the UHEP seminar on Urban Family Planning and Health Services, ICDDR,B, 30 May.

Baqui, A. H., N. Paljor, C. Lerman and D. Silimperi (1993), 'Mother's management of diarrhoea: do urban volunteers of Dhaka have an impact?', Urban FP/MCH Working Paper No. 8, Urban Health Extension Project, ICDDR,B, May.

ICDDR,B (1993), *Annual Report 1993*.

ICDDR,B (1994), *Annual Report 1994*.

Islam, N. (1991), 'The social implications of urbanisation', in *Report of the Task Forces on Bangladesh Development Strategies for the 1990s*, Vol. 3.

Islam, N. (1993), 'Urbanization, urban poverty and the environment', unpublished paper presented at the Global Forum on Environment and Poverty, Sonargaon Hotel, Dhaka, Bangladesh, 24–7 July.

Jamil, K., A. H. Baqui and N. Paljor (1993a), 'Knowledge and practice of contraception in Dhaka urban slums: a baseline survey', Urban FP/MCH Working Paper No. 3, Urban Health Extension Project, ICDDR,B, May.

Jamil, K., A. H. Baqui and N. Paljor (1993b), 'Modes of family planning services in the urban slums of Dhaka: effect on contraceptive use', Urban FP/MCH Working Paper, Urban Health Extension Project, ICDDR,B, September.

Khatoon, M. and N. Paljor (1993), 'Volunteer service delivery model', paper presented at the UHEP seminar on Urban Family Planning and Health Services, ICDDR,B, Bangladesh, 30 May.

Khatun, J. and H. Nazrul (1993), 'Socio-demographic profile of the urban volunteers', paper presented at UHEP seminar on Urban Family Planning and Health Services, ICDDR,B, 30 May.

Laston, S. L., A. H. Baqui and N. Paljor (1993), 'Volunteer and community perceptions of volunteer services', paper presented at UHEP seminar on Urban Family Planning and Health Services, ICDDR,B, 30 May.

Mahbub, A. Q. M. and N. Islam (1990), 'Extent and causes of migration into Dhaka metropolis, and the impact on urban environment', *Proceedings of the Seminar on People and Environment in Bangladesh – UNFPA, UNDP*, February, Washington/ Dhaka, Bangladesh.

Pyle, D. (1991), *Final Evaluation – UVP*, USAID, August, Washington/Dhaka, Bangladesh.

Silimperi, D. R (1995), 'Linkages for urban health – the community and agencies', in T. Harpham and M. Tanner (eds), *Urban Health in Developing Countries*, London: Earthscan.

United Nations (1987), *World Population Policies*, Vol. 1.

PART SIX

Organising in the City for Equitable Partnerships

CHAPTER 21

Urban Management through Decentralisation

Inke Mathauer and Sandra Ng

It has been said that: 'In dealing with arrangements for urban management, we are dealing with diversity' (Davey, 1993: 1). However, urban management remains an 'elusive' concept and is often taken, without clarity of meaning, as a point of departure in analysis and practice (Stren, 1993). For the purpose of this chapter: 'Urban management is the activity of attempting to mobilise diverse resources to work in a cooperative manner in the fields of planning, programming, budgeting development and operation and maintenance of a settlement' (Forbes Davidson, in Sidabutar et al., 1991: 142) in order to ensure 'the daily functioning of a city which will both facilitate and encourage economic activity of all kinds and enable residents to meet their basic needs for shelter, access to utilities and services and income-generating opportunities' (Rakodi, 1991: 542).

In the wake of blueprint, masterplan and grandiose planning approaches, as well as centralised and various forms of decentralised government, the currently favoured institutional arrangement for urban management is urban partnership. This is understood as the coordinated and cooperative effort by public, private, non-governmental and community actors in meeting the challenge of urban management. At their best urban partnerships have the potential of expressing institutional diversity, and of reflecting and guaranteeing a perspective that recognises difference and works with diversity within a social relations approach. Urban partnerships can be flexible, and can promote the participation and empowerment of all actors involved. However, none of this is automatic or assured. It depends on the willingness of all partners to cooperate; for weaker partners to take risks rather than refuse partnership arrangements on the grounds that they might potentially be co-opted; and for stronger partners not to be instrumental in their use of less powerful people or less skilled professional organisations, in order to win contracts or to ensure successful implementation on their terms.

This chapter will examine two contrasting attempts at institutionalising partnership approaches: the Integrated District Development Planning in

Peru and the Integrated Urban Infrastructure Development Programme in Indonesia. These accounts illuminate the difficulties and obstacles of establishing institutional diversity. Through this overview of past and present approaches to urban management and urban partnerships, we attempt to show that best practice in urban management is not only an end product but a continuing process requiring long-term commitment.

Integrated District Development Plan (IDDP) with community participation in San Juan de Miraflores, Peru

San Juan de Miraflores is one of the 39 districts of Lima. It underwent very rapid and almost unplanned urban expansion and had a population of about three hundred thousand in 1991 (Dawson, 1992a). Most parts of the district consist of shanty towns. The resources and capacity required significantly to improve the living conditions of the population are presently lacking within the municipality of San Juan de Miraflores. Peruvian local government reforms in 1981 resulted in municipal government adopting responsibility for basic services such as the management of local schools, policing, water, sanitation and electricity provision. The Municipal Law of 1984 includes a section on community participation, which can be initiated by mayors in the form of 'neighbourhood juntas' and 'community committees'. This provides the opportunity to consult the electorate, which is thereby charged with supervising the provision of services or carrying out public work (Dawson, 1992a).

When the Lima provincial municipal administration was headed by the United Left under Mayor Alfonso Barrantes (1983–86), it dedicated itself to the integration of community organisation in the decision-making process. The administration lost power in the election of 1986 and the former deputy mayor, Henry Pease, gathered interested municipal officers together to establish a think-tank. The specific remit of the think-tank was to continue to promote new ways of involving the community in district decision-making. Pease was supported by five Peruvian research NGOs, all of which had experience in community development in Lima's low-income areas. The result of this initiative was the foundation of the Institute of Local Domocracy (IPADEL), which brought together a wide range of experience and skills in urban and social planning.

The institute aimed at developing a prototype scheme to engender democratic community participation in local government through incorporating community organisation within the political decision-making process. The prototype included generating consultative mechanisms, linking representatives of community organisations and trade organisations with municipal authorities in each zone of the district, and further decentralising and democratising the administration of local government by establishing local offices, thus realising the 1984 Municipal Law's provision for community participation. The overall aim was the design of an integrated district development plan that accurately reflected and catered for the needs and aspirations of the population (Dawson, 1992a).

The process IPADEL designed a simple, rapid and inexpensive methodology for performing a survey of the district as preliminary baseline research for the project (IPADEL, 1992a). This took the form of a diagnostic study and a consultation process with the population, combined with the processing of information and ideas, based on the initial survey. IPADEL started by providing training on the preparation of a district plan for the leaders of the community organisations and trade associations of San Juan de Miraflores.[1] The workshops aimed at motivating leaders to raise awareness among their constituencies of the relevance of a district plan and of a diagnostic study to provide the basis for the district development plan (Dawson, 1992a).

The most committed organisations were those run by women as part of their collective survival strategies in the face of falling real incomes – such as bulk buying schemes, soup kitchens and self-help welfare activities – together with micro-enterprise associations represented by three independent organisations. IPADEL succeeded in facilitating inter-organisational cooperation to formulate common proposals and to continue elaborating these proposals. For the first time, small business organisations started to coordinate their activities with other organisations and associations of the district, resulting in the planning of a joint employment programme. Furthermore, a survey of a sample of 1,000 households covering each area of the district of San Juan de Miraflores was carried out in order to gather more detailed information about the socio-economic situation, service demands, income resources, transport patterns, perceived problems and the proposed solutions of local residents. IPADEL's expertise in urban planning meant that the data received by aerial photographs could be utilised in increasing the viability of infrastructure planning proposals (Dawson, 1992a).

Throughout the process, the newly elected mayor of San Juan de Miraflores did not show the same interest and willingness to cooperate in the project as had his predecessor. This was because IPADEL was perceived as a political opponent, since the institute grew out of the initiative of United Left politicians. Thus the initiative of setting up official neighbourhood juntas, reliant on the initiative of the mayor, was blocked. IPADEL had then to change its strategy, as there was no central and unified body at the district level to whom the proposed district plan could be addressed. In 1990 IPADEL initiated the formation of a centralised body, the Central Committee of Community Organisations, which consisted of various community organisations and associations. It rapidly dissolved, however, as differing organisational goals and attitudes manifested themselves in power struggles that impeded the elaboration of common future perspectives for the district. IPADEL therefore changed focus and concentrated on bringing together the various NGOs working in the district to coordinate their participation in the development of the district plan. The forum it provided was intended to share and exchange project experiences and studies, resulting in a joint document consisting of a situational analysis and sector proposals (Dawson, 1992a).

In 1991, recognising the significance of joint actions in lobbying local government, community organisations once again gathered and established a new centralised body, the District Management Committee, charged with campaigning for proposals in order to improve services. The results of the surveys and the proposals of the consultation processes were synthesised in a final document, the main conclusions of which were shared within the District Management Committee and used for further dialogue with the municipal authorities. Accordingly, realising the interests of the population working with IPADEL, the municipal authorities signalled more interest in developing the Integrated District Development Plan (Dawson, 1992b). The strength of the plan was the fact that it drew on existing resources, aiming at assessing how these could be best used and what organisations could provide best benefits and services. The plan thus contained very specific proposals on how to improve the financial and commercial potential of the district. Furthermore, it included practical and locally informed proposals on a wide variety of issues including land use, transport and roads, service provision, housing, environmental health measures, economic development and employment (Dawson, 1992a).

The Integrated Urban Infrastructure Development Programme (IUIDP) in Indonesia

Indonesia has one of the world's highest national urban growth rates at 5.4%, and thus is presented with considerable urban challenges (Suselo, Taylor and Wegelin, 1995). Indonesia's positive experience with the Kampung (informal or low-income settlement) Improvement Programme provided the impetus for the Directorate General of Human Settlements in the Ministry of Public Works to expand its approach in 1985. Essentially, the IUIDP consists of a package of activities informed by an integrated approach to planning and management whereby the allocation of available resources comes to local government from a traditionally highly centralised national government. The provincial level was given a pivotal role in trying to merge top-down and bottom-up planning processes.

The process   Planning and programming for the IUIDP is encompassed in a multi-year investment plan generally lasting from five to seven years. The objective of the Program Jangka Menengah (PJM – multi-year investment programme) is to serve as a means of prioritising infrastructural investment according to population trends and needs, relative to the availability of resources from local revenues, central grants, local borrowing capacity and local institutional capacity. IUIDP investment concentrates on sewerage, solid waste management, drainage and flood control, urban roads, market infrastructure and housing.

Activating the IUIDP can be disaggregated into four major phases. The process begins with the preparation of an IUIDP development assessment plan (IDAP) by local governments assessing infrastructural deficiencies and needs according to predicted urban growth in districts and municipalities. These predictions form the basis of a financial plan, which is a reference point for the PJM. Second, a draft investment plan, including resource requirements, leads the way in the drafting of a municipal revenue improvement action plan (RIAP) and a local institutional development action plan (LIDAC). These in turn facilitate the implementation of activities and involve the concentrated input of centrally appointed technical consultants. Third, a 'locally' designed PJM, based on technical, financial and institutional criteria, is presented to the provincial government level for assessment. Finally, the local government budget is integrated into the provincial budget. This is assessed at the national level by three highly bureaucratic ministries: the Ministry of Public Works, the Ministry of Home Affairs and the Ministry of Finance. It has been estimated that the whole process has a minimum time-span of ten months.

The legal basis for community participation is embodied in Indonesian law. For example, Law No. 4 of 1982 on the environment states that: 'everybody has the right and obligation to participate in environmental management' (including infrastructure provision, operation and maintenance). Equally, the Ministry of Home Affairs Regulation No. 9/1982 advocates for bottom-up planning approaches to identify the needs of communities in the preparation of programmes (Fritschi et al., 1992). The concept of joint financing by both government and non-governmental sectors has a long history in Indonesian development. Thus the IUIDP guidelines explicitly state that the private sector and the community need to be mobilised to make human and financial resource contributions. The guidelines do not, however, include statements on community participation in decision-making.

The IUIDP started in 1986 in the province of East Java. The programme was initially presented to local government as a general concept, rather than as a comprehensive programme incorporating specific objectives, administrative procedure and a tripartite structure. As a result, two years after initiation there was still little understanding of the programme and only partial support for participation at the local level (Pol, 1995). The provincial government moved from its original coordinating and technical provisioning role to influencing the formulation, review and appraisal of implementation of local IUIDP programmes (Hoff and Steinberg, 1993).

A unique component of the IUIDP is the comprehensive training that serves as a mechanism to support implementation. The rationale for training is that groups and areas critical to the successful implementation of the programme at the policy level, in management and in technical support, benefit from an enhanced ability to deal with issues arising from this highly ambitious exercise of decentralisation. The core training programme is directed at provincial and local government. The provincial IUIDP operational policy seminars, designed for decision-makers in the two levels of government, give policy-makers a forum in which to discuss and establish operational issues for programme implementation. The provincial IUIDP workshops, aimed at middle-level managers, are influenced by the results of the policy seminars. A course planned around the programme cycle for the technical staff of local government provides classroom teaching in combination with supervised fieldwork. It is designed to enable participants to become familiar with the PJM process and to increase awareness of policy issues. Aside from this core programme, special seminars and workshops are held for central government staff directly involved in the IUIDP assessments.

A particular strength of the overall training is that the workshops highlighted the diversity in interpretation of the underlying concepts of the IUIDP both regionally and among the various agencies involved. Recognising this fact, central government acknowledged the need for greater clarification, but others appreciated a liberal interpretation as it allowed for differences in interpretation and allocation of available resources and local priorities (Dimitriou, 1991).

Assessment: bridging the gaps through urban partnerships?

This chapter will now assess the principles of inclusive partnership that have informed the Peruvian and Indonesian experience by evaluating the following aspects: cooperation and coordination, participation and empowerment, and training and institutional capacity-building.

Cooperation and coordination The starting position for the Peruvian experience is the existence of devolved bodies at municipal level and the 1984 Municipal Law allowing for bridging the community with the municipal government, although this institutional set by itself in no way gave priority to the private and voluntary sector according to the principle of subsidiarity. Unfortunately, IPADEL was hindered in achieving its overall objective of institutionalising community participation in local government decision-making processes by unwillingness and lack of cooperation within local government authorities. However, the institute was successful in developing a mechanism to channel and coordinate community cooperation

and participation around the joint goal of an integrated district development plan. A District Management Committee – representing a range of
associations and different zones of the district, the joint employment
planning of the small business organisation, and the NGO study forum
– formed the links in a grid of cooperation and coordination relations,
expanding the concept of partnership. While clear links to the public
sector remained absent, the committee centralised private and voluntary
sector initiatives at the district level and provided the potential of realising
connections to the municipality and the public sector in the future. It is
important to note that the District Management Committee did not reflect
the entire composition of its constituency. Only one-fourth of its members
were female, and trade and business organisations were rather over-
represented (IPADEL, 1992b), inhibiting a diverse perspective for articu-
lating needs and planning. The initial breakdown of the Central Committee
of Community Organisations indicated the lack of mechanisms to deal
creatively with difference and conflicts in a sustained way.

In the Indonesian case, it is clear that intra-government urban
partnership was in fact the only focus envisaged in the IUIDP process.
The design of the PJM was limited to cooperation and coordination
between the three tiers of government. The non-government sector was
recognised primarily for its potential in realising financial resources for
investment in infrastructure and the provision of services. By relying
mainly on administrative decentralisation, the programme gave minimum
attention to developing practical mechanisms that made possible greater
involvement by other actors. The design of the PJM at the local level
created opportunities for cooperation with the community and the private
sector, but these were generally not used. Disappointingly, when the
strategic plans of local government were directed at mobilising other urban
actors, these were frustrated by the lack of local institutional capacity.

Clearly the goals of cooperation and coordination between different
levels of government, between the public and other sectors and among
different actors and interest groups within particular sectors have to be
pursued with great sensitivity as to who is initiating the partnership and
to what end. The involvement of central government might be important
and useful, especially if this includes a more equitable distribution in
terms of resources among regions or between the central and local levels.
However, this will be undermined if local government is denied the
autonomy to identify priorities. Likewise, the involvement of local government is essential, not least for coordinating and facilitating equitable
investment and management, but only if it can engage with the organisations of civil society outside of a top-down, hierarchical or party political
framework. Finally, processes of coordination and cooperation need to be
alert to how representatives of the private and community sectors emerge
and whose interests they represent.

Participation and empowerment In the Peruvian case popular participation in the formulation of a district development plan was realised through the consultation process among the 200 community organisations and associations. It can be argued that an emphasis on mobilisation and consciousness-raising provides fertile ground for empowering members of the community to consider the implementation of the IDDP, including decision-making, planning and monitoring. The significance of empowering residents through organising around a central issue lay in the fact that it constituted the basis for joint pressure via local government. This process of applying pressure was strengthened by the NGOs coordinating their activities, which contributed to a broader dynamic on an intermediary level. However, although the goal of community participation may have been achieved, this did not guarantee that all interest groups were involved and represented at all levels. The jury needs a further sitting before deciding whether, in this example from Peru, community participation was synonymous with or incorporated sensitivity to differences in the community or diversities in approach to organisation and process.

Overall assessments of the IUIDP in Indonesia conclude that the potential benefits of decentralising the planning of urban service delivery are limited by inadequate user participation and poor integration of private and non-governmental actors (Fritschi et al., 1992; Hoff and Steinberg, 1993; Atkinson, forthcoming). Clearly the example of the IUIDP shows that an 'integrated' and 'decentralised' process is not synonymous with participation, nor with inclusive partnerships, involving and enabling diverse groups. Active community participation is not incorporated into the PJM formulation process, and most local government offices are not amenable to community-based projects or greater community involvement with existing projects as they are seen as being time consuming (Hoff and Steinberg, 1993). However, with community participation legitimated by the IUIDP policy and constitutionally enshrined in local government, the potential exists for the involvement of a wider range of actors. But without significant changes in the practice of urban management and, some would argue, in the socio-political context as well, this is by no means ensured.

Training and institutional capacity-building In the Peruvian case the need to change the practice and mind-set not just of communities and businesses, but also of the public sector and politicians, was acutely recognised. Institutional development, in fact, was both the strategy and the objective of the IDDP. IPADEL's regional training events for local government officers were attended by councillors and mayors and have to be noted with assessing the role of training and institution-building (Dawson, 1992a). Enhanced by IPADEL's general standing with local government (Dawson, 1992b), these training events could influence the municipalities to integrate community participation into their practice.

Moreover, a side-effect of IPADEL's IDDP initiative was institutional capacity-building in the NGOs and the community organisations and associations, in addition to the District Management Committee's developing the skills necessary to proceed with the plan.

The strong training component incorporated into the IUIDP, designed specifically to build capacity into implementation, in Indonesia failed in its efforts. Davidson and Watson (1995) conclude that even in training, priority was assigned to the speed of production of the PJM rather than to the process of its production. Despite the existence of information and communication activities, no institutional structures existed for training in research, development and delivery (Sidabutar et al., 1991). Partly because of relatively weak local government structures and partly because of lack of clarity as to who was to manage training, there was confusion over who was to be trained, by whom and on what subjects. Coupled with these problems, the lack of adequate resources resulted in the number of planned training cycles being dramatically reduced. Effective training could have significantly enhanced the possibility for integrating private sector and community actors and for stimulating a participatory IUIDP process.

Conclusions in context

Elements of IPADEL's experience in Peru in urban partnership initiated from the bottom up might be transferable or replicable. Indeed, a second main objective of IPADEL was to produce a methodology that was open in terms of its outcomes, yet replicable and adaptable to other contexts in terms of its processes. In the rural Southern Andean province of Puno, IPADEL found an application for the methodology in an adapted form (Dawson, 1992b). It also must be noted that contingent factors such as expertise within IPADEL and the existence of a pluralistic organisational spectrum played an important role in the organisation's achievements. Finally, because of the high degree of organisation, there is a strong identification of the population with and strong engagement for the neighbourhood. These factors might not be present under other political, social and economic conditions or in a specific regional or country context and thus cannot be facilitated automatically elsewhere.

The experience of the IUIDP in Indonesia suggests that although the outcomes failed to include inter-organisational urban partnership, there are elements of the process that provide useful lessons. The fact that local governments are now designers of the PJM provides a framework for an urban management that could move towards a more inclusive and locally based approach. Although financial constraints remain, planning and design are now institutionalised within local government, and as this becomes an accepted norm, there is potential for the process to proceed towards effective urban partnerships. Keeping in mind the traditionally centralised government framework in Indonesia, the IUIDP process has provided an entry point at which private enterprise, non-governmental institutions and the community can proceed to work together, with the proviso that commitment, including resource commitment, from both national government and the international donor community remains.

Neither the bottom-up approach of Peru nor the top-down approach of Indonesia implies an adequate diversity perspective. The Indonesian experience exemplifies how the non-involvement of the private and the non-governmental sector can be the first barrier to the inclusion of alternative voices, especially in a context where central government is also not committed to representing the interests of or redistributing resources towards less powerful and more disadvantaged groups. In Peru, partnership involved the private and the voluntary sectors, and full participation was implicitly assumed. However, this experience shows that participation does not automatically mean the recognition of difference or working with diversity. Only a section of the population, those organised within community and business organisations, were consulted. Even within these groups, it is questionable to what extent their interests conflicted with those of more dominant groups. For example, beyond increasing the labour productivity of women, which was prioritised in the IDDP or a mere amelioration of some of their immediate felt needs, it is not clear whether the strategic gender interests of women were advanced. Similarly, it is not clear how conflicting interests are accommodated within and between sectors.

These issues point at two implications. First, institutional diversity is a precondition for having a diversity perspective in the first place. Hence urban partnership can facilitate a diversity perspective only when there are constructive mechanisms for recognising difference and resolving conflict. Second, urban partnerships that reflect a diversity perspective are contingent on the political will of those in power. Nevertheless, the experiences of Peru and Indonesia demonstrate potential entry points for establishing and elaborating an institutional arrangement that generates and internalises a diversity perspective. For Peru, the starting point for taking diversity into account lay in the existence of organisational pluralism. The task remains to include in the participation process a wider spectrum of organisations, encompassing and representing a broader range of interests. The same task remains for consultation processes within organisations, since it cannot be assumed that members' interests are homogeneous. Most important is the identification of social groups that are not visibly organised, so that they may equally participate in the process of developing a District Plan. In Indonesia, disappointingly, the IUIDP to date has had limited consultation with communities. However, the literature concludes optimistically that, because the IUIDP favours partnership and participation, the entry points for needs to be met in a diverse manner are there.

In conclusion, the Peruvian and Indonesian experiences are encouraging examples of first steps towards arrangements of urban partnership. The above discussion illustrates that best practice in urban management and urban partnerships is not only an end product but a continuing process. This implies that there is no blueprint approach and that the creation and institutionalisation of urban partnerships should comprise the adoption and adaptation of principles in combination with the consideration of the political, technical, social and financial feasibility, rather than follow a formulaic approach.

Note

1. In San Juan de Miraflores, there are over a thousand grassroots organisations dealing with the various problems of the residents. About two hundred organisations have been involved in the process.

References

Atkinson, A. (forthcoming), 'Development in urban environmental planning and management in Indonesia: the secondary cities of Sulawesi', *World Development*.

Dawson, E. (1992a), 'District planning with community participation in Peru: the work of the institute of local democracy – IPADEL', *Environment and Urbanisation*, 4(2): 90–100.

Davey, K. (1993), 'Elements of urban management', Urban Management Programme discussion paper, Washington, DC: World Bank.

Davidson, F. and D. Watson (1995), 'Training for IUIDP: ideas, integration and implementation', in H. Suselo et al., *Indonesia's Urban Infrastructure Development Experience*.

Dawson, E. (1992b), 'NGOs and public policy reform: lessons from Peru', *Journal of International Development* 5(4): 401–14.

Dimitriou, H. T. (1991), 'An integrated approach to urban infrastructure development: a review of the Indonesian experience', *Cities* 8(3): 193–208.

Fritschi, B. et al. (1992), 'Community participation and the IUIDP experiences and potentials', in R. van der Hoff and F. Steinberg (eds), *Innovative Approaches to Urban Development*, pp. 151–80.

Hoff, R. van der and F. Steinberg (1992), *Innovative Approaches to Urban Development*, Aldershot, UK.

Hoff, R. van der and F. Steinberg (1993), *The Integrated Urban Infrastructure Development Programme and Urban Management Innovations in Indonesia*, IHS Working Papers, The Netherlands.

IPADEL (1992a), *Proyecto de Planificacion Popular en San Juan de Miraflores, Lima, Peru*, Lima: IPADEL.

IPADEL (1992b), *Propuesta para el Plan Integral de Desarrollo de San Juan De Miraflores*, Lima: IPADEL.

Pol, E. van der (1995), 'East Java case study' in H. Suselo et al., *Indonesia's Urban Infrastructure Development Experience*.

Rakodi, C. (1991), 'Cities and people: towards a gender-aware urban planning process?' *Public Administration and Development*, 11(6): 541–59.

Sidabutar, P., N. Rukamana, R. van der Hoff and F. Steinberg (1991), 'Development of urban management capacities: training for integrated urban infrastructure development in Indonesia', *Cities*, 8(2): 142–50.

Stren, R. (1993), 'Urban management in development assistance: an elusive concept', *Cities*, 10(2): 125–38.

Suselo, H., J. Taylor and E. Wegelin (eds) (1995), *Indonesia's Urban Infrastructure Development Experience: Critical Lessons of Good Practice*, Indonesia: UNCHS.

CHAPTER 22

The Single Regeneration Budget and Urban Planning in Oxford

Sophie Peace

Urban planning in the United Kingdom is in a process of rapid change. Planners have learned a number of valuable lessons from past mistakes and have new opportunities for taking a more integrated approach via urban partnerships stimulated by the new Single Regeneration Budget (SRB), introduced in April 1994 by the Department of the Environment. Some critics have suggested that the SRB is merely an attempt by the government to save money by rolling all former sources of funding into one single source, which bidders have to compete for. Others have been more positive about the change that the SRB represents to urban planning approaches, believing that it encourages different groups involved in the task of urban regeneration management to cooperate to a greater extent, and hope that it may result in a more holistic improvement for the urban communities concerned. This chapter is a case study of a successful SRB bid for Pegasus Court in Blackbird Leys, Oxford. It aims to illustrate the considerations involved in this new approach to urban planning in the UK, and leaves readers to decide whether or not they think the process is replicable in other areas of the world.

Oxford City Council and Ealing Family Housing Association successfully bid for capital funding from the government's new SRB, and this chapter is drawn from their proposal. The urban planning process in Britain has moved away from the emphasis of the 1960s and 1970s on physically improving housing conditions and ensuring the greatest availability at the least cost. The aim is no longer simply providing good-quality housing but facilitating integrated schemes to stimulate employment and training opportunities, reduce crime and enhance wider health and security concerns. Fundamental to this shift in emphasis are effective partnerships between city councils, housing corporations, tenant associations and other local groups involved in planning and delivery processes. The SRB thus represents a potential departure from the hitherto piecemeal approach to urban regeneration in Britain and presents an opportunity for funding an integrated, holistic approach to the multi-faceted issues of council housing estates. The specific project at Pegasus Court in Blackbird Leys, Oxford, aims especially at addressing the needs of young unemployed people. Originally, there were also proposals for special high-cost accommodation for the elderly. However, due to the recent withdrawal of capital funding from the Oxfordshire City Council Social Services Authority, these plans have been shelved.

The Single Regeneration Budget (SRB)

The SRB is targeted at the regeneration of a physical area while improving training, employment, housing, environmental and business opportunities for local communities. The mechanism for change has been to roll 20 existing aid programmes from five national government departments into one fund: the Single Regeneration Budget. The SRB was initiated in April 1994, with a budget of £1.4 billion for 1994/95 from the Department of the Environment. Ministers have indicated that they will be looking to the SRB to support initiatives that build on good practice, represent good value for money and meet one or more of the following overall objectives, as stated in the *Bidding Guidance* (DOE, 1994):

- enhance the employment prospects, education and skills of local people, particularly the young and those at a disadvantage, thus promoting equality of opportunity;
- encourage sustainable economic growth and wealth creation by improving the competitiveness of the local economy, including business support;
- improve housing through physical improvements, greater choice and better management and maintenance;
- promote initiatives of benefit to ethnic minorities;
- tackle crime and improve community safety;
- protect and improve the environment and infrastructure and promote good design; and
- enhance the quality of life of local people, with regard to health and to cultural and sports opportunities.

The rationale behind the SRB is to tailor grants more closely to local needs, make them easier to obtain and thus increase the effectiveness and equity of funds. Bidding is on an annual basis and the schemes to be supported are selected by government ministers. Competition is intense and the majority of schemes put forward are unsuccessful. A quote from Denise Chevin from Ealing Family Housing Association illustrates how demanding the SRB is on housing providers:

> This new funding strategy is the biggest shake-up in urban regeneration policy for a decade ... In future, every £1 of government money for rejuvenating towns and cities will be fiercely fought for in competition. In this free-for-all,

resources will be scarce and partnerships the name of the game. Bidders will be expected to bring much to the table: not just finance from the private sector but support from local communities. They will have to paint visions for creating jobs and reducing crime as well as refurbishing homes (Chevin, 1994: 18).

The SRB brings the issue of the role of housing associations into sharp relief. It reflects government thinking that housing associations should not merely be providers and managers of housing, but rather, in partnership with others, should attempt to meet the wider needs of tenants. A similar shift from a less sectoral to a more integrated approach to urban regeneration and urban management has been noted in many other countries (Devas and Rakodi, 1993). The major drawbacks to this competitive process for providers are the high cost of unsuccessful bids and the increased bureaucracy created by the introduction of a quarterly monitoring system of all successful bids. There is also the risk of disappointment within communities, mobilised to support partnership initiatives.

The Blackbird Leys Redevelopment Initiative (BLRI)

The BLRI was successful in attracting just over £1 million from the government to add to the £3.68 million raised by Oxford City Council and the Housing Corporation as well as £1.3 million from the private sector. The BLRI is a project designed to tackle extremely poor housing conditions and by so doing significantly enhance the training, employment and business opportunities for local people living in the Blackbird Leys area of Oxford.

This initiative is linked to the other major housing developments at Blackbird Leys that the city has set up in partnership with housing associations – for example, the Greater Leys Estate, which is the largest social housing project of its kind in the United Kingdom. In working up the bid, Oxford City Council worked closely with a number of agencies, in particular Ealing Family Housing Association (EFHA), Oxfordshire Community Development Agency and the Pegasus Court Tenants' Association (PCTA). Other consultative partners include the John Mowlem Training Trust, Oxfordshire County Council Social Services Authority, Oxfordshire County Council Community Education Ethnic Minorities Team, Oxfordshire Community Health NHS Trust, Blackbird Leys Parish Council and the Young Builders' Trust (YBT). This SRB project is expected to generate real and lasting business and employment opportunities for local people at exceptional value for money. Central to the project is that working in partnership with local people, local groups and other key organisations creates the means to ensure real and long-standing benefits to the local community of Blackbird Leys. The targets aimed for are:

- 200-plus new training places;

- over 150 people obtaining accredited training qualifications;
- approximately 25 new long-term jobs for local people;
- 108 households rehoused from defective housing;
- 2 community businesses set up; and
- 60 new homes to be built.

There will be at least seven separate training packages. These include construction skills, building maintenance, business management, joinery for disabled people, training in community care skills, housing management and carpentry. The two community enterprises will provide long-term employment opportunities for local people.

The area

Blackbird Leys was developed in the 1960s as a large council estate on the edge of Oxford. According to the 1991 census, there are 8,500 people currently living in Blackbird Leys, against a total population for Oxford City of 134,000. Despite 'right to buy' schemes, over 50% of homes are still council tenant households, more than twice the average across the city. The downsizing of the nearby Rover car plant with the loss of over 5,000 jobs by the early 1990s led to increased unemployment of male unskilled and semi-skilled workers. However, it was the attention of national television on the prevalence of 'joy-riding' of stolen cars in the area and graphic pictures of 'youth riots' in the spring of 1992 that focused wider attention on Blackbird Leys. Those working in the area have suggested that this increased media attention actually contributed towards increased capital funding for social regeneration in the area. Although Blackbird Leys has poor deprivation indices, other areas of Oxford also fare poorly but have received considerably less input in terms of planning and capital funding. However, Blackbird Leys suffers from a range of housing, social and economic problems that put the situation of Blackbird Leys in the broader context of the Oxford area:

- Research undertaken by the University of Oxford as part of the City Council's anti-poverty strategy reveals that around 40% of the residents of Blackbird Leys are in receipt of housing/council tax benefit, and nearly 25% are on income support. Claimants on means-tested benefit have increased by 30% since 1991.
- According to the 1991 census figures, Blackbird Leys has the highest concentration of unskilled workers in the city and the greatest concentration of single parents, over 85% of whom receive income support.
- Rates of unemployment currently stand at 12% in the area, compared to 8.8% in the city as a whole. The Employment Intelligence Unit reports youth unemployment in Blackbird Leys at 27%.
- Over 10% of the population are from black and ethnic minority groups,

against a city-wide percentage of 6%. Within these groups, a disproportionately high number are unemployed. The 1991 census figures show that unemployment was 20.7% for ethnic minorities in Blackbird Leys compared to 13.1% for Oxford as a whole.

- A high incidence of debt and financial problems characterises household finances, with many households needing recourse to loans at very high rates of interest.

Pegasus Court

Pegasus Court is a development of 108 'Resiform' (a compound of asbestos and timber) system-built dwellings within four three-storey blocks in Blackbird Leys. The flats are of extremely poor standard and tenants suffer some of the poorest housing conditions in Blackbird Leys, with problems such as damp and lack of heating prevalent. A survey commissioned by Oxford City Council in July 1994 demonstrated that the dwellings in their present state have a life of only another three years and that the only cost-effective solution is to demolish them and redevelop the estate.

There is a small communal grassed area around the bottom of the flats, but no tenants have their own garden. This is a problem, especially for young families, as there is nowhere for their children to play or for washing to be hung out. Pegasus Court has experienced much vandalism over the years. There have been fires in the bin sheds and one block of garages was so badly vandalised that it had to be demolished. There are graffiti on the stairways and litter is regularly dumped in the area. Spatially, the large number of units in each block and the density of blocks result in many badly lit corners and alleyways around the estate. These factors, along with the lack of private garden areas, are being addressed in the architectural design of the new two-storey houses. These will be built at a lower density, to higher standards and with improved layout for maximum security for residents.

The project has four distinct but interdependent elements: housing, community enterprise, training and employment.

Housing The dwellings are currently tenanted and the tenants will be offered a choice of three rehousing options: a grant to purchase on the open market, a grant for shared ownership, or an offer of rented accommodation from either a housing association or the council. A realistic and efficient decanting (the moving out and rehousing of present residents) programme is the first and most essential requirement of this project.

In order to facilitate a decanting programme the Housing Corporation, subject to the SRB bid being successful, will make available to the city up to 108 tenant grants made up of a mixture of tenant incentive scheme (TIS) grants and do it yourself shared ownership (DISYSO) grants. In order to ascertain tenants' preferences and their suitability for each of the above rehousing options, a survey was undertaken by EFHA in August 1994. This showed that very few tenants wanted or had the financial resources for either shared ownership or assisted purchase by means of the TIS grant. Consequently the vast majority will have to be decanted to alternative rented property in either council or local housing association sectors.

The site will be demolished block by block and the vacated site will then be redeveloped as a mixture of housing comprising a self-build scheme and housing association dwellings for rent. The mix of housing reflects an approach to create a more balanced household mix within Blackbird Leys as a whole, with a relatively small proportion of the new housing for households with children. The flats in the four three-storey blocks will be replaced by two-storey houses with private fenced gardens. The redevelopment of the site will underpin a number of training and employment programmes for local people.

A 15-dwelling self-build scheme for local young people will be developed in partnership with the Young Builders' Trust. The YBT is a national organisation with expertise working with young self-builders and with whom Oxford City Council is presently working on a successful self-build scheme in another area of the city. With the level of interest already expressed, the council, EFHA and the YBT are confident in targeting this self-build scheme exclusively at unemployed and ex-offending young people, who live in Blackbird Leys.

As noted above, a significant part of the vacated site was to be developed for a 24-unit high-care scheme for the elderly. This was to be built to the highest specification, reflecting the needs and preferences of this client group. But because of the high cost involved, the county council has not been able to raise the amount required to fund this part of the project. As a result, the units for the elderly have had to be abandoned, meaning that there will be 64 houses for general renting.

Two major contingencies for the effective delivery of the bid proposals are the availability of appropriate housing for present tenants of Pegasus Court and the cooperation of the Pegasus Court Tenants' Association in the decanting process. Sylvia Moore, coordinator of the PCTA, notes that the present residents feel that they have been informed of rather than adequately consulted about the plans. Although they are keen to be rehoused there is considerable anger that they will not be allowed to move back into the new accommodation constructed on the site of Pegasus Court. The reason for this is unclear, but the EFHA argues that a smaller number of dwelling units will be available than presently exist and that it is more practical to rehouse the present residents permanently according to individual housing needs. The new accommodation will be allocated to those on council waiting lists. It is argued that this presents the possibility of creating a mix of tenants who may form a less polarised and more balanced community.

Community enterprise There are to be two community businesses, providing buildings maintenance services and care in the community services respectively. This component of the bid will be 'sub-contracted' to Oxfordshire Co-operative Development Agency (OCDA), which has the skills and experience to ensure success. OCDA will employ a community enterprise development worker based at Blackbird Leys whose core objective will be to develop the potential, commitment and energy of the local community to enable it to take advantage of the business opportunities in buildings maintenance and care in the community services.

While the bid does include construction-related training, this will not lead to a high level of long-term employment in the locality. Given that there will be over 1,400 new housing association dwellings completed in the city in 1992–98, the total housing association stock in the city will have risen to over 3,000 by the turn of the century. Unlike the temporary nature of construction employment, there will always be a need for maintenance services to the housing stock and the bid sets out an aim to access these stable and local employment opportunities for long-term unemployed people, through a community business. It is estimated that the equivalent of 15 full-time jobs will result from the buildings maintenance business.

The Pegasus Court SRB bid is linked with the city council's partnership development of a pensioners' centre with Oxford Housing Partnership on land adjacent to Blackbird Leys. This centre will be the premises from which the community care business will operate. It will be completed in June 1997 and will be open to all people of pensionable age in Blackbird Leys, estimated at over 1,300 people. It has been designed to provide a full range of social, welfare and care services for both able-bodied pensioners and frail elderly people. The business will provide services including hairdressing, bathing and chiropody and will offer locum services for residential care homes throughout the city. The clients for the community care services, procured through appropriate tendering procedures, are the Social Services Authority, the Oxfordshire Community Health NHS Trust and other relevant agencies.

Training and employment The training in construction skills programme will offer 210 training places for local people and specifically the groups targeted by the proposal. Of this number, 155 will be accredited places and where they are linked to longer-term employment opportunities arising from the community businesses they will be customised for that purpose. The programme will include buildings maintenance skills; business management skills; joinery skills for disabled people; housing management skills and plant maintenance. The project is expected to produce a significant boost in local employment opportunities: 135 jobs in the redevelopment construction projects; 15 long-term jobs in the community buildings maintenance business; and 10 long-term jobs in the community care services business.

Forward strategy and output monitoring

Oxford City Council will continue with its partners to monitor the longer-term effect of these initiatives and consider further ways of ensuring that lasting benefits for the local community can be secured. The outputs will be subject to regular monitoring of both quantitative and qualitative aspects. At the end of the project in 2001 there will be two community businesses in operation which will have continuing opportunities to bid for and procure contracts for buildings maintenance and community care, thus providing local employment opportunities. The benefits from the new housing will be enduring and it is hoped that the tenant management organisation will act as a catalyst for future management initiatives in the city.

Conclusion

The SRB provides urban planners with the opportunity and incentive to form partnerships with community associations, voluntary groups, households and the private sector in the delivery of urban services within the context of a more integrated approach to urban development. The emphasis laid on the necessity for consultation with and participation of the local community can only mean an improvement on development that is non-consultative and top-down. There are many, however, who have criticised the introduction of the SRB. It has meant a reduction in real terms in the availability of funding for urban regeneration, and the costs of the increased bureaucracy are transferred to local authorities and private agencies. Despite the potential pitfalls of the SRB and the planning process outlined above, this new approach to regenerating disadvantaged areas of British cities via the establishment of partnerships appears to be a promising attempt to make integrated, area-based social policy more effective and efficient in meeting the needs of diverse groups of urban dwellers.

Informal opinion among people who have been involved in the Pegasus Court bid and other SRB projects suggests that the Blackbird Leys Redevelopment Initiative at Pegasus Court is a reasonably good example of the SRB mechanism. In particular, the focus on directly tackling the short- and longer-term needs of local residents is highlighted. This focus is absent in many other bids involving SRBs, which end up being co-opted by large local business interests, lobbying for improvement of the physical, transport or aesthetic aspects of the target area instead of concentrating on the social aspects of urban regeneration.

In Blackbird Leys, as elsewhere, mechanisms for identifying and reaching diverse groups in the community need to be carefully developed and applied. The ethos of the project at Pegasus Court has been and will continue to be to work in partnership with local people, local groups and other key organisations as the best means of ensuring real and long-standing benefits to the local community. However, an ethos remains hollow if not followed in practice. The perception of the Pegasus Court residents of being 'informed' rather than consulted is of concern and, in itself, belies the notion of partnership.

The forward strategy and output monitoring elements of the proposals appear to be proactive and will assist the sustainability of the project objectives, but the monitoring is to be carried out by one of the key actors involved, thereby jeopardising objectivity and holding the potential for missing the views and voices of the less vocal and the least powerful. It is perhaps not surprising that the component of the original project that has already been sacrificed is that of catering for the elderly – a group without much influence.

In conclusion, this project will have winners and losers. It is not clear who will benefit from the necessarily limited training, employment and enterprise opportunities. Additionally, the fact that the present tenants will not be allowed to return to the original site once it is redeveloped means that established social networks could well be destroyed by their permanent relocation, thus denying the importance of social history and social space in the city.

Note

Thanks are due to Ealing Family Housing Association, who very kindly gave me access to the BLRI SRB bid proposal and who answered any queries that arose from the research. Thanks also to Sylvia Moore, who works for the Pegasus Court Tenants' Association and very kindly spoke to me about the proposals from the tenants' perspective.

References

Chevin, D. (1994), 'One for all: a contractors' guide to the new Single Regeneration Budget', *Building*, 29 April: 18–20.

Devas, N. and C. Rakodi (1993), 'Planning and managing fast growing development', in N. Devas and C. Rakodi (eds), *Managing Fast Growing Cities*, New York: Longman Scientific and Technical, pp. 41–62.

DOE (1994), *Bidding Guidance, a Guide to Funding from the Single Regeneration Budget*, April.

Oxford City Council and Ealing Family Housing Association (1994), *The Blackbird Leys Redevelopment Initiative: A Partnership Bid for SRB Challenge Funding Led by Oxford City Council and Ealing Family Housing Association*, October.

CHAPTER 23

Mediation and Participation in a Delhi Slum

Rakesh Mehta

This chapter examines the role of an NGO in empowering a community living in an urban Indian slum in Tughlaqabad in Delhi. It explores the relationship between the landowning agency (Delhi Development Authority) and the urban municipality (Municipal Corporation of Delhi) *vis-à-vis* the urban slum and how their conflicts affected the work of the NGO. The chapter also examines the functioning of land markets and how informal-level markets work when formal markets are monopolised by a single agency. This situation has adverse effects on the urban physical and social environment, since both agencies seek to avoid responsibility for providing basic civic amenities. This provides short-term advantages for slum-dwellers who establish themselves through official neglect, political patronage and by inserting themselves into the informal economy.

The chapter shows the dependence of householders in formal housing near the slum on services provided by people living in the slum. However, this does not translate into support for finding viable solutions to the problem of access to land and services by the slum-dwellers. This is essential for their long-term well-being and sustainable living and working environment. This chapter ends on the optimistic note that NGOs can play a vital role in the conscientisation of slum-dwellers in a democratic society and can enable them to demand access to resources essential to improve their life chances.

Urban development, slum upgrading and land markets

Traditional urban planning dominated by zoning regulations has significantly failed to take account of the needs of urban populations for land. Land markets controlled by governments have provided housing for the economically better off and commercial spaces for influential or large-scale businesses. The inevitable result has been thriving irregular land markets for the rest, which meet needs but violate municipal regulations. They are evident in slum and squatter settlements and the unauthorised colonies carved out in the peripheral areas around cities. Since these areas are technically irregular or illegal and are not a source of revenue, municipalities have been unwilling to provide them with essential services such as water supply or sanitation. There is a prevailing feeling that besides 'legalising' their 'illegal' status any assistance given to unauthorised occupants only encourages others. This then makes it even more difficult for the authorities to move people if the land is required for any planned purpose. The growth of slums is a result of the failure of urban and municipal planning to cater for economic migrants and to recognise the growth within cities.

Urban land use planning and urban extension in Delhi is the responsibility of the Delhi Development Authority (DDA), an autonomous body constituted by central government. It functions as the land development agency and acquires land for urban development. The DDA in its planning does not make provision for slums. The resettlement of slum-dwellers in peripheral areas of the city is done on a case-by-case basis. The policy of large-scale land acquisition for the expansion of urban limits by the DDA often excludes areas of unauthorised settlements, so that they are not treated as eligible for civic amenities.

The Municipal Corporation of Delhi is charged with the responsibility of providing civic amenities like water supply, electricity, sewerage and sanitation to different colonies. This is done by collecting revenues from house tax user charges and octroi (a tax on all goods entering the city). However, such facilities are provided only in 'authorised colonies'. These are areas where, after their development, responsibility has been transferred from the DDA to the municipality. Slums are not eligible for such facilities unless declared 'authorised' through a politico-administrative process. Therefore slums are unable to get official facilities from either the DDA or the municipality.

In Delhi, any agency requiring land that has been encroached upon by slum-dwellers must pay relocation charges to the DDA to rehabilitate the people involved. In theory this replaces the widespread use of forcible eviction of occupants. Faced with eviction and invariably reluctant to move from central locations to peripheral areas, slum-dwellers have been successful in getting 'stay orders' against redevelopment from the civil courts and have obtained court orders mandating their resettlement should the land be required for urban renewal. Thus the new policy is to relocate slum areas. This relocation initiative has not been effective, since those agencies requiring land are often reluctant to pay the relocation charges.

The DDA has therefore proved unsuccessful in relocating slums. The impact of this is that slums continue to exist in their original locations but are still seen as dysfunctional. The relationship between the municipality and the DDA in Delhi is characterised by mutual antagonism. The DDA would be happy to see the 'problem' of slums being tackled by the municipality, which it sees as responsible for providing civic amenities. The municipality, on the other hand, considers slums to be a reflection of the failure of the urban policies of the DDA and would like the DDA to provide the civic amenities. Central government has tried to resolve this urban planning conflict by transferring responsibility for slum areas to the municipality as a prelude to setting up a Slum Board. Thus the DDA has successfully absolved itself of any responsibility for providing civic amenities for slums, and this has enabled the municipality to set its own standards for slum upgrading. However, the board will be responsible for providing civic amenities only to those slum colonies that are 'transferred' to its charge by the DDA. This ensures that the task of preventing the regularisation of new slums belongs to the DDA, which is the monopoly landowner in Delhi. The process of transferring slums to the proposed Slum Board is a political one and depends on the extent of pressure and influence exerted by the organisation of slum-dwellers.

Because of the long-established systems of 'vote-banking', residents of slums are in a position to lobby local politicians to ensure some facilities. This builds up political pressure at election time to extract promises for 'regularising' the existing settlements. The DDA is subsequently put under political pressure to recognise these colonies and make them eligible for civic amenities. Slum-dwellers in Delhi are caught in the conflict between and also manipulate the two bodies. Both agencies view slums as an aberration in city life, to be ignored or, at best, to be given reluctant attention following the pressures of politicians who depend on their votes.

CASP-PLAN and the slum community in Tughlaqabad

Tughlaqabad is located in south Delhi in the middle of a large residential colony constructed by the DDA. There are approximately three thousand dwellings in the slum, which is inhabited by some fifteen thousand people. The slum is located along the north-west wall of the Fort of Tughlaqabad. The slum residents were labouring families involved in the construction of public housing in the area, who stayed there following its completion. Thus there is an integral link between the slum colony and the public housing colony and this has persisted, with a large percentage of the women in the slum involved in domestic work for families resident in the public housing. Rag-pickers and garbage-collectors from the slum also keep the area clean and recycle waste.

Since it is an unauthorised settlement there is a complete lack of infrastructure in the slum. Moreover, the slum has not been 'transferred' to the Slum Board. Most slum-dwellers are politically active and their votes count for the local elected representatives. The slum-dwellers have therefore been able to extract promises from elected councillors. They have put pressure on their local councillor, who has facilitated the construction of water supply stand-posts.

CASP-PLAN (Community Action in Slum Projects-PLAN) is an NGO that started working in the slum seven years ago with the object of involving the community in adult literacy. Its objective was to promote literacy as part of a process of awareness creation and towards this a community hall was constructed by the community with funds provided by CASP-PLAN. In the process of literacy work, other issues were raised by the people. Residents identified as their main priority a lack of access to finance, which prevented them from engaging in income generation. CASP-PLAN responded by initiating a group financing programme. Income-generating activities are financed through a system of group loans wherein small sums of money are advanced to meet the credit needs of individual members from a revolving fund. Loans can be taken for consumption as well as income-enhancing activities. The group manages the fund on its own. Women are encouraged to join the group and hold posts of responsibility. A number of other activities have been taken up by CASP-PLAN in conjunction with the residents. However, credit has shown itself to be a powerful way of empowering low-income groups.

The women and girls were able to start income-generating activities within the slum area. This enabled women to supplement household incomes and enhance their productive roles. A bakery unit was started by a group of women and provided bread and other bakery products to the colony with training and equipment provided by CASP-PLAN. A knitting unit and tailoring unit were also started by groups of women. These provided income opportunities for the girls and women of the colony.

Initiatives involving the public sector

Although CASP-PLAN established a good working relationship with this slum community of ten years' standing and initiated a number of useful projects, in order to meet the pressing needs of access to urban services and amenities it was necessary to seek the assistance or cooperation of either the DDA or the municipality. This was not easy, but there were some small and significant successes. One was the introduction of solar cookers in response to slum-dwellers cutting trees from the woodlot nearby because of the high price of other fuels. Solar cookers were sold to CASP-PLAN by the Delhi Energy Development Agency, a state government enterprise that promotes the use of non-conventional energy. CASP-PLAN in turn supplied them to the households. Solar cookers saved fuel expenses for the households and introduced an environment-friendly technology. They also signified an early cooperation between the public sector and an NGO.

The municipal authorities were not willing to provide street lights since it was an unauthorised colony. However, street lights were necessary for night-shift workers and for the safety of women. CASP-PLAN decided to install solar street lights with the help of the Delhi Energy Development Agency. The groups were trained in the maintenance of the lights. The area lacked any form of sanitation and the people were encouraged to construct low-cost twin-pit pour-flush latrines. CASP-PLAN provided mobile mounted sanitary latrines so that people could see the advantages before constructing their own. However, the DDA objected to the construction of the latrines since they would strengthen the claim of the slum to remain at the location. The residents approached the local councillor to get permission for latrine construction, but this would require the colony to be transferred to the Slum Board. Since the colony is more than a decade old, its claim for civic amenities is strong, but objections have been raised by the Archaeological Survey of India as the colony adjoins the old fort wall. Despite support from CASP-PLAN the issue of land has stalled the construction of latrines. The community and CASP-PLAN are continuing to apply political pressure to begin work on the latrines.

Garbage disposal in the area was a problem. The municipal authority refused to collect the garbage on the ground that the area was an unauthorised colony. While rag-pickers collected and sold recyclable material, organic garbage was not collected. The possibility of vermi-composting organic garbage was explored by CASP-PLAN, and a group of rag-pickers was trained in the process of vermi-composting. Vermi-composting requires land, and again site selection was problematic because of opposition from the local authorities. Eventually it was agreed that the composting would be done near the main drain running through the settlement. The rag-pickers were provided with hand-carts to collect the garbage. After selling the recycled material they vermi-compost the biodegradable garbage. The idea was that the compost would be sold, after packing, to the city's Kitchen Garden Association. This association was involved in the vermi-composting training so that a ready market for the compost existed through them. The response was enthusiastic as it provided rag-pickers with an extra source of income and at low labour cost, as the site did not need constant work. The DDA, however, did not allow this activity to begin since it feared that the land would be permanently encroached on by the slum-dwellers. Strong lobbying by the organisation of residents with support from CASP-PLAN is being conducted along with political pressure to get the activity started.

Conclusion

The conflicts between the DDA and the municipality over providing civic amenities to the slum colony exacerbated the problems for CASP-PLAN which, despite its best motivation, was unable to progress on some projects because of insecurity of land tenure. But its role in organising the people enabled it to exert pressure on the authorities. CASP-PLAN was successful in building on and facilitating the involvement of slum-dwellers in improving their own environment. This is an example of bottom-up community participation with an NGO providing top-down encouragement. CASP-PLAN also acted as a catalyst in enabling the people to articulate their problems and present their case to the authorities. Government agencies were better able to deal with one agency than with a lot of beneficiaries. The intermediary role adopted by CASP-PLAN proved significant in allowing residents more 'voice' in the city. With the growing organisation of the people and their increased self-confidence in dealing with government agencies, their position in the slum was secured and the threat of eviction was averted. CASP-PLAN empowered the slum-dwellers, which enabled them to place demands with the authorities to get access to civic amenities.

The diversity issues highlighted by this case primarily concern the different interests of two sets of neighbours – those in formal housing and formal unemployment and those in informal housing and informal unemployment. The slum is integrated with the surrounding formal housing colony by virtue of its proximity and economic ties. Despite the mutual interdependence that characterises their relationship with each other, land markets and real estate values influence the reception of the weaker group by the stronger one. While different groups contribute to city life in different ways and exert influence over and have access to greater or more limited resources, the different parts of the city are organically linked.

Linkages are not only spatial and economic but also organisational. The political process in a democratic framework makes it possible for vulnerable groups like these Delhi slum-dwellers to secure their livelihoods, even if in small measure, and to put periodic pressure on politicians for support through offering themselves as 'vote-banks'. The need is to enable people's organisations to function in an organised way and to demand access to resources and legalisation of tenure in a sustained way. Incremental improvements in smaller slum settlements are often more viable than large-scale projects, and this case study illustrates the value of NGOs playing a facilitating and intermediary role in these endeavours. In this example it is clear that urban planning regulations need to be drastically revised to take account of the growing diversity of city life and to recognise the contribution of informality to the city.

References

Bamberger, M. and K. Shams (1989), *Community Participation in Project Management. The Asian Experience*, Kuala Lumpur: APDC.

Chambers, R. (1994), *Poverty and Livelihoods: Whose Reality Counts?* An overview paper prepared for the Stockholm Roundtable on Global Change, 22–4 July , Internet.

Clark, J. (1991), *Democratising Development,* London: Earthscan.

Mitlin, D. and D. Satterthwaite, (1994), *Cities and Sustainable Development*, background paper prepared for Global Forum '94, Manchester, London: International Institute for Environment and Development.

Moser, C. (1989), 'Community participation in urban projects in the Third World', *Progress in Planning,* 32(2).

Nientied, P., S. Benmhenni, and J. De Wit (1990), 'Community participation in low-income housing policies: potential or paradox', *Community Development Journal,* 25(1), January.

Rondinelli, D. (1993), *Development Projects as Policy Experiments*, London: Routledge.

Rose, K. (1992), *Where Women are Leaders: The SEWA Movement in India*, London: Zed Books.

Van der Linden, J. (1986), *The Sites and Services Approach Reviewed*, Aldershot: Gower.

Verhelst, T. (1989), *No Life without Roots: Culture and Development*, London: Zed Books.

World Bank (1991), *Urban Policy and Economic Development. An Agenda for the 1990s*, World Bank Policy Paper, Washington, DC.

World Bank (1993), *Housing: Enabling Markets to Work*, Washington, DC.

Wratten, E. (1995), 'Conceptualizing urban poverty', *Environment and Urbanization,* 7(1), April: 11–36.

CHAPTER 24

Women in Solidarity in Mexico

*Lucy Tacher and Lourdes
Mondragon Padilla*

Low-income urban Mexican women have historically faced poverty with a strong will. Through individual and household collective survival strategies and by establishing organisations at neighbourhood and community levels, these women have successfully secured their families' basic needs. In their struggles, they have continuously confronted officials with demands for the long overdue public services in their *colonias populares* (shanty towns). The growing participation of urban women in organisation that goes beyond their traditional reproductive role and income-earning activities has strengthened their participation and has provided some concrete solutions to their families' problems, within a complex social and political arena. This has embodied a cultural, social and political fight against poverty and the status quo. They have struggled to defend their rights not only as mothers, but as women and citizens. Notwithstanding their crucial participation in the social and political life of Mexico, women's participation has until recent times been only partially recognised, analysed and interpreted. It was not until the second half of the twentieth century, and specifically during the 1980s and 1990s, that women's involvement in social and political struggles was acknowledged to any extent. These decades saw changes in Mexico that altered political culture and challenged the traditional mechanisms of political control and the conventional schemes of decision-making and decision-taking of the elite. Women's participation and contribution, if invisible, has nevertheless been crucial.

Urban popular movements

Urban popular movements have been prominent in Mexico's contemporary history. This can be attributed partly to the impoverishment of a great portion of Mexico's urban population and their particular concentration in Mexico City and its metropolitan area. It is also a result of the deterioration of the Mexican political system and its bureaucratic and managerial incapacity to respond to and meet the requirements and needs of the growing urban population. Urban popular movements and their component organisations have been decisive in social change, as Castells (1976) has pointed out. They are the real driving mechanism of change and innovation in the city. Defining popular movements is a controversial business. According to Foweraker (Foweraker and Craig, 1990), social movements are defined not so much by the interests they represent, but by their political practice and the demands they make. These demands emerge through the process of popular organisation but are also determined by the laws, institutions and state policies that bear on popular organisation.

This has been precipitated by two decades of economic reform and stabilising macro-economic variables, so that investment in social welfare programmes has been cut (Cordera and González Tiburcio, 1991). Urban popular movements in Mexico have been concerned mainly with the achievement of social welfare and security services: employment, wages, housing, water, sanitation, health, food, education. In short, they have focused on acquiring the basic services through which immediate needs can be met.

The invisibility of women's social and political participation in urban conquests

Throughout Mexican history, women have played a significant part in historical movements such as the independence war, the revolution, Catholic movements (La Cristiada) and many small and local struggles. Joe Foweraker (Foweraker and Craig, 1990) points out that today women play a key part in the organisation of low-income neighbourhoods and that female mobilisation is a notable dimension of contemporary urban struggles. Women develop reciprocal relations within which they provide each other and their families with mutual support that has made them less vulnerable, has challenged the traditional relationship between the state and civil society, and achieved important improvements in their *colonias populares*. There is no doubt that the participation of women in urban struggles has been crucial to urban movements. Their 'invisible victories' have been poorly acknowledged as victories by authorities, movements and sometimes even by women themselves in the context of an extremely anti-democratic political system. Finding a way to articulate women's particular gender and social demands with those of the rest of the population, at the same time engaging them or their representatives in regional and national policy-making and social development planning, is a minimum requirement in order to construct a more democratic system.

The establishment of the National Solidarity Programme

On 1 December 1988 the Mexican government, headed by President Salinas from the Institutional Revolutionary Party (PRI), presented a revolutionary development programme. Under severe political pressure, President Salinas recognised that the adoption of macro-economic policies was not enough to obtain economic stability; political, social and institutional development were also key elements in procuring such a goal (Consejo Consultivo del Programa Nacional de Solidaridad, 1994). Thus he hoped to assure the party's position in power by adopting a social programme that could efficiently gain the confidence and votes of the people while guaranteeing their vote and support (Dresser, 1994). Governmental response to this objective was the creation of the National Solidarity Programme, commonly known as 'Pronasol' (SEDESOL, 1995). Pronasol was designed to invest in both physical and social infrastructure that would foster and set the foundations for more effective social development systems in Mexico. In general terms, Pronasol's primary objective was to respond to the most urgent needs of the poorest groups of the Mexican population by granting them the opportunity to restore and consolidate their productive capabilities. This programme was seen to be the only way in which stability and continuity could be given to future welfare achievements (Dresser, 1994).

Pronasol constitutes a substantial change in the way in which social welfare policy in Mexico is perceived. The government has ceased to be the only source of social welfare provision and has become a facilitating agency helping the poorest groups of society to achieve the ends of individual and communal welfare. This concept has set a new relationship between the Mexican government and its people. A mutual responsibility has been established in the fight against poverty between the state and the individual or the state and the community. Social participation is seen as being as fundamental as the resources supplied by the government. Pronasol has successfully incorporated the idea of diversity in its development and has attempted to empower some of the less privileged groups within Mexican society, such as indigenous peoples, *campesinos* (peasants), poor urban dwellers and vulnerable women.

Programmes under Pronasol can be classified into three main categories, which span both rural and urban areas: target sectors such as welfare, health and education; target groups such as women or children; area-based strategies such as regional development programmes in the poorest states, public service programmes in rural and urban areas; and productive support programmes for rural and urban enterprises (Consejo Consultivo del Programa Nacional de Solidaridad, 1994). According to the projected budget for 1992, social welfare programmes received 70% of the allocated expenditures of Pronasol while productive support programmes and regional development programmes were allocated 15% each (Trejo and Jones, 1994).

Promoting participation

One of Pronasol's major innovations has been its working method. In order to participate within any programme, Pronasol requires evidence of previous community organisation. In order to receive the funds for a particular project, a community has to organise into a 'Solidarity Committee'. Once formed, the committee can then formally present its proposals and demands to its local government body. According to official records, 80,000 organised and officially listed committees were accounted for under the scheme in 1992 (Consejo Consultivo del Programa Nacional de Solidaridad, 1994). These committees have varied according to the nature of the organisation. They can be classified as follows:

- virgin committees that arise spontaneously without pre-existing organisation;
- committees that are organised in response to a local government initiative;
- committees that originate out of organisational structures within the Institutional Revolutionary Party itself; and
- committees whose origins can be traced to previously existing organisations such as opposition political parties or politically independent groups.

The forms of organisation and engagement with the political process are strongly linked to the nature and origin of the committees (Trejo and Jones, 1994). As more new and autonomous committees are established by communities the Solidarity Programme is giving rise to a new dimension in Mexican social policy. The reason behind this argument is that, as these committees originate within the community, they acquire an authentic capacity to organise and negotiate while weakening the traditional corporate structures that have traditionally been associated with the PRI. Thus the Solidarity Programme carries within it the potential to challenge and undermine the very political structures that set it up, rendering the programme vulnerable to changes in political power or indeed its own success.

'Women in Solidarity'

In December 1988, the programme 'Women in Solidarity' was created as part of Pronasol, with the sole objective of improving the conditions of impoverished rural and urban women. The targeted group was women in those regions with poor malnutrition, health, shelter and education levels and the programme was aimed at empowering women as well as at liberating them from hardship (SEDESOL, 1994b). The Mexican government had the mobilisation of women in mind when it introduced the National Solidarity Programme. Even though women did not necessarily participate in the formulation of the Women in Solidarity Programme, their participation in its implementation, and in Pronasol as a whole, was considered. However, Pronasol has also opened a space for women to participate actively in Mexico's broader social and political arenas.

Under the Women in Solidarity Programme women have organised into committees that define, promote and carry out different projects. Activities undertaken with the private and social sectors are coordinated by representatives of federal, state and local governments as well as by Women in Solidarity committees. An agreement between a local government and an interested women's committee has to be established in order for the committee to be eligible to receive Pronasol funds. At a centralised level, the authorised budget is set annually by the Ministry of Finance. It is channelled on a quarterly basis to the state entity that distributes the resources to the women's committees under their jurisdiction. The Federal Comptroller Ministry, the Committee for Planning State Development and the Ministry for Social Development form a delegation, which is then made responsible for monitoring and evaluating the project.

Women in Solidarity was formed by an umbrella federation of approximately three and a half thousand organised women's committees in charge of planning, executing and evaluating the projects carried out during the past administration (1988–94). It is worth noting that out of the total number of committees that were created, 65% were organised by highly marginalised women (Consejo Consultivo del Programa Nacional de Solidaridad, 1994). Women in Solidarity is not treated as an isolated programme and the participation of women in urban areas has not been limited to Women in Solidarity. Urban women, in particular, regularly participate in joint ventures with the rest of the community in other projects.

Women who live in popular urban *colonias* or shanty towns carry out domestic work in extremely poor conditions. In the majority of cases, they work with insufficient and deficient public services and are exposed to environmental hazards at their place of work, usually the home. They constantly confront domestic violence with little legal protection (CONAPO, 1995). As they enter the labour market under unfavourable and disadvantageous conditions, they encounter harsh economic, social and ideological barriers that make it hard for them to provide their dependants with food and access to proper health, education and other public services (ibid.). Furthermore, their social participation has been limited and their voices rarely heard in planning processes. Communities, through their committees, decide on and prioritise the projects that need to be implemented in their particular settlement or part of the city.

The most common types of urban social programme carried out under the Women in Solidarity umbrella are related to housing, water and complementary construction projects, including working in the construction of drainage systems and the provision of clean water. Men and women in the community dug the ditches and carried the electricity poles, pipes, wires and cement on their backs or with their mules in order to secure the public services they prioritised. In terms of productive action, women established *tortillerías* (places in which tortillas are made and sold), sewing shops, provision stores, popular kitchens and bakeries (SEDESOL, 1994b).

There is growing evidence that women are not simply being used instrumentally in cost-sharing exercises but are benefiting. They perceive Women in Solidarity and other components of Pronasol as having positive effects. For example, Mrs Dolores Sánchez Ramírez from the Drainage Solidarity Committee for San Pedro de los Metates, Acambey, State of Mexico said: 'Before [the programme was completed], everybody would throw the garbage everywhere, people would defecate in the open air, they would shower and cleanse, leaving the dirty water to pollute the roads; children would play in it. Now with the drainage system, dirty and black waters are bound to disappear' (SEDESOL, 1994b; author's own translation). Rosa Ofelia Coronado from the Solidarity Committee of Fraccionamiento Fomerrey in Nuevo León reported that: 'We feel very happy because after seven years and for more than ten years for others, we were lacking a very vital liquid: water. Today, finally, we have seen one of our dreams come true.' María Mayorga Rosales of Electricity Committee for Azafrán, el Rosario in Sinaloa was similarly optimistic about progress:

> We have to unite because we had no electricity, now the project is almost finished, we are just missing the transformers. This is going to benefit all of us because we can now buy a radio of some sort for entertainment because we do not have anything, not even a tape-recorder. Now that we have electricity, we can purchase a tape-recorder or a television so we can at least see the cartoons. And as well as a refrigerator that someone in the community can purchase. Also, there are a lot of scorpions in the streets – now, instead of using matches, with the street light we will be able to spot them.

Conclusion

One of the merits of Pronasol has been to recognise and build on the fact that 'solidarity' is a rooted concept among Mexican people, particularly among the poor and very poor. For years, Mexican communities have independently organised themselves to confront difficult situations (Consejo Consultivo del Programa Nacional de Solidaridad, 1994; Chant, 1996; González de la Rocha, 1994). Pronasol's orientation towards poor people's reality has made it successful because an understanding of people's own priorities 'supports their initiatives and draws upon their [the community's] ingenuity, energy and commitment' (Oxfam, 1995).

Although there is much ground to be covered in order to alleviate and improve women's conditions in Mexico, Women in Solidarity has been a cornerstone in setting a precedent for long overdue reform in Mexican social and political structures and values. It has alerted both the Mexican government and the nation as a whole to the particular needs of women that, up to now, have been ignored and have not been taken into account in policy decision-making processes. It has also highlighted and built upon women's attributes and contributions to social and cultural life and may potentially pave the way for their greater political participation. In this sense, one of the major successes of the programme has been the institutional action, initiated at a national level, for constructing a new participatory planning strategy that has broken with traditional practices and has set the basis in responding to women's actual needs and demands in the field of social policy (Trejo and Jones, 1994; SEDESOL, 1994a). Complementary to this are the social welfare programmes implemented by Pronasol and Women in Solidarity. Through them, long working hours and arduous workloads for women have been eased, giving them more time to participate in activities that benefit themselves, their families and their communities (SEDESOL, 1994a).

However, as the Oxfam report on poverty states:

> while community mobilisation is a necessary condition for development, it is not a sufficient condition. Local efforts to protect employment, improve services, and maintain security are unlikely to succeed in the face of economic crisis and the general collapse of social welfare provision ... Community initiatives can help people to cope with crisis and to survive; but it is up to governments to create the enabling environment through which such initiatives can transform societies (Oxfam, 1995).

Thus the proponents, planners and participants in Pronasol have to be constantly vigilant and cannot expect too much from the programme. Notwithstanding its achievements, Solidaridad is a politically vulnerable initiative at risk of being a 'fad' of President Salina's administration. The lack of continuity in Mexican politics makes it problematic for any social policy to succeed in the long term, especially policy that could potentially lead to power-sharing and even redistribution. Yet the basis has been established, and it is the responsibility of the present administration and the Mexican people to institutionalise the programme and to build upon it.

References

Castells, M. (1976), *Movimientos sociales urbanos*, Mexico City: Siglo XXI.

Chant, S. (1996), 'Recession and adjustment: gendered outcomes and implications in Mexico and the Philippines', Research Papers in Environmental and Spatial Analysis No. 31, Department of Geography, London School of Economics.

CONAPO (1995), *Situación de la Mujer: Desafíos para el Año 2000: IV Conferencia Mundial de la Mujer*, Mexico City: Consejo Nacional de Población.

Consejo Consultivo del Programa Nacional de Solidaridad (1994), *El Programa Nacional de Solidaridad: Una Visión de la Modernización de México*, Mexico City: Fondo de Cultura Económica.

Cordera, R. and E. González Tiburcio (1991), 'Crisis and transition in the Mexican economy', in M. González de la Rocha and A. Escobar Latapí, *Social Responses to Mexico's Economic Crisis of the 1980s*, Department of USA-Mexico Studies, University of California, San Diego: San Diego Press.

Dresser, D. (1994), 'Pronasol y política: combate a la pobreza como fórmula de gobernabilidad', in F. Vélez (ed.), *La Pobreza en México: Causas y Políticas para Combatirla*, Mexico: Fondo de Cultura Económica, pp. 262–99.

Foweraker, J. and A. Craig (1990), *Popular Movements and Political Change in Mexico*, Boulder, CO and London: Lynne Rienner.

González de la Rocha, M. (1994), *The Resources of Poverty: Women and Survival in a Mexican City*, Oxford, UK and Cambridge, MA: Blackwell.

Oxfam (1995), *The Oxfam Poverty Report*, Oxford: Oxfam Publications.

SEDESOL (1994a), *Programa Nacional de Solidaridad: Información Básica Sobre la Ejecución y Desarrollo del Programa*, Mexico: Porrúa.

SEDESOL (1994b) *Solidaridad: Seis Años de Trabajo*, Mexico City: Secretaría de Desarrollo Social.

SEDESOL (1995), *Informe Sobre el Desarrollo Social: Cumbre Mundial Sobre Desarrollo Social*, Mexico: Secretaría de Desarrollo Social.

Trejo, G. and C. Jones (1994), *Contra la Pobreza: Por una Estrategia de Política Social*, Mexico City: Cal y Arena.

CHAPTER 25

Urban Grassroots Organisation in Nicaragua

Leah Schmalzbauer

An effective democracy is one which consists of a permanent dynamic and the people's participation in a variety of political and social tasks. It is the people who give their opinions and are listened to; the people who suggest, construct and direct, organise themselves; who attend to community, neighbourhood and national problems; the people who are active in their sovereignty and the defence of that sovereignty, and who also teach and give vaccinations. It is a daily democracy and not one that takes place every four years (Nicaraguan Vice President Sergio Ramirez, July 1983).

This chapter analyses the vital contribution of community participation and empowerment to the building of diverse, accessible, healthy cities. Via a case study of the Nicaraguan Communal Movement (Movimento Communal de Nicaragua, MCN), it is argued that community empowerment and the mobilisation it ignites are keys to the development of strong, vibrant urban communities.

On the practical side, the MCN undertook concrete work in the areas of health, education and land distribution. This is analysed with a focus on 'who participated' in and 'who benefited from' the individual programmes. The strategic interventions of the MCN included reconciliation, mobilisation around the impact of economic reforms, evolving a working relationship with the state, and building power from the 'base' of the urban communities in which they worked. The conclusion stresses that while true empowerment and participation cannot be instigated from above, NGOs and development agencies can and should facilitate the process. Grassroots initiatives can work in partnership with government policy to produce communities that are not only liveable, but prosperous, diverse, dynamic and kind.

The concept of participation espoused in the quote that opens this chapter is not just to do with efficient and effective development. Rather, participation here is a key component of democracy. It is linked to and recognised as images of freedom, autonomy, efficiency, productivity and self-reliance. However, in the face of diminishing basic service provision and state support, participation has also become a survival strategy. When the government has stepped out of the provider role, the community has been encouraged to step in. It is mainly this kind of participation that has been celebrated by governments, international agencies and NGOs alike.

To link participation and democracy, it is necessary to broaden the idea of participation beyond self-help projects and basic needs provision, towards structural change. Participation need not be an end in itself. Indeed, some would argue that democracy should be the goal and participation a route to it. Participation can serve as an evolutionary process through which the ideals of democracy can be pursued. But this means people surpassing 'project participation' and mobilising to challenge directly the policies and power structures that often dictate the conditions of their existence.

The MCN is a dynamic 'best practice' example of an inclusive urban movement that has unified people against poverty and ensuing urban decay. By combining grassroots political mobilisation with broad participation in neighbourhood projects and campaigns, the MCN strives to meet practical needs while pursuing the strategic vision of Nicaragua's urban communities. The MCN is also an example of the advantage of a close working relationship between the city/state and the grassroots. It demonstrates that whether of the left or the right, governments, as well as citizens, can benefit greatly from an empowered and participatory populace.

The case of Nicaragua is truly unique. Its history has been one of resistance and revolution in which movement-building has been an organic process. Hence it is acknowledged that the path of the MCN cannot serve as a 'blueprint' model for urban mobilisation in every context. However, by illustrating the achievements of organisation, it can act as an impetus for communities in both the North and the South to mobilise around a clear, collective and strategic vision. The Nicaraguan example is inescapably a political one, and this text follows suit. It is written from the critical perspective of an activist, supportive of the Nicaraguan struggle but not blind to its difficulties.

The Nicaraguan Communal Movement: empowerment in practice

The historical context   In 1936, Anastasio Somoza founded a brutal dictatorship in Nicaragua that was to last for 43 years. During this period Nicaragua, in addition to having rampant poverty, landlessness, illiteracy and inadequate nutrition, is known to have had one of the worst human rights records in history. By the 1970s, Somoza's greed and brutality had led all but his National Guard to oppose him, and on 19 July 1979 he was ousted by a popular revolution led by the Sandinista National Liberation Front (FSLN).

The uniqueness of the Sandinista revolution lies in its inception as a 'grassroots' mobilisation of popular organisations that broke down gender, age and class barriers. Women and men, old and young, intellectuals, peasants, workers and entrepreneurs all joined forces with the common vision of toppling the dictatorship and building a new, just society that operated 'for the people'. This common vision of a new Nicaragua empowered the masses, inspiring tremendous participation.

Nicaragua's cities played a critical role in the revolution. Managua, the nation's capital and home to one-third of the population, suffered tremend-ously under the dictatorship. During that time, health care was unavailable to the majority, illiteracy was high, and land was concentrated in the hands of the very rich. In addition, an earthquake in 1972 demolished the city's centre and severely damaged its infrastructure. International aid for re-construction was subsequently siphoned off by Somoza for personal use, and for years the city lay in disrepair. Discontent among urban dwellers was high. Under the leadership of the MCN this discontent was channelled into activism, and the city became a major focal point of organisation and mobilisation that propelled the revolution.

At its birth, the MCN was a popular organisation of Sandinista Defence Committees (CDS) that provided logistical support for the urban in-surrection. After the 'Triumph' in 1979 the CDSs became key policy instruments of the FSLN. Although officially non-partisan, they were utilised by the state to carry out many important tasks. In a sense the CDSs became neighbourhood governments, serving as the impetus for some of the most celebrated achievements of the revolution. With very high levels of participation, the committees paved city streets and built community centres, cafeterias and health centres. They instigated sanitation campaigns, constructed water systems, oversaw urban land redistribution and improved schools (Quandt, 1993: 43). In addition, they organised health and literacy campaigns that were applauded worldwide.

In the very first months of the revolutionary government the FSLN, in collaboration with the popular organisations, held community meetings all over the country in which citizens were able to express their needs and vision for a new society. Health, education and property rights were prioritised. After decades of social neglect, Nicaraguans were anxious to move forward. The CDSs took a lead role in organising national literacy and health campaigns. These campaigns, which were carried out by urban volunteers, penetrated the poorest areas of the country's cities. Yet they also filtered into the countryside, alleviating much of the 'urban bias' that had previously dominated Nicaragua.

In the first year of the revolution the CDSs, in cooperation with the

Ministry of Health, trained 30,000 volunteer health workers, who were selected from their neighbourhoods to administer vaccinations against diphtheria–pertussis–tetanus, measles and polio. The results of this grass-roots campaign were phenomenal and by 1983 polio had been completely eradicated (Plunkett, 1995: 198). In the area of education the success of the CDSs was equally impressive. On 15 March 1980, only eight months after the fall of the Somoza dictatorship, the CDSs, in partnership with the Ministry of Education, launched a national Literacy Brigade. One hundred thousand urban volunteers, predominantly young people of high school and university age, set up study groups in urban neighbourhoods, towns and villages (ibid.: 197). No one was excluded from the opportunity to learn. Even the elderly poor, who had been denied the right to basic education as youths under the dictatorship, took their places next to children and adolescents, as they all learned how to read and write.

Nicaraguan women were the main actors in the health and education campaigns, comprising the majority of the volunteer corps. Their partici-pation can be attributed in large part to the long and unique history of women's mobilisation in Nicaragua. During the struggle against Somoza, for example, women comprised approximately 30% of the FSLN's combat forces, and at its peak in 1979, the women's organisation of the FSLN, the Association of Women Confronting the National Problem, or AM-PRONAC, had over eight thousand members (Molyneux, 1985: 227). Yet despite their success in penetrating the areas of activity generally dominated by men, Nicaraguan women's traditional social burdens were not lifted. Hence the politicisation of women's social roles can rightfully be criticised as maintaining the sexual division of labour within the revolution. Even so, it should be acknowledged that women's participation and leadership in the major social campaigns, most importantly the FSLN's health and education projects, were critical in the move towards greater female influence in municipal, regional and national policy-making.

Land redistribution was the third major area in which the CDSs were active. Approximately two hundred thousand people benefited from the Sandinista agrarian reforms of the 1980s, which redistributed all land that was deserted by Somoza and his inner circle (Plunkett, 1995: 203). As a result of the reform, 65,000 families in Managua were also given land titles (Quandt, 1993: 47).

The transition to autonomy Mass participation by an empowered populace is what enabled the success of the first campaigns of the CDSs. Yet while the CDSs enjoyed mass grassroots support, a valid concern developed within the committees that the priorities set by the FSLN for the urban neighbourhoods were not always in line with communities' individual needs. An organisational self-critique pointed to the risk of exclusiveness and instrumentality involved in remaining part of vertical state structures. In 1985 discussion therefore began around the issue of autonomy, and the CDSs began to shed their political character.

By 1988, after completing open dialogues with people in the neighbour-hoods as well as FSLN leaders, CDSs had decided to form an autonomous organisation based on the material needs and social vision identified by communities. The CDSs were replaced by a communal movement (the MCN) that had no political ties and vowed to work with whichever government was in power (Ampie, 1995). Omar Cabezas, the leader of the MCN in 1988, envisioned 'a vast and vigorous movement where the people, independent of creed, religion, political ideology or sexual orienta-tion, work for the good and development of their community' (Lomba, 1988: 45).

In 1990, the FSLN suffered defeat in the national elections and was replaced by the right-wing United National Opposition party (UNO). Nicaragua, which was already suffering economic crisis, was to undergo a complete socio-economic restructuring by the new government and international lending agencies. Within the first months of the UNO government, a strict structural adjustment programme was instituted and the government's provisioning and welfare role was all but abandoned. The MCN has struggled to use the economic reforms, austerity and consequent social suffering as stimulus to pull communities together. As stated by Cabezas: 'The more difficult the economic situation, the more necessary the unity of the people, not as individuals, but as a collective ... The crisis must be the motive for popular participation to resolve the problems' (Mariuca, 1988: 48).

The MCN began to organise people not around a specific ideology, but around opposition to the economic reforms and ensuing poverty (Plunkett, 1995: 195). Through the programmes and vision of the MCN, a reconciliation has taken place between Contras and Sandinistas. Enemies in war only six years ago, they began working side by side to ease the effects of the severe poverty that has claimed victims on both sides. This has widened the MCN's base of support to include urban sectors that were once its adversaries. The current director of the MCN, Enrique Picado, says the movement is maturing. 'At its inception, when approached by aid-givers, communities would ask, "What are you going to give us?" Now there's more of an idea of self-management. Now they ask, "What are we going to work together on"' (Ampie, 1995: 19).

In 1992 the MCN's national assembly, which includes elected repres-entatives from every member neighbourhood, laid out a 'Three-Year Plan of Action' that reprioritised health, education and housing. The results to date include the following: participation of 11,000 volunteer health workers in several day-long (annual) vaccination campaigns; 136 latrine projects; 226 drinking water projects; construction of 75 schools and repair of 37 classrooms; construction of 54 community health centres; 127 electricity projects; and the opening of 344 children's centres which include health-care units, community day-care, and lunch programmes (ibid.: 22). The MCN has also been invaluable in defending the land titles of the urban poor as UNO, with strong support from the right wing of the US Congress, attempts to reverse the Sandinista land reform. With funding assistance from international NGOs and solidarity organisations, legal aid offices have been set up in several neighbourhoods throughout Managua to provide the poor with affordable legal assistance to defend their property titles. At the same time as these projects are being achieved, the MCN is continuing a dialogue with the FSLN and UNO over how the three can better work together to overcome the urban effects of poverty.

Because of the high level of neighbourhood organisation and partici-pation inspired by the MCN, Nicaragua's cities have been able to stave off many catastrophes that have devastated other cities throughout the world. Cholera, for example, which ravaged many Latin American urban areas in the early 1990s, was avoided in Nicaragua because of the successful organisation of sanitation campaigns in the neighbourhoods and urban markets. There is also a strong argument that the emphasis that the MCN has placed on reconciliation has contributed to the avoidance of re-emerging civil conflict, and a political or military coup. Each neighbour-hood in the MCN has a clearly defined list of prioritised needs, as well as knowledge of the individual talents and skills of its members. This has enabled NGOs, both large and small, better to facilitate participatory urban projects in Nicaragua that respond to the people's needs and reflect their vision.

Conclusion

In Nicaragua, community empowerment and participation were built internally. They were instigated not by international agencies or NGOs, but by a grassroots struggle against poverty and oppression. Empowerment and participation were facilitated by the evolution of popular organisations, like the MCN, from parastatals into autonomous bodies who set out their needs and expectations and opened dialogue with all political parties, while continuously fostering the participation of those at the neighbourhood base.

Today, the need for high levels of organisation and participation within communities is more critical than ever. Following six years of economic structural adjustment policies and political reorganisation, Nicaragua is the poorest country in Latin America and has the highest per capita debt in the world (Plunkett, 1995: 201). Even conservative government statistics state that 2.7 million out of 3.9 million Nicaraguans are living in poverty (Soto, 1992). Urban unemployment stands at 60%, only 42% of city-dwellers have access to safe water and electricity, and illiteracy, which hovered at around 12% during the Sandinista government, has more than doubled to 25% (Gutierrez, 1992).

Norma Stoltz Chinchilla in her research on Nicaragua says:

> There is no question that material conditions are a limiting factor or parameter for the character of societies, classes, and individuals' lives, but politics and ideology can, in their own ways, be transformed into a material force that increases the possibility and probability of finding solutions to material problems (Chinchilla, 1995: 263).

The spirit of the Nicaraguan people has endured. Much of this spirit comes from their unique revolutionary past.

NGOs and international agencies wanting to improve cities and communities through enhanced participation must acknowledge that this is a political issue. It is not possible to encourage participation in urban development projects and then deny political mobilisation. The idea of good governance is to make governments responsive to their constituents. This seldom happens without activism. The success of the MCN stems from the projection of its political voice as much as from the participation it has built within the neighbourhoods.

References

Ampie, G. (1995), 'The community movement: defending its autonomy', *Barricada International*, XV(389), October: 17–24.

Chinchilla, N. (1995), 'Revolutionary popular feminism in Nicaragua: ideologies, political transitions, and the struggle for autonomy', in N. Bose and E. Acosta-Belen (eds), *Women in the Latin American Development Process*, Philadelphia: Temple University Press, pp. 242–65.

Gutierrez, S. (1992), *Interview: Movimiento Communal*, Managua, 19 February.

Lomba, M. (1988), 'Entrevista a Omar Cabezas', *Pensamiento Propio*, VI(52), July–August: 45–8.

Molyneux, M. (1985), 'Mobilisation without emancipation? Women's interests in state and revolution in Nicaragua', *Feminist Studies*, 11(2): 227–54.

Plunkett, H. (1995), 'The Nicaraguan Community Movement: in defence of life', in G. Craig and M. Mayo (eds), *Community Empowerment: A Reader in Participation and Development*, London: Zed Books, pp. 194–205.

Quandt, M. (1993), *Unbinding the Ties: The Popular Organizations and the FSLN in Nicaragua*, Washington, DC: Nicaragua Network Education Fund.

Soto, L. (1992), *Interview: Executive Secretary, National Workers' Federation*, Managua: 17 February.

Stieffel, M. and M. Wolfe (1994), *A Voice for the Excluded: Popular Participation in Development*, London: Zed Books.

Box 6.1

Learning to Participate: A City-wide Experience

Luz Dary Bueno Carvajal

My name is Luz Dary Bueno Carvajal, and I am a lawyer. I am involved in two community-based organisations in Southwest Bogota in Colombia. Fundacion Papazo has worked for over sixteen years with education development in the south-west region of the city, promoting local and regional development projects utilising skills and experiences from within its own communities.

The experience I want to talk about has its beginnings in the early 1980s, when I was in my last year of high school and we were involved in social service projects run by Fundacion Paz. A literacy programme offered the possibility of supplementing primary education for both adults and children and when we completed our social service practice we decided to continue in the programme as volunteers. When Fundacion Paz left we realised that it was necessary to carry forward the programme and to change its structure to involve community-based organisations in all aspects of the work. This is how we worked towards the establishment of Fundacion Papazo.

As we developed into a community organisation, we were confronted with the problem that we did not know how to lobby. We knew that we needed clean water and education, but we had never thought about the political process and what this meant for us as a community organisation. When we went to see the municipal officials we were asked: 'Who can vouch for you? Who is your political godfather?' We rapidly learned that we were not prepared for the political process in Bogota. We recognised that we, as the community, had to work together more broadly in the city, not just through a local project but through a city-wide programme.

In 1992 we participated in local administrative meetings and an election process. Although we were not a political party, we were asking people to vote for us. This was a very dangerous situation and we did not get enough votes in the election to generate the social movement that we had hoped for. Therefore we built upon our programme and began networking and lobbying and, when elections were called again, we gained 430 votes. These were votes for our credibility and indicative of people's trust in the organisation. Although we did not achieve political power, we learned that we needed to start an education process that could deal with the realities of the political processes such as the one we had just confronted.

I believe that we, as an organisation, have learned a lot about these processes, have a lot to share and have a lot to learn.

Source: Fedevivienda, Bogota, Colombia: a project that collected taped accounts of 'Our Practices' in Human Settlements Development for Habitat II, June 1996.

Box 6.2

How I Built my House

Orfidia Osorio

In 1982, I, my *compañero* (partner) and our first son shared a two-bedroom rented house. The rent and payment for services consumed more than half of the money we earned from working in the print shop. On several occasions, we had to refrain from buying essential things, such as milk for our baby, and we had difficulties in coming up with the money for rent or public services.

One day, while we were talking in our bedroom, I mentioned to my *compañero* that I had heard that some people from the outskirts of town were building their own houses. I suggested that we should join them in order to try to secure a roof over the heads of our children and ourselves. After thinking over my proposal for a few minutes he said: 'You know, it's not a bad idea to get our own house because it would reduce our living costs and give us the security, stability and peace in which to raise our children. But there are disadvantages. This is a very small town, its people are traditional, the authorities are very conservative and they are not going to allow us to do it. I would get the reputation of being a trouble-maker. If they do not kill us, they will drive us away from here. Still, I don't think it is totally hopeless. I think we should get other people interested, some friends that have the same problems. That way we can organise ourselves, we can work collectively to try to gather ideas, get the people and resources to succeed. It is also safer to be part of a group. Land there is cheap and there are some good lots for sale.'

The next day we went to the print shop and printed out 20 copies of a pamphlet inviting people to join our cause. It was a

BOX 6.2   285

great surprise and a delight to us that more than sixty people turned up on the day of the meeting. My *compañero* suggested that we organise into an NGO, name a board of directors and begin to work towards some solutions. This is how the Junta Provivienda Popular de Roldanillo Valle came about. With 85 members, it gained legal recognition in March of 1982. Municipal officials put all sorts of impediments in our way so that they would not have to collaborate with us in the project. The paperwork related to the housing project kept being delayed for no apparent reason.

Understanding that obtaining a house was not an end, but a means whereby community participation could help us attain better things for our family has been central to our cause. Despite all the obstacles we faced, we were eventually able to build our home. The sad thing is that the process of community participation and individual development has dissipated because of conflicting political interests within the group.

Source: Fedevivienda, Bogota, Colombia: a project that collected taped accounts of 'Our Practices' in Human Settlements Development for Habitat II, June 1996.

Afterword

*Gerard Howe and
Rajeev Patel*

The chapters in this book were written by members of both the urban-isation and social planning and the gender, development and social planning classes of the M.Sc. in Social Policy and Planning at the London School of Economics. We are offering an Afterword because we felt it might be interesting for readers to have some flavour of the *process* by which this book came about, both as a practical demonstration of working and learning through diversity and as an example of how ownership of a project implies increased likelihood of success. Both factors are salient for development practitioners.

The project itself began in December 1995 as a result of growing interest among students in the Habitat II process. As outlined in the Preface and Introduction, this led to us forming a voluntary group which became known as 'LSE for DiverCity' and eventually to our participation in the conference itself. The members of the group were a diverse set of people from different social, professional and cultural backgrounds. They included engineers, nurses, social workers and development professionals, with experience of social policy issues from grassroots to government, to international institutions, working in Asia, the Americas, Africa and Europe. However, given our position as students, we were initially unsure about our potential contribution, thinking it would be arrogant to offer policy options or papers. None the less, we were also aware that between us we had a wealth of experience and enthusiasm that might be channelled constructively. Under the expert guidance of the course lecturer, Jo Beall, it was decided that we might best use our comparative advantages by presenting a series of cases studies highlighting particular social policy and planning issues in urban development. To bind our work further to the Habitat II process, we took the criteria for 'best practice' generated at the Dubai conference as a point of departure, either adopting or offering a critique of them.

The group divided its administrative labour into three committees. The first was in charge of administration and communication of progress. The second committee was responsible for accreditation and registration of our student associations as an international NGO (LSE for DiverCity) which would represent the group at Habitat II. The third group concerned itself with fund-raising activities in order to pay for the five delegates allowed to represent us and, as we formalised the process of compiling case studies, the editorial process of getting them ready for dissemination. In addition to our own efforts, through Jo Beall we were able to raise funds from the Department of Social Policy and Administration, from the LSE, from the Women and Human Settlements Development Programme at UNCHS (Habitat) and from the ODA. We are very grateful to all those who contributed to the project for providing us with this unique opportunity.

The *process* included brainstorming sessions to match the interests and experience of group members with Habitat themes. We met periodically to discuss interim preparations and to share problems and ideas. In intellectual as well as social diversity, it was proved that the stronger the connections made between the parts, the greater the robustness of the whole. In between meetings there were periods of reflection and redrafting, before a first formal submission to the editing process. The editor, Jo Beall, and the editorial assistant, Gerard Howe, offered advice and assistance on content, focus and style. Writing abilities were varied and the group and editors worked to support less experienced members and to overcome fears in the group that the process might discriminate against those whose first language was not English.

The present book was showcased at the NGO Forum at Habitat II, where comments from interested parties were welcomed. Representatives of the class also participated in a special parallel event at Habitat II in which the guiding themes and illustrative case studies of the book were presented. The discussion and feedback were rich and fed into a final drafting process. It was the wish of the representatives of our group that the testimonies of women who contributed to the event at Istanbul were also included in this volume.

This book, then, is the product of a commitment by Jo Beall and her students to a process of 'learning through teaching and teaching through learning'. Significantly, the lessons learned by the group through the process of creating the book were as important as, if not more important than, the content. It was not always easy. There were worries that most of the people on the committees were from developed countries. Most difficult was the decision about who should represent the group in Istanbul and what they should and should not be allowed to say and do on the group's behalf. In Istanbul itself, there were tensions because some felt more involved than others. We tried to resolve difficulties and disputes through open discussion and compromise. Inevitably, this left some frayed nerves but if the book communicates a fraction of what we learned, we will have done well.

Index